NEAR NATURE'S HEART

&

E · P · ROE

HARDPRESS.NET
HOME OF HARD-TO-FIND BOOKS

Near to Nature's Heart
by Edward Payson Roe

Address:
HardPress
8345 NW 66TH ST #2561
MIAMI FL 33166-2626
USA
Email: info@hardpress.net

Near
to Nature's Heart

By
REV. E. P. ROE

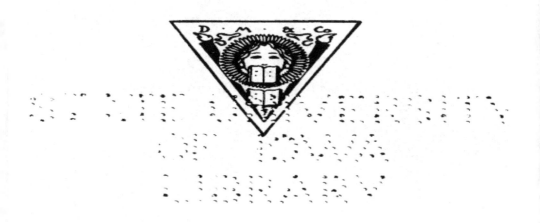

New York
Dodd, Mead and Company
Publishers

PREFACE.

THE autumn winds are again blowing, and the evenings are growing longer. At the time when the fires are kindled once more upon the hearth, I send this story out to visit those whom I can almost hope to regard as friends. If it meets the same kind welcome and lenient treatment which my previous works have received, I shall have more than sufficient reason to be satisfied. If, in addition to being a guest at the fireside, it becomes an incentive to the patient performance of duty in the face of all temptation, I shall be profoundly thankful. I am not afraid to inform the reader that these books are written with the honest, earnest purpose of helping him to do right ; and success, in this respect, is the best reward I crave. I do not claim for these books the character of beautiful works of art. Many things may have good and wholesome uses without exciting the world's admiration. A man who cannot model a perfect statue may yet erect a lamp-post, and place thereon a light which shall save many a wayfarer from stumbling.

It is with much diffidence and doubt that I have ventured to construct my story in a past age, fearing lest I should give a modern coloring to everything. But, while the book is not designed to teach history, I have carefully consulted good authorities in regard to those parts which are historical.

Captain Molly has her recognized place in the Revolution, but my leading characters are entirely imaginary. Still, I hope the reader may not find them such pale shadows that their joys, sorrows, and temptations will appear mere sickly fancies, but rather the reflex of genuine human experiences. They have become so real and dear to me that I part with them very reluctantly.

CORNWALL-ON-THE-HUDSON, N. Y.

CONTENTS.

NEAR TO NATURE'S HEART.

CHAPTER I.

A CHILD OF NATURE.

THE granite mountains that form the historical High-lands of the Hudson have changed but little during the past century.   On the 17th of June, about one hundred years ago, a day inseparably associated in American memory with Bunker Hill, and the practical severance of the cable of love and loyalty that once bound the colonies to the mother country, these bold hills undoubtedly appeared much as they do now.   In the swales and valleys, the timber, un-touched as yet by the woodman's axe, was heavier than the third or fourth growth of our day.   But the promontories overhanging the river had then, as now, the same grand and rugged outlines of rock and precipice.   The shrubbery, and dwarf trees, that catch and maintain their tenacious hold on every crevice and fissure, softened but little the frowning aspect of the heights, that, like grim sentinels, guard the river.

But nature in her harshest moods can scarcely resist the blandishments of June ; even as the sternest features relax under the caresses of youth and beauty.   On this warm still day of early summer, when over the city of Boston the wild-est storm of war was breaking, the spirit of peace seemed supreme even in that rugged gorge into which the Hudson passes from Newburgh Bay, and a luminous haze softened every sharp outline. The eastern shore was aglow with the afternoon sun, like a glad face radiant with smiles. The western bank with its deepening shadows was like a happy face passing from thought into revery, which, if not sad, is at least tinged with melancholy.

From most points of observation there were no evidences of other life than that distinctively belonging to the wilderness. If the pressure of population has brought so few inhabitants in our time, there was still less inducement then to settle where scarcely a foot-hold could be obtained among the crags. Therefore the region that is now filling up with those who prefer beautiful scenery to the richest lowlands, was one of the wildest solitudes on the continent, though amidst rapidly advancing civilization, north as well as south of the mountains.

While at that time the river was one of the chief highways of the people, the means of communication between the seaboard and a vast interior, so that the batteaux of voyagers and passing sails were common enough, still the precipitous shores offered slight inducement to land, and the skippers of the little craft were glad to pass hastily through this forbidding region of sudden flaws and violent tides, to the broad expanse of Tappan Zee, where the twinkle of home lights and the curling smoke from farm house and hamlet in the distance reminded them that they were near their own kind.

But there was neither boat nor sail in sight on the memorable afternoon upon which my story opens, not a trace of the human life that now pulsates through this great artery of the land, save a small sail-boat drifting slowly under the shadow of Cro'nest. The faint breeze from the west died away as the sun declined, and the occupant had dropped the sail that only flapped idly against the mast. The tide was still setting up in the center of the river, but had turned close in-shore. Therefore, the young man, who was the sole occupant of the boat, reclined languidly in the stern, with his hand on the tiller, and drifted slowly with the current around the mimic capes and along the slight indentations of the shore, often so close that he could leap upon a jutting rock.

Though the almost motionless vessel and the seemingly listless occupant were in keeping with the sultry hour, during which nature appeared in a dreamy revery, still their presence was the result of war. A nearer view of the young man who was mechanically steering, proved that his languid attitude was calculated to mislead. A frown lowered upon his wide brow, and his large, dark eyes were full of trouble— now emitting gleams of anger, and again moist in their sympathy with thoughts that must have been very sad or very bitter. His full, flexible mouth was at times tremulous with feeling, but often so firmly compressed as to express not so much resolve, as desperation. In contrast to nature's peace, there was evidently the severest conflict in this man's soul. In his deep pre-occupation, he would sometimes permit his boat to drift almost ashore ; then his impatient and powerful grasp upon the tiller bespoke a fiery spirit, and a strong, prompt hand to do its behests.

But, by the time he had crossed the flats, south of "Cro'nest," he seemed inclined to escape from his painful revery, and take some interest in surrounding scenes. He looked at his watch, and appeared vexed at his slow progress. He took the oars, pulled a few strokes, then cast them down again, muttering,

"After all, what do a few hours signify ? Besides, I am infinitely happier and better off here than in New York ;" and he threw himself back again in his old listless attitude.

His boat was now gliding around that remarkable projection of land that has since gained a world-wide celebrity under the name of West Point. When a little beyond what is now known as the old Steamboat Landing, he thought he heard a woman's voice. He listened intently, and a snatch of wild melody, clear and sweet, floated to him through the still air. He was much surprised. for he expected to find no one in that solitude, much less a woman with a voice as sweet as that of a brown-thrush that was giving an occasional prelude to its evening song in a shady nook of the mountains.

He at once proposed to solve the mystery, and so divert his thoughts from a subject that was evidently torture to dwell upon ; and keeping his boat close to the land, that it might be hidden, and that he could spring ashore the moment he wished, he pursued his way with a pleasant change in a face naturally frank and prepossessing.

As he approached the extreme point where now the lighthouse stands, the notes became clear and distinct. But he could distinguish neither air nor words. Indeed, at his distance, the melody seemed improvised, capricious, the utterances of a voice peculiarly sweet but untrained.

It soon became evident that the songstress was on the south side of the rocky point, on which grew clumps of low cedar. Standing with an oar in the bow of his boat, and causing it to touch the shore so gently that the keel did not even grate upon the rock, he sprang lightly to land, and secured his vessel. He next stole crouchingly up behind a low, wide-spreading cedar, from whence he could see over the ridge.

It was a strange and unexpected vision that greeted him. He naturally supposed that some woodman's or farmer's daughter had come down to the bank, or that a party of pleasure had stopped there for a time. But he saw a creature whom he could in no way account for.

Reclining with her back toward him on a little grassy plot just above a rock that shelved down to the water, was a young girl dressed in harmony with her sylvan surroundings. Her attire was as simple as it was strange, consisting of an embroidered tunic of finely-dressed fawn-skin, reaching a little below the knee, and ending in a blue fringe. Some lighter fabric was worn under it and encased the arms. The shapely neck and throat were bare, though almost hidden by a wealth of wavy, golden tresses that flowed down her shoulders. Her hat appeared to have been constructed out of the skin of the snowy heron, with its beak and plumage preserved intact, and dressed into the jauntiest style. Leggings of strong buckskin, that formed a protection against the briars and roughness of the forest, were clasped around a slender ankle, and embroidered moccasins completed an attire that was not in the style of the girl of the period even a century ago. She might have passed for an Indian maiden, were it not for the snowy whiteness of her neck, where the sun had not browned it, and for her good pronunciation of English. In her little brown hand she held a fishing-rod, but she had ceased to watch her floral float, which was the bud of a water-lily tied to the line. Indeed, the end of her pole dipped idly in the water, while she, forgetful of the sport or toil, whichever it might be, sang her passing feelings and fancies as unaffectedly as the birds on the hills around, that now were growing tuneful after the heat of the day.

Thus far, our hero, whom we may as well introduce at once as Theron Saville, had been able to distinguish only disjointed words, that had no seeming connection ; mere musical sparkles, rising from the depths of a glad, innocent heart. But imagine his surprise when she commenced singing to an air that he had often heard in England :

"I know a bank whereon the wild thyme blows,
    Where oxlips and the nodding violet grows."

She broke off suddenly, sprang up, and commenced wind-
ing the line upon her pole.   Then Saville saw that, though
very young seemingly, she was taller and more fully developed than he had supposed.   At first glance she had
appeared to be little more than a child, but as she stood
erect, he saw that she was somewhat above medium height
and straight as an arrow.

He was most eager to see her face, thinking that it might
help to solve the mystery, but she perversely kept it from
him as she leisurely wound up her line, in the mean time
chattering to herself in a voice so flexible and natural that it
seemed to mirror every passing thought.   Now, in mimic
anger she cried, "Out upon you, fishes, great and small—
whales, leviathans, and minnows!   'Canst thou draw out
leviathan with a hook?   Canst thou put a hook into his
nose?'   No, I can't; nor in the nose of a single perch,
white or yellow.   Did I not whisper when I first came,
'Come home with me to supper?   Scaly, unmannerly
knaves, out upon you; I'll none of you."

Then, with instant change to comic pathos, she continued, "'Alas, 'tis true, 'tis pity; and pity 'tis, 'tis true.'
I'll none of you—when I wanted a dozen."

Suddenly, with a motion as quick as a bird on its spray,
she turned, and appeared to look directly at Saville.   He
was so startled that he almost discovered himself, but was
reassured by noticing that she had not seen him, but was
looking over his sheltering cedar at something beyond, with
a pouting vexation, that he learned a moment later was
only assumed.   He now saw her features, but while they
awakened a thrill of admiration, they gave no clue to her
mystery.   The hue of perfect health glowed upon her oval
face, while her eyes were like violets of darkest blue.   The

mouth was full, yet firm, and unlike Saville's, which was chiefly expressive of sensibility and suggested an emotional nature.

Altogether, she seemed a creature that might haunt a painter's or a poet's fancy, but have no right or real existence in this matter-of-fact world. Saville could not account for her, and still his wonder grew when she exclaimed in tones as mellow as the notes of the bird she addressed :

"What are you saying there, saucy robin? You're so proud of your scarlet waistcoat, you're always putting yourself forward. 'The sun's behind the mountain, and it's time for evening songs,' you say. Well, I can see that as well as you. Go sing to your little brown wife on her nest, and cease your 'mops and mowes' at me.

> "'I can sing in sunshine,
> I can sing in shadow,
> In the darkest forest glen,
> O'er the grassy meadow,
> At night, by day, 'tis all the same,
> Song is praise to His loved name.'"

Then she lifted her face and eyes heavenward, as if from an impulse of grateful devotion. Her white throat grew full, as in slower measure, and with a voice that seemed to fill the balmy June evening with enchantment, she sang as a hymn those exquisite words from Isaiah :

> "For ye shall go out with joy,
> And be led forth with peace ;
> The mountains and the hills
> Shall break forth before you into singing,
> And all the trees of the field shall clap their hands."

Saville was in a maze of bewilderment and delight. Was this a creature of earth or heaven? A fairy or an ideal Indian maiden, the perfect flower of sylvan life? All his classic lore flashed upon him. Oreads and dryads, nymphs

of the mountain and forest tripped through his brain to no
purpose.   She seemed to him as much a being of the imagination as any of them, but was so tantalizingly near and
real, that he could see the blood come and go in her face,
the rise and fall of her bosom, the changing light of her
eyes ; and yet he feared almost to breathe lest she should
vanish.   Moreover, a pure English accent, and familiarity
with Shakspeare and the Bible, savored not of the wigwam
nor of Greek mythology.   He resolved to watch her till she
seemed about to depart, and then seek to intercept her, and
by questions solve the enigma.

The girl stood quietly for a moment as the last sweet
notes of her voice were repeating themselves in faint echoes
from the hill-sides, and then in a low tone murmured,

" How can I be lonely when God makes all His creatures my playmates?''

In the quick transition that seemed one of her character-
istics, she soon snatched up her fishing-rod, exclaiming :

" Old Will Shakspeare, I know more than you.''   And
she sang again,

> " ' I know a bank ' where the strawberry ' blows,'
> Where the red ripe strawberry even now ' grows,'
> ' Quite over-canopied with luscious woodbine,
> With sweet musk roses and with eglantine ; '
> These I can gather long before the night,
> And carry home to mother ' with dances and delight '—

with dances and delight''—and as she repeated this refrain,
she lifted her slight pole like a wand over her head, and
commenced tripping on the little grassy plot as strange and
fantastic a measure as ever wearied Titania, the fairy queen.

There was another low cedar nearer to her, and Saville
determined to reach this, if possible.   He did so, unperceived, and for a moment gazed with increasing wonder on
her strange beauty.   Though she seemed a perfect child of

nature, as unconventional as a fawn in its gambols, there was not a trace of coarseness or vulgarity in feature or action.

Suddenly the girl ceased her improvised dance, and looked around as with a vague consciousness of alarm. It was evident she had not seen nor heard anything distinctly, but as if possessing an instinct akin to that of other wild creatures of the forest, she felt a danger she could not see. Or, perhaps, it was the influence of the same mysterious power which enables us in a crowded hall to fix our eyes and thoughts on one far removed, and, by something concerning which we hide our ignorance by the term '' magnetism,'' draw their eyes and thoughts to ourselves.

From her quivering nostrils and dilating eyes Saville saw that his nymph of the mountain, wood, or water—the embodied enigma that he was now most curious to solve—was on the eve of flight ; therefore, cap in hand, and with the suave grace of one familiar with the salons of Paris, he stepped forth from his concealment.

But, seemingly, his politeness was as utterly lost on the maiden as it would have been on a wild fawn, or the heron whose plumage mingled with her flowing hair ; for like an arrow she darted by him up the steep ascent, with a motion so swift, so seemingly instantaneous, that he stood gazing after her as helplessly as if a bird had taken wing.

It was not until she had gained a crag far above him, and there paused a moment, as if her curiosity mastered her fears, that he recovered himself, and cursed his stupid slowness.

But, when he again advanced toward her and essayed to speak, she sprang from her perch, and was lost in the thick copse-wood of the bank. Only her light hazel fishing-rod, and the line with the water lily bud, remained to prove that the whole scene was not an illusion, a piece of witchery that comported well with the hour and the romantic region.

Correctly imagining that though invisible she might be watching him, he took the flower and put it in his button-hole, leaving the pole on the bank ; then, taking off his hat, he again bowed in the direction whither she had fled, with his hand upon his heart, which pantomime he hoped contained enough simplicity and nature to serve in place of the words she would not stay to hear.

He then pushed his boat from the shore (for he no more thought of following her than he would a zephyr that had gone fluttering through the leaves), and permitted it to drift down with the tide as before.

With the faint hope of inducing her to appear again, he took up a flute, of which he had become quite a master, and which he usually carried with him on his solitary expeditions, and commenced playing the air to which she had sung the words,

"I know a bank ——"

He was rewarded by seeing first the plumage of the snowy heron, then the graceful outline of the maiden's form on a projecting rock where now frowns Battery Knox. He again doffed his hat, and turned the prow of his boat in-shore, at which she vanished.

Believing now that she was too shy to be won as an acquaintance, or resolute in her purpose to shun a stranger, he pursued his journey with many wondering surmises. But partly to please himself, and with some hope of pleasing her, he made the quiet June evening so resonant with music that even the birds seemed to pause and listen to the unwonted strains.

Thus he kept the shores echoing and re-echoing till his boat was gliding under a precipitous bluff, where it would be impossible to land. Here a light northern breeze came fluttering down the river with its innumerable retinue of ripples, and Saville threw down the flute and hoisted his sail. As he glided out from the shadow of the bluff to the center of the river, the same weird and beautiful voice resounded from the rocks above him, with a sweetness and fullness that filled the whole region and hour with enchantment,

"I know a bank whereon the wild thyme blows."

Then he saw the plumage of the snowy heron waving him a farewell, and distinguished the half concealed form of the maiden. The northern gale tossed her unconfined hair for a moment, and then the vision vanished.

The wind freshened, and soon the water was foaming about the bow of his boat. Taking up his flute, he gave as a responsive farewell the simple melody which had become a kind of signal between them, the one link of mutual knowledge. the gossamer thread that might draw their lives closer together.

The maiden, who no longer needed the sheltering foliage, but was concealed by the deepening twilight, listened till the faintest echoes had died away in the distance, and then, quite as bewildered and full of wonderment as the hero of our story, slowly retraced her steps toward West Point.

Saville gazed lingeringly and regretfully back upon the landscape that grew more picturesque every moment in the uncertain light, and felt that he was leaving a fairy land for one of stern and bitter realities.

CHAPTER II.

VERA AND HER HOME.

WITH slow and thoughtful steps, the young girl pursued her way, finding a path where, to another, there would have been only a tangled forest, growing among steep ridges and jagged rocks. But the freedom and ease with which she picked her way with almost noiseless tread, might have deepened the impression that in some occult manner she was akin to the wilderness in which she seemed so much at home. Having crossed a rocky hill, she entered a grassy foot-path, and soon approached a dwelling whence gleamed a faint light. Though her steps apparently gave forth no sound, they were heard, for suddenly innumerable echoes filled the silent valley, and two dogs, that must have been large and fierce, judging from their deep baying, came bounding toward her. With a low laugh she said :

"Here's 'much ado about nothing.' There, there, Tiger and Bull ; two precious fools you have made of yourselves, not to know me."

The great dogs fawned at her feet and licked her hands, and, by the humblest canine apologies, sought forgiveness for their rude greeting.

The light from within fell upon the somewhat haggard and startled face of a man who stood upon the door-step and peered out into the darkness.

"It's only I, father ;" and in a moment the girl was at his side.

'The man responded but slightly to her caress, and, entering the one large living-room of the cottage, sat down, without a word, in its most shadowy corner, seemingly finding something congenial in its gloom.

" What has kept you so late, Vera ?" asked a woman who was taking from a rude cupboard the slender materials of the evening meal.

" I was watching a queer little sail-boat, mother."

" Sail-boat, sail-boat ; has it landed near us ?" asked the man, starting up.

" No, father. I watched till it disappeared down the river," said the girl, soothingly.

" That's a good child. Still it does not signify ; no one could have any business with me."

But the slight tremor of excitement in the girl's tone caused the mother to give her a quick, searching glance, and she saw that something unusual had occurred.

Vera looked smilingly and significantly into the pale, anxious face turned to her, and her glance said, " I will tell you all by-and-by."

The woman continued her tasks, though in a manner so feeble as to indicate that the burden of life was growing too heavy to be borne much longer, while Vera assisted her with the quickness of youth and the deftness of experience.

From a little " lean-to" against the side of the house, used as a kitchen, an aged negress now appeared. A scarlet handkerchief formed a sort of turban above her wrinkled visage. She was tall, but bent with years, and there was a trace of weird dignity in her bearing, that was scarcely in keeping with her menial position.

" Did de young missis bring anyting ?" she asked.

" Nothing, Gula," said the young girl, lightly. " The unmannerly fish laughed me to scorn. Though I tempted them above with a lily bud, and beneath with a wriggling

angle-worm, not one would come home with me. They
were afraid of you, Gula."

"Den dare's nothin' for supper but milk and bread,"
muttered the old woman.

"It will suffice for me. To morrow I will be up with
the lark, and have a dish of strawberries for breakfast."
And she hummed to herself:

> "I know the bank whereon they grow—
> A thing Will Shakspeare does not know."

The mother looked at her fondly, but her smile ended in
a sigh. With her, almost everything in life was now ending
with a sigh.

The frugal repast being ready, the father was summoned,
but before he would leave his partial concealment, he asked
Vera to close the window-shutters, so as to preclude the
possibility of any one looking in from the outer darkness.
The man seemed haunted by some vague fear which was
not shared by the rest of the family, but which, in his case,
was tacitly recognized and humored. He ate his supper
hurriedly, and then retired again to his dusky corner, where
he sat the remainder of the evening, silent, save when
spoken to by his wife and daughter, who evidently tried to
retain him as part of the family circle, though he morbidly
shrank within himself.

The mother and daughter were left alone at the table, at
which they sat even after Gula had removed to the kitchen
the slight remnants of the meal. A dip-candle burned
dimly between them, and lighted up, but with deep con-
trasts of shadow, two remarkable faces—not such as one
would expect to find in a rude log cabin of the wilderness;
for the uncertain rays revealed the fact, though disguised by
many a dainty rural device, that the walls of the dwelling
were of rough-hewn logs. But the homely surroundings

only brought out more clearly the unmistakable refinement of the faces of mother and daughter, now turned toward each other in a subtle interchange of sympathy that scarcely needed words. They seemed to have formed the habit of communicating with each other by significant glances and little signs apparent to no one save themselves, and there existed between them a love so deep and absorbing that it was ever a source of tranquil pleasure to look into each other's eyes. This silent communion was rendered necessary in part, because there was much of which they could not speak in the presence of the father and husband in his present warped, morbid condition of mind. To her mother Vera embodied her name, and was truth itself, revealing, like her playmates the mountain streams, everything in her crystal thoughts. To her father she was equally true, but was so through a system of loving disguises and concealments. If she had told him of her adventure of the afternoon he would have been greatly excited, and sleep were banished for the night.

The mother saw that Vera had a confidence to give, and quietly waited until they should be alone; and as she looked tenderly upon her child, her pale, spiritual face might have realized the ideal of pure motherly love. As such, in after years, Vera remembered it. It was well that she should look long and fondly upon those dear features, for in their thin transparency they promised soon to become *only* a memory.

But Vera knew nothing of death. She had never seen a pallid, rigid human face, and the thought that the dear face before her could ever become such, was too dreadful to have even entered her mind.

The mother, with a secret and growing uneasiness, had been conscious of her failing powers. Her usual household cares became daily more burdensome. She panted for breath, after tasks that once seemed light. Her rest, instead of being sweet and refreshing, was broken through the long night by a hacking cough, which the bland air of June did not remove as she had fondly hoped. But, in the strange delusion of her disease, she ever expected to be '' better in a few days,'' and she never had the courage to blanch the joyous face of Vera with the vague fear which in spite of her hopes sometimes found entrance to her mind. The malady had been so slow and insidious in its advances, that Vera had not noticed the daily yet almost imperceptible changes, but old Gula sometimes shook her head ominously, though she said nothing. The husband was too deeply shadowed by one oppressive fear to have thought for anything else ; and so the poor exile (for such she was) unconsciously to herself and those she loved, daily drew nearer to the only home where the heart is at rest.

Upon a rustic shelf above Vera's head were two books that originally had been quite handsomely bound. They were the products of a time when things were made to last ; and yet such had been their vicissitudes and constant use that they looked old and worn. They were the only books Vera had ever seen. They had been the story-books of her childhood, and long before she could read them, her mother had beguiled her by the hour with their marvelous tales. They had been the school-books in which she had conned her letters ; and, following her mother's pointing finger, she had spelled her way through them, when the long and unpronounceable words were to her lisping tongue what the rugged boulders around their home were to her little feet. She had often stumbled over both ; still she had learned to love the mossy boulders and the equally formidable words, and the latter had gradually become stepping-stones to her thoughts. These books were now yearly developing for her deeper and richer meanings, and were having no small part in the formation of her character. The gilt letters on their backs were not so faded and worn but that the titles could still be read—the "Plays of William Shakspeare," and "Holy Bible."

The former had been given to Vera's mother in other and happier days, and in another land, by the man, now but a wreck of the handsome, spirited youth, who then gave glances and words with the gift, which she valued more than the book. She had given him the Bible in return, and he formerly had read it somewhat for her sake, though seldom for its own. The Bible was much the smaller and plainer volume, and suggested that the purse of the donor might not have been as large as her love. In the sudden and dire emergency which made them exiles, these two gifts of affection had been hastily snatched among the few other things they had been able to take, in the confused and hurried moment of departure.

At a sign from her mother, Vera took down this Bible, and drawing the failing candle nearer, read a few verses from the 14th chapter of St. John, commencing, "Let not your heart be troubled." At the close of each day, for many sad and anxious years, the poor woman had tried to sustain her faith by these divine, reassuring words. They were read first, not only for her own support, but in the hope that they might have a soothing, calming effect upon the disquieted mind of her husband. To Vera, also, she believed that they might eventually become a legacy of hope and strength. After they were read, some other passage was also chosen.

The mother had opened the kitchen door that Gula might hear, if she would, since she never could be persuaded to be present at the family altar. Gula had been stolen from her African home, where, as she once hinted in a moment of anger, she had possessed some rude and savage kind of royalty, and since that time she had suffered cruelty and wrongs without stint from those who called themselves Christians ; thus she naturally chose to remain a pagan.

As Vera read the sacred words, the mother's face, where she sat, a little back from the light, was sweet and shadowy enough to be that of a guardian spirit.

The corner in which the father remained had grown so dark that only the gleam of his restless eyes could be seen. Vera's voice was sweet, low, and reverent. It was not a form, but a heartfelt service in which she was leading, and one that she knew to be dear to her mother.

She made a pretty picture, with the dim candle lighting up her classic profile and a bit of her golden hair. All the rest was in partial and suggestive shadow.

After the lesson of the day had been read, they sat a few moments in prayerful silence. With the shrinking timidity which some women find it impossible to overcome, this Christian wife had learned to pray unceasingly in her heart, but could never venture upon outspoken words. Her nature was gentleness itself, and strong only in its power to cling with unselfish, unfearing tenacity to those she loved. Had her husband been condemned to suffer any form of death, her meek spirit would have uttered no protest, but only force could have prevented her from sharing his fate. If, by interposing her own life she could save her daughter's, she would give it up so naturally and instinctively that the thought of self-sacrifice would not even occur to her. Years before, she had renounced, for the sake of her love, everything save honor ; and though knowing that exile and soon death itself would result, she never considered the possibility of any other course, but in resignation accepted what she regarded as her inevitable lot. Where she loved most, with the certainty of gravitation, her steps would follow, while the power remained. She was one whom the world would call weak, but whose strength God would honor, because possessing in her humble sphere His loftiest attribute, patient, all-enduring love.

Before seeking her own little nest, Vera went out to speak to the old negress, whom she found sitting on a low doorstep, smoking her pipe.

"Art lonely, Gula?"

"No, chile, I'se got past dat. Dare's lots talkin' to ole Gula."

"Why, I hear nothing save the whippoorwills, and the frogs in the marsh."

"I doesn't hear dem. De voices dat come to me come from far back o' dese mountains. I isn't lonely any mo'."

"How queer!" said Vera musingly. "But you were lonely once, Gula?"

"Yes, chile; for nigh on twenty summer and winter my heart was a-breakin'. I was so homesick like, dat I wanted to die ebery minute. Den I died. My heart was jus a heavy stun in my bres'; only my body was kind o' half alive so it could work when dey whipped it. But de heart inside didn't tink nuffin, nor feel nuffin, nor know nuffin. On a sudden, one night, I kind o' woke up and heerd voices a callin' me to run, and I got up and run, and trabbled for days and nights till I got here; den de voices tole me to stop. And I'se a stoppin' and a waitin' to see what de voices say nex."

"I can't understand it," said Vera wonderingly.

"No, chile, you needn't try."

"Where do these voices come from?"

"From way back o' dese hills—from farder dan de great water whar dem floatin' miseries, dey call ships, go—from whar de sun shine hotter dan it did to-day, all de time. Oh, dis poor ole heart's nebber been warm since dey carried me, screamin', on de floatin' misery. Go to bed, chile, g⌐

to bed ; ole Gula hopes you'se body'll nebber be alive arter your heart's dead."

" Poor old Gula," said Vera, in a voice so gentle, so sympathetic, that it would have moved the stoniest nature. " I'm very sorry for you.   ' Let not your heart be troubled,' Gula. "

The old woman was touched by the young girl's compassion ; but she had a strange, rugged pride, that prevented her from ever receiving openly what still was balm in secret. Probably the voices that had induced the fugitive to stay at the humble cottage were those of her present mistress and Vera, speaking in the long unheard accents of kindness, though in the poor creature's disordered fancy they had blended with those she imagined coming from her old tropical home.   Therefore, the roughness with which she said,

" Dare, dare, chile, none o' dat, don't keep you'se mudder waitin' ; go to bed," was only assumed to disguise the sudden relenting which usually takes place when the flintiest heart is touched by the potent wand of kindness.

" Good night, Gula," said Vera.   " Among your voices you shall always hear mine ; and I hope it won't be cross often ;" and she followed her mother, who had already gone on before to her child's sleeping apartment.

It was as strange a little nook as one could imagine ; and if Vera had been a nymph of the mountains, as her appearance had suggested to Saville, this resting-place would have been in harmony.   The rude cottage had been built at the sloping base of the rocky height crowned in later years with the frowning walls of Fort Putnam.   Just above the cabin on the southern side, a huge crag projected so far from the rocky steep as to form a natural shelter or sort of cave. This little niche had been enlarged by excavation, and the granite eaves extended by rough-hewn boards, so as to form quite a roomy apartment, which Vera and her mother had disguised into as dainty a rural bower as any grotto of the Grecian nymphs. It was connected with the main living-room of the cabin by a covered way securely thatched and protected at the sides by heavy logs, fastened in the securest manner. Indeed the entire dwelling had been built with almost the strength of a fortress, and Vera's father seemed to find a growing satisfaction in strengthening its various parts with stone and wood. The brief ascent to her "nest" —as the young girl called it—was made by stone steps. When her mother grew feeble, Vera brought home a slender grapevine that she had found swinging from a lofty forest-tree, and stretched it from her door to that of the living-room. By laying hold of this, the ascent could be made with greater ease. A stout cord passed along the roof, so that if anything happened, summons or alarm could be given instantly. But though the poor man who arranged all these precautions seemed burdened with an increasing dread, the years had passed, and they had been unmolested in their wilderness retreat.

The mother placed the candle on a little bureau, and sat, panting from her climb, on the edge of Vera's couch. The daughter drew a bench forward, and dropping on it, leaned her arms on her mother's lap and looked up into her face as she did when a little child. Indeed, in her guileless innocence and ignorance of the world from which she had ever been secluded, she was still a child, though fully sixteen.

"Now, mother, you have been working too hard again to-day," she said reproachfully. "See how tired you are."

"No, dear—I am only a little breathless—from climbing to your nest. I get out of breath so easily of late. Now tell me what has happened."

Vera described her adventure of the afternoon, which in her tranquil life was a notable event. She dwelt long and somewhat admiringly upon the stranger's appearance and manner, especially his act of putting the water-lily bud in his button-hole.

" If he roves flowers, mother, he can't be bad."

But it was upon the notes of his flute that she descanted most enthusiastically. " And do you know, mother, he played the same air that I had been singing, and which you taught me years ago. But he must have thought me wild as a hawk."

" No, dear, as timid as a dove."

" Well, I was greatly startled at first. When I got a good look at him I was not so much afraid. But you, and especially father, have so often warned me against making acquaintances. You don't think I was rude, now ?"

" No, dear, no more than the birds that take wing when you come too near."

" The birds are getting very presuming, mother ; they either think that I am one of them or not worth minding. They only cock their little heads on one side and give me a saucy look, and then go about their business just as if I were not near."

" They know and do not fear their friends," said the mother abstractedly, " and you have been their harmless playmate so long that they know all about you." And the poor woman gave a long sigh.

" Now what does that mean, mother ?"

" That you cannot always have such innocent and harmless companions. You are growing up, Vera. You cannot always be a little wild-flower of the woods. You must make acquaintances erelong. It is needful that you should. But how are you to make them ? Where are you to find them ? We are strangely situated. I wish we had some good neighbors, and your father did not feel as he does."

" Ought I then to have stayed and spoken to this young man ?"

" No, darling, you did right.   He was an utter stranger. And yet such are all the world.   The ordinary ties which unite us to our fellow creatures seem utterly broken, and our isolation is so complete that I see no escape from it. For myself I do not mind it.   I am content.   But for your sake, Vera, I do indeed wish it were otherwise."

" I too am content, mother.   The woods are full of play-mates for me, and we chatter away to each other as merrily as the day is long.   We are beginning to understand each other too.   Do you know, mother, that the sounds of nature seem a sort of language which I am fast learning?   I went out on the hills the other day after the shower, and found a brook and a brown-thrush singing a duet together, and I sat down and mocked them till I learned what they were saying"—and in almost perfect mimicry she first gave the gurgling murmur of the stream and then the mellow whistle of the thrush.

" You are a strange child, Vera.   But what did the brook and bird say?   I do not understand their language."

" Why, it's plain as can be.   They said, ' Cheer up, Vera.   Let not your heart be troubled.   After the shower comes the sunshine.'   What else could they mean?   There was the brook sparkling in the sunlight, and singing the louder for the shower ; and there was the little bird, which neither the lightning nor the rain had hurt."

Tears came into the mother's eyes, and kissing her child, she said :

" Good night, Vera ; you are so innocent that God talks with you, as He did with Adam and Eve in the garden."

The mother returned to the main room, which was also used as a sleeping apartment.   Gula had already retired by some rude steps to her loft overhead.

With the dawn of the next day, the mother was awakened by Vera's receding voice, mingling with the songs of her music-masters, the birds, and knew that she had gone for the promised strawberries. Before very long, she returned with an oddly constructed basket of broad leaves, heaped up with the daintiest fruit of the year, and a moment later the cabin was filled with their wild aroma, as, with scarlet fingers, Vera quickly prepared them for breakfast.

"How kind it was of you to get us these berries," said her mother. "I thought I had lost my appetite altogether, but these taste so good that I must be better. Perhaps they will make me well."

The flush of pleasure that came into Vera's face vied with the ruby fruit, and she said, joyously:

"You shall have them, mother, as long as there is one to be found in the shadiest nook."

The light of day now revealed clearly the character of their abode, which, in its exterior, did not differ greatly from the ordinary log cabin of the frontier. There had evidently been an effort to make it exceedingly strong, and on every side were loop-holes, through which could be passed the muzzle of a rifle.

But the usual bareness and unsightliness of these primitive dwellings had been quite removed by festoons of the American woodbine (or ivy) which Vera had planted at the corners, and trained along the eaves and to the very ridge. There were also attempts at flower-beds, in which she had sought to tame some of her wild favorites of the woods.

But the interior was an interesting study, from the effort of refinement, everywhere manifest, to triumph over the rudest materials. Such of the furniture as had been bought, was strong and plain, and had evidently been selected from motives of economy. This had been added to and supplemented as far as the ingenuity of the inmates permitted, and on every side were seen pretty little things that were not childish, and yet would please a child.

Autumn leaves, still brilliant, which Vera had pressed, with great pains, between dry leaves preserved for the purpose, festooned the unsightly walls, producing an effect that gave the young girl more content then Gobelin tapestry gives to its princely possessors. Mingling with these festoons were button-balls, cut the preceding autumn from the plane-tree, and bright red berries. In one corner was a huge hornet's nest, suspended from the branch where its savage little architects had built it the year before, and whose construction Vera had watched with great interest, until, in the fall, the paper citadel, that an army would hesitate to attack, was evacuated ; then she had carried it home as a trophy. But she found that it still contained a small garrison, which occasioned no little commotion as they recovered from their torpor in the warmth of the room. On a spray beside this fortress, was placed, for contrast, an abode of peace—a humming-bird's tiny nest. In place of prosaic pegs and hooks, the antlers of the stag were fastened here and there, and served many a useful purpose. Rustic brackets, and a cross of gray bark, with a mossy base, divested the apartment of all appearance of the squalid poverty that often characterizes the pioneer's cabin.

But the principal feature was the wide stone fireplace into which for many years Vera could pass without stooping, and in the corner of which she still sat on winter evenings, reading by the light of the blazing fire, her inexhaustible story book, the " Plays of William Shakspeare." Over the hearth was a great iron crane ; and it was a proud day for Vera when she learned to relieve her mother by swinging it in and out, deftly hanging thereon the sooty kettle, without smirching her hands or dress. Above a rude mantel, on which Vera had placed some odd little ornaments gathered in her rambles, were suspended a long rifle of very fine workmanship, and a silver-mounted fowling-piece, which the exiles had brought with them, rightly estimating their value when seeking a refuge in the wilderness. The shot-gun was light but strong, and of exquisite finish, and had in other days brought down many a pheasant in English parks. It carried just as truly now, and Vera had learned to be almost as unerring in its use as her father. In conse-quence, a plump partridge frequently graced their board that too often was meagre enough. For a large part of the year game was their principal food, as her father supported his family by hunting and trapping. But of late he had grown so moody and uncertain in his actions, that for days he would sit in his shadowy corner brooding over · some dark secret of the past. It would then devolve on Vera alone to supply the needs of the household, and at times the poor child's heart was heavy, as weary and discouraged she re-turned in the evening only to report her ill-success. Then her father would rouse up as if his manhood were struggling against the paralysis creeping over his mind, and he would be more like his former self. But as Vera grew older, and more acquainted with the habits and haunts of game, and learned in what waters to drop her line successfully, she became more self-reliant and confident that she could at least maintain a supply of food if the worst came to the worst. On days when the man's mind was most unclouded, he would, at his wife's solicitation, take the skins and prod-ucts of the chase to some village down the river, and barter them for such things as were needed. A little of the hoard of gold which they had brought with them still remained, and was kept for some emergency of the future.

Thus the years passed on, and Vera was ceasing to be a child in appearance, though still a child in guileless sim-plicity, and content with the pleasures and duties which had filled her time thus far.

CHAPTER III.

THE ICONOCLASTS.

THE northern breeze caused Saville's boat to glide rapidly through the looming shadows of the lower Highlands, and in comparatively brief time lights glimmered invitingly from the village of Peekskill, which was situated at the head of a wide bay upon the eastern shore. Here he decided to seek refreshment and spend the night, intending to pursue his homeward journey the following morning.

The episode of the afternoon had formed a pleasing but temporary diversion to the thoughts it had interrupted ; but now, with increasing power to pain and agitate, they came trooping back. In the consciousness of solitude and in the enshrouding darkness, he made less effort at self-control. His features were distorted by contending emotions, and he often gave vent to passionate exclamations. It was evident that a painful question was pressing upon him for immediate solution, and that the results of his action in any case would be very serious.

But by the time he reached the rude wharf he regained his self-command, and having moored his boat, sought a dwelling which combined the character of farm-house and tavern. Here he received a welcome that was but in part professional, for in those days of limited travel, a stranger was an event, and a guest in reality as well as in name, being often made much of, and becoming an object of absorbing interest, it might be added also, of curiosity, to his entertainers. .

Saville found the little inn already in a state of excitement and bustle over the arrival of an old acquaintance of his own, a wealthy, pleasure-loving young gentleman from the city below, who was off on a fishing excursion, and who eagerly sought to gain Saville as a companion.

" What is the news from the army before Boston ?" asked Saville, gloomily.

" ' The army before Boston ' be hanged, and the army in Boston also.   I could not sit down to dinner but a fire-brand of a patriot would pluck one sleeve, and demand, ' Are you for Liberty ? ' and an ancient fossil who had brushed against a duke, or mayhap a duchess, would pluck the other sleeve, and querulously question, ' Are you not for the King ? '   It was in vain that I anathematized both, and said, ' No, I'm for dinner.'   There is no such thing as peace down there, unless you are ranting on one side or the other.   So I snatched my fishing tackle, and showing a clean pair of heels, am here among the mountains.   It's a confounded poor world for a man to enjoy himself in. There are always two parties in it bound to devour each other, and if you won't raven on one side or the other, they'll both turn in and rend you.   I don't care whether the laws are made in Philadelphia or London, if they will only let me alone.   There, I'm through with the accursed squabbles of the hour.   I'm here to get rid of them, and intend for the next few days to forget the existence of both Parliament and Congress.   So come with me, and keep out of purgatory as long as you can."

In spite of his prolonged mental conflict, Saville still felt himself unequal to solve the question that burdened him ; and so to gain time and distract his thoughts, he complied with his friend's wish.

On the following morning they started, equipped for the sport.   It was the Sabbath, but in Saville's estimation the

day was no more sacred than would be a Decadi of the coming French Revolution. He had lived in infidel France
sufficiently long to regard the Sabbath as a relic of superstition. He was a disciple of the " New Philosophy," and
had faith in naught save man, and man was a law unto
himself.

But the sport which completely absorbed his companion
dragged heavily with Saville, and after a few days he returned
to his boat, resolving to put off his decision no longer ; so
the latter part of the week saw him again beating southward
against the wind with many a long tack, as the river broad-
ened before him.

Saville's position was a trying one, and yet not peculiar
in that day when the plowshare of division ran, not only
through communities, social circles, and churches, but also
through families, severing the closest ties. In order that
his present circumstances and character may be better understood, it will be necessary to take a brief glance into the
past.

Theron Saville combined both the French and Dutch elements in his parentage. On his father's side he came from
that grand old Huguenot stock which has largely leavened
for good the American character. He had thus inherited a
legacy of prayer and sacred memories from his ancestry,
and might if he would, receive the blessing which descends
to children's children : a " covenant-keeping God " would
faithfully seek to reclaim him from evil. But he had utterly
abandoned the faith of his fathers, and was now an open
unbeliever.

His moral state was the natural result of the influences he
had fallen under during his education. In accordance with
a custom quite common among patrician families in colonial
days, he had been sent to Europe to finish his studies.
After a few years at an English university he went to Paris to

acquire his profession, that of military and civil engineering. But his tastes did not lead in the direction of exact and practical science, and he appreciated the French opera far more than French roads and fortifications. But it was the new and skeptical literature of that chaotic age that chiefly fascinated him. The brilliant theorists and iconoclasts who were then, with jest and infinite wit, recklessly sapping the foundations of the slowly built structures of human belief, of social custom, and of established government, seemed to him the heroes of the world. He, as little as they, foresaw the crashing ruin for which they were preparing. Bigoted violence had succeeded only too well in stamping out and exiling the Huguenot element, and what then passed for religion in France, was such a wretched imposition as to be despised even by its consecrated priests. Social distinctions were arbitrary and unnatural. Etiquette ruled in the place of fidelity and principle, and behind this tinsel mask gross license rioted. Government had become simply the oppression of the many by the few—an organized system to rob the people that the titled might indulge in unbounded extravagance. The corner-stone, which is the family, with its sacred and guarded rights, had crumbled, and the whole social and political fabric was consequently tottering in inevitable weakness. The character of the times made it far easier to scoff and strike at all institutions that should be sacred than to reform them ; and the leading minds of the day were great only in their genius for satire and innovation. But it was the fearful degeneracy in the institutions themselves that gave point to the sarcasm, and it was their crumbling weakness that made blows, which now seem puny, then to appear herculean.

Young Saville, unschooled by experience, had just the temperament to be carried away by the railing and irreverent spirit of the age. Naturally visionary, enthusiastic, and gifted with far more imagination than judgment, he reveled in the " Atheistic Philosophy," and exulted over it as the groundwork of a new and better order of things. Voltaire enchained him by his boundless wit. Diderot, and even Helvetius with his gross, materialistic theory, that sensation originates all that there is in man, became his masters, while in political creed he was a disciple of Jean Jacques Rousseau. Liberty, which was of an impossible kind —liberty, which from the absence of safeguards and foundations must, and in fact did, degenerate into the wildest license, became his dream ; and he hoped to become eventually an apostle of this French ideal of freedom, in his own land.

Yet when the time came for Saville to return to New York, he had not become utterly vitiated by the evil influences which were then demoralizing a nation. Something in the old Huguenot blood and in his early training still remained in his nature as a germ that might be developed into healthful growth. He was not false, though unrestrained by religion, or even by what was regarded as morality in his own land ; he accepted the world's code of honor and unlike the world in which he had been living, was true to it. His word bound him ; and though capable of very wrong action, he shrank from anything mean, base, or ungrateful. He was not coldly, selfishly, and deliberately depraved at heart. He scoffed with his favorite author, Voltaire, not at what he believed sacred, but at what, in that false age, pretended to sacredness, and was in fact a solemn and venerable farce. The truth back of this, which had been corrupted or abandoned altogether, he did not recognize nor even believe in its existence. A false priesthood had made religion a byword and a hissing. As ignorant and superficial as the leaders of opinion, he did not distinguish the purer faith of his fathers from the gross superstition from which it had separated itself, but condemned all religion as the folly of credulity, the evidence of a weak and unenlightened mind.

He was heartily in sympathy with Rousseau's best characteristic, hatred of the artificial and unnatural, and joined in his protest against the absurd and arbitrary tyranny of etiquette and monstrous custom.   He believed with the great innovator, that after the rags had been taken from the peasant, and the titles and court dress lifted from the noble, in each case remained that essential atom of society—man ; and he held that this human unit, with its innate rights and qualities, naturally developed, must be the starting point in the reorganization of the political fabric.

He could not then see that he and his teachers would ever build in vain, even were they to attempt reconstruction ; for they ignored man's moral and spiritual nature and its needs.   Let man build his side of the arch never so well, the work would crumble, because the opposite side, which is God and the pure morality of his law, and the key-stone, which is intelligent faith and obedience, would be utterly lacking.

But there was hope for Saville, because he was so sincere in his skepticism ; because he accepted so enthusiastically theories, the majority of which now have in history a record like that of brilliant meteors only.   He had not reached the most hopeless of mental attitudes, that of coldly doubting everything, nor had he sunk into the apathy of discouragement, or plunged into the recklessness of those who see nothing good or sure save present gratification.

His authors were demi-gods, and adorned a temple of fame which he might enter.   He was not near enough to know the selfishness, meanness, and often baseness of their lives.   If he had read the confessions of Rousseau, he might not so readily have become his disciple.   The fact that he could honestly believe in these writers and their teachings, proved him capable of accepting the truth with equal heartiness, when once apprehended.

Saville heard with pleasure of the growing restlessness in the American colonies under British rule, and ardently hoped that he might there become a leading advocate of the broad liberty of the new philosophy.

It became his favorite dream that he might be one of the founders of a republic in the new world, in which liberty and equality should be the corner-stones, human reason the sole architect, and nature the inspiration. During his voyage home, he spent much of his time in the imaginary construction of this Utopia of the future, in which he hoped to have no mean place. Nor was it at all surprising that one of his age and temperament should have fallen completely under the influence of the philosophy that was then sweeping over the world.

CHAPTER IV.

" FOR WORSE."

SAVILLE had not been long in his native city before an event occurred that changed the spirit of his dreams, or rather blended them with others of a different nature. The nebulous goddess of liberty, at whose feet he had been worshiping, was exchanged for a creature of flesh and blood, earthy indeed, material even to her mind.   But Saville had a faculty of seeing things, not as they were, but through a transfiguring mist of his own imagination.

During his voyage home, his father had died suddenly, and, in consequence, young Saville, for a few months immediately after his return, was much secluded from social and political life.   Sorrow renders the heart more tender and receptive, and there were long and vacant days to be beguiled.   His mother, who had inherited the thrifty traits of her Dutch ancestry, availed herself of this opportunity to secure an alliance which worldly wisdom would commend, inasmuch as the young lady in question was the heiress of property which would double the large wealth of her son, and thus, of course, double his happiness.   Their mutual acres were so situated that they could be joined together with great advantage.   Whether the moral and mental qualities of the parties themselves were equally adapted to union, was not considered, and indeed seldom is, by your sagacious match-maker, who to the end of time will be filled with self-congratulation on having united estates.   That two poor souls must henceforth dwell in purgatorial fires of discord, or become polished icicles under the steady frost of indifference, is a mere matter of sentiment. Two acres instead of one is a solid consideration, and ought to satisfy any heart.

Mrs. Saville loved her son after her fashion, and was serving him, as she supposed, in the best and most enduring manner. She was aware that society would regard the match as brilliant ; and to have the world nod approval was as great a thing a hundred years ago as to-day. She had met the parents, the uncles, and aunts of the coveted neiress, in solemn conclave on the subject, and found them quite as ready to enter into the arrangement as herself. With many fine speeches they disguised the property considerations uppermost in each mind, and it was agreed that the young lady's disposition should be delicately inclined to assist. That willful factor in the problem, however, bluntly said, " I'll wait and see him first. "

This very natural decision disturbed Mrs. Saville but little ; for she knew that unless her son had changed greatly, his appearance would be in his favor. Her chief ground of anxiety was the action of the young man himself.

" Men are so unreasonable," she said ; " but unless Theron is utterly blind to his own interests, he must see things as we do. The young lady I have chosen for him is rich, handsome, and of one of the first families in the colony. Indeed her relatives in England are titled."

All this was true. Mrs. Saville had weighed exfernals carefully. Julia Ashburton was very handsome after her type and style. The prudent mother had considered everything save the viewless, subtle spirit which dwelt within the beauty, and which would prove, to the sorrow of all concerned, the spirit of a Tartar.

Verily Saville was utterly blind to his own interests ; for, soon after his return, he delighted his mother and the other schemers by action that accorded with their plans.

Miss Ashburton was eminently gifted with the power to awaken passion ; and in one who, like Theron Saville, saw everything through the transfiguring haze of his own fancy, she could even inspire an approach to love. But a man who desired a wife, a home, and domestic peace, would look askance at her. Her black eyes were too near together, and emitted scintillations rather than the pure, steady light of a womanly nature. They could fascinate and beguile with something of a serpent's power, but they would drop abashed before the searching gaze of an honest man. Her forehead was none too low, but it was narrow. The development of her lower face was full ; not too much so, perhaps, for sensuous beauty, but to a close observer it would suggest the trait of stubbornness, and the possibility that passion might triumph over all restraint. But it was the perfection of her form—which she was not at all chary in displaying—and her grace of carriage, which constituted her chief attractions. She was as lithe and supple as a leopard, as well as feline in many of her qualities.

But Saville glorified her into ideal womanhood, and she for a time fostered his delusion. Having seen the handsome young stranger, who possessed all the courtly bearing and polish that could be acquired in French salons, she readily joined in the family conspiracy. She was as gentle and sympathetic as it was in her nature to be, and gave him most of her time. A spirit less exuberant than Saville's would have had a vague sense of dissatisfaction—a consciousness of something wanting in both her words and manner ; but his heart, generous to a fault, was deeply touched by her show of regard for his recent bereavement, and his love for her was mingled with gratitude. Soon she saw him a captive at her feet, and could make her own terms.

During the long hours spent together, he, hoping to find a sympathetic and congenial spirit, had often enlarged (to her horror) on his favorite dreams of broad, democratic liberty and equality. He even permitted her to see his bitter hostility to everything that bore the name of religion, or superstition, as he would characterize it, and he regarded all forms of faith as the chosen instruments of tyranny. He believed that he could soon kindle in her an enthusiasm equal to his own for the new and glorious ideas that he had acquired abroad, and for the reception of which, he imagined, events were rapidly preparing America.

Now, Miss Ashburton was, by nature and education, as hostile to these ideas as it was possible for any one to be. She was a Tory and royalist to her heart's core, as were all her family ; and their descent from a titled house in England was the cherished source of their abounding pride.

The girl to whom Saville often discoursed of his Utopian dreams, in a manner so rapt and pre occupied that he scarcely noted her effort to disguise her apathy and distaste, was not capable of enthusiasm for anything save herself. Selfishness, the bane of all character, especially of woman's, had consumed the kindly endowments of her nature, and sometimes, when her lover's face was flushed in the excitement of his own thronging thoughts, which were at least large and generous, if mainly erratic, there would come a crafty, and even vindictive, gleam into her eyes, which seemed to say, " I will endure with such patience as I can, until the uniting links in the chain are forged, and then you must listen to me."

If, at times, her manner chilled him, and he imagined her lacking in sympathy, he consoled himself by the thought that she did not yet understand these great themes, and that he could not expect her to reach in a few weeks the advanced views, which, in his case, had required years, and that, too, where they formed the political and social atmosphere in which men lived.

As for Miss Ashburton, she soon perceived what she regarded the weak point in his character – the one that would give her the advantage in the inevitable conflict that must come after marriage ; and that was his loyalty to his word —a scrupulous, generous, though perverted sense of honor. He was a true gentleman, after the fashionable French ideal, and not according to the French reality. It was a sad fact, that in that debauched and chaotic age, the ninth commandment, and, indeed, every other in the Decalogue, rested as lightly on the French conscience as the seventh. Of course there were many honorable exceptions, and to these Saville belonged.

Therefore, when in due time he poured out his passion, she was full of demure hesitancy and doubt. "Would he be faithful to her?" she asked. "He had lived too long in Paris, where men's eyes and fancies were given too great freedom. He believed in such new and strange French doctrines, which seemed to unsettle everything, even religion, and was captivated by French ideas in general. How could she be sure that she had secured a steady, loyal English husband?"

In view of Saville's theories and rhapsodies she might perhaps have urged these objections with some reason. But the astute maiden had no fears on these grounds. She was skillfully playing part of a pre-arranged game. She would bind him by many and varied pledges. She would keep him from the course on which his heart was bent, by promises that now seemed silken cords of love and loyalty, but would afterward prove galling fetters by which she would hold him captive under a merciless tyranny.

Unsuspicious of her object, he gave her pledges innumerable, which could readily be made to bear the meaning she designed, but which in his mind had no such purport. Having ensnared and woven a web around her victim, she gracefully permitted herself to be won.

It was a rude awakening that Saville had from his delirium of love, and dream of inspiring sympathy in his career as an apostle of the broadest liberty, wherein all kings, human and divine, were to be overthrown. His wife had been under restraint too long already for one of her willful, self-pleasing nature, and she threw off the mask with unseemly haste. To his dismay he found that he had married a pretty bigot, who would not hear a word against church or state, the venerable abuses of which were even dearer to her than their excellencies. Nay, more, she told him that by all his oaths of loyalty to her he was bound to the Tory side, which was then rapidly becoming defined in distinction from the Whig, or patriot party ; and such was the ingenuity of her feminine tact, that in his bewilderment he half feared that she was right ; and that he, like the Hebrew slaves, would be compelled to build the structures he would gladly tear down.

At first, he chafed like a lion in the toils ; but on every side she met him with the meshes of his own unwary promises. In vain he protested that loyalty to her did not involve loyalty to institutions that he hated.

"I am identified with these causes," she would coolly reply.

By this chain of loyalty to her, she would even drag him to church, and made religion seem ten-fold more hateful by the farce she there enacted. His eyes were now opened, and he readily saw that she was a bigot to the forms of worship, and that the doctrines of her church were neither understood nor considered. Her spirit was that of the Italian bandit, who will shed his own blood to carry out the purposes of his priest, and the blood of any one else that his interest or revenge may require.

Thus the wretched months dragged on, and Saville was a moody captive.   As the stirring events thickened which prepared the way for the overt acts of the Revolution, he was often greatly excited, and inclined to break his fetters ; but he was ever confronted by a will more resolute than his own.

"To whom do you owe the more sacred duty," she would ask ; " this wretched cabal of blatant rebels who will find halters around their necks if they go much further, or your wife to whom you have pledged your honor ?"

His young friends in the patriot ranks were greatly disappointed in him.   Before marriage, his utterances had been pronounced and radical ; now he was silent and kept himself aloof.

There were many sneers about the " apron-strings of a Tory wife," and the " difference between large swelling words and the giving and taking of honest blows."   Some of these flings reached Saville, and stung him almost to frenzy.

Of course anything like love or even passion died out between these two, whom relatives had so complacently matched, but who never could be mated.

At first, Saville often appealed to her, earnestly and even passionately, to be a wife in reality, and not to thwart every hope and aspiration of his life.

She would exasperate him by coolly replying. " Only as I check and thwart your wild fancies and mad action can I be a true wife.   Can't you see that you are bent on ruining us both ?   Your mind is full of monstrous innovations. It is as if you should say in the dead of winter, I have a vague plan of a better home than this.   Let me tear down our house, and I will build something different.   Not while I keep my senses.   What would our property be worth under the ' *nouvelle ordre* ' as you call it ?"

" But, madam, you do not consider me at all, but only

the property. Am I to have no other career than that of a steward of our joint estates ?"

" That is better than a rebel's halter. But let us end this useless discussion. You are a man of honor, and your word is pledged."

The tidings of the battle of Lexington almost brought things to a crisis, and resulted in a stormy scene between husband and wife. His passion and invective were so terrible as to alarm even her for a time. And yet it only served to intensify the settled obstinacy of her nature. It also greatly increased a growing dislike for him, which needed only time to develop into hatred.

At the close of this memorable interview, she said harshly,

" I have endured this folly long enough. You must either give up this madness wholly and utterly, or else trample upon your honor and duty, and proclaim yourself a perjured villain. The day you join the rebel crew, you desert your wife ; and I will never so much as touch your hand again."

" Do you mean that ?" he asked hoarsely.

" The God you dare to despise is my witness. I do."

" Pitiful are the gods which attract such worshipers," he sneered, and turning on his heel, he left her.

He now saw that the crisis had indeed come. He had learned to know his wife sufficiently well to be aware that neither appeals nor circumstances could change her views and actions. She formed her opinions and purposes solely on the grounds of her own prejudices and wishes ; and a nature without generous impulses made her coldly obstinate in their maintenance.

And now what should he do ? The epithet " perjured villain " stood in the path to patriotic action, like a grisly spectre, for perjured he knew that she would make him appear to her family.

If his own interests only were involved, he would not have had a moment's hesitancy. But was it right to risk his property and life in rebellion, and perhaps bring his mother to poverty and danger in her old age ? For she, too, by many an eloquent appeal assured him that he would be false to the sacred duties which he owed her in her widowhood ; and by the whole force of the filial bond, sought to chain his generous nature to inaction. He was thus torn by contending emotions, and tortured by conflicting claims. His cheeks grew wan, and his face haggard, in as cruel a captivity as ever man endured. But both mother and wife looked on unsympathetically. They were in the most aggravating condition of mind toward the sufferer, complacently sure that they were right and he wrong ; that they were acting for his best good, and that he, like a rash, foolish child, must be held in steady restraint until he should pass beyond the folly of his youth. Their treatment was as humiliating as it was galling.

And yet he did not know what was right, for he had no true moral standard. He had cast away that book of divine ethics, which clearly defines the relative force of each claim upon the conscience, and which, in an emergency like this, calmly lifts a man up to the sacrifice of himself and every earthly tie, that God may be honored, and humanity at large served.

But, in his creed, as we have seen, man was his own law ; and while his heart said, " Join the cause of freedom," a perverted sense of honor said, " No, your word has made you the slave of your wife's bigotry, and your mother's fears."

In vain he appealed to his mother, telling her how patriotic ladies in the city were urging their sons to heroic action, and teaching even their little children the alphabet of liberty She would only weep and prophesy dismally.

"When these mothers see their sons brought home mangled corpses, and their pleasant homes burned, and their children turned adrift upon the heartless world, they will shed tears of blood over their folly. I love you too well to permit you to rush to your own destruction as truly as to mine."

She always assumed that it would be impossible for him to go without her permission.

His bitter reply at last became, "Your love will be my death by slow torture."

"Nonsense, my child," the old lady answered, almost petulantly. "You will soon see the day when you will thank me from the bottom of your heart for having kept you out of this wretched broil, which will ruin all who engage in it."

Thus there was not even sympathy for him at home, but only a riveting of the fetters which were eating into his very soul. So he came to indulge in long and lonely expeditions, by which he sought to escape, in some degree, the painful conditions of his city life.

CHAPTER V.

WASHINGTON'S SERMON.

THE explanatory digression of the two previous chapters left Saville returning from one of these flights from the tormenting difficulties of his position. In due time he approached his native city, passing for miles along rugged and heavily wooded shores, that now are occupied by spacious ware-houses, and wharves crowded with the commerce of the world.

By the time he reached a point opposite where Canal Street now ends at the North River, his attention was drawn to a large flotilla, just leaving the Jersey shore. Remembering that it was Sunday afternoon, he was still more surprised to find that on grounds adjoining his own estate, near the foot of Murray Street of our day, an immense concourse of people were assembled. His boat soon reached his private quay, where he found his body-servant, who had come down to the shore, with thousands of others, to witness some great event.

His master's face was sufficient interrogation to garrulous Larry, and he at once launched forth.

"Glad ter see yer honor. Yer jist in time. Faix, sure, there's great doin's on foot. The rebels, as yer leddy calls 'em, are gittin' bold as lions, an' will eat us up if we don't jine the bastes. I'm half a mind to turn rebel meself."

"Stop your nonsense, Larry. Who are those coming yonder across the river, and what does this concourse mean?"

"It manes more than I can tell ye in a breath, yer honor. But that's Gin'ral Washington himself that's a comin' there, and the rebels have knocked bloody blazes out of the red-coats in Bosting."

These tidings were sufficient to arouse Saville's ardent spirit to the highest pitch of excitement. Mingling with the throng at the spot near which the disembarkation must occur, he met an acquaintance from whom he obtained a more satisfactory, if not succinct, explanation of what he saw.

The battle of Bunker Hill had been fought, and behind a slight breast-work constructed by a few hours' labor, his countrymen had met and thrice repulsed the veterans of Europe. In the torrent of blood which flowed that day, the Revolution had become a fact to which men could close their eyes no longer. The time had arrived when all must take sides ; and Saville recognized the truth that he must now choose with which party he would cast his lot. He was in an agony of conflicting feelings, and hoped that something in the stirring events of the hour might settle the question which he felt scarcely able to decide himself.

He gained a standing-place upon a projecting rock on the beach, from which he had a good view both of the crowded shore and the approaching flotilla, and his enthusiastic nature kindled momentarily as he gazed on the scene.

It was a lovely summer afternoon. The sun shone bright but not too warm, and gave a touch of beauty and lightsomeness even to things prosaic and commonplace in themselves. But there was little that was ordinary on this occasion. There, facing him on a sloping bank, was such a throng of his fellow townsmen as he had never before seen together, their faces aflame with excitement. Near him were drawn up in martial array a thousand men with glittering accoutrements, and bayonets whose points the declining sun tipped with fire.

When the boats approached the land, even the heavy booming of the cannon was drowned by that most awe-inspiring sound of earth—the shout of a multitude, wherein the thought, the intense feeling and resolute purpose of the soul finds loud, vehement utterance. It is a sound that stirs the most sluggish nature. How then would the spirit of one be moved who, like Theron Saville, believed that the voice of the people was the voice of God? He did not shout with the others. His excitement was too deep for noisy vent, but his face grew stern, and his lips compressed with his forming purpose. He was growing desperate, and was passing into a mood in which he was ready to trample every tie and extorted pledge under foot that he might join what he believed would prove a crusade against all tyrants, temporal and spiritual.

But his chief desire now was to look into the face of Washington, of whom he had heard so often, and who had even now gained much of that remarkable influence which he was destined to possess over the young men of the country. His rural and hunting tastes, his romantic, military experience on the frontier, and his reputation for the most daring courage, had already made him a hero in a new country where such qualities would be most appreciated. But to Saville, he was more than a hero, more than a patriot and chivalrous soldier : he was a forerunner and inaugurator of the golden age of liberty and equality, which his fancy portrayed in the near future. Groaning himself under the thraldom of the old and hated régime, he regarded the coming commander-in-chief as a captive in hard bondage might welcome a deliverer. He expected to see a face that was a revolution in itself, eager, fiery, kindling others into flame by its intense expression.

But, when a tall and stately man in the prow of the foremost batteau uncovered, as he drew near the shore, in acknowledgment of the resounding acclamations, he was at first disappointed. He was not looking on the bold, defiant features of an innovator. There was scarcely a trace even on that calm, noble face, of the enthusiasm that was burning like a flame in his own heart.

Wherein lay the man's greatness and power? In his eagerness to see more nearly the one he now felt would largely shape his own destiny, as well as that of others, he sprang down the rock, and unconsciously stood in the shallow water. Washington noted his eager action, and turned his face full upon him with a kindly look and half-inclination, while Saville removed his hat at once.

As Washington again lifted his eyes to the waiting thousands, the young man scanned his face as if he would there read his own fate. Here was a man who had larger wealth and higher social position than himself, and yet he had joined his fortunes to a cause which Saville's relatives characterized as both desperate and disreputable. Here was the man toward whom the national heart instinctively turned, and hailed as leader and chief. As Washington looked to God for guidance and help, Saville looked solely to man, and as we have said before, with all the eagerness which the hope of his own deliverance and the realization of his dreams could inspire, he scrutinized the face before him to gather if this were the coming man of the *nouvelle ordre*.

He did not see what he expected—the embodied principles of the French iconoclasts and reckless innovators, but the native quickness of his race enabled him to apprehend the spirit which animated Washington, and which found expression in his honest face. There was no elation, no appearance of gratified pride, which such a reception would have evoked, had the elements of personal vanity existed largely in his nature. There was an absence of all complacent self-confidence and self-assertion, and yet he inspired confidence, and more—something of his own heroic and patient spirit of self-sacrifice in behalf of a sacred cause. His face wore the solemn aspect of one who felt himself charged with awful responsibilities. As he saw the thousands turning toward him in hope and trust, the burden of the nation's weal pressed heavier upon him. And yet there was not a trace of weakness or shrinking in view of his mighty tasks. His face had the calm, strong expression of one who had counted the cost, who was wholly consecrated, and who, without a thought of self, proposed to serve a cause in which he fully believed, leaving to God the issue. Like the ancient Hebrew leader who climbed Sinai's height to the presence of God, he also had been prepared above the clouds to lead the people who tarried on the plain below.

Though Saville could not understand the source of Washington's strength, still the calm, noble face quieted him. Half unconsciously he was taught the difference between mere enthusiasm and personal ambition, and a resolute purpose combined with unselfish devotion. He was generous and noble enough himself to appreciate the heroic qualities embodied before him, and to be won to something of the same spirit for the time being. Washington's appearance and character reconciled Saville's heart and conscience, which had long been at variance, and made him feel with the certainty of intuition, that the cause which had won such a man was so sacred, that he could be true to it, and at the same time true to every duty he owed his wife and mother.

There are times when the mind, thoroughly aroused, works with marvelous rapidity ; and the few moments that intervened between the near approach and disembarking, gave that face, toward which so many were turning for inspiration, time to preach Saville the only sermon which he had ever heeded. The most effective sermons, after all, are those which are embodied. The Word of God was a living person—a Divine Man.

He who had been harassed so long by conflicting claims, hesitated no longer. With his eyes fixed on the man that, in his humanitarian creed, he was ready to worship, he said in the low, deep tone of resolve—

"His cause is mine from this hour forth. Liberty, equality, or death."

Washington had landed, and Saville was possessed with a desire to hear him speak, and so pressed toward him with many others. General Schuyler, who stood at his chief's side, had noticed the eager and interested air of the young man. He knew Saville slightly, and the thought occurred to him that it might be a good opportunity to secure the adherence of one who had thus far stood aloof, but whose wealth and talents would be a welcome addition to the cause. He spoke in a low tone to Washington, and then stepping up to Saville, said,

"Let me present you to his Excellency, with others of your fellow-citizens."

Before Saville could realize it, the man he adored had taken him by the hand, saying,

"Mr. Saville, I hope you are with us in this good cause."

With deep emotion, Saville replied,

"I am with you in any service—the humblest—which your Excellency may require."

"Rest assured," said Washington, kindly, "that it will be honorable service, for which your country will reward you."

The young man stepped back, more proud and pleased than if he had been decorated by all the sovereigns of Europe.

The procession was now commencing to form.   Saville pushed his way out of the throng to where Larry was gaping at the strange sights, and called,

"Bring me my horse, saddled, within five minutes."

"Och, by the holy poker," gasped Larry, as he ran to obey the order, "the maister is a goin' to turn rebel.   Thin I'll be a rebel, too ; for there's nary a man of 'em all that can fight ould England wid a better stomach than meself. Didn't she take the last praty out of me bin at home ?"

A little later, Saville, mounted on his favorite horse, took a flying leap over his garden wall, and joined the cavalcade of leading citizens who were to escort the Commander-in-chief down Broadway ; while Larry followed with the populace on foot, chaffing right and left to the amusement of many listeners.

At length the pageantry was over, and in the purple twilight Saville sought his home.   Everything in nature that Sabbath evening breathed of peace and tenderness, but he justly feared that a scene of bitter and unrelenting hostility was awaiting him.   The coming battles in which he would take part, would never require the nerve and self-control that he must maintain this quiet June evening, and in his own home.

In his exalted and generous mood, he determined to make one more appeal before the final separation with his wife took place.   But meeting her on the piazza, he saw by a glance that it would be a vain and humiliating waste of words.

Her features were inflamed with passion, and upon her full lower face rested the very impress of willful stubbornness.   She had evidently heard of his action during the afternoon, and surmised the result.   Having never been thwarted in her life, she now hated the man whose course and motives were so utterly repugnant to her.

She stood in the doorway, dressed for walking, and, not waiting for him to speak, said harshly :

" Well, sir, in a word, what is your decision ?"

" I have decided that I am a free man and a patriot."

" A rebel and a perjurer, you mean."

" That is your unjust version, madam," he repliec quietly, for Washington's calm, strong face was before him.

Her features grew fairly livid, but she was about to pass out without a word.

" Julia !" he exclaimed, intercepting her, " listen for one moment before you take this rash, irrevocable step. If I am true to the sacred cause of Liberty, I can be true to you. I——"

" Stand aside !" she cried, imperiously stamping her foot. " I will not hear one word of your idiotic drivel. The idea of you being true to anything, who break pledges made at God's altar, and cast off your wife to join a herd of ragged, blaspheming rebels ; I shall never darken your doors again."

" Well-chosen phrase, madam. You have indeed darkened my door, and darkened my life. But farewell : I will not reproach you. I will be loyal to the name of wife : the reality I never had."

She deigned no reply, but passed down the path that led to the adjoining residence of her parents, with such hot wrath in her heart that it was strange the roses did not wither as she passed.

Saville breathed more freely after she was gone. It seemed as if a deadly incubus had been lifted from him.

But he soon found that the meeting with his mother would be a far severer ordeal. When he entered her room, and saw her, who was usually so stately and composed, utterly broken down, rocking back and forth as if in mortal agony, with her gray hair hanging in disorder over her face, he felt as if a sword had pierced him.

"Ruined! ruined! all is lost!" groaned the wretched woman.

"Why are we ruined," he exclaimed impetuously, "more than thousands of families who have joined the patriotic cause?"

"We shall soon be homeless and penniless."

"No, mother, not at all. I shall have it distinctly known that you still adhere to the crown. I will put all the property in your name, and content myself with a soldier's fare."

"And I shall then be childless and alone in the world!" she continued in the same despairing tone.

"Oh, cease, mother; you may break my heart, but you cannot change my purpose. My word is pledged to Washington and Liberty."

"It has been pledged before," was the reproachful reply.

"No!" said the young man sternly; "do not charge me with dishonor. I can endure that from the woman to whom the miserable hap-hazard chance of this world and priest-craft temporarily joined me, but not from you. I never deliberately and consciously made a pledge against my present course; and to-day I have seen a man who has taught me how I can be true to you, and at the same time true to Liberty. You say, 'my child,'—do you not realize that I am a man, who must be guided by his own independent will or be despised by all? I have chosen my lot."

With these decisive words, Saville retired to his room, that he might regain his calmness and form some plans for the future.

Among his first acts during the next few weeks was the transfer of a large sum of money to Paris, subject to his own or his mother's order. Having thus cast an anchor to the windward, he felt that he had done much to provide against the vicissitudes of that stormy period, and thus could give his thoughts more fully to the stirring work of the hour. He explained his situation, as far as a scrupulous delicacy would permit, to Captain Sears, more generally known by the sobriquet of "King" Sears, and told this recognized leader of the populace in all daring revolutionary acts, that after the few weeks required to settle his affairs and provide for his mother, he would be ready to enter the regular service, and that, in the mean time, if any enterprise were on foot, he could be depended upon at any moment. His young Whig acquaintances had no further cause to complain of his absence from their councils, or of a disposition to shrink from "honest blows" if any were to be received. He found a congenial spirit in a fiery young student of King's College, whom his companions nick-named "the Little Giant," but who is now known to the world as Alexander Hamilton ; and the two young rebels plotted treason enough, in Tory estimation, to satisfy the shade of Guy Fawkes, and were quite as ready to blow up Parliament and all other anciently constituted authorities.

Mrs. Saville's manner was for a time that of cold and stony despair, and considering her views and feelings, it was more real than assumed. But beneath the thick crust of her worldliness and conservatism, there was a warm, motherly heart, which soon began to yearn toward her only son, who, she now feared, might any day be lost to her forever. Her coldness soon gave place to a clinging tenderness, which she had never before manifested, and which made it a hundred-fold harder for her son to carry out the steadfast purpose which the expression of Washington's face had inspired. Moreover, such are the contradictions of woman's heart, she secretly admired her handsome son, in his buff and blue uniform, and respected him far more than if he had been content to remain merely the steward of the large joint estates which her thrifty scheming had united.

Both pride and indifference prevented Saville from making advances toward his wife, and there was nothing in her nature that would prompt to any relenting. On the contrary, as her husband's outspoken republicanism and skepticism were bruited through the city, her hatred grew more intense and vindictive. Not only was his opposition to church and state most offensive, but the fact that he could break her chains and ignore her existence was humiliating, and taught the spoiled beauty, for the first time, that her despotic will could be disregarded. Nothing so exasperates some natures as to be first thwarted, and then severely let alone.

He scrupulously re-transferred her dower and every vestige of property to which she had the slightest claim ; and she, in impotent spite, refused to be known any longer by his name ; but the irrevocable marriage vows had been spoken, and this past act of folly, like a hidden rock had seemingly wrecked the happiness of both. They might hate each other, but they were forbidden to love any one else.

CHAPTER VI.

"A SCENE AT BLACK SAM'S."

ON the evening of the 23d of August, 1775, a large mansion standing at the corner of Broadway and Dock (now Pearl) Street, appeared to be the center of unusual excitement, even at that time of general ferment. The place was well known as the down-town tavern of Samuel Fraunces, who, from the swarthiness of his complexion, went by the sobriquet of "Black Sam." This tap-room and restaurant was a general resort, not only because Fraunces was the Delmonico of that day, and could serve a dinner and cater in wines better than any other man in the city, but also because Sam's patriotism effervesced as readily as his champagne or strong beer ; and, it may be added, for the reason that they were often served by his pretty, black-eyed daughter, Phœbe Fraunces. To her, perhaps, in the following year, Washington owed his life, since she was able, through the confidence given her by a lover who was one of Washington's body-guard, to penetrate a Tory plot to destroy the dread Commander-in-chief by poison. True-hearted Phœbe was not to be won by a lover who proposed to administer such potions, so, having smilingly beguiled from him his secret, she furnished him with another noose than that of Hymen's make, and donning her brightest petticoat, went cheerfully to his hanging.

But upon this memorable occasion, she was the embodiment of exuberant health and spirits, and seemed as sparkling as the wines she brought to the guests that thronged this favorite haunt of the city.   It was warm, and her round, stout arms were bare, and her swelling throat and bosom snowy white, while her eyes were black as coals.   But while she was coquettish and piquant, there was nothing pert or bold in her manner, and he was either drunk or brutish who gave her a wanton word the second time.   In her ready tongue she carried a keener weapon than the swords that dangled and clattered at the sides of the incipient warriors on whom she waited ; and when provoked she gave thrusts which brought the hot blood at least to their faces.   But while she inspired a wholesome respect, she was generally bubbling over with good humor and arch repartee, and so was a general favorite.   Her mercurial nature readily caught the spirit of the hour, and to night her dark eyes were ablaze with excitement, and her white teeth, which frequent smiles displayed, and her white neck and arms, gave to her quick movements a glancing, scintillating effect. As she flitted here and there among the noisy patriots, many an eager sentence was suspended and but lamely finished, as the speaker's eyes followed her admiringly.

Little wonder that she was the blooming Hebe of this bacchanalian Elysium, for the majority habitually craved the boon of drinking to her health.   She would graciously comply, and then chuckle with her father over the coins resulting, when, at the late hour (at that primitive time) of ten at night, they counted the gains of the day.   It is to such places that men resort who appear to value public and purchased smiles from those who sell to all alike, more than similar glances from wives and children, which they rarely seek to win, and more rarely deserve.   Phœbe was not above reaping this harvest from fools ; but she did it so fascinatingly that they felt well repaid.

Black Sam, broad and swarthy, stood behind his bar,

controlling and directing his large establishment from this central point like a captain on the deck of his ship. His eyes were a trifle duller than Phœbe's, and indicated that he indulged occasionally in more than the sips of a connoisseur. But to-night they glanced rapidly and shrewdly around, seeing that his daughter and her assistants neglected no one ; and he found time, in the mean while, to add a word in his heavy bass to the various pronounced political discussions and utterances going on around him. It was very evident that Sam and his patrons had little reverence for the "divinity which doth hedge a king," and these quasi subjects of George III. spoke of him with a refreshing candor which it would have been well for him to have heard, for it might have saved a world of trouble. It has ever been the chief misfortune of potentates that they are surrounded by a dead wall of courtiers that excludes every rude but warning sound.

Phœbe's excitable temperament correctly interpreted the occasion. There was something abroad in the air which charged the summer night with subtle and electrifying power. Though many were evidently in ignorance, it was noted that Fraunces exchanged significant glances with several present, and seemed dilating with some portentous secret. His suppressed excitement grew more apparent, as his rooms filled rapidly, and the crowd increased about the doors. It was also observed that all the newcomers were armed, and that among the rapidly appearing faces were those which, like beacon fires, always betokened some doughty undertaking. The general stir and hoarse murmur of voices was greatly augmented when Saville entered with young Hamilton, followed by fifteen students from King's College, all fully armed. The latter were soon chaffing with Phœbe as they took from the tray she brought them, glasses brimming over with rich Madeira, for which the tavern was most famous.

"With father's compliments," said Phœbe, courtesying.

Then, boy-like, they proposed three cheers for the prince of caterers and the fair Hebe who had borne them the nectar which he alone could furnish ; and they were given with deafening heartiness and glasses raised aloft.

They were scarcely drained, before a young man, leaning upon the bar, and who was more noted for his drinking powers than his discretion, cried,

"I propose another toast—Saville, who is doubly to be congratulated, since he has escaped a double bondage—that of King George and also of his Tory wife ; having slipped the cable of her apron-string by which——"

Before he could finish his sentence, Saville's fist was planted upon his mouth with such force as to send him reeling to the floor, with his glass clattering after him. Standing over the prostrate and half-tipsy man, and trembling with rage, Saville said, threateningly,

"The man who dares to cast a slur upon my wife shall do so at his peril."

There was the usual uproar and confused sound of conflicting voices, when a cry arose which drowned all else, "Sears, Sears, King Sears," and that great firebrand of the American Revolution, whose headlong zeal and courage kindled so many fires of contention with the royal authorities, stood among them.

"Come, come, comrades," he cried, "no need of interchanging blows here among yourselves. Come with me, and I will give you a crack at our common enemy. Colonel Lamb, with his artillerymen, and Captain Lasher, with his company, are marching down Broadway to take the guns at the fort, without saying so much as ' by your leave.' Who will follow me to their aid ?"

There was a loud acquiescing shout, while Black Sam sprang over his bar, crying,

" Lead on, King Sears, and the man who refuses to follow may choke with thirst before my hand serves him again.''

In Fraunces's estimation, this was the direst threat he could make, and in fact, to many present, the fulfillment would be like cutting off the springs of life.

Hamilton took Saville's arm, saying,

'' Come, comrade, fall in. What do the maudlin words of that drunken fellow signify? Come, you know we've grand work on hand to-night.''

In a few brief moments the crowded, noisy rooms were deserted. The street became full of hoarse shoutings, and the confused sound of many feet, as Sears, Hamilton, and other extemporized officers marshaled the citizen-soldiery in something like orderly array. Then from the head of the column rang out those stirring words which, though causing many hearts to bound with hope and thrill with grand excitement, have yet been the death-knell of myriads.

'' Forward—march !''

With strong and steady tramp the dusky figures receded toward Broadway, while Phœbe, with eyes ablaze, stood in the door waving a farewell with her handkerchief, its flutter meaning anything rather than a truce with King George's agents of oppression.

Black Sam's buxom wife took his place behind the bar, while Phœbe repaired to an upper window that she might see if the English man-of-war in the harbor had anything to add to the drama of the evening. The hitherto thronged hostelry became silent, being deserted by all save a few old men whose age precluded them from taking part in the events of the night. It was an occasion when not even the famous Madeira of Sam's tavern could tempt any loyalists thither ; and such of the Whigs as were too prudent to join the raid, skulked away, much preferring to face a dozen

English batteries than to hear the comments of Phœbe Fraunces upon their discretion.

As for the young woman herself, she repined bitterly at the usages of society which prevented her from taking hand in the promised mêlée, and was half inclined to don her father's habiliments, and be a man in spite of fate.

CHAPTER VII.

NEW YORK UNDER FIRE.

COLONEL LAMB and Captain Lasher with their companies halted on Broadway till Sears and his following of citizens joined them ; then they proceeded at once to Fort George, which had its front on Bowling Green, and was located within the space now bounded by State, Bridge, and Whitehall Streets. Tory informers had revealed to the authorities in charge of this work the intended attack. In view of the overwhelming force, no resistance was made by the small garrison. Unmolested at first, the patriots went to work with feverish zeal to dismount the cannon from the bastions, and load them on the heavy wagons that came lumbering down Broadway for the purpose.

To Alexander Hamilton and his party was given the task of capturing Grand Battery, another and smaller work nearer the river, which was also accomplished without resistance.

But the fiery young spirits composing this band were much disappointed at the quiet and peaceful nature of the enterprise thus far.

" We might as well have come armed with only pickaxes and crowbars," growled Hamilton.

" Yes," responded Saville, in like discontented mood. " A brigade of carmen was all that was required on this occasion. I had hoped that the night would be enlivened by a few flashes at least. Suppose we go down to the water's edge and take a look at the *Asia*."

Securing the approval of their superior officers, and leaving a guard in charge of the work, the rest of the party commenced patrolling the shore, casting wistful glances at the ship, whose masts and yards were faintly outlined against the sky.

" Now, if we had only a dozen whale-boats," said Hamilton, " and could go out and board that old tub, we would have a night's work that would stir one's blood."

" Not a little would be set running, no doubt," replied Saville ; " and it would not all be on our side either, I imagine. But see, they are waking up on board. We may have a bout with those water dogs yet."

It soon became clear that there was an unusual stir and excitement on the vessel. Lights gleamed and glanced rapidly from point to point, and faint and far away came the sound of orders hastily given.

Then there was a heavy splash in the water.

" Hurrah !" cried Hamilton, " they are manning a boat. We will resolve ourselves into a committee of reception."

The measured cadence of oars confirmed the surmise just made, and the young men eagerly pressed to the furthest point of land, and looked well to the priming of their firelocks. The barge was pulled steadily toward them until at last a dusky outline emerged from the night, and then the shadowy figures of the crew.

" Make not a sound, and let them land if they will," said Hamilton in a low tone.

But the barge approached warily, with lengthening rests after each dip of the oars. At last, the officer in command detected the little party in waiting, and shouted :

" Who and what are you ? What deviltry's on foot to-night ?"

" Come and see," cried Hamilton laconically.

But the officer's night-glass, together with the ominous

sounds from Fort George, clearly showed that this was not good advice under the circumstances. There was a hurried consultation, and then, whether by order or not cannot be known, some one in the boat fired a musket, and the hot young bloods, for the first time, heard the music of a whistling bullet.

" Give 'em a volley—quick !" cried Hamilton.

Obedience to the order was indeed prompt, and yet not so hasty but that the marksmen, familiar with the rifle from boyhood, took good aim, and several in the barge were killed and wounded. The silent oars at once struck the water sharply, and the boat rapidly disappeared toward the man-of-war ; but the young men heard enough to satisfy them that their shots had taken effect.

Immediately upon the report of the first musket, Colonel Lamb, Captain Lasher, and King Sears hastened to the shore with many others, and learned from Hamilton what had occurred. In the mean time the barge reached the vessel and reported, satisfying Captain Vandeput of the *Asia* that the intimations he had received of the proposed attack upon the forts were correct. The British authorities hitherto had hesitated in taking decisive action, knowing that it would precipitate the conflict at once. But now the point of forbearance seemed passed, and he ordered the port-holes opened and the rebels dispersed by a few shots. In quick succession three flashes came from the ship's sides, and three balls plowed into the Battery.

But so far from dispersing quietly, Lamb ordered the drums to beat to arms, and the church bells to be rung, and soon the silent city was in an uproar.

English blood, as well as American, was now at boiling point, and the defiant sounds from the shore were no longer answered by single shots but by broadsides, the thundering echoes and crashing balls of which awoke both Whigs and

Tories to the realization of the true meaning of war. The experiences of Boston, the very thought of which had caused many to tremble, were now their own in the aggravated form of a midnight cannonade. Men, women, and children, many but partially clad, rushed into the streets and joined the increasing throng of fugitives that pressed toward the open country, away from the terrible monster in the harbor, whose words were iron, and whose hot breath threatened to burn their homes over their heads. Tories, as they ran, cursed the rebels, whom they regarded as the cause of the trouble ; and the Whigs anathematized British tyranny. But faster and hotter than their oaths the heavy balls crashed into their houses or over their heads, with the peculiar, demoniacal shriek of a flying shot.

A night bombardment is a terrible thing for strong, brave men to endure. The roar of cannon is awe-inspiring in itself ; but when it is remembered that every flash and thunder peal has its resistless bolt which is aimed at one's life, only those who have nerved themselves to risk their lives calmly, or who, like the patriots on the Battery, are lifted by mad excitement above all fears, can stand unmoved. But how could the sick and the aged—how could helpless women and children endure such an ordeal ? Only the pitying eye of God noted all the fainting, mortal fear of those who tremblingly snatched children, treasures, or sacred heirlooms, and sought to escape. Hearts almost ceased their beating, as the terror-stricken fugitives heard balls whizzing toward them. The messengers of death might strike out of the darkness any where and any one. Broadway has witnessed many scenes, but never a more pitiable one than when, in that August midnight, a hundred years ago, it was thronged with half-clad, shrinking, sobbing women, and little children wailing for parents, lost in the darkness and the confusion of flight. When, at last, the open fields beyond the range of the *Asia's* guns were reached, the strangely assorted multitude, from whom the gloom of night and common misfortune had blotted out all distinctions, sat down panting and weary, and prayed for the light of day.

Many who were helpless and a few who were brave remained in their homes, either in an agony of fear or in quiet resignation. Among the latter was Phœbe Fraunces. But there was not a particle of resignation in her nature, for she chafed around her father's tavern like a caged lioness ; and when a round shot, well and spitefully aimed at the " pestilent rebel nest," as it was called on the *Asia*, crashed through the house, shattering a decanter of Madeira that the gunner would rather have drained himself, she forgot the softness of her sex utterly, and seizing a huge cutlass that hung over the bar, and leaving her mother to recover from a fit of hysterics as best she might, she started for the scene of action in a mood that would have led her to board the *Asia* single-handed, had the opportunity offered. But, as she approached Fort G or e and hear the rough voices of the men at work, her modesty regained its control, and she realized that it was scarcely proper for a young woman to be abroad and alone at that time of the night ; so, she who was ready to attack a man-of-war, turned and fled before that which a true woman fears more than an army—the appearance of evil. But it would have been a woful blunder for any rude fellow to have spoken to Phœbe that night, armed as she was with the old cutlass, and abundance of muscle to wield it. His gallant advances would have been cut short instantly. .

Although there was panic in the city, there was nothing of the kind within the dismantled walls of Fort George, from which the cannon were fast disappearing ; nor upon the Battery, where Colonel Lamb's artillerymen, flanked by

Hamilton and his students, were drawn up, to prevent the *Asia* from interfering with their operations by landing a force from the vessel. But Captain Vanderput prudently contented himself with striking from a distance, supposing that the terrors of a night bombardment would soon bring the contumacious rebels to their knees. To make the warning lesson still more effectual, and to increase their punishment greatly, he ordered the guns to be loaded occasionally with the deadly grape-shot.

But, in the morning. both he and the populace had a surprise. The Battery was not covered with killed and wounded. In fact, there was not a Whig to be seen, dead or alive. But neither was there a cannon to be found in the royal forts. While he had been thundering his disapproval from the harbor, the "raw militia," who, his officers jocularly asserted, "would not stop running south of King's Bridge," had steadily completed their tasks, and spirited off every gun to parts unknown.

And when, in the peaceful summer morning, the fugitives, who had spent the night in the open air, concluded they had better go home to breakfast, and appear in less picturesque toilets, they found, instead of death, carnage, and gutters running with blood, no wounds save those which the carpenter and joiner could heal. It was another remarkable example of how little destruction may be caused by a bombardment even in a crowded city. The mercurial temperament of the people, which their descendants seem to have inherited, led those of Whig proclivities, who were overwhelmed with terror but a few hours previous, to react into cheerfulness and exultation. Many doughty citizens, who stole into their back entrances, strangely appareled, soon afterward appeared, dressed in different style, at their front doors, hoping that their flight had been covered by the darkness ; and not a few, who had made excellent time toward

King's Bridge, ventured, over their dram at the corners of the streets, to descant on " the way *we* carried off the British bulldogs from the fort."

The Tory element in the city was very quiet that day ; but a sullen, vindictive expression lowered upon many faces. The timid and conservative sighed, again and again,

" Where is this thing to end ?"

In a beautiful up-town villa, the face of one fair woman was often distorted with passion and hate, as she hissed, through her teeth, " *He* was foremost in this vile night work." But when Saville, hungry and exhausted, reached his home, his mother, who had been a sleepless watcher, only folded him in her arms, murmuring,

" Thank God ! you are yet spared to me."

Then she gave him a breakfast that in future campaigning caused many a longing sigh as he remembered it.

CHAPTER VIII.

LARRY MEETS HIS FATE.

HAVING completed all the arrangements possible for his mother's comfort, and settled his affairs as far as the times permitted, Saville made known his readiness to enter the regular service at any point where he could be most useful. His education as an engineer led to his being sent to Martelear's Rock (Constitution Island) in the Highlands of the Hudson. He would have much preferred serving under Washington, before Boston, but had too much of the spirit of a soldier to think of aught save prompt obedience. Having been commissioned as lieutenant, he repaired to the scene of his duties about the last of September, and found that he was to serve under an officer by the name of Colonel Romans, who had arrived on the ground with a small working force about a month earlier. He was assigned to the duty of superintending the details of labor and the carrying out of the plans of the chief engineer in respect to the incipient fortifications.

While strolling around the rocky island, the evening after his arrival, he soon came in full view of the extreme point of land on the western shore, whereon he had seen such a strange vision a few months previous. In the press and excitement of succeeding events, the circumstance had quite faded from his memory ; but now, with the purpose of diverting his mind from painful thoughts, he decided to solve the pretty enigma by which he had been so unexpect-

edly baffled.   He made some inquiries of the small garrison
with whom he was associated ; but they, like himself, were
newcomers, and knew nothing of the few inhabitants of the
region.   For several days he was too much occupied with
the effort to obtain the mastery of his duties to think of
aught else, and, when evening came, was well contented to
climb some rocky point on the island, and rest, while he
enjoyed the wonderful beauty of the landscape ; for this
historic region was just as weird and lovely then as now,
when it is admired by thousands of tourists.

But one warm afternoon, early in October, he took with
him the garrulous Larry, his body-servant, who had followed
the fortunes of his master, and started in a little skiff down
the river to a cottage on the western bank, which he had
noted on his journey up.   This might be the home of the
wood-nymph, or he there might learn something about her.

" Come, Larry, I want time for a little shooting after I
land," said Saville, impatiently ; " so pull away, and I
will steer, for the tide is against us."

" I'm obleeged to yer honor," replied Larry, dryly, tug-
ging at the oars ; " there's nothing like dewision of labor."

" You can rest while I am tramping round with my gun,"
said Saville, who gave Larry something of the license of a
court jester.   " I shall expect you to wait for me where
I leave you, so that there may be no delay in our return."

" Faix, sur, I hope ye's gun will be more ready to go off
than I'll be, arter this pull."

Having descended the river half a mile below the foaming
cascade now known as Buttermilk Falls, they fastened their
boat and ascended the bank to the cottage, or, more correctly, log cabin.

Saville quickly saw enough to convince him that this
could not be the home of the young girl who sang

    " I know a bank whereon the wild thyme blows."

A huge, fat hog reclined in the sun near the step, and chickens passed in and out of the door, as if they had equal rights with the family, while the cow-stable formed an extension to the dwelling, and was quite as well built as the rest of it. Were it not for his wish to make inquiries, he would have turned away in disgust.

But for Larry the scene appeared to have unwonted attractions. With arms akimbo he struck an attitude of admiring contemplation, as he exclaimed,

" I'm glad I come wid your honor, for I've seen nothink so swate since I left the ould counthry. Now, isn't that a beautiful soight? Pace and plenty! 'Twas jist such a pig as that as grunted at me father's door. Faix, sur, it makes me a bit homesick;" and Larry's shrewd, twinkling eyes grew moist from early memories.

As they proceeded a little further, Larry saw that which proved quite as attractive to him as the vision of Vera had been to Saville a few months before; but the elements of mystery and romance were wholly wanting. In a small inclosure back of the house a young Irishwoman was digging potatoes. As the men approached, she leaned leisurely upon her fork-handle, and stared at them unblenchingly. Her head was bare, but well thatched with thick, tangled tresses which were a little too fiery to be called golden. Her eyes were dark, expressive, and bold; her stout arms were red and freckled, as was also her full and rather handsome face. In simplicity and picturesqueness no fault could be found with her dress, for it appeared to consist only of a red petticoat and a scant blue bodice; but it might well have been mended at several points. Her feet and ankles were as bare as those of Maud Muller, if not so shapely and slender. But, as she stood there, aglow with exercise, in the afternoon sun, she seemed to Larry a genuine Irish houri—the most perfect flower of the Green Isle that he had ever seen ; and he hoped that his master, who had accosted an old woman knitting in the doorway, would keep him waiting indefinitely, so that he might make the acquaintance of this rare creature.

" I'm glad to see you well, madam, and enjoying the fine afternoon," began Saville, with French suavity.

" Umph !" responded the old woman, and after looking him over briefly, went on with her knitting.

" Have you any neighbors in this region ?" asked Saville, undaunted by his forbidding reception.

" Mighty few as is neighborly."

" But there are other families living near.'

" A small sprinklin'."

" Haven't you some neighbors further up the river, and nearly opposite the island where we are building the fort ?"

" Indade, an' we have not. Our neighbors be dacent folks who own their land, and not skulkin' and hidin' squatters."

" Would you mind taking a shilling for a bowl of milk ?" said Saville, pursuing his object with a little finesse.

" Now ye talk sinse," replied the old woman, rising. " No, nor two on 'em. I ax your pardon for being a bit offish, for I've seen sogers in the ould counthry, an' no good came o' 'em. Yer grinnin' man there is not a soger, be he ?"

" No, indeed ; Larry is a man of peace."

" 'Kase I want 'em all to understand that if any sogers come a snoopin' round here arter Molly, they'll be arter catchin' me 'stead o' her."

" I don't think any will come, then," said Saville gravely. " But I'm sorry you give your neighbors up the river such a bad character."

" It's not meself that gives 'em a bad character, but their own bad dades."

" Wny, what have they done ?"

" That's more'n any one knows ; sumpin' the ould man's mighty 'shamed on, for he won't look honest folk in the face ; and as for that wild hawk of a gal o' his'n, the less said 'bout her the better. She's kind of a witch, anyhow, and 'pears and dodges out o' sight while yer winkin'. She needn't turn up her nose at my Molly there, that's come o' dacent folk.''

" And has she been guilty of that offense ?''

" Dade an' she has ; Molly comes 'cross her now an' thin, out berryin', and fust she tried to speak her fair, but the ill-mannered crather would kinder stare at her a minute, and thin vanish in a flash. She's larnt more o' that ould heathen black witch, as lives wid 'em, than anythin' good. "

" What is the name of the family ?"

" That, too, is more'n anybody knows. They calls 'emselves ' Brown ;' but I know 'tain't their name ; for it was meself that did a bit o' washin' for 'em once when the woman was sick, and there was two names on the linen, but nary one nor tother was Brown. I couldn't jist make out what they was, for I hain't good at readin' ; but one thing is sartin, husband and wife don't have two names.''

" Have they done anything wrong since they came here ?"

" Well, I can't say they are robbin' and murderin' every night, and yet how they live nobody knows. But it's 'nuff that they're hathen. They did widout the praste in the fust place, and nary a thing have they had to do wid praste or parson since. The ould black witch worships the divil, for Molly's seen her in the woods a-goin' on as would make yer har stan' up ; and I'm a-thinkin' the divil will git 'em all ; an' he may, for all o' me. "

By the time Saville had finished his bowl of bread and milk, he came to the conclusion that the crone had more spite and prejudice against her neighbors than knowledge

of them. It was the old story of resentment on the part of
the ignorant and the vulgar toward superiority and exclusiveness. It was very probable, however, that some guilty
secret of the past led to this utter seclusion. Saville well
knew that there were many hiding in the wilderness whose
antecedents would not bear much light. And yet his curiosity, so far from being satisfied, was only piqued the more
by the old woman's dark intimations. Taking his gun, he
said to Larry, who was now digging potatoes vigorously,

" So that is the way you are resting."

" Diggin' praties is an aisy change, and kind o' homelike ; and thin, yer honor, ye wud not have me a-standin'
like a great lazy lout, while a fair leddy was a-workin'."

" Very well ; but save enough muscle to row me home."
And he went back upon the hills in quest of game, leaving
his deeply smitten factotum to the wiles of Molly, who,
with hands upon her hips, contemplated his chivalric labors
in her behalf with great complacency.

" The top o' the mornin' to ye," Larry had said as he
approached, doffing his hat.

" Faix, an ye're a green Irishman not to know the afthernoon from mornin'," was Molly's rather brusque greeting.

" The sight o' ye wud make any time o' night or day
seem the bright mornin'," was Larry's gallant rejoinder.

" Ye kissed the blarney-stone afore ye left home, I'm
a-thinkin'."

" An' ye'll let me kiss yer own red lips, I'll dig all these
praties for ye."

" I see ye're good at a sharp bargain, if ye be a bit green.
But I'll wait till ye dig the praties."

" But ye'll give me jist one buss when I'm half through,
to kinder stay me stomach."

" There's plenty lads as wud be glad to dig the praties
for me widout a-drivin' hard bargains for it."

"So they'll tell yees afther the praties is dug. They'll be very swate about it whin the cowld snow kivers the ground."

"An' ye think ye're very swate about it now," said Molly, with her head coquettishly on one side.

"No, but I'm a-hopin' ye'll be swate about it."

"What's yer name, anyhow?"

"Larry O'Flarharty; an' ye may have it yerself any day that ye'll go wid me to the praste."

"Is that what ye say to every gal ye mate?"

"Faix, an' it is not. It's to yersel that I've just said it."

"Ye're better at talkin' than doin'. I thought I'd git at least one hill o' praties dug by yees."

"Give me the fork, thin, and I'll show ye that Larry O'Flarharty can take care o' ye and a dozen childer into the bargain."

"Och, ye spalpeen! Ye'll have me coorted, married, and a gran'mother, afore ye git a praty out the dirt."

Larry set about his labor of love with such zeal that the potatoes fairly hopped out of the ground, carroling, as he worked,

> "I'll dress ye up in silks so foine,
> An' ye shall drink the best o' woine.
> Be jabers! but we'll cut a shoine
> The day when what's yer name is moine."

How's that for a dilicate way of axing ye yer name?"

"What do I want wid a name since ye're goin' to give me yourn?"

"What shall I call ye till the happy day comes?"

"Molly, for short."

"Let it be for short, thin, and not for long."

"D'ye think I wud marry a man o' all work? I'm goin' to marry a gallant soger boy"

"No ye hain't, nayther," struck in her mother, whose age had evidently not impaired her hearing.

Molly gave her head a defiant toss which indicated that the maternal leading-strings had parted long ago. Larry paused abruptly in his work, and leaning his chin on the fork-handle, asked,

"Are ye sarious about that now ?"

"Ah, go on wid yer work and sthop yer foolin'," said Molly, who saw that she had made a false move in her little game to get her potatoes dug by another.

"Divil a praty will I dig till ye tell me."

"Divil another shall ye dig any way, ye impudent spal-peen !" retorted Molly, who was touchy as gunpowder ; and she took the fork out of his hands, and turning her back upon him, struck it into the potato hillocks as only a spiteful termagant could. Discomfited Larry in the mean time perched himself on the fence, that he might take an observation, and hold a council of war in his own mind. But the more he looked the more the charms of this wonderful creature grew upon him, and his soft, impressible heart became as wax. He soon hopped down from his rail, and said,

"Come now, Molly darlint, what's the use o' a-goin' agin fate ? Ye shall marry a soger bhoy, I see that by the cut of yer perty jib, as the sailors say. Ye've spunk and fire enough for a rigiment. Give me the fork agin, and one o' yer own swate smiles."

"Well, since ye're a sort o' baste o' burden, an loike workin' better nor fightin', ye may have yer way."

"Faix, an' I will be a baste wid the burden of a sore an' heavy heart, if ye talk to me in that way."

Molly could come out of a pet as quickly as she fell into it, and so she said,.

"I'll be swate thin till ye git the praties dug."

" Yis, an' many a long day afther.   I know the soger bhoy ye're goin' to marry."

" No, ye don't."

" Yis, I do."

" What's his name ?'

" Larry O'Flarharty.   The masther may git a new man, for I'm goin' to 'list.   The nixt time ye see me I'll be a gay and gallant soger bhoy.   I'll———"

" Hush, mother's comin'."

Larry delved after the potatoes as if they were halfway down to China.

The old woman looked sharply and suspiciously at them, but only said,

" Molly, go afther the cows.

" I'll go wid ye," cried Larry, throwing down the fork.

" No, ye won't," retorted the old woman ; " yer masther ould ye to bide here till he come."

" I'm a-thinkin' I'll be me own masther," said Larry, straightening himself up ; " everybody's gittin' free an' indepindent, and I'll thry a hand at it meself."

" Go along and git 'em yerself, mother," added Molly, who began to entertain some thoughts of her own in regard to this ardent admirer that was so subservient to her will and moods.   " They hain't far off ; and ye wud not have me treat the man what has been a-workin' for me all the afthernoon so oncivil as to lave him alone.   Go along, and we'll have the praties dug agin ye git back."

The old woman was in straits what to do, since in either case she must leave her daughter alone with one at least nearly connected with the dreaded " sogers ;" but at last she hobbled grumblingly after the cows, the tinkle of whose bells proclaimed them near.

With the usual perverseness of human nature, Molly grew friendly toward the soldiers as her mother showed prejudice against them. The more she learned about their life, the more attractive its publicity, vicissitudes, and excitement became to her bold, restless spirit, and she had already resolved to enter the camp in some capacity at the earliest possible moment. The thought now occurred to her that perhaps she might find in this plastic, garrulous stranger just the chance she hoped for. Molly was aware of her infirmity of temper, and if she could find a "soger" that could be kept submissively under her thumb, she would consider herself blessed with better luck than she had ever dared to expect.

Larry made his first favorable impression when he good-naturedly dismounted from his rail, and recommenced the work which she was ready enough to leave to him ; and she was not long in coming to the conclusion that if this pliable and useful man of all work could be transformed into a regular soldier, and then be captured as a sort of base of operations, which would enable her to lead a free, wild, rollicking life, she had better make the most of the opportunity. But she went direct to her point with feminine indirectness, and so when her mother was out of hearing, said,

"Ye're not brave enough to be a soger."

"An' ye are not brave enough to marry one."

"Some foine day, when ye're a-blackin' yer masther's boots, ye'll find yerself mistaken, for ye'll see me a-walkin' into camp the wife o' the handsomest man o' the lot o' yees."

"Now what do ye mane be that ? ' asked Larry, abruptly suspending his labors, while his chin and troubled phiz again surmounted the fork-handle.

"I mane," said Molly yawning, "that I 'm only a-waitin' to make up me mind which of me soger swatehearts to take."

"An' how many have ye, sure?" said Larry, in something like dismay.

"Oh I sumthin' less than a dozen."

"But ye hain't made up yer mind on any on 'em yit?" queried the anxious lover.

"Well, not yit. There's two or three on 'em I could worry along wid if I thried."

"Yis, an' it would be worryin' along, Molly, me dear; while wid me ye'd be happy as a quane."

"But I telled ye afore I was goin' to marry a soger."

"And I telled ye afore I was a goin' to be a soger."

"Yis, a-goin' an' a-goin', but I'll belave it when I see it."

"An' one wake from this day ye will see it," protested Larry, with hearty emphasis.

"Now ye begin ter talk a little sinse," said Molly, more complacently. "Well, well, I'll thry ye, and give ye an aven start wid me other swatehearts. If ye're down by the wather a wake from this afthernoon dressed as a gay soger boy, I'll think ye mane sumthin', but all yer foine words now is loike spilt wather."

"Och, Molly, me darlint," cried Larry, and pitching away his fork, he threw his arms around the bewitching creature, and took full payment for his labor of the afternoon.

"Hold on, Larry," cried his master, who had returned just in time to witness this last demonstration; "hold on, or you will never be able to row me back to camp."

"Faix, yer honor," said Larry, somewhat abashed that his gallantry had been observed, "I fale much refreshed."

"Well, come along, then; it's time we were off."

"Good-by, thin, Molly, my dear, for one long wake."

"Ye're nothin' but a wild Irishman," said Molly, half angry, and half laughing; "but mind ye, come in the toggery I tould ye on, or don't ye come at all."

"Don't ye fear. Whin I come agin, yer other swate-hearts will be like the stars when the sun comes over the mountain."

"An' hist!" continued Molly; "don't ye come up to the house, or mother'll take yer life. I'll mate ye at the wather."

That night Larry made known his purpose to enlist at once. In vain Saville protested. Like the immortal Romeo, Larry had found his Juliet, and was in feverish haste to don the uniform that would give him an "aven sthart wid the other spalpeens of swatehearts," whose imagined rivalry, Molly had shrewdly guessed, would be a most powerful incentive to prompt action.

"But don't ye mind, yer honor; it's in the 'tillery I'm goin' to 'list, and so I can do yer odd jobs jist the same."

"Are you going to marry that carroty-headed girl over there?"

"If ye spake of the swate crathur in that way, divil a turn will I do for ye agin."

"Mark my words, Larry, you are giving up one master to find a harder one," at which his quondam servant went growling and muttering away.

Larry was true to his tryst, and the reader may be assured that the strategic Molly was not absent. After two or three meetings, in which she nearly tormented the poor fellow out of his senses, with fear and jealousy of the mythical "swatehearts" who were just about to carry her off, Molly permitted the entrancing concession to be wrung from her, "I will stale away wid ye to the praste, if I kin only git a pair o' shoes."

Having received this sweet assurance of affections won, Larry, on his return, made pacific overtures to his former master.

"Ye know that I served ye long and faithfully."

" Well, that will do for preface. What do you want now, Larry ?"

" Faix, sur, an' if ye'll give me a pair o' yer shoes, I'll do many a good turn to pay for 'em."

" With all respect for your understanding, Larry, I don't think they'll fit you."

" I've taken the measure of a fut as they will fit, yer honor."

" Oh ! I see now ; yes, yes, there are the shoes ; and by the way, Larry, I have a pair of leather breeches which you may take her also ; for she struck me as one who would be sure to wear them before long."

" Bless yer honor, ye mustn't judge all the women o' the world by yer own bad luck." And with this home-thrust, Larry went chuckling away with the shoes that were to consummate his happiness.

Before a week of wedded bliss had passed, the newly fledged artilleryman found that he had, indeed, exchanged his old master for a more exacting one, and he dubbed the redoubtable Molly " captain," long before she won the title by her military prowess.

CHAPTER IX.

LEFT TO NATURE'S CARE.

THE changes that war was about to make, in the wild and secluded region which Vera's father had chosen as his retreat and hiding-place, soon began to manifest themselves. The arrival of the engineer, Colonel Romans, with his working force, at Constitution Island, was discovered almost immediately by the young girl, while out upon one of her excursions, in the latter part of August. Nor could the advent of the soldiery be kept from her father, as the morning and evening guns, and the notes of the drum and fife, announced their presence, with startling distinctness, in the quiet summer air.

At first the morbid and conscience-stricken man was in great excitement and alarm, and, with the tendency common to persons in his condition, connected the unlooked-for event with danger to himself. His fears led him to propose that they should all leave their home, and seek some more secluded spot far back in the mountains ; but for once his meek and gentle wife was firm in her opposition to his will. She saw that her husband's mind had become so warped that it was no longer capable of correct judgment in any matter where his fears were concerned. The reason for the military occupation of the island opposite she had not yet learned, but could not see how it necessarily threatened them with danger. Moreover, her desire that Vera might form acquaintances, who could rescue her eventually from a seclusion that might at last leave the girl utterly alone in the world, increased daily. In spite of her false hopes, which were a part of her disease, and an earnest desire to live, she had failed so rapidly, during the oppressive heats of summer, that vague fears for the future often gave her great uneasiness. She clearly recognized her husband's growing distemper of mind, and old Gula was still less to be depended upon. How could she leave her child so friendless and unshielded?

In her terrible anxiety, the gentle creature would at times become almost stern and fierce in her appeals to heaven, crying :

"O God! as thou art good and true, preserve my child, and bring her to me at last, pure and unspotted from the world. I commit her to thy care, and I hold thee to thy many promises."

While her growing weakness made it apparent, even to her husband, that she could not be moved, and he was thus induced to remain in his present home, he continued steady and unrelenting in his determination that no acquaintances should be formed with the new-comers. Of this purpose Vera and her mother had a very disheartening illustration about the middle of October.

One day, just as they were about to sit down to their meagre dinner, the two huge dogs bounded out from the door-step, with fiercest clamor.

Mr. Brown, as he may be called at present, sprang up, and was only in time to prevent a conflict between a stranger and the savage beasts.

Vera also ran to the door, in order to see the cause of the alarm and her heart throbbed quickly, as she recognized in the stranger the young man who had surprised her, in the manner already described, while fishing.

"Back, Tiger and Bull," said their master ; and, as the

dogs reluctantly obeyed, he advanced with a dignity which Saville was quick to recognize, and said, coldly,

" Have you any special business with me ?"

The young man commenced replying suavely, and in a manner which he hoped would pave the way to an acquaintance ; but, still more coldly and sternly came the interrupting question :

" Have you any business with me, sir ?"

" I cannot say that I have, save that as a temporary neighbor I would be glad to show myself neighborly."

The man regarded him suspiciously, but continued, with the same repelling coldness,

" You have the bearing of a gentleman."

" Yes, sir ; and the character and standing of one."

" I shall put that assertion to the test," was the forbidding response ; " and if you fail to make it good, I shall know how to act hereafter. I desire seclusion for myself and family. This cottage, though very humble, is my castle, and I regard any visits to it or to this locality as an intrusion."

Saville flushed deeply, for, if this man were a guilty outlaw, he could assume a hauteur and loftiness which were oppressive. He felt almost as if an ancient baron were ordering him, as a poacher, off his grounds. But in the face of Vera, who stood excited, trembling, in the doorway, he thought he detected a different and friendly expression ; so he made one more effort to remove the suspicious exclusiveness of the father.

" But suppose I come in the spirit of kindliness," he said.

" I thought I made it clear that I desired no visits whatever," was the stern reply.

" You are unwise, sir," said Saville with corresponding haughtiness. " I am an officer and a gentleman, and as such might have extended protection to you and your family. This region will soon become full of armed men, and how can you escape visits from the rude soldiery, who may not always be over-scrupulous?"

"They will come at peril to life and limb," said the man savagely; and he began to show symptoms of great agitation.

Saville saw that the young girl's eyes had overflowed with tears, that her hands were clasped, and that her whole manner was a mute appeal. But whether it was to leave them at once, or to give unasked, the protection against the danger at which he had hinted, and which her father had so harshly refused, he could not tell. He also saw that the man was becoming excited and dangerous, and that the dogs, quickly catching their master's spirit, were bristling toward him. Vera sprang down with words of rebuke, and soon had the fierce animals crouching at her feet. As she stood between them in her simplicity and unconscious beauty, tears gemming her eyes like dew upon violets, she made a picture that Saville did not soon forget.

With a silent bow and smile to her, which she returned by a grave and graceful inclination, he turned away, and soon disappeared among the trees. He had seen enough, however, to kindle his vivid imagination, and on his way back among the hills, in search of game, indulged in many wild surmises in regard to the people who so resolutely secluded themselves. But he could scarcely fail in reaching the conclusion that fear was the motive, and that the man was hiding from the consequences of some act of the past, the discovery of which would lead to terrible punishment. It was still more certain that he had belonged to the superior and educated classes, for his unkempt appearance and rude attire could not disguise his proud and stately bearing. At the same time, even the brief glimpse that Saville had caught of the externals of the cabin, proved that some one dwelt there who had an eye and a love for beauty.

The rude logs were prettily disguised by crimson festoons of the American ivy. Clumps of eglantine with equally brilliant foliage stood on either side of the open door, through which he could see a little of the rustic decoration within. The impression, however, that the man was a criminal chilled his desire for personal acquaintance, and save some generous pity that the fair young girl should be left to develop under such forbidding circumstances, he soon became indifferent to the inmates of the cabin from which he had been so rudely repelled. With the exception of the maiden, the other inmates were probably subjects for the detective and constable. Whether right or wrong, Saville was as open as the day, and had no taste for mysteries or crime.

But the results of his attempted visit were not so slight or transient in the little cabin among the mountains. Vera, and especially her mother, were bitterly disappointed. To the latter it seemed as if a providential opportunity of gaining some hold on the outside world had been lost ; and when her husband became calmer, she so remonstrated with him that he half regretted his own action. But the trouble was that he could not be depended on, for when his mind had been enabled for a moment to struggle toward a correct judgment, another dark and engulfing wave of fear would sweep over it, carrying him back into the depths of his old despondency and morbid dread of strangers.

But the remark of Saville, that the region would soon be filled with armed men, while it greatly increased his uneasiness, also kindled a faint gleam of hope. In his occasional expeditions to distant villages for the purpose of barter, he had heard faint mutterings of the storm that had now broken over the land. The only hints which he had obtained were

from the casual remarks of others, for he had feared to ask
questions, as this would give the right to question him.   He
was regarded, at the few places where he traded, as an odd,
half-deranged man, and received but little thought or attention.   Indeed, it was his policy to assume something like
imbecility on all matters save that of securing a fair return
for his merchandise.

The few expressions which he had happened to hear, in-
dicating trouble between England and her colonies, had
made but little impression on him, however, as the idea
that there could be any resistance to her mighty power never
entered his mind.   But now what else could the presence
of so many soldiers mean, save resistance?   Were the
soldiers that had already come, and that were coming,
under British rule or hostile to it?   If they were English
troops, nothing could induce him to remain.   If they were
American forces in armed rebellion, then there would be
hope that in their success he might finally escape the juris-
diction of English law.   His mind became so far aroused
and clear that he was enabled to act intelligently, though
characteristically.   Instead of going over to Constitution
Island, where he might readily have learned the situation,
he prepared a large pack of articles for barter, and started for
a distant village down the river.   Here he assumed his old,
stolid manner ; but he heard enough to so stimulate his
curiosity and awaken his hopes that he at last brought himself to question an old and inoffensive appearing man who
was working alone in his garden.   Learning from him the
principal facts which had thus far transpired, and the open
resistance into which the colonies had gradually passed, he
started for home in a state of wild and almost exultant excitement.   At first, he half proposed to take an open part
in the struggle.   But long before he reached his cabin, the
old wave of morbid fear returned, and the habit of secretive-

ness, and disposition to shrink from every one, resumed their mastery. He decided to remain in his present home as a post of observation.

"I'll wait and see what headway the rebellion makes," he muttered ; "for if it fails after I have committed myself to it, I am lost utterly." The man had become such a wreck of his former self that his only thought was for his own personal safety. His terrible secret had seemingly blasted every generous and noble trait with its deadly shade.

During his absence Vera and her mother ardently hoped that the young stranger might come again. Vera even went down to the shore, and looked wistfully at the island opposite, from which the din of labor on the fortifications came faintly across the river. But she saw not the one to whom she now felt she could almost find courage to speak, and ask for that protection which he had intimated they might need.

During the summer and autumn, they had been left utterly alone. Even Vera, in her youth and inexperience, had become alarmed at her mother's feebleness and hacking cough, and her thoughtful efforts to alleviate and help were as pathetic as they were beautiful. She felt that they had a very trying winter before them, and knew that her father could be depended upon less and less as a support. But she induced him to repair the cellar under the cabin, so that the vegetables from a small garden might be stored securely. She also had persuaded him to enlarge a spring near the house into a little pond, and in this her skill enabled her to place quite a number of fish. She did her best to follow the example of her wild playmates of the woods, that were busy most of the time in providing against the cold, dark days to come, and she even diminished the squirrels' hoards, by the quantities of nuts which she gathered and dried for winter use. She also carefully noted the haunts of rabbits, partridges, and quails, and prepared traps and snares which could be used when the snow covered the ground.

But, as the autumn winds sighed through the mountains, she sighed also ; for a strange depression and boding of evil was stealing over her.   Her face, which had been full of sunshine and mirthfulness even in darkest days, grew un-wontedly thoughtful and oppressed with care ; but her features were none the less lovely, as they began to express womanly solicitude and responsibility instead of a child's light-hearted confidence.   In her mother's presence she ever sought, however, to maintain her cheerful hopefulness. But the mother's love pierced all disguises, and it was one of the bitterest drops in her overflowing cup that her child should be so early and heavily burdened.

The bond of clinging affection appeared to grow stronger and tenderer between mother and daughter, as their relations toward each other changed, and Vera began to give the failing parent the care she had once received herself. There were days when the poor woman could scarcely leave her bed, and then Vera's every touch was a caress.   But the bracing air of autumn and winter appeared to agree with the invalid better than the relaxing heat of summer.   The generous diet of game which Vera carefully prepared did much also to keep up her strength.   But perhaps her gain in vigor was due to the element of hope which her sympathetic spirit caught from her husband ; for he had at once informed his wife of the struggle that was commencing with the Power he dreaded, and both felt that in its success would come a calming sense of security.   The wife urged her husband to take an open part in the conflict, correctly judging that daily contact with others would be the best antidote against his habit of morbid brooding.   But in his unnaturally developed caution and shrinking fear of discovery, the man was not equal to this, and, for the time, became only a secret and anxious watcher of the events which he hoped might work out his deliverance. The habit of suspiciously shunning every one had grown to be a disease. Indeed, so warped had he become that he began to dread lest his wife—the only one in this land who knew his dire secret—might reveal it to Vera in some unguarded moment ; and at times he even harshly cautioned her against such a possibility.

Thus the winter passed rather sadly and drearily away. Vera's powers were taxed to their utmost as nurse, watcher, and housekeeper. Her father also had bad days when nothing could induce him to leave his dusky corner, and then her hands and feet were pinched with cold, as she visited the traps and snares among the hills, carrying the fowling-piece also, in order that their meagre larder might not become utterly bare.

In the midst of her deepening anxiety and increasing burdens her mystic sympathy with nature increased, and she found comfort and companionship even in the wintry landscape. Bible ideas and imagery blended with what she saw around her. As with the lightness of a fawn she bounded through the newly fallen snow, she would exclaim with an ecstatic thrill of hope,

" My robe, one day, will be as white and sparkling, and the gems in my crown brighter than the icicle's gleam hanging over yonder ledge of rocks. God teaches me, even in winter, by such pretty things, what He is preparing for His children."

When at times every branch, spray, and twig was encased with snow, and the evergreens were bending beneath their fleecy burdens, she would be half wild with delight at the beauty of the scene, and would cheer her mother by saying,

" See what God can do in a single night. Won't our

mansions in heaven, which we so often read about, be beautiful, mother? for he has had ever so many years in which to prepare them. Don't you think he is making them prettier all the time?"

"Yes, Vera," her mother would reply; "as we grow better, God makes them prettier. Never distrust Him, for you see what He can do even in this world which is so full of evil and trouble."

Thus, every beautiful object in nature became to the young girl an evidence of her Heavenly Father's good-will and love, and an assurance that He would fulfill at last all the wonderful promises of the Bible. And dark and dreary days, and disagreeable things, were expressions of the evil in the world, from which she had His promise also, that she should be protected, and finally delivered.

Often, when the cold, bitter wind was blowing, and the trees and shrubbery were tossing in its power, she would draw a slender spray with its securely encased buds against her glowing cheeks, as she said, caressingly,

"Don't fear! We shall be taken care of. Next May will be like last May, and the wind will come softly from the south."

Again, she would stand in the snow upon a violet bank, and call,

"Heigh-ho, down there, tucked away in your winter bed! Do you ever dream of me in your sleep?"

Thus nature, even in mid-winter, suggested to her child sleep rather than death; and hope, instead of fear and despair; and when her heart grew heavy and full of vague forebodings of evil, as she saw her mother's weakness, and her father so deeply enshrouded in gloom, she would take her trusty gun and one of the great dogs, and spend hours among the defiles of the mountains, finding peace and good cheer, where to another would have been only blackness

and desolation, or the awful solitude and grandeur of a
mountain landscape in winter.   While Vera's character was
simplicity itself, this noble companionship with things that
were grand and large, though at times stern, took away
utterly the elements of silliness and triviality which make
many young girls at her age a weariness to all save those as
empty as themselves.   And the sternness of many scenes was
more apparent than real ; for in frowning ledges of rocks
Vera found cosy nooks in which she was protected from the
winds as she rested, and the sun would often light up the
face of the precipice, as a smile might illumine the rugged
features of one who seemed harsh and cold in nature, but
who, on closer acquaintance, would be found to possess
traits that are kindly and gentle.

The winter passed, and Vera was being prepared for the
part she must take in life—for temptations and ordeals
which would test the strength and integrity of the strongest.
Her teachers were not such as the fashionable would choose
or desire—sickness and sorrow at home, and the solitude of
wintry mountains without ; and yet these stern-visaged in-
structors made their pupil more sweet, unselfish, and
womanly every day.   They endowed her with patience,
and, at the same time, inspired her with hope.   Moreover,
she had the two grand books of the world, the Bible and
Shakspeare ; and often as she watched in the corner of the
wide fireplace, she half read and half brooded over their
glowing pages, until her own mind was full of thronging
thoughts and fancies, which, in their beauty and character,
were at least akin to those she read.

Still, she often had a sense of loneliness, and the natural
craving for a wider companionship and sympathy.   From
the day on which she had at first met Saville, there had
been in her mind a vague, faint unrest, and a desire to
know more of the world to which he belonged.   His

attempted visit had greatly increased this desire, and concen-trated her thoughts upon him as the only one concerning whom she had any knowledge, or who had shown any interest in her.   She often found herself vividly recalling the two occasions on which she had seen him, and which had ended so unsatisfactorily.   His manner, appearance, and his words and tones even, were dwelt upon ; and he became to her like one of Shakspeare's knightly and heroic char-acters—half real, half ideal.   She would end by sighing,

" He has probably gone away, and thinks of us only as rude, ill-mannered mountaineers."

As spring advanced her mother failed rapidly, and Vera's heart and hands became too full for thoughts of aught else save the deepest and tenderest solicitude.   Old Gula shook her head more frequently and ominously, and Vera had the most painful misgivings.

. One day, after her mother had recovered from a terrible paroxysm of coughing, she followed the old negress to the little kitchen, and asked,

" Why do you shake your head so discouragingly ?"

" Ise a tinkin' dat missis is a hearin' voices as well as ole Gula."

" What voices ?"

" You'se can't understan', chile ; but you will, some day.   Dey come to de homesick like."

" Where do they come from ?"

" Why, from home, honey.   You'se mudder is like ole Gula—far from home.   I heerd her a talkin' in her sleep of a green, flowery island, way off 'yond de big water.   She, no more'n ole Gula, hab allers lived 'mong dese cold, stony mountains.   An' now de voices is a callin' her home."

" Do you think—do you think mother—oh ! can mother die ?" said Vera, in a terrified whisper.

" Dunno nuffin 'bout dyin', child ; don't tink dere's any

such ting.   But some day you'll find dis ole body lyin' cold
and still, but 'twon't be Gula, 'twon't be me.   I'll be far
away, a followin' de voices ober de big wabes, where de
floatin' miseries go, and Gula will be home where de sun
shines warm all de time, and de palm-trees wave.   Oh !—
oh !—ole Gula's heart is sore ; sore wid waitin'.''   And
the poor creature threw her apron over her head, and rocked
herself back and forth in all the tropical demonstrativeness
of grief.

But Vera's heart was sore also, and finding that she was
losing self-control, she hastened out into the twilight, and
sitting down upon a rock back of the cabin, sobbed as if
her heart would break.

Gula soon forget her own grief in the young girl's distress,
and removing her apron, her quaint, wrinkled face became
full of commiseration.   At last she rose and hobbled to her,
and laying her hand on the bowed head, said in husky tones,

'' Dare, dare, po' young missis ; don't take on so.   You
mustn't be sorry dat you'se mudder's goin' home.   When
she gits back where she lived afore, she won't be sick any
mo'.''

'' Oh !—oh !—oh !—there's no use of trying to be blind
any more.   Mother is going hom . ; but not to England—
to a better home than that.   But, oh !—to be left alone—
what shall I do ? how can I bear it ?''

Calming herself by a great effort, she at last returned to
her mother, who had surmised her daughter's distress, and
looked at her so wistfully that Vera again lost self-control,
and kneeling by the bed, gave way to an agony of grief.

'' O mother,'' she sobbed, '' how can you leave me ?''

The poor woman gave her child a startled look, and then,
more fully than ever before, realized the inevitable separa
tion soon to come ; she also saw that the sad truth could be
no longer concealed from Vera   Reaching out her feeble

hands, she took her child into her arms, and they wept together till both were exhausted.   Then the mother whispered
the old sweet refrain that had soothed and sustained her
through so many troubled years :

" ' Let not your heart be troubled, neither let it be afraid.
In my Father's house are many mansions'—I think I shall
soon be in mine, Vera ; and I will watch and wait for you."

" I don't want another mansion, mother.   I'll ask God
to let me live with you.   One mansion will be enough for
us both.   Oh, why can't I go with you ?"

" Your father needs you here, Vera.   Oh, my poor husband !   For my sake he fell into this gulf of darkness.   Had
it not been for me——"

" Hush !" said a stern voice ; and mother and child became very still, the one oppressed by a dark secret known,
and the other by the same secret unknown, but which the
girl, even in her inexperience and ignorance of evil, began
to realize must be very sad and dreadful.   She retired for a
time to her little grotto-like apartment in the side of the hill,
and then came back calm and strengthened, and entered
upon her patient watch.

The husband, who had been a silent, and, up to the time
of his harsh interruption, a forgotten witness of the scene
just described, was terribly agitated by contending emotions.
The words he had heard had aroused him from his deep
preoccupation, and he too began to realize for the first time
that his wife might be near her end—that this was more than
a temporary illness.   His mind was not so utterly warped
but that he foresaw his loss with the keenest anguish.   He
had loved this faded, dying woman with all the strength of
his nature, and the thought that she could die and leave
him had never been entertained.   But now it came like a
revelation—a lightning flash into his darkness, making everything the darker thereafter.   At one moment his heart would

yearn toward her with an infinite tenderness and remorse ; and then the thought would come surging up, born of his guilty secret and demoralizing fear, that if she died, no one, at least in this land, would know the past. It seemed to him that he had arrested her just as she was on the point of revealing the secret to his child. She might do so still. He remembered that the dying were prone to unburden their hearts to some one. He determined that this must be prevented at all hazards ; and in spite of his morbid suspiciousness, he still had such trust in the woman who had been so true to him, as to be satisfied that if she gave him her solemn promise to be dumb—never to tell even Vera— she would keep her word.

When their daughter had left them alone, he said abruptly, and yet in a tone that trembled,

" Esther, are you going to die ?"

" Yes, Guy," said the wife, wearily and faintly.

After a moment, and still more tremblingly, the man said,

" Will you protect me to the last, as you have in all these years ?"

" Yes, Guy."

" Will you give me your word, which you have never broken, not to tell even Vera ?"

" Yes, Guy ; not even Vera."

" Will you swear it ?" he said hoarsely.

" God is my witness, I will be silent. The deed was not done in malice—God will forgive you, Guy. Oh, let the ' Lamb of God which taketh away the sins of the world ' lift the load from your heart. He has from mine. But how—how can I leave you and my darling child ? And yet you may be better off without me. I fear I have become a burden."

The man gave way, and throwing himself down on his

knees beside his wife, groaned and sobbed in a perfect tempest of grief.

" I've blighted your life, Esther," he cried.   " Think what you might have been.   You might have dwelt in a palace."

" Hush, Guy," said his wife solemnly.   " If all could be done over again from that night when you came and told me what had happened, I would act just the same.   I loved you then.   I love you now, and God loves you."

" What kind of a God is he that permits such horrors ?" groaned the wretched man, showing that even the love of the unbelieving can in such emergencies do little else than wound and pain those who cling to them.

" He is the God who only can deliver from such horrors, and remedy the fatal mistakes and deeds of this life," said his wife eagerly.

" How has He remedied them ?   You are dying, and we will be left alone in this dreary wilderness, in which we must cower and hide till we also die."

" O Guy, Guy, time is short, and eternity very long. So trust, so live, that all may be well hereafter.   I shall wait for you and Vera ; and it seems to me that heaven will not begin till you both come to me."

The man was silent, and became more composed.

" And Guy," continued his wife faintly, for she was growing very weary, " I fear this utter seclusion is unwise and unsafe.   It may be fatal to Vera's happiness.   Go out and take an open part in this conflict for liberty.   You will be your old self after you have mingled awhile with your fellow men."

" Not yet," groaned the man.   " I dare not yet."

The wife sighed deeply, but said no more.   But her sore heart was comforted when her husband rose and for the first time for years bent over her, giving a kiss and gentle caress, as he said,

'' Poor little wife, you have been faithfulness itself.''

Then he went back to his dusky corner ; but the watchful glitter of his eyes was often dimmed with tears ; and Vera found on her return that her mother had fallen into the deep sleep of utter exhaustion.

The spring night deepened and darkened, but a shadow darker than the night had fallen across the cottage ; for all at last realized that death was near. Toward morning the man dozed in his chair, but Vera's eyes were fixed with a wide and fearful gaze into that dread future when she should be alone in the world that to her was so strange and unexplored. More than once the thought crossed her mind in reference to Saville,

'' If he knew, would he come ?''

And yet all through that interminable night, she was sustained and comforted by the memory of One who she felt sure would know and care.

But in the light of the lovely May morning, and in view of the fact that her mother seemed a little stronger and easier, hope revived.

'' Father, I think a surgeon might help mother,'' said Vera with decision.

The man gave his daughter a startled look, and her words had evidently awakened a sudden conflict in his mind. But his aroused and better nature prevailed.

'' Perhaps he might,'' he faltered ; '' perhaps he might.''

'' Then where can one be found ?''

He strode up and down the room a moment, then casting a compassionate look at his wife, muttered,

'' She shall have the chance, cost me what it may.'' Then aloud to Vera—'' There is no doubt a surgeon at the garrison on the Island. ''

'' I will go for him at once,'' said Vera.

" Will you—will *you* go ?" said her father with an air of great relief.

" Yes, if I could only keep mother with us, I would go anywhere and face anything."

The poor woman smiled faintly, but shook her head.

But old Gula barred Vera's exit, till she had finished her morning bowl of bread and milk.

" You'se not a sperrit, honey, do' you'se growin' to look mighty like one." Old Gula had considerable sense still in spite of her weird ways.

" I will take our little skiff out of its hiding-place and launch it for you," said her father ; " and I will be on the watch with my rifle all the time to see that no harm comes to you."

In less than an hour Vera's light shell shot out of a little cove above the point of land opposite Constitution Island, and was soon dancing on the waves raised by the southern breeze blowing against the tide.

Saville was engaged as usual, directing the work upon the fortifications, when a casual glance toward the river revealed to him the approaching skiff. Its occupant so puzzled him that he hastened for his glass, and soon recognized the shy maiden who had eluded him on the point just opposite, and whom he had half forgotten. But now she seemed coming boldly to the shore a little below where he stood. As Vera looked around and saw who it was, she seemed startled, and rested on her oars.

" Are you, too, afraid of me ?" asked Saville kindly.

Her reply was a few vigorous strokes which brought her boat to his feet, and then rising steadily, she stepped lightly to the shore, before he could offer his hand.

" You see I trust you, sir," she said simply, as she stood tremblingly before him with downcast eyes.

" And am I such an ogre that you fled from me once,

and now tremble before me as if I might eat you up? Though if I were an ogre I should be sorely tempted to fall to ; for I doubt if one ever sat down to a daintier meal.''

The young girl's eyes overflowed with tears, as her only reply to this light badinage.

'' You are in trouble,'' said Saville quickly, and in a very different tone.

'' Yes,'' was all that Vera could say.

'' Tell me what I can do for you ?''

Putting her hand upon her bosom to still its wild throbbing, caused by embarrassment, excitement, and her violent exercise, she at last was able to say,

'' Is there—I would see a surgeon.''

'' Sit down, my child, and rest. Do not be afraid ; you may trust me fully. I will bring the surgeon to you. ''

'' I am much beholden to you for your courtesy,'' said Vera, naturally falling into the quaint language of the book with which she was so familiar, and whose courtly phraseology seemed to her appropriate in addressing a stranger.

Saville was interested in the contrast between her stately words and simple, grateful manner, for she was much relieved at finding that she need not face the stare of the garrison.

Calling one of his men, Saville told him to stand guard, and permit no one to approach his protégée, and then hastened for the surgeon. Neither he nor the man who stood mechanically at his post, though with many a curious glance at the strange visitor, realized that their good behavior was greatly to their advantage ; for if they had been capable of anything else, an unerring rifle would have spoken from the opposite shore.

Saville soon returned with a stout, burly, but kindly-featured man, who, on learning Vera's errand, looked with dismay at the slight skiff.

"Look ye here, my child," he said brusquely, "I'm not a fairy like yourself, and can't swim. Did you imagine you could take a fully developed surgeon across the river in that shell ? I wouldn't venture in it for twelve months' pay in advance."

Vera turned her face, full of distress and disappointment, in mute appeal to Saville, who immediately said, cordially,

"That's right ; you can trust me to keep my promise of help ; so don't spoil your pretty eyes with tears. You can lead the way in your skiff, and I will take this healing monster over in a pontoon boat, or ship-of-the-line, so that he be kept from the element he most dreads. But wait a moment, and I'll get you something that will do your mother more good than all his medicines," and he hastened to his quarters, and brought Vera a bottle of French brandy. "There," he said, "I put that in your charge ; for it won't do to trust the doctor with it. He will tell your mother how to use it, but do not let him show her."

But not a glimmer of a smile came into Vera's face at Saville's light talk. Indeed, it grated harshly on her ears, as she remembered her mother's critical state.

"Now, cheer up," added Saville kindly, "and lead the way. If our good doctor is helpless on the water, he is skillful on the land, and no doubt will soon restore your mother to health."

Vera, whose sore heart was in such need of sympathy, lost her control at Saville's kindly tones and manner, and bursting into tears, said,

"I fear mother is sick unto death ;" and turning hastily sprang into her little boat, and was soon out in the stream, where she kept the light craft waiting in position, with the care and precision of a water-fowl.

Saville's pontoon proved to be a handsomely modeled boat of his own, which he kept for his private pleasure or for patroling the river should occasion require, and he soon struck out vigorously after Vera's guiding skiff. She led them to a point from which the ascent to the cottage could be made with comparative ease. Saville was about to accompany them, having again become interested in the unique character of the maiden, and feeling assured that if the cabin was the hiding-place of crime, none of its occupants could be vulgar criminals ; while the thought of evil was not to be entertained in regard to the maiden. But Vera arrested his steps, by saying, with painful embarrassment,

"Father said I must bring no one save the surgeon."

Saville's quick spirit was hurt, and he flushed resentfully. Vera felt herself cruelly trammeled, but was unable to see how she could explain the apparently rude requital of his kindness. Her troubled face, however, almost instantly disarmed him, and he saw that her words were not at all prompted by her own feelings ; and when she suddenly stepped up to him, and said in a low tone.

"'Charity suffereth long and is kind,'" he took her hand and answered gently,

"Charity also 'thinketh no evil.' You are a good girl, though you are rather odd. Good-by, and don't worry about me. May your mother soon get well."

"And may God require thy kindness," Vera said so earnestly, that for the moment he felt as if she had appealed to One who had an existence. But a moment later, after she was gone, he shrugged his shoulders, and soliloquized,

"That's the way it always is—crime and superstition go together. That girl's parents, who no doubt are hiding from the constable, are very religious, and have taught this poor child their pious jargon. Still she seems to have the natural grace to use it with skill and taste. She is, indeed, very odd, and her seeming familiarity with the two greatest works of fiction in the world is unaccountable in one so young and isolated. I must find some means of propitiating her churlish father ; for I would like to pursue this strange acquaintance further.''

The surgeon's practiced eye at once saw that Vera's mother was in the last stages of consumption, and to the questioning and entreating eyes that were turned upon him, could only shake his head and say,

'' Neither I nor any one else can do much for you, madam ; you must prepare for a better world. ''

Vera gave a faint cry, as if she had received a mortal wound, and was about to give way to her grief, when her mother restrained her by saying,

'' Be calm, darling, for my sake.　It is just as I supposed. Let us patiently submit to God's will. ''

'' That's a good child, '' added the kindly surgeon. '' Try to control yourself and listen to me, and you can make your mother's last days much easier ;'' and he gave full directions, and left alleviating remedies.　'' But Saville was right, '' he concluded, '' the brandy will do more to sustain your mother at times than anything else.　You needn't come back with me.　I can find my way to the boat.''

The doctor's visit had not been so brief but that he had been much impressed by the mother's refinement, and the appearance of the cottage.

'' You may depend upon it, '' he said to Saville on his return, '' those people there are very far from being ordinary mountaineers.''

Thus the young man's interest was still further stimulated, and he resolved, though with no motive of vulgar curiosity, if possible, to penetrate the mystery.

The lovely spring day without, was a dark and dreary one within the cabin, for the last hope of recovery had vanished.　The husband sank into the deepest gloom, from which nothing could arouse him ; but he was unwontedly tender and thoughtful of his wife. From that day he so managed and provided for the family that Vera could give all her time to the sick-room. But this seclusion from her outdoor life, combined with her broken rest and burden of sorrow, told heavily on the young girl, and she was beginning to look almost like the ministering spirit Gula had spoken of. The mother would often urge her to go out and take the air, but Vera would always reply, in the pathetic words of one whom in simplicity and fidelity she resembled, " Entreat me not to leave thee."

And yet it was an unspeakable comfort to the dying woman that her husband so provided for the household as to leave her beloved child a continuous watcher at her bedside ; for had Vera been compelled, as had often been the case in the past, to spend much of her time roaming the hills and following the brooks in order to keep up a supply of food, the cup of her bitterness would have overflowed. As well as she could, in view of her own ignorance of the world and the peculiarities of their situation, she tried to advise and guard her child in reference to the future.

" Let your name," she said one day, " which your father gave you because he said I had been true to him, express your character. Be true to your God and your faith, be true to my poor teachings and your own pure womanly nature. Let the Bible guide you in all things, and then you will always have peace in your heart, and find sympathy in nature without. But rest assured, Vera, however wise and greatly to your advantage anything may seem, if your Bible is against it, do not hesitate to turn away, for it would not end well. Keep thy heart with all diligence. When it troubles you—when your old playmates, the innocent flowers, look at you reproachfully, something will be wrong. Keep true, my darling, and our separation won't be long.

But, oh !—how can I leave you in the world, so unshielded and alone ?   O Thou who callest thyself a ' covenant-keeping God,' fail not my child.''

Again, at another time she said, '' Vera, one of the most painful things in your future lot will be that you cannot trust the judgment of your father.   Indeed, you will have to be his guardian and protector more truly than he will be yours. Be very tender and patient with him, for my sake as well as from your own love, and yet be firm when your own and his interests require it.   I do not think this utter seclusion wise or safe.   It will draw rather than avert suspicion and trouble.''

'' Why does father shrink so from strangers ?   Though I have often asked, you have never told me much about your old life in England.''

'' Well, my darling, you must be content to know little, for your life will be burdened enough, I fear, with your own troubles, and I would not add to them those of the past. Let it satisfy you to know that your father met with a sudden and great misfortune, and was compelled to leave his native land.   I loved him, and followed him, as I would again, if I were free to choose.   But, Vera, he took me to a minister of God before we left England, and with this plain ring, and with sacred words, we were joined in holy wedlock.   I had thought to be buried with this ring, but it can serve better uses.   I now put it on your hand, as a kind of charm against evil.   Give no man any rights, Vera ; permit not even a caressing touch from one that you may even love, unless he will wed you with your dead mother's ring, and in the presence of God's minister, in accordance with the teachings of God's book.''   And she placed the plain gold band upon Vera's finger.

Did not God inspire the act ?

Of course Vera had spoken often of Saville's kindness, and

the mother seemed to have a presentiment that he might have much influence upon her daughter's destiny. "I wish I could have seen him, for it is said that the dying often have great insight into character," she sighed, one day, as Vera was speaking gratefully of his words and manner ; and the girl deeply regretted that she had not permitted him to come.

"If he ever does seek your acquaintance, find out if he is true, above all other things. If truthfulness is wanting, you can depend on nothing else. I pray God that he, or some other strong, honest friend may be raised up for you ; for when I remember the words, ' This region will soon be full of armed men,' my heart fails me. I fear your father's manner will only draw suspicion and hostility."

Thus the dying mother tried to counsel Vera against the time, when, though still a child, she should be entirely dependent for guidance on her own judgment and conscience.

After all hope of life had been removed by the surgeon's visit, she failed quite rapidly, until at last her life seemed but a breath, that might cease at any moment. She felt that her end was very near, and one day, in the latter part of May, would not permit her husband to leave the house. Still, she slept most of the time, only rousing, now and then, to give the watchers a faint smile. The man sat most of the time with his face buried in his hands, overwhelmed with remorse and gloom. But Vera's eyes were continually fixed on her mother's face, as if she feared her treasure might vanish should she turn away an instant.

As the sun sank below the mountains, the sleeper aroused, and her face was so peaceful and painless that Vera said :

"You are better, mother."

"Yes, darling, I shall soon be well. Where's old Gula ?"

Vera called her, and the aged negress, with her wrinkled face working strangely, stood at her bedside.

"Good-by, Gula. Oh! that among your voices you

could hear that of our Saviour, saying, ' Come unto me, and
I will give you rest.'   I shall wait and watch for you, too,
my poor old friend.''

" You'se will git home 'fore ole Gula, but I'se a goin'
soon—wery soon.''   And the poor old creature threw her
apron over her head, and going back to the door-step, rocked
back and forth, crooning a low, continuous wail of sorrow.

" Guy,'' said the wife.

Her husband came and took her hand, already cold with
approaching death.   She fixed her large and unnaturally
bright eyes upon him while he trembled like an aspen in
his effort at self-control.

" Guy,'' at last she faltered, " I left all things to follow
you ; won't you follow me to the home where we shall be
safe and at rest ? '

" I will try,'' he groaned.

" Be gentle with Vera—be thoughtful of her.   If he who
so kindly aided her in bringing the surgeon comes again, do
not drive him away.''

The man could not trust himself to speak, but bowed his
head in assent.

" Oh ! my husband,'' said his wife in sudden and passionate earnestness, " I love you ; I would follow you again
to the ends of the earth.   ' Let not your heart be so troubled.' ''

With a cry like that of one desperately wounded, he rushed
from the room, exclaiming, " My punishment is greater than
I can bear.''

Her eyes followed him with infinite regret and tenderness,
and the expression of her face must have been akin to that
of Christ, as he wept over the doomed and unbelieving city.
For a few moments she was silent, and her lips moved in
prayer.   Then she turned, and took her child in one last
close embrace.

"Vera, darling," she whispered, "it's only for a little while, and then we'll not part any more. Assurance has been given me that He who took into his arms the children that mothers brought Him, and blessed them, will take my place to you. My heart is not troubled, neither is it afraid. I leave you in His charge, and no one shall be able to pluck you out of His hands."

"Mother," said Vera suddenly, "do you think God would permit any one to have two guardian angels? Might he not let me have two, at least till I find some one who will take care of me?"

"Well, dear, if He will, what then?"

"It may be selfish, mother darling, to ask you to leave heaven; but God says in His Book that after we go to Him we shall be 'like unto the angels.' If He will let you, would you mind coming down sometimes to watch over me? I shall be so very, very lonely without you, and if I thought you were near me at times, it would be such a comfort."

"I believe he will let me come, darling, and it seems to me that not all the joy of heaven could keep me from being continually at your side. But whether I can come or not, He has said, 'I will never leave thee nor forsake thee;' and His words seem very sure to-day."

The mother's voice, in her mortal weakness, had sunk to the lowest whisper.

After a few moments, she said, "Can you sing me the twenty-third Psalm, darling?"

Vera had long before passed beyond sobbing and tears, and now possessed the strange, unnatural calmness of those who are lifted by some great emergency of sorrow far above their ordinary moods and powers.

Rising from this last close embrace, she chanted those sublime yet tender words, which have been like an all-powerful and sustaining hand to myriads of weary pilgrims in the last dark stage of the journey home. The music was simple and improvised, but so sweet and full of pathos, that even her father, who had returned, was calmed and melted by it, and sat down by Vera's side to watch and wait for the end. The mother's face was very peaceful, and she seemed to be sleeping. Suddenly her eyes opened wide and her face appeared illumined by a coming light. Her lips moved, and Vera, bending over, heard her whisper,

"Oh, my Saviour, hast Thou deigned to come Thyself for me? 'Behold the handmaid of the Lord.'"

Then, as if remembering those she was leaving, she looked back to them with a smile that Vera never forgot, for it seemed spiritual rather than human, and said quite plainly,

"Good-by for a little while. All is well. Let not your heart be troubled, neither let it be afraid."

Her breast rose and fell with two or three long sighs, and then the frail, earthly tabernacle was tenantless, but upon the pallid face the departed spirit had left the impress of peace. To Vera, in her excited and exalted state, the dusky cabin seemed filled with the rustle of angels' wings.

"Is she dead?" asked the husband in a hoarse whisper.

"No," said Vera gently, "she is in heaven."

Her father went back to his dark corner, and sat there through the long night, motionless, sleepless, and scarcely seeming to breathe. Vera, still holding her mother's cold hand, watched mechanically, too stunned and bewildered to think or to realize her loss, and yet sleepless from excitement and the long habit of wakefulness. Old Gula brought her a cup of milk, but she shook her head.

"Now, missy, mind your mudder jus' de same. Wouldn't she say take it?" and Vera drank it eagerly.

The night deepened, and was full of the strange, weird sounds to which she had always loved to listen, but she did not hear them. The silent stars passed over her head as unnoted as the hours. With the same steadfast gaze she looked toward the dead face, which, though hidden by the darkness, was ever distinctly before her. At last, as the morning dawned, the face began to take shape to her outward vision. At first it was shadowy and spirit-like, then that of a quiet and peaceful sleeper ; but at last a broad ray of light, streaming through the casement, fell full upon it, giving it a strange gladness, and the effect of recovered youth, health, and beauty. God seemingly transfigured the wasted features, suggesting to the desolate young watcher what had really taken place in the sunny land " wherein the inhabitant shall no more say, I am sick." To Vera's strong and simple faith it was like the vision of her mother's glory in heaven, and the ray became, and was ever remembered, as an angel of light and comfort.

Then Gula entered and said, " Keep a-doin' jus' as you'se mudder would like, honey. Go to de spring and bathe your face, and den come and see what I'se got for you."

Vera went at once, and the cool water, coming from the heart of the mountain, calmed her feverish excitement. She sat down on a mossy rock, and looked around like one who had entered a new world and a new life, and could not yet comprehend it. But gradually the familiar sights and sounds of nature gained her attention, and began to speak to her in the language she loved and understood so well.

" Look at us," said the violets, blooming at her feet. " All last winter we slept in seeming death, as your mother is sleeping now ; but at the right time God awakened us, and here we are to comfort you."

" Look at me," said the bubbling spring. " The black ice shut me in, as the black earth will cover your mother, but it did not hurt me ; and, sparkling again this morning as brightly as ever, I am here to comfort you."

" Listen to us," said the birds over her head. " We did

not sing here last winter, but we were singing where the cold winds never blow. So your mother has only flown away to a sunnier clime, and we are here to comfort you.''

'' Look at me,'' cried the sun, rising in unclouded splendor over the eastern hills. '' Do I not come back to you after the darkness of the night ? So will He, whose light I reflect, shine away your sorrow, and He has sent me to comfort you.''

'' Watch me a little while,'' said a drop of dew, hanging on a delicate wind-flower that she had unconsciously pluck- ed ; '' and, ere you are aware, the sun will draw me up toward himself into the sky. So God has taken your mother, and soon he will take you, and he himself will wipe away all tears and comfort you.''

Then, to the fancy of the solitary girl, who had little com- panionship save that of nature's children, these voices all seemed to join in a swelling chorus :

> '' Oh ! trust with us the great Creator,
> Whose law of love our love enthralls ;
> Unnoted by our Heavenly Father
> Not e'en a fluttering sparrow falls.''

> '' Let not your heart be faint and troubled,
> And neither let it be afraid :
> For God will guard, with care redoubled,
> The child in his own image made.''

Thus the peace and hopefulness of nature were breathed into her heart, and she went back to the cottage, trusting in Him to whom all things seemed to point.

But, when she entered the cabin, and the sleeper did not awake with the wonted smile of recognition and words of welcome ; when she kissed the cold lips, and found that they were indeed cold and unresponsive, a mysterious dread chilled her own heart, and the realization of her loss, loneliness, and helplessness was so vivid as to be well-nigh overwhelming.

But tears, nature's relief, came at last, and she wept and sobbed until she grew quiet from exhaustion. Then Gula again resumed her homely ministry, and after inducing the stricken orphan to take a little food, was at last pleased to see her escape from sorrow for a time in the deep oblivion of sleep.

The husband, who for many hours had seemed stunned and paralyzed by his loss, at last aroused himself, and told Gula that he would go with the skiff up the river for a coffin, and that it would be late before he returned. Having taken some provisions, and leaving the two dogs as protection, he departed.

Vera slept quietly until the time her mother had died the previous evening, when something, perhaps, in the recurring hour caused her to start up as if called. But time had been given for her healthful nature to recuperate, and though the sense of desolation, all the more oppressive from her father's absence, was indeed terrible at times, she was able to resume her post of watcher for the night, saying to Gula,

" I will feel better sitting here by mother, as if she were still alive, than I would anywhere else."

" I'se a gwine to stay here wid de young missy," said Gula resolutely ; and she crouched down in the wide fireplace, the faint flicker of the flames often giving a strange effect to her face and form as she crooned weird snatches of the barbarous music learned long ago in her tropical home.

It was a remarkable group : the mother, once beautiful and abounding in hope, now faded and dead in the mountain cabin ; the exile, the old African princess, who had been stolen from her home, and wronged, until her mind had become even a greater wreck than her scarred and shriveled form ; and the young maiden, who was like some of her favorite mountain flowers, that grew into fragrant love-liness among rocks and cliffs, where it would seem they could scarcely live at all.

The night deepened, and it may be well believed that other and viewless watchers gathered round the sorrow-stricken girl.

CHAPTER X.

THE ROBIN HOOD OF THE HIGHLANDS.

AS the lovely spring day, which had brought to Vera a brief respite from her sorrow, was drawing to a close, a man might have been seen issuing from a log cabin located among the mountains west of the Hudson, and at a considerable distance from the river. His manner was brisk and decided, as if he were looking forward to the labors from which, in view of the hour, he should naturally be returning. His house was built very strongly, and appeared as if it might be used as a refuge and defense, as well as a dwelling. The place had a certain rude air of thrift, and yet there was nothing to indicate from whence the owner's revenue came. There was no cleared and arable land near, and certainly the beautiful horse, that cropped the grass in the small inclosure around the cabin, had never served as one of a woodman's team.

The man's action was still more irreconcilable with any peaceful pursuit ; for he rapidly ascended the lofty hill back of his house, which was one of a succession of wooded highlands, stretching away toward the river, and having gained the summit, scanned the valley to the westward, giving especial attention to some object far distant upon the road leading southward.

As he stood there, partially concealing himself among the low trees, glass in hand, we may sketch him briefly. He was a little past middle age, tall, and most powerfully built ;

his quick movements, however, adding an impression of lightness and something like grace to that of strength.   The aspect of his face was bold, even to recklessness.   He had the bearing of one gifted with unlimited natural daring, rather than the calm, patient courage which would lead a man to die at his post.   His restless black eyes had the habit of glancing rapidly from side to side, as if he were on a perpetual reconnoissance.   The light that came from them was not the diabolical gleam of those who know themselves to be villains, but rather the keen, alert expression often seen in beasts of prey.   There was scarcely anything to indicate the presence of a moral nature.   The eagle, perched upon his eyrie, scanning the valley to see where he could swoop down to the best advantage, would be the most correct type of this man, Claudius Smith by name, and the terror of the whole region, during the early years of the Revolution.

Apparently satisfied by his scrutiny, he went rapidly back among the hills, instead of returning to his own house. Within less than half an hour he reached a secluded glen. Before descending this, he again took an observation—not of the exquisite landscape, with valleys lying in shadow, and rugged highlands aglow with the setting sun, and all decked in the tender and tinted foliage of May.   The gleam of a rifle barrel would catch Smith's eye instantly, but the perception of beauty was not in his line.

Again everything appeared satisfactory, and he descended the hill-side nearly to its base, and then, instead of giving the conventional signal of thrice whistling, he imitated with marvelous exactness the neigh of a horse.   A flat stone, quite hidden by some copse-wood near where he stood, was thrown back, and eight men emerged, as it were, from the bowels of the earth, and the leader and his band were together.

" It's all right, boys," he said hurriedly. " I watched the squad of militia till they disappeared to the southeast. The coast is clear. Meet me, mounted and armed, at my house within an hour ;" and with the lightness and celerity of movement that characterized him, he vanished among the trees.

His men well understood their part, and were seemingly glad to be released from confinement. The presence of soldiery in the neighborhood made the resort to this hiding-place (of which they had several in the mountains) a precaution which their leader insisted on, for this Tory gang had already become so notorious that parties had attempted their capture. After carefully covering the mouth of the cave, they went to their secluded mountain homes, or where their horses were in hiding, and within the time named, were reassembled at Smith's house, armed and mounted in true moss-trooper style.

Never was a group of Italian bandits among the Apennines more picturesque and suggestive of ruthless deeds than these highland Tories and Cowboys ; and not a classic brigand of them all was more unscrupulous.

They were all dressed somewhat as their leader, in red flannel shirts and short coats, which could be buttoned tightly or hang loose like a cavalryman's jacket. Buckskin breeches, and topboots armed with spurs, completed their simple attire ; but their leathern belts bristled with weapons, while across each one's back was slung a short musket. Though little more than midnight plunderers, they were ever prepared for desperate fighting, should the emergency require it. As they hastily devoured the rude meal which the wife of their leader had prepared, they certainly were a savage-looking crew, with their unshaven faces, and eyes gleaming out from under slouched hats, which they had not the grace to remove.

But of their horses, the beautiful and innocent accomplices of their crimes, too much could scarcely be said in the way of praise.   And little wonder, for the freebooters had taken the pick of the whole country side.   The splendid and spirited beasts made the quiet evening resonant with their neighing, as they impatiently pawed the earth while waiting for their ignoble masters.

At last, in the dusky twilight, the men formed a circle about the door, and Claudius Smith held aloft a flask of whisky, as he cried,

"Here's to a big night's work;" and he took a heavy draught.

"Tip it well, boys," he added; "for you've plenty of rough, hard riding before you, and mayhap some fighting."

A shout greeted this announcement, and the flask was drained, and filled again for the emergencies of the night.

Slinging their muskets over their shoulders, they sprang lightly into their saddles, and were soon following Smith along a rough road which skirted a mountain side.   Where the road was rough and precipitous, they walked their horses; but at times they would break into a sudden gallop over level reaches, showing that they knew every inch of the way. At last they descended to the valley, and struck out rapidly across the open country, till they approached a secluded farm-house, where, drawing rein, they entered the gateway, and surrounded the dwelling.

"This is the right kind of a Whig, boys, for he's got a pile of hard money stowed away somewheres; so don't let him escape.   Bring him out, Cole."

The man thus addressed dismounted, and taking from the adjacent woodpile a log of wood, crashed in the door, thus rudely arousing their victim from his slumbers.

"If you want to save your life, come out and speak to

me,'' shouted Smith ; '' but if you pull a trigger you are a dead man.   You know Claud Smith.''

The wretched farmer knew him only too well, and called, '' I'll come as soon as I get my clothes on.''

'' No matter about your clothes.   We ain't over modest, and it's not women you've got to deal with, I can tell yer.''

The man, partially dressed, appeared in the doorway, with face so pale that it looked white even in the starlight.

'' Now,'' continued Smith, '' I've got two things agin you.   Fust, you're a Whig ; and second, you're hoardin' up money that others need more'n you do.   If you want me to let yer off on the first offense, you must bring out every shiner you've got.''

'' Now, Smith,'' began the man tremblingly, '' you are entirely mistaken.   I haven't got any——''

'' Stop your jaw,'' said the robber coarsely.   '' A man that's so near eternity as you be ought to look out how he lies.''

'' But I tell you I haven't——''

'' String him up, boys ; we'll help his memory.''

They were provided with a rope for such style of persuasion, and throwing it over the well-sweep, they fastened it around the neck of their victim, and lifted him off his feet for a moment.

'' Can you remember where it is now ?'' asked Smith unfeelingly.

But they had misjudged their man, for he had that kind of passive courage and obstinacy which rises up against outrage, and is strong to endure.   Moreover, his gold was his heart's treasure, and he doggedly resolved to part with life first ; so he said,

'' I know you, Smith ; you've no more feeling than a stone.   I expect you'll take my life any way, but you shan't have my money.''

" Oh ! you want some more persuasion, do you ?   Up with him again, boys."

They kept him struggling and strangling as long as they dared and still preserve the breath of life, and then let his feet rest on the ground.

" Now you see how mistaken you are, and how tender-hearted I am.   Here I've given you another chance for life ; but be quick, for this is only the beginning of our night's work."

" No," gasped the man doggedly.

" No ? curse you !   I'll soon change that tune.   Up with him again."

With oaths and ribald revilings, the bandits, whose dusky figures seemed those of demons, obeyed the diabolical order. When they again let him down, the farmer was unable to stand ; but, in response to their kicks and questions, he maintained an obstinate silence.

" Shall we string him up and leave him ?" asked Cole.

Smith hesitated, and for a moment the man's life depended on the caprice of the bandit's lawless will.

Then he said, carelessly,

" No, let him alone.   I rather like his grit, and I've nothing agin him.   If I had, old feller, I wouldn't even give you time to say your prayers.   Let us look for ourselves, boys.   Mayhap we'll find enough to pay us for coming out of our way."

The victim crawled to his door-step, on which he sat in sullen silence while they ransacked his house in no gentle style, breaking their way where locks resisted.   But the farmer had concealed his coin too well for discovery.   In order to spite him, however, they carried off many valuable papers, and all light articles of value on which they could lay their hands, and with the parting salutation of a kick to their half-murdered host, they vanished in the darkness as rapidly as they had come.

The inmates of farm-houses and cabins trembled as they clattered by, but they were safe for that night, as the next point at which Smith meant to strike was far distant. It was a part of his policy to mislead and bewilder the authorities by depredations so far apart as to make it seem impossible that he and his gang were the authors in each case.

Their long, swinging gallop soon brought them to the mountains again, and for an hour they slowly ascended the precipitous sides ; then, like the wind, they crossed a level plateau, and afterward continued through wild and unfrequented roads known to few save themselves, finding breathing places for their horses when the ascent or descent was steep. In about three hours they commenced defiling down what was little more than a path, from various points of which the gleam of the Hudson River could be seen in the starlight. The way was rough and rocky, but their horses had been trained for their work by many similar expeditions. At last they drew near the recently commenced military works at Fort Montgomery, and their approach became quiet and stealthy.

" We must capture one of the garrison," said Smith ; " for if we can send a full account of what the Whigs are doing here, our Tory friends in the city will pay us well for it."

Leaving their horses in a clump of dark, overshadowing trees, with several of the party in charge, Smith and three others cautiously reconnoitered on foot until they reached the unfinished line of the works. Stealing along this a little distance, their steps were soon arrested by a slight sound. Listening intently for a few moments, Smith turned and whispered succinctly,

" It's some cuss asleep. Leave him to me."

Advancing cautiously a few steps further, he saw the faint

outline of a sentinel leaning against a small tree, with his hands crossed on the muzzle of a musket, above which a bayonet gleamed. The Tory, quick at expedients, instantly formed a plan for his capture. Summoning his three comrades, he directed them how to support his undertaking. He then took from one of them his leather belt, and stole noiselessly up behind the tree against which his victim was leaning, and whose nasal organ made the night anything but musical. Then, like a flash, he threw the belt around both tree and man, and secured his prisoner by drawing the buckle tight.

"Och, Molly, me darlint, hold on a bit. Bloody blazes ! what's——"

Smith's hand stopped further utterance, and then a handkerchief was tied securely over his mouth. The other bandits came up, and before the unwary sentinel (who was no other than the unfortunate Larry, and whose faculty of getting into trouble never deserted him) was fairly awake, he was bound and spirited away, giving the garrison he was set to guard no other warning than the remonstrance which Molly's sharp tongue and heavy hand had made habitual.

When they reached the secluded spot where the others were in waiting, Smith put a pistol to Larry's head, and said,

"Now speak low, and speak to the point, if you ever want to speak again. Answer my questions ; I can tell whether you are lying or not. At your first lie my men will cut your juggler." And removing the handkerchief, he asked rapidly about the number of the garrison and the nature of the work.

Larry's discretion preserved him to die for his country upon a more auspicious occasion, and he answered as well as his chattering teeth would permit. Smith was soon convinced that he had drawn from him all he knew, and then said coolly,

"Now you are going to desert, you know. If I should kill you and leave you here, it might make me trouble. You will have to disappear, and make your cursed Whig commander believe that you have gone off to parts unknown. We shall have to take you with us till we find a good place for you to desert in."

These words had such a mysterious import that Larry resolved to make a desperate effort to escape. But his hands were tied behind his back, and the rope they had used on the farmer was about his neck, with which they hustled him along as they resumed their march northward, tending toward the river bank.

"Sure an' ye're not goin' to murther me ?" gasped Larry.

"Well, I s'pose that's about it, in plain English," said Smith.

"Surely ye'll not shed innocent blood ?"

"Your blood isn't innocent. In the first place, you're a —— Whig ; in the second place, you were sleeping on your post, and your own officers would shoot you for that to-morrow ; at least they ought to, and we'll save them the trouble."

"What are yees goin' to do wid me ?" asked Larry hoarsely.

"Oh, put you quietly out of the way, where you will do no harm," said Smith, who rather enjoyed Larry's terror. "They say dead men tell no tales ; but it's an infernal lie. There are times when I don't want either dead or live men on my trail."

Larry was now satisfied that if he ever saw Molly again he must act promptly, and with almost superhuman strength he tugged at the cord that bound his hands. With a thrill of hope he was at last able to draw one hand out of its confinement, and thus relieved them both, but had the presence of mind to keep them together as before, so that their freedom was unnoted, and continued on a little further with the gang, till they came to where a steep bank shelved down into the darkness on one side of the road. Then, with the celerity which his desperate emergency prompted, he drew his knife, cut the rope around his neck, and bounded over the bank, rolling, tumbling, springing, he knew not whither, in the mad desire to get away.

For a moment his captors were so astonished that they did not move ; then Smith cried,

" Don't shoot. After him ; cut his throat, and hide his body."

Two of the most active sprang from their horses, and commenced descending the rocky, precipitous bank. But Larry had the start, and his pursuers were not willing to go at his breakneck pace. For a wonder, he reached the bottom of the ravine sound in limb, and darted off in the darkness among the concealing copse-wood, soon becoming utterly lost to view. The baffled brigands gave up the chase, and returned, grumbling and swearing, to their horses. Nor were their ruffled tempers soothed by the volley of curses received from their leader.

" I could have shot him if you hadn't stopped me," said Cole.

" Yes, and brought the garrison clattering after us. I had other work on hand before I crossed the mountains, and I won't be balked either ; so come." And away like a thundergust they sped to work destruction elsewhere.

In an incredibly short space of time, Larry regained his post, and found, to his joy, that the time for the relief of guard had not come. Dodging around in shadow, he reached his quarters, and awakened Molly as roughly as he had imagined she was rousing him when the Tory pinioned him to the tree.

" Bloody murther !" spluttered Molly.

" Hist, or I'll throttle ye. It's me—Larry. If ye don't want to see me shot in the mornin', git me a musket in a wink."

" Faix, an' I'll shoot ye meself, if ye don't be quiet. Ye've been drinkin'."

" Now, Molly, me darlint, I'll tell ye all in the mornin'; but if ye don't stale out an' git me a musket, I'm the same as a dead man. They won't mind yees if ye is seen, but if they cotch me, it's all up. Don't ye see? I'm off me post. I've been robbed and murthered, an' to-morry I'll be shot. Yees can stale to the armory an' git me one in a jiffy. Go quick, or I'll haunt ye all yer days."

This dire threat roused Molly to action, and she now began to realize, from Larry's desperate earnestness, that the emergency was pressing. Her husband threw a gray blanket around her, and with bare feet and noiseless tread, she slipped to a forge near by, where arms were repaired, and soon returned, saying,

" There, now, look to yerself, for I don't want to be bothered wid ye after ye're dead." A moment later Larry was back to his post, where he stood, straight as a ramrod, often rubbing his eyes, to make sure it was not all a dream. But his torn clothes, aching wrists, and bruised limbs proved the reality of his strange experience, and he was only too glad that the loose discipline of the incipient fort had enabled him to gain his beat without detection. When, a little later, the officer of the guard came around with his squad, Larry challenged him with great promptness, and went rejoicing to his quarters with an encomium on his vigilance. But his tale was so strange that Molly would not believe it, and her only comment was,

" I thought ye'd be mare-ridden afther the supper ye ate. Ye'd better find that firelock in the mornin'."

But when, in the morning, she saw his wrists and bruises,

and the gaps in his clothes which she must mend, she consoled him by saying,

"Och, ye spalpeen! it was the divil himself as had ye; better mend yer ways."

Larry shook his head, but resolved that he would put chestnut burrs in his shoes before he slept on his post again.

Smith and his followers soon reached the vicinity of the lonely log cabin back of West Point, where Vera was keeping her patient watch. As they struck up the glen leading to the dwelling, Cole sidled up to his leader, and said,

"Claud, you're not goin' to Brown's?"

"Yes, I am. Why not?"

"Well," continued the superstitious robber, "they say everything is not right there, and that the old black witch as lives with them can do with a feller just what she pleases. I'm not afraid of flesh and blood, but our weapons ain't o' much account agin the devil."

"I'm not afraid of man or devil," said Smith surlily. "They say there's a lot of hard money hid in that cabin, and I'm not goin' home empty-handed, after such a ride as we've had to-night."

Cole's words, however, oppressed the mind of the leader, for superstition is rarely divorced from ignorance and crime. He also saw that Cole's fear was shared by the rest of the gang; so he caused them to halt, and passed around the flask of whisky again. Under this stimulus they advanced, and were glad to hear sounds that were earthly, as the great dogs bounded fiercely toward them. Two shots in quick succession dispatched them, and after their dying whine ceased, all was still—it seemed to them strangely and unnaturally still. They supposed the owner of the cabin would appear, but there was not a sound.

Smith took another pull at the flask, and then approached the door, but the same oppressive silence continued; a dread and restraint that he could not understand chilled his heart, and the fire that flickered on the hearth filled the cabin, as seen through the windows, with fitful and fantastic shadows.

"Come away, Claud," muttered his companions ; "this is no place for us."

But the hardihood of the man prevailed. Taking another fiery draught, he cocked his pistol, and went straight to the door and knocked.

There was no response.

He lifted the latch, and it yielded to him. Stepping within, he stood transfixed. Gleaming out upon him from where she crouched by the fireplace was the weird, unearthly visage of old Gula, whose fixed gaze of terror was to him a Gorgon stare. More awful to the guilty soul was the white, dead face turned toward him from the bed. Vera knelt by her mother with clasped hands and eyes turned heavenward, and her beauty, pallor, and attitude gave her a spiritual rather than an earthly aspect. But not a sound broke the silence that had now become awful to the man of blood, and it seemed to him that he could not break the spell himself. A jet of flame leaped up suddenly from the hearth, and the strange inmates of the cabin seemed to dilate as if in supernatural light. A panic seized upon the robber. He turned upon his heel, and, without a word, sprang upon his horse and galloped away with his trembling companions ; not did they draw rein till far up among the mountains. Speaking of it afterward, Smith said it seemed to him as if a great hand took him by the shoulder and thrust him out.

At the first fierce clamor of the dogs, Vera felt a sudden shock of terror, which the firing increased ; but her training and her own instincts led her to lift her heart at once to God. Then came the impulse to trust Him only, and stepping to the door, she unbarred it, and then knelt by her mother's side, in which attitude she remained until the clatter of the flying bandits died away. When she arose, she said,

" ' Fear not,' Gula, ' for they that be with us are more than they that be with them.' If God should open our eyes as he did the eyes of the young servant of Elisha, we, too, would see that ' the mountain is full of horses and chariots of fire round about' us.''

" Your God seems mighty po'ful,'' said the negress, with awe in tone and manner, " but Gula's too ole to be changin' Gods at her time o' life. De captain ob de floatin' misery dat brought me from my home, and de mas'r dat used to whip my ole dead body, sot great store by your God, and was allus axin' him to dam folks, whatever dat was ; and I'se afeard if I should pray to him he'd take me to whare old mas'r is, and I doesn't want to see him no mo'. I wants to go back to my ole home.''

Vera sighed deeply, for Gula's harsh experience, which she could not fail to associate with the Divine name that she heard so often, raised perplexing questions. But after a little the young girl said thoughtfully,

" I do not think your old master will be where mother is. God does not mix winter and summer together. No more will he join the cruel and brutal with the loving and gentle. Suppose my God should take you to where mother is ?''

Old Gula shook her head, saying, " I'd like po'ful well to see old missus, an' p'raps dey'd let me visit her. But I doesn't want to take no risks ob meetin' ole mas'r agin, and I does want to see my ole home. Oh ! dat I might go dis minute.''

With such quaint, unearthly talk the Christian maiden, who was scarcely more than a child, and the pagan slave beguiled the heavy hours. In their beliefs, as in their appearance, there was seemingly wide diversity ; but in the only kinship that is abiding—that of love—and in God's eyes they were not so far apart as many who bow together at his altar. The fathomless chasm of evil did not divide them, and perhaps at last old Gula would find her tropical home so blended with Vera's paradise as to be content.

NOTE TO PRECEDING CHAPTER.—Claudius Smith is not a fictitious character, but was once the terror of the region adjacent to the Highlands of the Hudson. The robbery of the farmer actually took place as described, and is only antedated little more than a year. When Smith was hung at Goshen, N. Y., January 22d, 1779, this farmer asked Smith where valuable papers he had stolen were.

" Meet me in the next world and I will tell you," was the grim reply.

His tall and splendid form, arrayed in rich broadcloth with silver buttons, combined with his fearless and almost manly bearing, made him an imposing figure on the scaffold ; and even in the hour of death he inspired something like dread and respect in the vast throng that witnessed his exit. His deep depravity, or, perhaps, more correctly speaking, his lack of a moral nature, was shown at the last moment by a characteristic act. Just before he was hung he " kicked off his shoes," with the brutal remark,

" Mother often said I would die like a trooper's horse with my shoes on ; but I will make her a liar."

CHAPTER XI.

THE MOTHER STILL PROTECTS HER CHILD.

THE winter had passed rather drearily and unsatisfactorily to Saville. The garrison at Constitution Island was small, and the works on the fortifications advanced slowly. Although his education as an engineer had been superficial, he was satisfied that Colonel Roman's draughts and lines of defense were very defective, and that time and money were spent to little purpose. Moreover, his visits to the western shore, and his excursions after game, had shown him that the island was overlooked and commanded by more advantageous points. But his frank statements to this effect had not won him favor with his superior officers, who were ignorant and incompetent, and had more than humanity's average dislike for criticism. Moreover, Saville was so often faulty in the details of his profession as to be frequently open to censure himself, and his prospects of promotion were not very flattering. He would have much preferred active service in the presence of the enemy; but such was the dearth of engineers that he was kept at labors much too peaceful for his fiery spirit.

He had, besides, another cause for dissatisfaction and uneasiness, which also increased his unpopularity in certain quarters. It was impossible for one of his frank and outspoken nature to nurse his unbelief in silence. He even felt it a privilege and a duty to advocate the new ideas acquired abroad, and soon had quite a following of young

and unstable men, to whom he often discoursed in his glowing style on what he termed " the absurd and antiquated beliefs and systems of the past, originated by shrewd old
schemers who constructed and maintained them for their
own advantage. They had been imposed upon men in
times of general ignorance," he said ; " but the age had
come when men would use their reason, and break away
from the tyranny of custom and the trammels of superstition.
Man should be true to himself, and obey the laws which he
found existing in his own nature, instead of trembling before
an imaginary God seated on a throne which no one had
ever seen. The idea of men in the eighteenth century bowing down to an ancient Hebrew divinity ! Why not also
before Isis, Jupiter, and Odin ?" But the practical results
of his bold, brilliant theorizing perplexed and troubled him.
So far as his sophistries found acceptance, and he succeeded
in removing from his listeners the idea of a personal God to
whom they were accountable, they became reckless, vicious,
and generally demoralized. It was said, and with seeming
good reason, that Saville had a very bad influence over his
associates. It was not, however, the man himself, but his
pernicious opinions, that did the mischief. Those whose
minds he poisoned were coarser-grained than he, and had
not his resources of culture, nor his repugnance to the gross
vices of the camp. It was in vain that he remonstrated with
them. His skeptical words had broken down the barriers of
a wholesome fear, which, with many, serves for a time in the
place of principle ; and the dark tides of evil flowed in unrestrained. Thus he unwittingly made them uncongenial
companions for himself ; and, as spring advanced, and his
life grew lonely and isolated as he recalled his wife's unnatural course toward him ; as he remembered that his mother
was grieving over his action as a great misfortune ; as he saw
those who had in a measure accepted his iconoclastic and

skeptical views sinking far below the level of true manhood, his spirit at times grew bitter and resentful, and he would say,

"Everything I touch blackens, and even to my mother I am only a source of sorrow and anxiety. What is the evil fatality of my life?"

But his nature was too sanguine and healthful for any continued morbid brooding, and he would soon throw off the burden of unhappy thoughts, and hope for better things.

Vera's quest of the surgeon had renewed his interest in one whose character seemed so unique that he felt quite a strong desire to explore further; for he had a Frenchman's love of companionship, providing it was tolerably congenial.

The difficulty of making the acquaintance of the family on the opposite side of the river now acted only as an incentive. Perhaps the man was a political refugee, and whatever was the cause of his seclusion he and his certainly did not belong to the class of vulgar criminals. Possibly, if he crossed the river with his flute, and, within hearing of the cabin, played the air which he and Vera had come to associate with each other, the air to which he had first heard her sing the exquisite words,

"I know a bank whereon the wild thyme blows,"

he might lure the young girl to an interview. But, recalling his experience with the fierce dogs, and their equally dangerous master, he also took his arms.

Remembering that the cabin was at the base of a rocky height, he concluded that, by scaling this, he might overlook the habitation unobserved. The lovely spring day was declining when he reached the summit of the hill, where now are the ruins of Fort Putnam, and found that he could there, among the sheltering evergreens, securely carry forward his reconnoissance. With his glass he was able to subject everything to the closest scrutiny ; but there was no one in sight, and even the great dogs were not visible. At first, he hoped that the man had gone away and taken them with him, and he was about to tune his flute to the musical signal which he was in hopes the daughter would answer, when his attention was caught by an ominous heap of newly turned earth under a wide-spreading elm not very distant from the house. Its meaning was soon shown, for the door of the cottage opened, and there issued forth the strangest funeral procession that he had ever seen. It consisted only of three : the husband, who carried upon his shoulder the coffin containing the light and wasted form of his wife ; Vera, and old Gula. Vera carried a large cross of flowers, composed of the white blossoms of the dog-wood and bloodroot, while the negress followed with two wreaths of evergreens. Slowly, and with bowed heads, they carried the wife and mother from one lowly home to the last and most lowly of all. Then Gula helped her master to lower the coffin into the grave, while Vera stood sobbing by. Nor would she permit any one to put the floral cross and wreaths of laurel upon the coffin of her mother save herself. Then all three stood a few moments in silence at the side of the open grave, as they might upon the shores of an ocean across which one very dear had passed beyond their reach. The man, with folded arms and bowed head, stood as motionless as a statue, while Vera, after a few moments, opened a book, which Saville afterward learned was the Bible, and with a voice choked with sobs and interrupted by bitter weeping, tried to read those sublime and inspired words which form part of the burial service in all Christian lands, commencing.

" So also is the resurrection of the dead."

Saville had become so intensely interested in the scene that he had stolen with noiseless tread through the sheltering cedars sufficiently near to catch the broken utterances ; and although he had heard bishops and eloquent men read those words, never before had he been so impressed with them. Tears of sympathy started to his own eyes, and he thought,

"Poor child, that beautiful fiction is a comfort to her now. It's a pity to disturb some of these superstitions, since they soften many of the inevitable ills of our lot to those who can believe."

After closing the Bible, Vera tried to chant the Twenty-third Psalm, which her mother had asked for just before her death ; but after a few broken, plaintive strains, her grief overpowered her. The thought of that dear form being covered with the cold, black earth was too terrible to be borne, nor would she remain as a witness, and so she fled to her own little retreat in the side of the hill back of the cabin. Old Gula soon tottered after, moaning and wringing her hands in her honest grief.

At last the man started out of his stony paralysis, and seizing the spade, worked with superhuman energy till the grave was filled and mounded. Then going to the house, he took his rifle and started up the glen. He was soon lost to view, and the place became as silent and apparently as deserted as when Saville first saw it.

He wondered what had become of the dogs. Venturing down into the valley, a little distance below he found their dead bodies. Here was another mystery. He waited for a time, hoping that Vera would come to the grave, for she seemed so alone in her sorrow that he longed to assure her even of a stranger's sympathy. He had been deeply touched by the scene he had witnessed, and his curiosity had developed into the most kindly interest. He felt that he could not go away until he had told her that if he could ever be of help to her she must come to him again. At first, he thought he would go directly to the door and ask to see her ;

but, acting upon another impulse, he sat down by the grave, and commenced playing a beautiful dirge that he had learned abroad.

He was soon rewarded by seeing the door open, and the maiden appear, looking wonderingly up, as if she thought the music came from the air. But, on recognizing him, she was much startled. Still she did not turn away, nor did Saville cease his music, but only sought to give it a more plaintive and tender character. After a moment's debate with herself, Vera approached with hesitating steps, like a timid fawn. Then Saville arose, and taking off his hat, awaited her coming.

"Will you forgive a stranger for intruding on your sorrow, when his only motive is sympathy?" he asked gently.

Vera essayed to speak, but found no words.

"I hope you are not sorry I came. I would not force my company upon you now."

"No—oh, no. I am not sorry. I think God sent you. I was so lonely, it seemed as if my heart was breaking. Pardon me, I have such a pain here (pressing her hand upon her side) that I can hardly speak."

"I feel very deeply for you," said Saville soothingly; and he took her hand and gave her a seat on a rock beside the grave. "Is there anything I can do to comfort you? Though a stranger, you surely can trust me in this sacred place. I do not think there is a wretch in the world who could harbor an injurious thought against you by your mother's grave."

"I am sure you could not," said Vera gratefully; "and you are less a stranger to me than any one else in all the world."

"Can it be true that you have no friends—no acquaintances—beyond the inmates of the cottage there?"

"It is true: while mother lived she was everything to me.

and when I saw her placed in the ground, the world turned black.   If she could only have taken me with her !''

'' But that would leave the world ' black' for some one else,'' said Saville gently.   '' That might be more than your father could bear.''

'' I know it's selfish and wrong for one to feel so ; especially when mother is, at last, well and happy ; though just how she can be when I am so unhappy is hard to understand.''

'' It is, indeed, poor child.''

'' It will seem right by and by,'' Vera continued, more calmly and patiently.   '' ' What I do thou knowest not now, but thou shalt know hereafter.'   Already I see He will not make the burden heavier than I can bear, for He sent you here when it seemed I could not endure my lonely feelings any longer.''

Saville was deeply stirred, for he was by nature very sympathetic and emotional.   But he must have been unnaturally callous, could he have looked unmoved upon Vera as she turned to him in her terrible isolation and sorrow.   Little other claim had she upon him save that of kindred humanity ; and yet it seemed to her that he was the only one that could be sent out of the strange unfamiliar world, whose words and presence would not be a burden.

To Saville, led as he was ever prone to be, by his generosity and imagination, it appeared that this orphan, in her loneliness and bereavement, had the most sacred claims upon him.   Because she was so friendless and defenseless, his chivalric spirit acknowledged her right to seek help from him.

When men are devoid of faith in a personal God who is intelligently shaping the destiny of his creatures, and controlling events, they are prone to believe in such vague abstractions as fate, destiny, and fortune.   That he should have met Vera as he had in the first instance, and then have received her at the island, when she came in the vain hope of finding help for her mother ; that the young girl should take his proffered sympathy as if famishing for human fellowship, and even in her strong superstition feel that her God had sent him,—all together combined to kindle his quick fancy, and impressed him with the feeling that in this case humanity asserted one of the strongest claims that would ever rest upon him. At the same time, he was not conscious of the degree in which Vera's beauty, youth, and uniqueness of character emphasized this claim.

With all his faults, he had no small vanity to mislead him, and was sufficiently pure and noble to understand Vera's innocent welcome and frank expression of relief that he had come. He regarded her feeling as an intense desire to escape from the awful solitude of sorrow. Sympathy from one's own kind is one of the deepest and most instinctive wants of the heart ; and there are times when it must be had or the consequences are disastrous. No nature that is human is self-sufficient in every emergency of life ; for even the pure and perfect human nature of our Lord, though allied with Divinity, pleaded with the drowsy disciples, "Watch with me." This request was not a mere form, nor a test of their loyalty, but the inevitable appeal for support which ever comes from suffering. The larger and more perfect the nature, the more deeply is this want felt. But, while human kindness and consideration can do much to assuage this eager hunger of the heart, it cannot satisfy. The experience of Gethsemane is well-nigh universal, and there come to all, hours of darkness when earthly friendship is as unavailable as that of the men who slept through their Master's grief when he was but a " stone's cast" away.

How true this was in Vera's experience will be seen here

after ; but now she saw that the stranger, toward whom her thoughts had so often turned, was strangely moved in her behalf, and it greatly comforted her. She felt almost sure that God had sent him, and that he would become such a friend as her mother desired her to gain,—one that would enable her to make further acquaintance with her fellow creatures, and escape from her dangerous isolation. The thought of anything like love, which might end in an alliance with this young man had never entered her mind. She did not know what love was, save that love which, in its tranquil phases had swayed her since childhood.

As has been said, Saville was large-minded enough to understand that she welcomed him as a captive might ; and that he, in some degree, satisfied a natural craving for sympathy and companionship. He also saw that she was as guileless and ignorant of the world, as she was friendless and in need of guardianship ; and every generous trait in his nature responded to her unconscious appeal. He took her hand, and said,

" You are, indeed, very much alone in the world. I never knew any one quite so friendless, who was as good as you are."

" You are almost the only one I have ever spoken to, save mother, father, and old Gula," replied Vera, looking into his face as frankly and gratefully as a little child.

" Would you like to speak to me often ? Would you like to have me as a friend to whom you could tell your troubles, and from whom you could ask help and advice without any fear ? I am willing to be a brother to you as nearly as I can."

Vera's lovely face was fairly illumined with gratitude ; but, without removing her frank and childlike gaze, before which a bad and designing man would have shrunk abashed, she said, earnestly,

" And can you offer so much to one who has so little claim upon you ?"

" Who could have a stronger claim ? Your need, your loneliness and sorrow, your youth, beauty, and ignorance of the world and its dangers, would awaken a chivalrous spirit in the basest of men ; and such, believe me, I am not, with all my faults. Let me, then, be a friend and brother, till you can find better and more helpful friends."

" And do you think that I could use you only as a stepping-stone on which to cross a rough place ?" said Vera, a little reproachfully. " Ingratitude is a ' marble-hearted fiend.' No friend can ever take the place of one who has been kind to me at this time. But, humble and friendless as I am, there are conditions of which I must speak first. I am, indeed, alone. There is no one to guide or counsel me, and I must follow mother's teachings and words, as far as I can remember them. She told me that if I ever made friends, the first thing I must try to be sure of was their truthfulness ; for she said no good qualities could take the place of truth, and that, if this were lacking, all else would fail. I feel sure that you are true and honorable. My heart tells me that you are. You would not deceive me anywhere, much less here," with a little, eloquent gesture toward the spot where her mother was sleeping. " Will you promise me that your friendship will ever tend to help me live and feel as that dear mother would wish ? I believe God will permit her to be near me, and I wish her to see no change, no forgetfulness of her, or any of her words. I would rather live alone all my life in these mountains, and never see any one, than grieve her. My only request is, that you will help me to remain true to her teachings, and to live in a way that I know will be pleasing to her."

Saville hesitated a moment, for Vera was asking more than she could understand. According to his opinions the best service he could render this young girl was to enlighten her mind, and break the chains of superstition. And yet his theory in this case failed signally, for that superstition was now her only comfort—the rock that sustained her above the dark waves of sorrow. He might better stab the girl looking up wistfully at him, than hint that her mother was not living and that there was no such place as heaven. Then the thought flashed into his mind : could his philosophy make her more true, innocent, and lovely in character, than had those mother's teachings, to which she was so pathetically seeking to be loyal ? His experience as its teacher had not been encouraging ; and had he not better leave the spells of early years unbroken, in this instance ? The moment's reflection convinced him that any other course would be most cruel, and perhaps disastrous ; and therefore he said solemnly,

"I promise what you ask ; and when I see what your mother's teaching and example have made you, I feel assured that I am acting right."

Thus again Saville gave a pledge which would in the future confront him, and rise like a wall across his path.

But Vera heaved a great sigh of relief, and said, "I am content. I now have done just as mother would wish," and she looked as fondly at the grave as if it were an intelligent face.

For a little while Saville watched her wonderingly in silence, and then asked abruptly,

"You have never told me your name."

"Vera—Vera Brown."

"Vera ! it's a most appropriate name."

"It was appropriate to mother, and it was given to me by father, because he said she had been so true to him. Oh ! how I wish you had come sooner," she added, with a sudden rush of tears.

" Why do you wish I had come sooner ?"

" Mother wished to see you."

" Indeed ! did she know anything about me ?"

" She knew all that I did. I never hid a thought from her, and never shall, for I think God will let her come back to me and be my guardian spirit. Can you think I did not tell her of your great kindness when I went for the surgeon ? She wanted to see you and thank you," and Vera's tears fell fast.

" Why did you not come for me ?"

" I did venture once to the shore, but there was a feeling which I cannot explain that made it impossible for me to ask you to come, though I so much wished you would," said Vera, unconsciously revealing the maidenly reserve, which, though not understood, controlled her. " I was in hopes you might come again of your own accord."

" I ought to have done so ; and yet I feared I might be an intruder."

" You have no reason to blame yourself, after the treatment you received from father and myself. I had no cause to *expect* you ; I only *hoped.*"

" I am still to blame," said Saville ; " for while your voice forbade me to come, I thought I saw in your eyes the need of sympathy and help."

" You saw what was true, indeed."

" Besides, you spoke your father's will, and not your own wish."

An expression of pain flitted across the girl's face. For a moment she sat still in deep embarrassment, trying to think how she should explain her father's action, past and prospective ; but she knew so little herself, and the whole subject was so mysterious and sad, that she was at a loss to find words.

Her truth, however, and her simplicity served her better

than skill or concealment; for at last she turned a little abruptly to Saville, and with eyes washed clear by many tears said,

"My father met with a misfortune in England. What it was I do not know; neither he nor mother ever told me. But he had to leave his home; so he brought mother here, and here I was born, and here we have lived ever since: now you know all that I do. Mother thought that father's troubles and his long seclusion from the world had a bad influence on his mind, and once told me that he had greatly changed from his former self. But, like Cordelia, 'I love him according to my bond,' and with her could cry,

> 'O my father! Restoration, hang
> Thy medicine on my lips; and let my kiss
> Repair those violent harms.'

But from you I can ask only forbearance; the same generous courtesy that you showed when you said to me, 'Charity thinketh no evil.'"

This statement, so simple, guileless, and yet enriched by an apt allusion to one whose character she seemed to possess, greatly pleased Saville. Whatever had been the act that clouded the father's life, not even the shadow of its knowledge rested upon the mind of the child.

"Your thoughts are as crystal as yonder spring," he said; "and yet you are enshrouded in mystery. How came you so conversant with the two great books of the world?"

"There is no mystery about that; they are the only books we have. I learned to read in them, and they have been my companions ever since. What I should have done without them, often, I scarcely know."

"Which of the two do you like the better?"

"Oh! the Bible, of course. But a year ago I found

more pleasure in the plays, and I never could get weary of them ; but when mother began to fail, and my heart to sink with dread, the plays would not answer. I wanted something like the kind voice of a living being speaking to me, and so I have read the Bible altogether of late."

"And does the Bible seem like a living voice speaking to you ?"

"Why, surely ; the Bible is God's Word. Sometimes I hear mother's favorite text so plainly—' Let not your heart be troubled '—that I look around, half expecting to see some one."

Saville sighed, as he thought, "What a pity her belief is not true !" but he said, changing the subject,

"Will you let me ask about another mystery ? How does it happen that your two great dogs lie dead yonder ?"

"There is a mystery concerning those two humble friends, which perhaps you can help us solve. When I found them dead this morning, I felt very badly. It seemed as if death still hovered around us ; and yet God preserved us so wonderfully from greater harm, that we have only reason to be grateful." Then she told him of the night alarm, and the intrusion of the robber within the cabin. "But after he entered," continued Vera, "he did not speak, and scarcely moved until he turned and abruptly left the room ; and then, judging from the sound of their horses' feet, they went as if flying for their lives. I unbarred and unbolted the door, so that we might be solely in God's hands ; and He protected us as He did the prophet, when cast into the lion's den."

"This is very strange," mused Saville frowningly.

"Do you think they were soldiers ? Their coming has troubled father terribly."

"You say they came up the valley from the south, and continued northward."

"Yes."

" I scarcely think they were any of our men.   It is more probable that they belong to a class of dangerous wretches that are becoming very troublesome.   They pretend to be Tories or Royalists, but usually plunder either party as they get a chance."

" Oh ! thank God, who kept us from the evil."

" I do indeed shudder to think of your situation last night," said Saville, growing pale at the thought of the young girl's peril.   " But, to quote from one of your favorite books, ' Conscience makes cowards of us all.'   These guilty rascals are very superstitious, and no doubt your mother's dead face was more protection than an armed man. But it troubles me greatly to think of you as so isolated and unshielded."

" I shall continue to trust in God," said Vera calmly.

" That is right ; keep up your faith and courage," replied Saville heartily ; adding mentally, " Poor child ! never was delusion more harmless and useful than in your case."

The twilight was now deepening fast ; still it had not grown so dark but that Vera's father could be plainly seen advancing toward them.   When he saw Saville, he stopped abruptly, and took his rifle down from his shoulder, with the instinctive action of one who suddenly thinks himself in the presence of danger.   But Vera rose promptly, and taking her companion's hand, led him forward, saying,

" Father, this is Mr. Saville, who was very kind to me when I went for the surgeon."

The man's recognition was so cold and distant as to be forbidding, whereupon Vera continued, in a tone whose firmness and decision excited Saville's surprise, and proved that she had unusual force of character,

" You remember mother said that if he came again you must treat him with kindness and courtesy ; and from henceforth mother's will must be your law and mine."

This reference to his dead wife disarmed the man at once. The known wishes of a loved one who has died are often far more potent than were strong entreaties when urged face to face ; and the husband's mind was not so warped but that he was suffering from the remorseful impression that he had not been as considerate of his wife as both duty and his own affection required, and he was in a mood to make amends. It was only his strongly rooted habit of shunning and repelling strangers that now stood between him and this the first visitor who had broken in upon his solitude for so many long years. But Vera was gladdened by seeing him master this, though evidently by a great effort, and give his hand to Saville in something like a welcome.

"The wishes of the dead are indeed sacred," he said ; "and I hope that neither myself nor my daughter will ever have cause to regret our acquaintance."

"I pledge you the word of a gentleman, you shall not," replied Saville heartily ; "and to the extent of my power as an officer I will extend you protection while I am in this locality."

"I hope you will not go away," said Vera in a low tone ; but there was more entreaty in her wistful look than in her words.

"The chief element in a soldier's life is uncertainty. I must obey orders, and there is prospect of a very active campaign. But wherever I am, I shall not forget you, nor cease to use what influence I possess in your behalf."

Mr. Brown now went so far as to ask Saville into the cabin, where Gula had prepared as good a supper as her slender materials permitted. Saville's high breeding and familiarity with the world enabled him to talk with ease and grace, while his tact and genuine sympathy for the afflicted household made his words like oil that calmed the troubled waters in the souls of each of his listeners ; for, beyond a few eager

questions on the part of Mr. Brown in regard to the progress
of the war, both father and daughter were well content to
listen rather than speak, when their hearts were so full of
sorrow, and their lips sealed by so much mystery.   Gleams
of hope and almost exultation came into the eyes of the fear-
haunted man, as Saville told him of the forced and hasty
evacuation of Boston, on the part of the British troops, of
which event vague rumors only had reached the mountain
cabin.

" But, after all," he asked, " can the American Colonies
make any prolonged resistance to the enormous power of
England ?"

" Yes," cried Saville enthusiastically ; " we are on the
eve of complete and final independence, and on this new
continent will be built up a system of life and government
which will revolutionize the world."

The haggard face of his host lighted up as he caught
something of the young man's spirit ; but soon the shadow
fell across it again, and he shook his head, saying,

" England's power is almost without limit, and English
blood is slow to heat and slow to cool.   Rest assured it will
be a long fight."

" Yes, and a hard one," added Saville thoughtfully ;
" and I am inclined to think that the severest part of the
struggle will be for the possession of this river.   For that
reason I may be of service to you, as this region becomes
crowded with troops."

While Saville and her father were dwelling on the military
and political aspects of the situation, Vera's eyes and thoughts
often wandered out into the darkness that concealed the little
mound which was still ever present to her mind, and as the
last words were uttered, she sighed,

" Perhaps mother has escaped from ills too great for her to
bear."

" It shall be my effort that you escape from as many as possible also, though not by flight into the unknown," said Saville, generously hoping to do more than circumstances would probably permit, to show his friendship. " And now, sir," he continued, giving his hand to his host, as he rose to depart, " you cannot fail to trust me after to-day ; for I have broken bread with you, and were I a wild Arab, I could never entertain an injurious thought against you or yours."

This cordiality toward his host was somewhat the result of policy ; for he saw that if he would be of service to the daughter, he must disarm the suspicions of the father. Moreover, he had come to the conclusion that the man's offense had been of a political nature, for in his words and bearing there was no suggestion of vulgar crime.

To Vera's hand he gave a strong pressure, as he said, " If anything I can say or do will cheer you, I will soon come again."

" You have cheered and comforted me more than I could have believed possible," said the maiden gratefully ; and she added, with the frankness of a child, " I hope you will come soon and often."

CHAPTER XII.

BEACON FIRES.

SAVILLE was not slow in keeping his promise, and became a frequent guest at the little cabin among the mountains.   His visits, which at first were made largely from sympathy, soon became sources of so much pleasure, that he was ready to avail himself of any pretext which gave him for a few hours the society of one who was more fascinating than if schooled in social arts.   And yet such was her youth and simplicity, and so undisguised was her wonder as he described scenes and life in New York and Europe, that she seemed to him only an intelligent child, whom it was a delight to instruct.   Congenial companionship was a necessity of the young man's nature ; and in Vera he found so much delicacy and refinement, combined with such utter absence of conventionality, and entire ignorance of the form and etiquette of the times, that she appeared to confirm his Utopian dreams of a liberty so large that the impulses of nature would become the only laws.   But nature, to Saville and Vera, had very different meanings.   To the one it was an existing order of things that he could not account for, but in which man was supreme, and a law unto himself.   To the other it was the creation and dwelling-place of a Divine, all-powerful Being, who was, at the same time, her Father and friend. In the beauty and purity of Vera's character Saville saw the effects of this belief, but he erred greatly in supposing all to be the result of earthly causes.   The development of the soul, under the influence of a Divine, ever-present Spirit, was a truth concerning which he had little knowledge and no faith.

Of his own great trouble and disappointment he never spoke to any one. His wife's conduct was more than a sorrow, and had become rather a bitter shame and disgrace, to which his proud spirit could not endure the slightest allusion. Not even to his mother had he mentioned her name since the evening she crossed his threshold for the last time. It was his wish to forget her existence ; for his blood tingled as he remembered how easily she had duped him, and how blindly and stupidly he had wrecked his happiness. While, therefore, he spoke frankly to Vera of his mother, and of his life abroad and in New York, he maintained the habit of silence, in regard to his wife, which was already fastened upon him.

Vera had disarmed at once the bitter and misanthropic thoughts, which a man with his experience is prone to cherish toward the entire sex. No mountain stream could be more transparent than this child of nature, who had learned none of art's disguises. When, from instinct, she manifested maidenly reserve, the cause was as apparent as the effect. Her perfect guilelessness deepened the impression, that Saville had formed from the first, that she was but a child ; and his warm and growing affection was that of a brother for a younger sister, who accepts wonderingly and trustingly his superiority in all things. And yet there was withal a certain womanly dignity which often puzzled Saville, and made it impossible for him to indulge in the innocent caresses which are natural between brother and sister.

As for the young girl, she no more thought of analyzing her feeling toward her new found friend than would the mind of a famished man dwell upon the chemical constituents of the food that was giving him a new lease of life. She

did indeed love Saville, and she knew it ; but her strong
and deepening regard caused no more unrest than had the
tender yet tranquil affections which had hitherto governed
her.   She loved him like a sister, and yet with more intensity than that relation usually awakens.   She loved him from
a deep and abiding sense of gratitude.   He had been a
friend in the sorest extremity of her life, and had come as a
deliverer when her heart was breaking in her terrible anguish
and loneliness.   He had rescued her from the agony which
pierced like a mortal thrust, as she realized that her mother
was buried from her sight ; and he had gently and tenderly
sought to comfort and divert her thoughts ever since.   She
loved him for the same reason that many others of her sex
would : because he was lovable, and possessed the traits that
usually win esteem.   He was brave ; he was manly in his
appearance and bearing ; frank and affable in his manner ;
and more than all, possessed tact, and the power of adapting
himself to the moods and characters of his associates.   He
could be most fascinating when he chose to exert himself ;
and both inclination and every generous impulse led him to
do all in his power to cheer the orphan, who looked to him
as the sole friend she possessed.   But perhaps the tenderest
element in her affection was the result of her mother's
knowledge of him, and her belief that he would prove the
deliverer who would open a way of escape from an isolation
which she saw, more and more clearly, would be fraught
with danger and unhappiness.   He had shown kindness to
her mother, and his gift of the brandy had made the pain
and weakness of her last days more easily borne.   Under
the circumstances, and with her nature, how could she do
otherwise than love this stranger knight, who had done so
much to help and relieve from sore distress ?

And yet there was a depth in her heart in which the name
of Saville had never sounded.   If he had told her that he

bad a true and loving wife in New York, her heart would have bounded with joy ; for in that wife she would hope to find another friend, of her own sex. She could love her at once for his sake. If, in brotherly confidence, he had told her of another maiden that he loved, no sister would have sympathized more unselfishly and heartily. Saville was right ; Vera was still a child.

With no disposition to monopolize her as a discovery of his own, Saville was perfectly ready to introduce other officers, whose characters warranted the privilege, at the mountain cabin. But it was found that its master was so morbidly averse, as yet, to any extension of acquaintance, that at Vera's request, he waited until circumstances should break down the barriers. Her father's intense interest in the progress of the war grew more and more apparent, and they believed that if he could be induced to take an open part in the struggle, his mental disorder would pass away. Although, at times, he seemed almost ready to yield to their wishes, his old habit of shrinking caution and demoralizing fear would suddenly resume its sway and disappoint them.

That this was true was most unfortunate ; for, as the season advanced, the whole country became pervaded with rumors of Tory plots and uprisings. The arrival of British forces was daily expected at New York, and it was said that the loyalists in the city and along the shores of the Hudson were in league to rise, on the advent of large bodies of supporting English troops. It was a time of general distrust. Near neighbors regarded each other with suspicion, and often with good cause. Spies were everywhere plying their trade of drawing from the unwary, secrets that might prove ruinous. It was a bad time for people who could not or did not fully account for themselves ; therefore, the man who, among the few that were aware of his existence, went by the name of "Skulkin' Brown," could not fail to become an

object of suspicion.   There were increasing rumors, which
had no other foundation than the excited imaginations of
people who feared danger on every side, and only the fact
that nothing definite was alleged against him, prevented a
self-appointed delegation from waiting on him with notice
to decamp to parts unknown.

But, in the garrison at Fort Montgomery, rumor began to
take more tangible and ominous form ; for Molly, sharing
in all her mother's prejudices against the neighbors who had
been so secluded and unsocial, began to give out many dark
hints of what she had surmised rather than seen ; and these
intimations constantly gained in evil suggestion as they became the staple gossip around the camp fire.

The artillery company to which her husband belonged
had been stationed for a time at Fort Montgomery, but had
recently been recalled to Fort Constitution ; and Larry was
glad to get back, for after his experience as sentinel, he regarded the east side of the river as the safer one.   He and
his wife naturally gravitated toward that class among the
soldiery who were as ignorant and superstitious as themselves ; and loquacious, rash-speaking Molly was not long
in convincing her associates that old Gula was a " haythen,"
and in league with the Evil One, and that Vera was her
disciple.

These rumors soon took such shape as to become the
topic of conversation among the officers, and thus Saville
heard of them.   Alarmed for the safety of Vera, he promptly
sought their origin, and was not long in tracing them to the
daughter of the old crone who had disgusted him with her
envenomed but baseless innuendo on the afternoon when
he and Larry first saw the nymph of the potato field.   At
first, he sought to reason with Molly, and awaken her sympathies for the motherless girl.   But, on the mention of
Vera, the coarse-fibered woman only tossed her head, with

something like a leer on her bold, handsome face ; and Saville, with indignation, saw that she gave him credit for very
different motives from those of commiseration and friendly
regard for the maiden he was seeking to protect.   Therefore
he said, with a sudden anger and sternness, before which
even the reckless termagant quailed,

"Beware how you or your husband whisper another lie
against those who are under my protection.   If you even
hint anything you cannot prove, I will have you drummed
out of camp."

This, to Molly, was a dire threat, which for a time had
the desired effect ; for, in her estimation, she could suffer no
greater misfortune than to be exiled from the camp, where
she had already become quite a potentate, with numerous
satellites, the unfortunate Larry being the most subservient
of all.   But her spite rankled and strengthened, neverthe-
less.   Saville was no favorite of hers ; for her husband had
reported his significant offer of his old breeches, as well as
his shoes, at the time she captured his quondam man-of-
all-work.

Saville was able, in part, to allay the suspicions of his
brother officers, by his strenuous assertions that the Whig
cause had nothing to fear from the inmates of the mountain
cabin ; but, when asked to give some account of them, he
could say but little, and so an evil-boding prejudice remained.

But the rapid events of a stirring campaign soon banished
all thought of possible dangers ; and in the approach of
legions of British troops, the exile suspected of Tory proclivities was forgotten.

As the month of June passed, the nearer approached the
time when all felt that the English men-of war and transports
must appear upon the coast.   Not a day dawned but the
tidings of their arrival at New York was expected by Colonel

James Clinton, who then commanded the forts in the High-lands ; and the feverish excitement of expectation hourly increased among both officers and men.

One lovely evening, about the last of June, Saville, after his labors upon the fortifications were over, pulled his boat across the river to a little cove near the cabin. He had suffered much, during the past year, and was finding in the society of Vera an increasing power to obliterate the painful impressions of the past. He felt, at times, like one con-sumed with feverish thirst, and that her conversation, at once so childlike and intelligent, so natural and yet tinged with the supernatural, was like a cool mountain rill, sweet and sparkling, as it issued into the light from its mysterious source in the heart of the hills. He often wondered at her ability to enchain his thoughts, to awaken questionings in regard to matters which he had considered settled, and un-consciously to arouse misgivings concerning his doubt and unbelief.

Of one thing, however, he was certain : her influence was making him a better and truer man, and bringing a strange peace and hopefulness into his soul, that hitherto had been full of unrest, and was at times embittered by impotent re-sentment at his destiny and again weighed down by deep despondency.

He was soon on the crest of the rocky height above the cabin, playing upon his flute the air which had become the summons to trysts that, thus far, had not been tainted by the thought of evil. A clear voice from the glen below echoed back the words,

"I know a bank whereon the wild thyme blows,"

and, a moment later, Vera gave him her hand in greeting.

After a little while their conversation flagged. The subtle sympathy between them had grown so deep, that they did not need a constant interchange of words to enjoy each other's society ; and, on this occasion, the exquisite beauty and peace of the landscape, as they scanned it from their lofty eyrie, so impressed both that they were content to gaze in silence.   Darkening and lengthening shadows from the western mountains stretched far across the river, whose glassy surface had gradually passed from the sheen of silver to a colder, steely gleam, as it washed its bold shores at their feet ; but the heads of '' Sugar Loaf'' mountain, and other lofty heights, were still crowned with light and robed in royal purple.   Coming night would soon uncrown them, even as death brings darkness and obscurity to those who, but a brief time before, shone pre-eminent in power and station.

At last Saville said,

'' Why is it, Vera, that while here with you, the real world, which is full of turmoil and trouble, recedes, and I seem near another world which I would gladly enter ; for even on its borders I find a strange peace and quiet joy. The people I am thrown with in the garrison are coarse, and their best idea of life is commonplace and material.   Our food is plain and even gross, and yet it seems wholly to occupy the thoughts of many.   How you live I cannot tell, unless the fairies feed you.   Every day has its harassing rumors, and we know that the enemy will strike us soon ; and the sooner the better, for the great question of Liberty can be decided now only by hard blows.   But you cannot know what a relief it is to escape from the dust, heat, and din of labor on the fortifications, and the oversight of men who seem little better than beasts of burden, to a scene like this, and to have you hover near me, my dainty Ariel.   Are you sure you are not a spirit of the air, an emanation of this romantic region and hour ?   When the cold, dark days come, will not you and your rustic bower vanish ?   If I come next

November, and give our musical signal, will not the sighing of the chilly wind be my only answer ?   Are you really flesh and blood ?''

'' I might answer with Shylock,'' repliedV era, playfully, '' ' Have I not eyes ?   Have I not hands, organs, dimensions, senses, affections, passions ?' ''

'' Still, you differ vastly from ordinary mortals.   How is it that when with you, such a sense of peace, rest, and deep content steals into my heart ?''

'' Another has said, ' My peace I give unto you, not as the world giveth give I unto you.'   It is that which you feel, I trust.''

'' Who said that ?''

'' The Prince of Peace—the God who loves us both.   Life is bringing to me, as well as to yourself, many sad and stern realities.   I live as you do, but am fed much as the ravens are, not knowing where to-morrow's supply is to come from ; only sure that it will come.   You know well, Mr. Saville, that there is now nothing sportive and fairy-like in my life, and yet deep in my heart abides perfect peace.''

Its reflection was on her face, as he gazed upon it long and intently.

'' May it never be disturbed,'' he said fervently.   '' I enjoy, while here, but the pale reflection of what you possess.   But it's all a mystery, like yourself.   What's that ?''

Far to the southward a faint light illumined the dusk of approaching night.   While they looked, another and nearer flame sprang into the sky, and soon the highest mountain-tops all along the river were ablaze.

'' What do they mean ?''   asked Vera, in an awed whisper.

'' They are beacon fires,'' said Saville excitedly ; '' the enemy is at last at hand.   Good-by, my little wildflower ; I must be at my post instantly.   May the hot breath of war never wither your bloom.''

" Good-by,'' said Vera sadly ; " but remember, I shall be here in November, just as certainly as in June.''

" While I live I will seek for you,'' he called back, as he sprang down the rocks and vanished in the darkness.

Vera watched the ominous glare of the alarm-fires for a long time, and then sighed, as she descended to her home,

" Alas ! war means death to many, and, perhaps, to him, my only friend. But not if prayer can shield him.''

She found her father watching the glare, also, in moody silence. Taking his arm, she stood quietly by him. How much those beacon fires might presage to both !

" They have come at last,'' he said, with a deep breath.

" Yes, father, no doubt the English ships are down the river, and now is the time for you to do as mother said— join Mr. Saville, and take an open part in the struggle for liberty. It will be so much better and safer.''

He only shook his head, and she felt his arm tremble beneath her hand.

" Do you think,'' he asked hesitatingly, " we could find a safer place than this ?—one further away ?''

" No, father ; none half so safe as this. We cannot leave this place, where mother died,'' she answered, so decidedly that he yielded to her stronger will, and permitted himself to be led quietly within the cabin ; but, in accordance with his old habit, he sat, a sleepless watcher, through the night, in his dark corner, his eyes moving restlessly at the slightest sound without. Vera tried to watch with him, but her head soon dropped upon the chair.

Gula, shading the light with her hand, looked at her calm face a moment, and then went muttering to her loft, " She doesn't hear no voices yet.''

CHAPTER XIII.

LIBERTY PROCLAIMED AMONG THE HIGHLANDS.

SEVERAL evenings passed before Saville appeared again, and then he went directly to the cabin, for he had tidings for both father and daughter.

"I wish you joy, Mr. Brown," he cried, as they went out to meet him. "You are no longer under British law. This is a free country." And in rapid sentences he told them of the formal declaration of independence on the part of Congress, and of its joyous and hearty ratification by the people, as far as they had been heard from.

His words greatly excited both his listeners, and a sudden gleam of exultation appeared upon the man's haggard face. Saville saw his vantage, and added eagerly,

"I have been selected to read this solemn declaration to-morrow, at evening parade, before all the troops ; and I have come to ask you and Vera to be present. I will put you under the charge of our surgeon, whom Vera knows, and will guarantee your safety. Indeed, your safety largely depends upon your coming ; for if you are known to be present and approving upon such an occasion, it will disarm suspicion, and all will recognize that you are on our side."

"We will come," said Vera decisively ; for she felt that it might be the turning-point in their lives.

"Oh, no, my child ; I cannot," cried the father trem-blingly.

" Yes, father ; you can and will," said Vera calmly. " I shall go, and you will not permit me to go alone."

Urged by his strong desire to verify the tidings he had heard with his own ears, and Vera's gentle coercion, he yielded. It was arranged that they should come the following day to a point, near the fort, where they would find Saville, who promised to give them a position which, while not conspicuous, would enable them to hear those pregnant words which had created a new and independent nation.

As may well be imagined, Vera's excitement was scarcely less than that of her father, though more controlled. She was, at last, to catch a glimpse of the world and its inhabitants, concerning which she had thought and dreamed so much. She was to be present on an occasion of pomp and military display, and the one she loved and honored as the most excellent man existing, was to be the central figure. To her, he embodied the Declaration which he was to read, and was a synonym for liberty. In her fancy, she compared him to the youthful David of Bible history, and the loftiest Shakspearian heroes ; and her heart overflowed in gratitude to God that He had raised up such a friend and deliverer for her and her father. Through his kind offices, she already, in hope, saw her father restored to sound reason and useful station, and both gaining a respected and recognized place in society. To-morrow would be the auspicious day which would inaugurate the happy change.

" Mother was a true prophetess," she said to herself a hundred times. " He is the true friend whom God has raised up to rescue us."

Temptation was indeed coming to Vera as an angel of light, but as yet no threatening cloud appeared above the bright horizon. As the thundergusts lurked behind her native mountains, to break at last as from a clear sky, so might the truth come to her.   But now, with the unquenched confidence of a child, she exulted over the vista of hope and promise opening before her, and with an affection and admiration which was essentially that of a sister for a strong and gallant brother, she permitted Saville to become to her the centre of all earthly expectation.

She was almost as sleepless that night as her father, and the next day, an hour before the appointed time for starting, was dressed in all the simple finery she possessed.   And simple indeed it was ; for neither from her mother nor her foster parent, nature, had she acquired any artificial or gaudy tastes.

Moccasins incased her feet.   Her dark-blue gown was made after the fashion in vogue when her mother was a maiden in her English home, and was fastened at her throat by a quaint and ancient brooch.   But her chief ornament was the wealth of golden hair that flowed, unconfined, far down her shoulders.   Upon her head, as jauntily as when Saville first saw it, sat the plumage of the snowy heron.

Saville wondered at her beauty, as she appeared, glowing with exercise and excitement, at the rendezvous.   Her father also had seemingly nerved himself up to the emergency, and maintained the stately bearing of a gentleman of a former generation ; while Vera, to a very great degree, had removed from his person and dress the habitual appearance of disorder.

Saville led them at once to his quarters, and placed before them such refreshments as could be obtained in a mountain garrison.   According to agreement, the bluff but kindly surgeon soon appeared, and did his best to entertain the visitors.   Saville would have introduced a few other officers, but Mr. Brown had stipulated that he should make the acquaintance of no other person than the surgeon.   To his disordered fancy, danger menaced from every one who obtained knowledge of him. Saville and Vera readily acquiesced, feeling that his habit of reserve and morbid fear could only be broken gradually.

But Vera was more than content, and would have been in a state of childlike wonder and delight, had she been left solely to the enjoyment of the new and strange scenes witnessed now for the first time. But with Saville, and the surgeon who was kind to her mother, at her side, to explain and protect, she felt that her cup was full to overflowing.

Saville noted with pleasure her simple grace and dignity of manner. She was his *protegée*, and he had felt some anxiety as to her appearance and bearing, and also lest she should be painfully embarrassed, or so odd in dress and manner as to attract unfavorable notice. But her bearing was that of a well-bred but diffident child. Her modest deference to the surgeon's words both charmed and disarmed him of the prejudice which her father's life and reputation had created ; and her keen and intelligent interest in all she saw, and the innocent wonder that often found expression upon her mobile features, amply repaid Saville for his effort to secure her presence. There was, withal, a trace of quaint Shakspearian stateliness in her words and manner, which, to one of his tastes, was far more pleasing than the artificial graces of the prevailing mode.

As the hour approached for evening parade and the ceremonies attendant upon so important an occasion, Saville conducted them to a commanding yet sheltered position beneath some overshadowing trees, from which they could see and hear all, and still not be full in the public eye. As Vera noticed this, and saw how relieved her father was that he could shrink partially out of sight, she said,

" Do you read one's thoughts, that your courtesy is so kind ?"

" I should be dull indeed," he replied, " if I could not

read your thoughts, and most unkind not to please one so easily pleased. Good-by, now, for a time. I must go and prepare for the part that I am to take."

"I am proud that it is the chief part," she said exultantly.

Saville's enthusiasm over the Declaration of Independence had scarcely known bounds, and so attracted the attention of his brother officers, that Colonel James Clinton, the commanding officer, said laughingly,

"You shall read it at evening parade, for, judging from the feeling you show, you can do the document more justice than any of us."

"I shall esteem it the greatest honor of my life, if I may," responded Saville eagerly ; "for I see in this instrument the inauguration of a totally new condition of society. I think its writer was inspired, and that it contains more than he realized. He wrought better than he knew. Take the words, 'all men are created equal, and are endowed with certain inherent and inalienable rights ; that among these are life, liberty, and the pursuit of happiness.' Push these pregnant sentences to their logical conclusion, and they level all arbitrary distinctions, and break all chains, spiritual and temporal. They will make all men sovereigns, instead of vassals and slaves of tyranny, existing on earth or believed to exist somewhere else."

"Hold on, Saville," cried Clinton ; "you haven't quoted correctly. The document reads, 'endowed by their Creator with certain inherent and inalienable rights.' A Creator that can endow, can also impose restrictions."

"I admit," Saville had replied, "that in the letter of its phraseology, the instrument accords with the waning superstitions of the times ; but, as I said, the writer wrought better than he knew, and placed there the germs of a golden age, wherein man will be supreme, reason holding the sceptre. Suppose we break the bonds of King George, how can we possess liberty and pursue happiness, if we are trammeled on every side by what some ancient bigots imagined was the will of an obscure Hebrew Divinity? If we must be governed by the myths of remote antiquity, in the name of reason, let us go to Greece ; for there, at least, we shall find some breadth and beauty.''

" If I saw in this document what you foreshadow, I'd burn it instead of having it read," said Clinton, with an oath. " I see in it only independence of King George, and allegiance to the God of my fathers.''

" The acorn grows slowly," Saville answered ; " but when it grows, the shell decays and drops away.''

"Very well," said Clinton ; "you shall read it, and every man can interpret it for himself.''

And so it had been arranged. Apart from Saville's enthusiasm, the selection would prove good in other respects, for he had a fine presence, and a strong, sonorous voice.

As the sun sank behind the western highlands, the tap of the drum summoned the garrison to their respective positions, and filled all minds with eager expectancy. Vera heard the confused and hurrying tramp of feet, and rapid commands from officers which, though unintelligible to her, soon crystallized the human atoms into compact masses. In every part of the fort and island that was visible, bodies of men appeared with bayonets gleaming above their heads. Then, with a precision and order which only military discipline can produce, each company was put in motion by a single word, as if all were swayed by one will. The rythmical tread of many feet echoed and re-echoed on every side, and soon the open, level space before her began to fill with angular masses of men. At first, they seemed to her untaught eyes like human blocks placed here and there by chance ; but, as company and battalion came marching forward to the music of fife and drum till they seemed to form an innumerable host, she saw the angular human masses take, as it were by magic, the outline of three sides of a hollow square. The martial sounds caused every nerve to tingle, and looking at her father, she saw, with a thrill of hope, that he was losing his shrinking manner, and that his eyes were kindling with a grand excitement akin to her own.

In very brief time the lines were dressed, and the men standing like serried ranks of statues. A word of command rang out, which was followed by a subdued crash, as every firelock came simultaneously to the ground, and the ranks became statuesque in another attitude. She also saw that in the mean time every cannon had been manned along the extensive line of breastworks. A little in the rear of the nearest stood a person whose strange costume did not prevent Vera from recognizing as the young Irish girl whom she had occasionally met in her mountain excursions. It was no other than the redoubtable Molly O'Flarharty, dressed in a blue petticoat, the scarlet coat of an artilleryman, and a cocked hat worn rakishly on one side. She also saw, from Molly's steady gaze, that she knew both herself and her father ; but, while the woman's bold stare gave her for a moment an uncomfortable impression, she soon forgot her existence in the interesting scenes in which she was a participant.

When all were in position, and silence had taken the place of the preceding din and tramp of feet, Colonel Clinton, with his staff officers, issued from the shadow of some large tents, and grouped themselves on the fourth and open side of the square, the commander being a little in advance of the others. To Vera, as they stood there in as brilliant uniforms as the times and their meagre purses permitted, they seemed heroes of the first magnitude.

But when Saville's tall form appeared, and he advanced

and saluted Colonel Clinton with the erectness and steadiness of a trained soldier, combined with the ease and grace of one who had seen court life abroad, tears of exultant pride suffused her eyes, and she murmured, " He towers above them all."

> " See what a grace is seated on this brow ;
> Hyperion's curls ; the front of Jove himself ;
> An eye like Mars, to threaten and command ;
> A combination, and a form, indeed,
> Where every god did seem to set his seal,
> And give the world assurance of a man."

A deep hush fell upon the garrison, broken only by the rustle of the parchment as it was unrolled. Even the most stolid of the soldiery could be seen craning their necks that they might hear more distinctly the words that were so fraught with destiny to them and their children. But there was no need of such effort ; for Saville's powerful voice, like a trumpet, sent every syllable even to the artillerymen standing at the distant guns.

When he came to the words, " We hold these truths to be self-evident : that all men are created *equal*," he gave to them such emphasis and meaning, that they thrilled all present, and touched the deep chord of human brotherhood in every heart. From the common soldiery, who felt their humble station, but believed that this truth made them peers of all mankind, there went up an irrepressible shout, whose echoes were long in dying away. Saville smiled, as he thought, " Did I not say that the germ of perfect liberty and equality is in these words ? ay, and the instinct of the masses will discover it, in spite of their rulers. Even the mere announcement causes these poor fellows to break the iron bands of military restraint."

More than once the reader was interrupted by outbursts of applause, or by groans and hisses given with emphasis by his recent subjects for King George, who, in this memorable document, was to hear the unvarnished truth in a form that would make his ears tingle.

It was indeed a remarkable occasion and scene. In the words themselves, in the feelings of those who then for the first time heard them, and especially in view of the results, the element of sublimity was pre-eminent. It was befitting that the surroundings should be sublime ; that there should rise on every side solemn mountains, some in shadow, some crowned with light and glory, suggestive of the checkered fortunes of those who must fight long years for the liberty they were now claiming. But when a strong current of popular feeling and opinion sets steadily in one direction, it will break through all barriers, and overcome all obstacles, even as the broad river at their feet had cleft its way through miles of granite hills.

As the last words fell from the reader's lips—" And for the support of this declaration we mutually pledge to each other our lives, our fortunes, and our sacred honor,"—a frenzy of enthusiasm seized upon all. The lines were partially broken, for the citizen soldiery were too recently from their democratic homes to be held in check, had restraint been attempted. The three-cornered continental hats were whirled high in air, and the prolonged and deafening shouts were but partially drowned by the cannon that, from every embrasure, thundered repeated salvos. The guns of Forts Clinton and Montgomery were soon answering like mighty echoes.

Though the reader had acquitted himself admirably, he was content to be forgotten in the wild excitement over what he had read, and escaped almost unnoticed to Vera's side. As he saw the deep intensity of feeling expressed in her dark blue eyes and earnest face, the thought occurred to him, " She is not a child ; she is capable of becoming, if she is not already, a heroic woman."

The father, also, was so changed that he scarcely knew him. He looked, not only like one who could fight for liberty, but lead others in the conflict. Not from him, however, but from Vera, came the request that they might now depart.

" I am overpowered," she said ; " perhaps if I had had former glimpses of the strange and unknown world, I would not feel so. But I am now overwhelmed, as I imagine one of the old prophets must have been just after he had seen a vision."

" The excitement has been too much for you," said Saville gently.

" Yes, for the moment ; but I have seen that which I can think over and dream about for months. I am very grateful to you for this wonderful experience ; but let us go now, and when you come again I shall have many questions to ask. Mother was right--you are the friend that she had a presentiment you would become. Oh, that she were with us to-day !"

" Your mother seems ever present to your mind," said Saville, in a low tone, as they walked to the boat.

" Dear mother !" sighed Vera, in a tone that trembled with tenderness ; " perhaps she is nearer to me than you, upon whose arm I lean."

It caused Saville a sudden and sharp pang to remember, as he believed, that her mother had vanished into nothingness, and had no longer any existence.

On parting at the landing, Saville took Vera's hand in both his, and said,

" I have learned to respect you very much to-day, my little friend. I think you are ceasing to be a child, and are becoming a woman."

" I would rather be a child as long as I can," said Vera humbly, " for I have so much to learn."

Her father wrung the young man's hand, and said,

" I shall be with you in this struggle actively, if not openly."

" Openly, my friend, openly, and all will be well," cried Saville, as they pushed from the shore.

If he had taken that advice, it might have saved him and his daughter years of suffering.

CHAPTER XIV.

ECHOES ALONG THE HUDSON.

EARLY in the season—indeed, as soon as it became probable that his native city, New York, would be the next point of attack—Saville had commenced to chafe at the orders that kept him so far from the prospective scene of action, and made him little more than an overseer of the soldier laborers, working upon fortifications. When, at last, the beacon fires and subsequent intelligence announced that the enemy were in the harbor, and the city was liable to assault at any moment, he could scarcely restrain his impatience, and at once made application to be transferred to the main army. He was now daily hoping to receive the orders he desired. In the uncertainty, he had decided to say nothing to Vera, since, if the request were denied, she would be saved from the pain of fearing his departure ; and, should it be granted, she would be preserved from days of anxious anticipation.

But in the mean time events occurred which intensified his desire to visit the city, and he began to feel that the duty he owed his mother was conflicting most painfully with that of a soldier. If he could only remove her to a place of safety, he would even be content to return to the mountain fort where there was no immediate prospect of active service. This anxiety kept him on the alert for every rumor from the city, and in that feverish and portentous time there were rumors innumerable.

But on the 13th of July, while directing a working par
in the construction of a bastion, he noticed two sloops com
ing up the river at an unusual speed. The wind was blow
ing very strongly from the southeast, and yet they carried s
much sail as to involve danger, and at times would careen
over to the water's edge. Saville was something of a sailor,
and he knew that none of the easy-going skippers of the
river craft would carry all the canvas they could raise, in
such a gale, unless there was urgent reason.

Scanning them through his glass, he was soon convinced
that there was reason, and that events of great importance
had occurred below. He was confirmed in this surmise
when the vessels, instead of standing on past the fort, approached the shore, and came up before the wind. Even
while casting anchor two boats shoved off, and a few moments later the captains of the sloops were clambering up the
rocky bank and asking for an audience with Colonel Clinton. Saville led them at once to the commandant's tent,
and the bluff skippers, almost in a breath, said :

" Colonel Clinton, look well to your guns. The Britishers attacked the city yesterday afternoon, and some of their
largest ships were a-standin' straight up the river when
night closed in. If they keep on they'll be here afore long."

Then followed several hurried questions and answers.
Clinton was a prompt man and a brave soldier, and though
his garrison and works were ill able to cope with English
ships of the line, he had no other thought save that of resistance to the last.

" Make all sail," he said to the captains, " for New
Windsor, where you will find my brother, the general. Tell
him what you have told me. Ask him to order out the
militia at once, and reinforce me at the quickest possible
moment."

The captains needed no urging, and scrambled aboard

their vessels, which were soon lying upon their sides again, in imminent danger, as every inch of canvas swelled with the freshening gale. But, even in advance of their swift progress, and in accordance with a preconcerted signal, Colonel Clinton sent the echoes of a heavy gun booming up the river, warning his brother, the warrior-governor, that the guardians of the Highlands must bestir themselves at once.

"I am sorry, Saville," he said to the anxious visaged young officer; "but there is no use in your thinking of getting away now. The garrison is ridiculously weak as it is. Out with every man who can handle a pick or spade. We must fight with these while the red-coats give us a chance." And, having put everybody in motion at Fort Constitution, he hastened down to Forts Montgomery and Clinton, to push forward the work there also, and arrange for signals, should the enemy's ships appear.

Saville, as a good soldier often must do, ignored all personal interests and affections, and, to his utmost, seconded the endeavors of his commander. In order to animate the men, he even laid hold of the tools himself, in emergencies that required unusual effort; and the ramparts seemed visibly to grow under the eager labors of officers and men.

Late in the afternoon, General George Clinton's barge, filled with men, was descried coming down the river, and the belligerent governor was soon concerting measures of defense with his brother, who, in the mean time, had returned. Having informed Colonel Clinton of the important steps he had taken, and of the various regiments that would speedily be on the march to reinforce the posts, he said,

"I shall make my headquarters at Fort Montgomery, as that is nearest the enemy. I want to take down with me one or two engineer officers, to help push forward the lines."

"Yonder is a man who is not afraid of work," said the colonel; and Saville was instructed to accompany the governor at once, and told that his baggage would be sent after him.

The day passed, and brought no enemy ; but the feverish excitement and expectancy were not permitted to die out ; for, as soon as darkness closed, the hill-tops far to the south began to blaze, and the Dunderberg, Bear Mountain, Sugar Loaf, Cro' Nest, and Butter Hill speedily assumed their crowns of flame.

From the rocky height above the cabin, Vera and her father watched the ominous glare, for a long time, with deep anxiety. However little she might know of its cause, one thing was certain—it portended danger to her only friend.

On her was imposed already the most painful experience of war—woman's helpless waiting and watching for those they love.

Not many hours later, swift riders brought tidings to the fort that the admiral, Lord Howe, had come to co-operate with General Howe, his brother, and that the active campaign would no doubt commence at once.

On the following day came a letter from Washington, urging General Clinton to do what had already been accomplished, for the energetic governor had stirred up the whole country. In the evening the notes of the drum and fife were heard along the river road, and three hundred of the hardy Ulster County militia marched into the fort.

During the night, Vera saw many lights on the mountainside, to the west ; they were the camp fires of five hundred men, who arrived in the fort early the next morning, and, after a brief respite, for rest and refreshment, all were at work upon the fortifications, every man acting, in the grand excitement of the moment, as if all depended on himself.

For two or three days Saville's labors were incessant, and he had scarcely time to obtain necessary rest. But, as matters quieted down somewhat, and the English ships remained quietly at anchor in Haverstraw Bay, he found an opportunity to slip across the river, on a visit to the mountain cabin. Vera was overjoyed to see him again ; for, from her eyries, even her unpracticed eyes had descried preparations for immediate conflict : while her father was tremblingly eager to obtain the latest tidings.

" I am out with my rifle," he said, " on the southern hills, as long as I can see ; and you have one vigilant scout in your service, if he is unknown."

" Let me report your services to the general," said Saville ; " it will be so much better for you both, if your position is known."

" Not yet, not just yet," said the man nervously.   " I am not equal to it yet : you must give me time."

And so the fatal delay to take a recognized part in the war continued.

Saville's visit was necessarily brief, for he could not long be absent from his post.   In parting, he said,

" Good-by, once more, my little sister ; I will see you again soon if I can, but in these times we do not know what an hour will bring forth.   If we should not meet in a long while, you must not grieve too much."

" I should not sorrow," said Vera tearfully, " as others who have no hope ; for I believe in another world, and a better life than this, where we shall not be disturbed by these rude alarms ; but grieve I would—and how deeply, you can never know.   Am I so rich in friends that I need not grieve ?"

" How will it be when you come to have many ?" he asked, half playfully.

Looking full into his eyes, without the faintest blush tinging her pale cheeks, she said earnestly,

" If that time ever comes, you will still be first."

They accompanied him to his boat, for every moment

with him was precious. As he pushed away the father said,

" I shall be watching on the Dunderberg to-morrow."

The presence of English ships so high up in the waters of the Hudson, created intense excitement along its shores, among both Whigs and Tories ; nor was the general ferment diminished by the fact that the enemy's boats were out daily, taking soundings far up toward the Highlands. Everything indicated that they were preparing to take possession of the river.

On the afternoon of the day following Saville's visit, signals were seen along the mountain-sides, which indicated that the enemy were approaching. The drums beat to arms, and all were ordered to their posts. The guns were manned, and the matches ready for lighting.

Before very long, one of the tenders of the British ships was seen beating up against a stiff northern breeze, which would enable her to retire rapidly in case of danger. But the occupants of the fort supposed that the men-of-war were following, and prepared for the worst. Larry, whose company had been again ordered down to Fort Montgomery, was stationed near a long thirty-two pounder which had the best range of the river, and was not a little nervous, now that his amorous enlistment had brought him face to face with something more than garrison duty ; but his wife, Molly, aflame with excitement, hovered near him, voluble now with gibes and taunts, and again with words of cheer. The element of fear seemed totally lacking in her composition, and in this respect her influence was good over the raw recruits, who dreaded to " show the white feather," as it was termed, where a woman was undaunted. Thus she became a privileged character, and was tolerated, as useful camp-followers often are. Many an awkward fellow, though badly frightened, would rather march to a cannon's mouth

than receive a scornful glance from Molly's black eyes ; and
if she gave a man an opprobrious nickname, it stuck to him
like a burr. Colonel Clinton would often laugh, as he
said,

" Molly makes soldiers out of the militia faster than the
drill officers."

But Larry had become proof against all her sarcasms. He
had philosophically accepted his matrimonial fate, and only
shrugged his shoulders at her keenest thrusts.

But that English vessel which was beating slowly up
against the wind, and the others that he believed to be following, might give him something harder to digest than
words, and he heartily wished himself back in the " Ould
Counthry," even though there was " not a praty in the
bin." But he had nerve enough to go through with his
duties, and that was all that was required of him.

At last it was thought that the vessel was in range, and
the governor himself, as well as the officer in command of
the artillery, ran his eye along the gun.

" Fire !" he cried.

Every eye was strained, and happy were they who had
glasses. A shout of exultation went up, as the ball was seen
to plow into the tender's quarter, and applause was again
and again repeated as she quickly went about and scudded
down the river before the wind. The echoes had scarcely
died away, before Larry breathed freer in the hope that the
attack would not be made, and that he should " live to fight
another day."

Saville asked and obtained permission to follow the tender
in his sail-boat, and observe her movements, and was soon
skimming along before the breeze at a rate that would make
it necessary to drop his sail, unless he wished to enjoy the
hospitality of a British prison-ship. As it was, he approached so near that a brass howitzer on the tender was

brought to bear upon him, and the ball passed over his head, striking the water a little to the leeward. He concluded to run his boat into a sheltering cove, until the tender sailed out of range ; but in doing so, had narrow escapes from two more shots. He did not know that the self-appointed scout was watching all from the sides of the Dunderberg, and that Vera would grow pale as she heard of his peril.

When the tender had receded sufficiently, he reefed his sail and followed more cautiously, contenting himself with the use of his glass. He had not proceeded far, before the English vessel suddenly rounded to, and cast anchor. A boat was lowered, and Saville first thought that they intended giving him a chase, in the hope that he might be captured, since he would have to beat up against the breeze. But, confident of the sailing abilities of his little craft, he determined to let them come within range of his rifle before going about.

But the boat, on the contrary, was pulled steadily toward shore ; and soon a farm-house, at the base of the mountain, was in flames, while the cries of its occupants came to him faintly against the gale.

" Do they call that war ?" muttered Saville indignantly. " I must have a shot at those base marauders." And he ran his boat in shore, behind a projecting rock, and unshipped the mast, so that nothing could be seen. Then, seizing his rifle, he sprang up the mountain-side, and made the best speed he could, over the rocks, through the copse-wood, toward the burning dwelling.

The work of destruction was complete, and the incendiaries had already embarked before he came within range. He feared they would be out of reach before he could get a shot. But the boat had proceeded from the shore but a little distance, when a sharp report rang out from the sides of the Dunderberg, and the stroke oarsman fell over backward. This caused some confusion and delay, and Saville gained on the boat rapidly. But, after a moment or two, the oars struck the water more vigorously than ever, and Saville was about to fire, and do the best he could, when a second well-aimed shot disabled the oarsman who had been substituted, and again delayed progress somewhat.

He now sprang down the rocks toward the water, and whipping out the glass that was slung over his shoulder, endeavored to distinguish, if possible, the form of the officer in command, feeling that he, more than any of the rest, deserved punishment. Though this man, with the cowardice in keeping with his deed of rapine, sought to hide himself among the crew, Saville's glass revealed his insignia of rank. Leaning his rifle over a rock, he took deliberate aim, and fired ; then, taking up his glass, he had the satisfaction of seeing the craven spring up, and fall overboard, while his cry of pain came distinctly across the water. He was immediately pulled on board, but whether dead or alive, Saville could not tell, and in a moment or two more the boat passed out of range. The few random shots that had been fired by the marines pattered harmlessly against the rocks ; for the two fatal marksmen were well concealed.

Saville now remembered that Mr. Brown had said that he would be watching on the Dunderberg that day, and he at once surmised that it was he who had fired the first two shots. In the hope of seeing him and taking him back in his boat, he sent his powerful voice far up the mountain,

" A friend—Saville."

" I believe you are, Mr. Saville," said a quiet voice at his side ; and to his surprise, on looking around, he saw the object of his thoughts standing before him.

" How, in the name of the impossible, did you get here without my seeing you ?"

"I told you that I could be something of a scout, and wished to prove it."

"You can be invaluable if you will," said Saville, shaking his hand heartily. "Those were splendid shots you made."

"Yours was a better one, and at a longer distance. I am glad you hit that miscreant in command. I would have sighted him, but I saw you coming, and wished to delay the boat till you got within range. But it would have been an infernal shame to have let that fellow escape, for he treated the inmates of the farm-house brutally. Good God! the thought of such a wretch coming to my cabin in my absence!"

"Mr. Brown, you owe it to your lovely daughter to place her in some position of safety in these troublous times."

"I believe you are right," muttered the father, with contracting brows.

"Let us find an asylum for her and old Gula at once, and then do you openly join the army. I will look after your interests."

"I believe I will," said the exile hesitatingly; and he suffered Saville to lead him to his boat.

If they had been near the fort all might have been well, and the man enrolled in the Continental service. But, as he sat quietly in the boat, while it tacked slowly up the river against the wind, his blood had time to cool. Reaction from the fatigue and excitement of the day set in. One of the old waves of fear and despondency began to surge over his unstable mind, and Saville heard him mutter,

"My God! I have shot two English soldiers. If ever apprehended, my fate is made doubly certain."

At last he said piteously, "Put me ashore anywhere; I can go no further."

Saville reminded him of his promise, and pleaded with

him to keep it for Vera's sake, but soon saw that it was in vain.

" Put me ashore," was the only response, and uttered in tones that were almost savage. Then he added, half apologetically, " I am not myself now, and all I can do is to cower and hide. I will see you again soon."

Saville reluctantly acquiesced.

" Say not a word about me till you have my consent," said his trembling companion ; and he dashed into the thickest copse-wood, as if his only thought were concealment.

Alas for Vera !

CHAPTER XV.

SAVILLE'S NIGHT RECONNOISSANCE.

SAVILLE proposed, on the following day, to visit the cabin, in the hope of finding its owner in a better mood. He was more and more convinced of the wrong of leaving Vera so exposed, and with no better protector than one who, at times, was ready to fly from his own shadow. He saw that her father's mind was more shattered than he had supposed, that he could not be depended on even from hour to hour, and was fast coming to the conclusion to act independently of his will, if possible.

But early in the day came the startling tidings that the British men-of-war—the *Phœnix*, carrying forty guns, and the *Rose*, twenty, were standing steadily up the river.

Again there was preparation for immediate conflict, but the vessels came to anchor within six miles of the fort, and there remained quietly.

With the enemy, however, in such close proximity, no one could leave his post that night or the next day.

Governor Clinton was greatly alarmed, and with good reason. The river was deep, and, with a fair wind, the ships could speedily pass his guns, unless disabled ; and, once above the Highlands, a rich and defenseless country was open to ravage. He feared that they might take advantage of some dark night, and slip by him in the deep shadows of the mountains.

To prevent this, the shores were lined with guards, and

the river patroled by boats. Huge piles of brushwood, and other inflammable materials, were placed at various points along the shore opposite the fort, and these were to be kindled after nightfall, the moment it was discovered that the ships were under weigh. Thus the fort would remain in darkness, while the men-of-war must pass distinctly through the transient glare, and so become excellent targets.

The cannoniers slept by their guns, while Molly's scarlet coat flamed along the ramparts by day, and she flitted hither and thither almost as restlessly at night. Every morning found her as morose and vixenish as one of the wildcats of her native mountains, because the signal fires had not blazed, and that all had remained quiet on the Hudson.

There soon came a day on which there was a steady downfall of rain, and it was feared that the brush-heaps and combustibles would become so dampened that they would not kindle. The night promised to be excessively dark, and Saville learned that the general was growing anxious.

He again volunteered to go in his boat on a reconnoissance, and his offer was gladly accepted.

"If we fire three shots in instant succession, you may know that the ships are under weigh up the river, but if we fire at intervals, give no heed, for it may be necessary in self-defense, or we may have a skirmish."

"Don't do anything rash," said the governor. "You are such a fire-eater, that I scarcely expect to see you again."

Saville chose two active young fellows, who had been boatmen, to accompany him, and with muffled oars they pulled vigorously at first, till they began to approach the hostile vessels. Then they permitted themselves to drift slowly with the tide, which was in their favor. The darkness had become perfectly intense, and there was not a sound save the heavy patter of rain on the water.

They drifted for a period that seemed interminable to their excited minds, and then Saville whispered,

" I fear we shall pass without seeing them. The fact that they have no lights out is very suspicious."

Scarcely had he spoken when the gentle breeze from the south caused a slight creaking of cordage so near that it seemed just over their heads. He at once crept cautiously to the bow of his boat, and put out his hands, so that it might not strike with even the slightest concussion.

It was not long before a faint black outline loomed up over him, and a moment later his hands touched the sides of a ship. Feeling stealthily along, he found that he was near the bow, and, by standing up, was able to hold his boat for a time in motionless silence. He could hear the confused sound of voices, and the step of the officer of the watch, but nothing definite.

At last, footsteps and voices approached the bow of the ship under which he stood. Some one said distinctly,

" It's cursed dark."

" Yes ; but that would be in our favor, if we only get a little more wind from the present quarter, and could feel our way up through these black hills. It's just the time to catch the —— rebels napping."

Saville concluded that he would now put a word in their counsels.

" Have my pistol ready," he whispered to the nearest of his companions.

Then, by a powerful effort, he pushed his boat well away from the ship, and shouted,

" But the rebels are not napping, and, as proof, take that," and he fired his pistol where he supposed the group to be.

There was a sharp cry of pain, followed by great confusion for a moment, and in the mean time Saville's companions pulled rapidly away.

"Here, a lantern, quick! Hold it over the side," shouted a hoarse voice.

This was all that Saville desired, and taking up his rifle he fired instantly, and man and lantern splashed overboard.

"Lights, lights! man the guns! every man to his post!" roared the same gruff voice. "This comes of playing bo-peep in the dark. The cursed rebels might put a keg of powder under our quarter, and blow us up."

"Would to the gods I had thought of that before," cried Saville; "but I thank you for the suggestion all the same."

"Stop his mouth with grape shot," thundered the officer. "Isn't there a musket or a pop-gun aboard, that no one can fire a shot?"

"Pull sharp to the left," said Saville to his oarsmen.

The confusion and uproar on the ship were so great that a moment or two elapsed before the officer's order could be obeyed, and then a bow-gun belched forth the iron hail, and a scattering fire from muskets commenced; but the balls only cut harmlessly into the water in the region where the bold patrols had been.

When once under the rayless shadow of the western moun-tain, Saville felt safe from pursuit. In the mean time nu-merous lights appeared on the other ships, and indicated their positions.

"I am going to ask you," said Saville to his compan-ions, "to do something that, after all, is not so dangerous as it seems. The ships there are lighted up, while complete darkness covers us. One of you can scull, I suppose."

"Yes; both."

"Who is the best shot?"

"I used to bring a squirrel out of the tallest trees," said one of the men.

"Well, by sculling we can move noiselessly around among the ships, now on one side, now on the other, and make them think there are a dozen boats here instead of one. I wish two shots fired in rapid succession occasionally, to increase the impression of numbers. In this way we can keep them in an uproar and state of alarm all night, while we, by moving rapidly from point to point, will run but little risk of being hit."

His companions had the nerve to enter upon the scheme at first with zest ; and one of them, seizing an oar, soon propelled the boat within range of the ship with which they had first come in contact. Dropping well astern, they approached slowly and cautiously her nearest quarter. Soon the outline of a human form gave Saville a fair mark, and his rifle again rang out with startling distinctness in the silent night.

The man with the oar then sculled rapidly toward the eastern shore, passing directly aft of the vessel. Again there was the trampling of feet, and a hurried giving of orders, and many shots were fired in the direction from whence had been seen the flash of Saville's rifle. But, in the momentary delay, the lively little craft had passed so far to the eastward as to be out of range.

" Now," said Saville, " let us give them two shots on the other quarter. The moment we fire, scull down the river. Come around well abreast, so that it will seem as if our shots were fired from another boat."

In a few moments, the firing from the ship ceased, as it seemed to produce no effect ; but there was evidently great excitement on board.

They had scarcely reached the position which Saville desired, when several men were sent aloft with lanterns, in the hope that their rays might penetrate the darkness more effectually.

" Steady and careful now," said Saville. " Let us each pick off one of those fellows in the rigging. Fire just after me."

Thus to the bewildered and harassed marines two flashes came from a new and unexpected point.

Saville's man dropped plump on the deck, the other let his lantern fall, and, after an ineffectual effort to climb down, fell also.

But the enemy were now better prepared, and bullets fell thickly around the unseen assailants.

Fortunately they escaped, and soon reached a point to the south where their position was unsuspected.

" They are getting too sharp for us here," said Saville ; " suppose we next have a skirmish with that big fellow yonder."

His companions agreed, but rather reluctantly ; for this measure of attacking an English fleet was more than they bargained for on leaving the fort.

" I will give you a crack across her bow," said the man at the oar ; " but would rather not go any lower down."

It was arranged that two shots should be fired again. Drifting with the tide, they slowly approached the second and larger ship, which was the *Phœnix*, and watched for their opportunity. In the meanwhile, comparative silence was again restored, though it was evident that all hands on both the ships of the line and their tenders were kept in sleepless vigilance at their posts by their ubiquitous assailants, who numbered but three.

At last, dusky forms appeared, and the two rifles again awoke the sleeping echoes, but with what effect could not be seen.

The commander of the *Phœnix*, however, warned by the experience of the other ship, had stationed marines all along the sides of his vessels, and the return volley was so prompt and accurate that Saville's fellow marksman was slightly wounded. Happily the man at the oar escaped, and they again passed out of range, by going toward the western shore.

and the English officers soon checked the useless firing at random.

But Saville had effected his object. There would be no sleep on the British vessels that night, nor any hope of catching the " rebels napping." So he hoisted sail, and quietly stood up the river, leaving the sorely puzzled and not a little frightened British crews standing at their guns and alarm-posts, so that any attempt at boarding, on the part of the indefinite number of rebels imagined in the surrounding darkness, might be repelled.

Saville and his companions received high praise for their conduct, and were soon sleeping peacefully, while the harassed enemy remained on the alert until daybreak.

NOTE.—The incidents of the preceding chapters are largely founded on fact. The tidings of the irruption of the British ships into the waters of the Hudson were brought as described. A tender of these ships ventured within range of Fort Montgomery, and received a shot in her quarter. On retiring down the river, her boat was sent ashore, a farm-house burnt, and the boat, on returning, was fired upon. The *Phœnix* and *Rose* approached within six miles of the fort, and, whenever opportunity offered the English vessels were annoyed by marksmen in boats or from the shore.

CHAPTER XVI.

DARK DAYS.

ON the following day the commanders of the British vessels satisfied themselves that fuller preparations for resistance had been made than they supposed ; and, not relishing the experience of the preceding night, nor considering it safe to remain in a position where the deep shadows of the mountains might afford concealment until an attacking force was close upon them, they ordered their ships down the river to the old anchorage.

Fear of immediate attack having passed, Saville's thoughts recurred to Vera and her father, and he proposed visiting them that evening, hoping that he might find Mr. Brown in a condition to carry out the measures on which his own and Vera's welfare depended. But during the afternoon he was hastily summoned to headquarters.

"I can now give you a quasi leave of absence," said General Clinton ; "and you have earned it. Go and look after your mother's safety. But first deliver these dispatches to his Excellency, General Washington. They are important, and must reach him at the earliest possible moment. Your escort will be ready within an hour on the further shore. I have mentioned your name with praise in my dispatches, and though I shall feel your loss, you will probably be assigned to duty in the main army. When things are somewhat settled, your heavy baggage will be sent after you. And now, sir, hasten. Give those papers into his Excellency's own hands, or into those of his private secretary."

Saville was greatly pleased at this turn of affairs, and, in the excitement and bustle attendant upon his hurried departure, forgot for a time the inmates of the cabin. When he did remember them, it was with a pang of genuine pain and regret, that he could not see Vera before his departure. As this was impossible, he penned a few hasty lines, explaining his sudden movements, and urging that she should find a safer retreat, and that her father should enlist openly in the war. This was sent to the surgeon at Fort Constitution, with the request that he would deliver it. Unfortunately, the missive was never received.

Having arrived in New York, and delivered his dispatches as directed, Saville received permission to provide for his mother's safety.

The old lady, however, would not leave her city home, asserting,

"I have naught to do with this unnatural broil, and shall demand protection from both parties."

But, after all, her chief motive was the desire to be near her beloved son, who, she hoped, might be assigned to duty upon the works that were going up at various points on the island. In this expectation she was ready to endure the terrors attendant upon the city's bombardment.

Saville therefore gave up his leave of absence, and at once reported for duty again. In consideration of his natural desire to see more of his mother after so long an absence, he was given charge of the construction of some redoubts not far from his own house, and at a point where his wife could plainly scan his movements with a glass. Often and darkly she scowled upon him.

But the disastrous battle of Long Island soon occurred, and was speedily followed by the retreat of the American forces from the city and island. Saville, in his sphere, and to the extent of his ability, seconded Washington's masterly ase of the pick and shovel in the disheartening campaign that followed. He now sought thoroughly to learn his profession, and became an efficient officer. Washington learned to know something of his value, finding that he had promptness and energy, which enabled him to accomplish much even with few men ; and at times, defenses reared in a night were worth regiments.

On the 4th and 5th of November, the British forces began to retire from before Washington's strong position in the interior of Westchester County, taking the roads leading southward and toward the river. As soon as it became evident that the enemy would cross into the Jerseys and menace Philadelphia, Saville was sent thither to aid in strengthening the defenses of that city. Thus his hope of seeing Vera at the close of the fall campaign was disappointed. He wrote to her again, as he had several times before, in care of the surgeon at Fort Constitution. But that officer had been assigned to duty elsewhere, and the letters never reached their destination. Saville comforted himself with the hope that Vera was informed of his movements and continued remembrance.

As day after day passed, and nothing was seen or heard of her friend, a great dread began to chill Vera's heart. Her father had come back from his watch on the Dunderberg in a wretched condition of mind. With scarcely a word, he had cowered all the long night in his dark corner. But, as the result of rest and quiet, the incubus lifted from his mind somewhat in the morning, and Vera heard of Saville's peril in following the tender down the river, and of his firing into the marauder's boat. Of his own share in the transaction her father was characteristically silent, even to his daughter.

On the dark and stormy night of Saville's reconnoissance, the southern breeze had borne faintly through the damp air

the reports of the guns.   To her, every such sound now
meant danger to him.

The days passed, and still he did not come.   Her father
told her that the ships had moved down the river.   As far
as she could judge, the garrison opposite had no apprehension of immediate attack.   She urged her father to go down
to Fort Montgomery and make direct inquiries ; but vainly.
Saville's prolonged and unexplained absence had awakened
his morbid suspicions and fears, and his mind was so shattered that he was not capable of the effort.

A look of wistful, anxious expectancy became the habitual
expression of Vera's face.   The slightest sound startled
her.   In her daily tasks, her face was ever toward the window.   The breaking of a twig, the bark of a squirrel,
brought her to the door.   She often ventured down to the
shore, and strained her eyes in the vain effort to recognize
him on the island opposite.   Constant prayer for his welfare
and speedy return was in her heart.

At the twilight hour, when he had been accustomed to
appear, she would climb to the rocky height behind the
cabin, and wait and watch, as they who are wrecked on a
barren island scan the horizon for a ship.   As dusk deepened
into night, her despondency would become more leaden
and oppressive.   Then she would drag her heavy steps back
to the cabin, and sigh and sob herself to sleep.

Not even Gula's entreaties could induce her to eat much,
and she grew wan and spirit-like indeed.   The old woman
began to shake her head ominously, and mutter,

" I'se afeard she's beginnin' to hear voices.   'Twill be
orful lonely if she goes home afore ole Gula."

One evening after she had been vainly watching, she tried
to sing the musical signal which he had so often answered
by voice and flute,

"I know a bank whereon the wild thyme blows."

She sang one line with a pathos that would have touched the stoniest nature, and then held her throbbing heart to listen. The weird notes of a whippoorwill from the lonely valley were the only answer.

She threw herself upon the ground, like a child, in an agony of grief, and wept until utterly exhausted. When she looked up, the lurid glare of the beacon fires was again upon the mountain-tops, but he had not come.

" O God !" she sighed wearily. " I am a weak child. I had but one friend —one brother. Where is Thy mercy ?"

" O mother ! are you happy in heaven, when I am so lonely ?"

Poor Vera was in the deepest mystery of earthly discipline. Her God, her mother, and her friend, all seemed to have deserted her that night, and she could scarcely drag her weary feet to the home where no gentle sympathy awaited.

Her father was away upon the hills with his rifle most of the time, and was wholly absorbed by his interest in the progress of the war, at which he could only guess, as he would speak to no one. Vera had hoped that he might again meet Saville, and whenever he returned, she eagerly questioned him.

Old Gula, in her strange superstition, sorrowed mostly for herself, as she saw Vera growing pale and weak like the parent who had died.

" Young missy is a gwine home to her mudder, and I'll be left all alone. Why can't de voices call me too ?"

On the evening after her almost despairing grief, Vera said to herself, " I can endure this suspense no longer. He is either sick, wounded, or dead ; for he could not have left without a word of farewell. I will go to the fort and find out. He may have needed my help, while I have been weakly mourning for him."

Nerved by this thought, she waited not a moment, lest

her maidenly timidity should obtain the mastery.   For his
sake--impelled by the thought that he might possibly be in
need of her care—she could venture to face the stare of
strangers.

It did not take long to row her light skiff to the opposite
shore, and bitter tears filled her eyes as she thought of the
two former occasions on which she had crossed at that place.

Near the spot where she had landed when in quest of the
surgeon, she saw a small group of men, and, from their
uniforms, surmised that they were officers.   It occurred to
her that she might question them, and be saved the ordeal
of meeting others.   She concluded to ask for the surgeon,
since, if Saville were sick, wounded, or—her heart sickened
at the thought—he would know all the facts.

Unfortunately, the officers whom she was about to address
were wild, reckless fellows, who had made their normal condition worse by liquor.

" There's a rare bird," cried one, as Vera approached.

" I would see Mr. Jasper, the surgeon," she said modestly,
with downcast eyes ; " and crave the favor of being shown
where I may find him."

" The surgeon, pretty miss ! you have no need of a surgeon.   It is a gay young gallant like myself you are looking
for."

" You do me great wrong, sir," she replied coldly ;
" and if there is a man of honor present, he will grant my
request."

" We have no surgeon," continued the first speaker recklessly.   " A soldier's only business is to die, and to have a
jovial time while he can.   So come, my pretty one, ex-
change your frowns for smiles."

" As you are men," cried Vera desperately, trembling
like a leaf, " have respect for a defenseless girl, and tell me
where I may find Surgeon Jasper."

The instincts of a gentleman still lingered in one of the party, and, in response to this appeal, he said soberly,

"He is right, miss; there is no surgeon at the present moment in the garrison, Dr. Jasper having been ordered away."

' Then—then—may I see Mr. Saville?" faltered Vera.

"Saville, Saville," laughed the first speaker coarsely. "She had him in mind all the time."

In pity for her distress, the second speaker again came to her relief, and said,

"Lieutenant Saville is not here, and I have heard that he was ordered hastily to New York."

"Come, my lass o' the hills," struck in the tipsy youth. "The crows have eaten Saville before this. I'll be to you a far better lover."

"For shame, Dick, let her alone. Saville will call you to bloody account, if he hears of this nonsense."

"Things have come to a fine pass," blustered the fellow, "if I've got to ask Saville's permission to speak to a mountain wench. By Jove! I'll kiss her, if I fight a dozen Savilles," and he started forward to give the insult.

Vera, with her old instantaneous quickness, which had once surprised Saville, eluded him, sprang into her skiff, and was out in the stream in a moment, while her insulter, unsteady from liquor, missed his footing, and fell into the water. His companions roared with laughter at his plight, and ere he could scramble out, sputtering and profane, Vera was half-way across the river.

Every nerve in the poor girl's body was tingling with indignation and fear, when she reached the shore. She scarcely had strength to climb over the hills to the cabin, and then fainted across its threshold.

Old Gula was in sore dismay, but had sense enough to carry her to the cool spring, and bathe her face. At last she slowly revived, but was seriously ill for several days.

Still, the bitterness of her mental trouble had been relieved, for Saville's absence was accounted for. He had been ordered hurriedly away. In her strong trust, she believed that there had been no opportunity for a farewell visit, and there was no necessity for thinking that he was either sick, wounded, or dead. Although he was exposed to the innumerable risks of a brave man in an active campaign, her confidence increased that God would spare him in answer to her prayers.

With reviving hope and faith, her strength and vigor returned ; for, in her case, the spiritual and physical organizations were so closely allied that one could not suffer without keen sympathy from the other. But in both she was naturally healthful, having been nurtured in the atmosphere of truth, and the bracing air of the mountains.

Her father, upon her illness, seemed at last somewhat conscious of his daughter's need, and, in his poor way, sought to meet it. He waited upon her with unwonted tenderness, and brought the delicacies of wood and stream ; but he had lost the power to speak soothing and appreciative words. His own disordered mind was tossed on such a sea of troubles, that he had no calming thoughts for another.

Thus, in her sad isolation, Vera was compelled to look heavenward, and, in her long hours of weakness, the unseen world of faith grew very near and real. She felt sure that her mother was watching at her side, and in the night, at times, fancied she saw the dear, familiar form. The impression was often so strong, that she would reach out her arms with expressions of endearment, or speak her thoughts with the freedom of olden time, when sure of loving sympathy.

Her mother's favorite text, "Let not your heart be troubled," acquired daily richer and fuller meaning, and the ability to trustfully cast all her burdens on her Saviour increased.

So, although the strain and nervous excitement of the past year had been very great, she slowly but surely rallied back into her old, vigorous health. She would need it all in her coming desperate struggle for bare existence.

By the time she had fully recovered, the autumn winds were prophesying of winter, and, with a forethought learned in the hard school of experience, she realized the necessity of making all possible provision. She knew how little her father was to be depended on, and he might grow worse. Therefore, as she grew strong, she became busily engaged with her old playmates, the squirrels, in hoarding everything that could be preserved for coming use.

As her father could not be induced to join the Continental service openly, she persuaded him, as far as she could, to resume his old hunting and trapping pursuits.

It might be a long time before she would see Saville again, or before her hope of finding friends and a recognized place in society would be realized. So, nothing remained but the patient performance of present duties.

And yet the dangers resulting from her position, and her father's vain effort to hide from all observation, were increasing. Nothing so attracts attention as unusual efforts to shun it, and nothing so piques curiosity as mystery and concealment.

Relieved from Saville's immediate presence, it was not long before Molly's tongue began to wag again, in dark hints as to the uncanny character of the inmates of the cabin. While such gossip had no weight with the officers, it had with certain of the ignorant soldiery, and gradually Vera and Gula were acquiring the titles of the '' white and black witches of the Highlands.'' If Molly had urged on some of the baser sort, over whom she had obtained almost all the power of a gypsy queen, Vera's homely duties might have found tragic interruption ; but a wholesome fear of Saville's vengeance restrained her.   And yet Vera, unconsciously, was living over a mine which might be fired at any time.

To the officers, also, Brown, from his seclusion, and the fact that no one could account for him, was an object of suspicion, and they would be inclined to deal summarily with him should any one bring a definite accusation.

But though wrong-doing in the past, and most unwise action now, must cause their legitimate evil results, God would not permit his child to suffer beyond her ability to endure.

During the month of October, the beacon fires had often flamed, and yet while Vera and her father saw that there was unusual stir and preparation in the garrisons, and extraordinary efforts to obstruct the navigation of the river, no attack was made, and they remained in almost total ignorance of the progress of the war.

At last the exile could endure his anxiety no longer, and he determined to find out the condition of affairs ; but, with his old characteristic caution, went across the mountains to an interior village, for the ostensible purpose of barter.   He had in his mind the inoffensive-appearing old man whom he had once before ventured to question, and felt that if circumstances favored, he could do so again without risk.

He found the aged gardener at work as before, and as talkative as ever.   But the dismal tale that he told of the American defeat on Long Island, of the evacuation of New York, of continued retreats, and, worse than all, of the second irruption of the British ships into the Hudson, caused Mr. Brown's cheeks, already pale, to grow more ashen.

" How is it you don't know 'bout these things ?" asked the old man with sudden curiosity.

" I live back in the mountains," was the hasty reply ;
and the fear-stricken man waited for no further questions,
but started for the hills, with the one desire to find in them
some impenetrable recess for concealment.

At first, he was bent upon leaving the cabin at once ; but
Vera, with gentle firmness, refused to listen to any of his
wild plans. She saw clearly that the time had come when
her judgment and will must be supreme. But he ventured
less and less abroad, and the impression appeared to grow
upon him that his dusky corner was the safest place. Here
he would often remain all day, and sometimes through the
night also, apparently dreading to move.

As one of the results of her father's condition, the task
of providing food devolved chiefly on Vera ; and the bleak-
ness of November and the biting cold of winter often chilled
her weary frame, as she wandered over the hills in quest of
game. But the chill at heart, the cold, dreary despondency
which often crept over her while engaged in these un-
womanly and unseasonable labors, was harder to bear. She
could not now anticipate the welcome of a gentle and sympathetic mother on her return. Even when cold and exhausted, she almost dreaded going back to the cabin where
her father crouched and cowered, haunted by fears that were
becoming contagious, and where weird old Gula muttered
and mumbled unceasingly of her unearthly voices. The
poor girl herself was growing morbid in her misfortunes and
unnatural surroundings.

The hard struggle for mere existence began to blunt her
finer sensibilities, and she was often too weary for even
prayer or thought. Like many others, under the increasing
stress of earthly care, she permitted herself to lose gradually
her hold upon the divine strength and patience, which her
mother had ever enjoyed through her confiding and un-
questioning faith. Not that she entertained doubts of God's

ability and willingness to help, or cherished resentful thoughts at her lot ; but, in the pressure of daily duties, prayer was neglected. She was drifting unconsciously from the quiet waters, where faith had kept her spirit moored in peace, out upon the restless sea of mere human endeavor and dependence. Like many another, she could still pray " Lead me not into temptation, and deliver me from evil ;" but for " daily bread " she turned practically to her traps in the thickets, to her fowling-piece, and to the diminishing stores that her own hands had gathered. Unfortunately, the question of daily bread was the absorbing one, and, as we have seen, it did not bring her near the Divine source of spiritual largeness and growth. Thus her life began to grow hard, material, and devoid of those influences which had made her appear to Saville more akin to the supernatural world in which she believed, than the tangible one which was all to him.

The poor child was learning to employ bodily fatigue as many use narcotic drugs, and sought to escape from her desperate loneliness in the oblivion of sleep, whenever her tasks permitted. In dreams, at least, she occasionally saw her mother's loved face bending over her, with the old expression of tenderness ; more frequently Saville's flute gave the musical signal from the rocky height above her grotto, and she, in spirit, hastened to the tryst ; but ever to awake and find it only a dream. Although she would sob herself to sleep again, she would still hope for the return of the vision, that she might once more see his face and hear his voice.

Vera began to realize, in some degree, that she was growing narrow, and dwindling toward a mere animal existence ; and she shed bitter tears over the truth. She sometimes tried to overcome the tendency, and would take down the Bible, or the Plays, after the labors of the day ; but her head would soon droop upon the page, and the pine knots sink into ashes, as had her hopes.

Her father was dreading lest he should become known, and compelled to carry his secret into the presence of questioning curiosity. With almost terror at the thought, Vera began to ask herself,

" Am I always to live this life ? Am I to be left here till I become little better than the beasts and birds of prey that hide in these mountains ? Indeed, I envy them ; for they, at least, have companions of their own kind."

She was able to feel her isolation more keenly since she had been given a glimpse of the world, and, in her intimacy with Saville, had learned to know the sweets of congenial society and friendship.

Though so very young, she was becoming one of earth's weariest pilgrims, and at times she almost felt, when benumbed with cold, like lying down in some wild mountain-gorge, and letting the snow drift over her as she sank to sleep. If she had believed, with Saville, that it would have been a dreamless, eternal sleep, she would undoubtedly have yielded to the temptation.

Thus the winter dragged heavily on, till the sun turned from its decline southward, and began to fill the mountains with brighter and more genial rays. But she, who had always welcomed this change, scarcely heeded it. Perhaps the sharp suffering and seemingly untoward events soon to come, would be better than the slow, increasing pressure of the sordid cares and loneliness of her lot. Immediate and pressing dangers might break up the apathy of practical unbelief, wherein God becomes a being who must be prayed to and served, but ceases to be a helpful, sympathetic friend. Anything that would drive her to Him as a refuge would be a blessing ; anything that broke the leaden monotony of her life, a healthful change.

CHAPTER XVII.

"THE WHITE WITCH OF THE HIGHLANDS."

IN the latter part of February, the stores in their little cabin ran so low that it was necessary they should be replenished by a visit to some country store.   But her father, from long inaction and brooding, was in his worst mood, and it was in vain that Vera besought him to go on the errand.   At last, in her desperation, she decided one morning to go herself.   On ascending the hill behind the cabin, she saw that the river was covered with smooth ice.   She went down to the point of land which enabled her to look up the river, and through the cold, clear air, the villages of New Windsor and Newburgh seemed not far away.   Returning, she took a little of their hoarded money, and, without a word to her father, started on what was, to her, like the voyage of Columbus, a journey into the unknown.   Her only weapon of defense was a light, strong staff, pointed with iron, which would enable her to try the ice, and also assist in walking.   She kept close to the western shore, so that, like a timid hare, she might fly to cover, if she deemed it necessary.   Though she found the way longer than she supposed, and the effort to walk on the smooth ice against the wind very fatiguing, she reached in safety the shores of New Windsor, where she saw a building whose appearance led her to hope that she might there obtain what she wished. To her joy the surmise proved correct, and she was saved further weary steps.   She asked and obtained permission to sit down and rest awhile. Many and curious were the glances cast upon her by the loungers that always infest such places, especially in winter.

Some tried to engage her in conversation, but there was something in their tones and manner that, though she did not understand, she disliked, and, with an innate dignity and reserve, which is a true woman's sure protection unless men are equal to brute violence, she silenced them. She would have gladly hastened away, had she not felt that rest and the warmth of the place were essential for a time before starting on the homeward journey with her laden basket.

Among the men present, when she entered, was a knot of rough-looking soldiers, who had impressed her most disagreeably. They had stared at her a few moments, winked at each other, and then to her relief, departed.

As soon as she felt equal to the effort, she started homeward ; but the sun was already declining ; the sky also was becoming overcast, and the rising wind betokened a storm. By the time she reached Butter Hill, the snowflakes began to fly, and not a solitary form was seen on the dreary expanse of ice, where, in the morning, travelers had appeared in the distance.

Still, this did not trouble her, for she did not dread a storm as much as she feared meeting rude fellows coming or going from the garrisons below. Her only concern was lest the snow might make her progress dangerous, by covering the occasional air-holes that almost always occur in the ice among the Highlands.

But, imagine her dismay, when, on passing around the point of a mountain, she came upon a group of soldiers, apparently lying in wait. With sickening fear, she recognized in them the ill-favored fellows she had seen in the store at New Windsor.

She hesitated, and was about to turn back ; but they, with devilish cunning, seemed to give her no heed.

" I have naught to do with them, nor they with me," she thought ; "and no doubt they will let me pass without a word."

Indeed, they moved out toward the middle of the river, as if intending to pursue their way without regard to her. This gave Vera renewed hope, and the chance to keep near the shore as she desired.

When she reached a point where the mountain shelved perpendicularly down to the water, rendering its ascent impossible, they turned sharply on her, one shouting brutally,

" So ho ! ye're the white witch o' the mountains, are ye ? But the divil himself can't help ye now, 'les ye fly up the rocks."

Vera gave the precipice a despairing glance : even she could not scale it. There was no chance for aught save flight ; and, for a few moments, she made desperate efforts to escape, once or twice barely eluding a grimy, outstretched hand.

Notwithstanding her wonderfully quick movements, and the abrupt turns which she was able to make on the smooth ice by the aid of her staff, they were gradually hemming her in toward the bluff. A few yards to the south, and near the land, she saw a small air-hole with open water, and at once formed the desperate purpose to lead her pursuers so near it that they would fall in ; or else, if failing in that, to find, herself, a refuge in death beneath the ice. She ran to its perilous edge, and then, by means of her staff, turned short toward the shore. Her nearest pursuer was so intent on grasping his victim, that he did not see the danger in time and fell in.

This created a diversion in favor of Vera, and two of her pursuers stopped to help their comrades, but the remaining three were adjured, with oaths and curses, to "head her off up agin the mountain."

"May the divil fly away with me if I don't believe she is a witch," cried one of the ruffians.

Vera had now reached a place where there was a break in the precipice facing the river, the rock making a sharp angle, and receding from the water a few feet ; and then it made another angle and trended away toward the southwest, leaving an increasingly wide margin between the precipitous bluff and the river. Despairing of escape on the ice, Vera had the hope that by springing ashore she could make her way along this margin, and so up among the hills.

But the tide was out, and huge cakes of ice were piled among the rocks where she attempted to reach the land ; slipping on one of these, she fell, and was delayed, seemingly, a fatal moment. Two of the men sprang ashore south of her, thus cutting off escape along the base of the cliffs, while one stood on the ice behind her.

"We've got her now !" they cried, with horrid joy ; "she's just druv into a corner o' the rocks, and must go through 'em to get away."

"Two on ye keep her there, then, and t'other come and help us git Barney out. I'm afeerd he'll droon. The cussed ice breaks wid us, and he's gittin' could and numb-loike."

Vera gave a swift glance and a sobbing prayer to Heaven, and then turned toward the granite rocks that beetled above her head, to see if there was the faintest possibility of escape. With a thrill of hope, she saw crevices in the inner angle of the rock, and from one of these, far above her head, a bush was growing. Here was her only chance. Availing herself of the moment's respite given by her pursuers in their solicitude for their half-drowned companion, she planted her long staff among the loose stones, and, by its aid, steadied herself up the almost perpendicular rock, till she reached the bush. It bore her weight, and seemed like a helping hand. Fear lent her wings, and, by the aid of the shrubbery, she reached a point not quite so steep, where the angle in the precipice turned off toward the river somewhat, and she was able to climb with more security and hope.

All this had transpired in a moment of time, while the eyes of the ruffians had been turned toward the one of their number struggling in the water. Having pulled him, more dead than alive, out upon the ice, they made a rush for their victim, when, to their unbounded amazement, they saw her, far above their heads, ascending what seemed, from their point of view, the perpendicular face of the rock. For a moment they could only stare in their wonder. Then one of the men whipped out a pistol.

"Don't fire!" cried another, "for if the divil hain't carryin' her up, she'll fall; an' if he is, the ball'll come back and kill yerself."

Fortunately this sage advice was taken, and, a second later, Vera had followed the angle in the rocks to the summit of the precipice, and was at least fifty feet above their heads. From this point the ascent was easier and safer, although still very difficult and dangerous. As every moment she mounted higher, scaling places that appeared impassable, a superstitious dread crept over them, and they slunk off with muttered curses to the opposite shore of the river, leaving the basket where Vera had dropped it. The angels that had charge over her, lest she should dash her foot against a stone, were, to their besotted minds, evil spirits, though certainly less malignant than themselves.

As she saw them depart, she sat down on a shelf of rock, panting and exhausted. Night was near, the sky overcast, and the snow whirling through the air. The great mountain of "Cro' Nest" rose between her and the cabin, while, from the wide rugged valley that she must cross, came the roar of the wind in the forest. She thought not of these dangers, however, in her unbounded gratitude for what seemed an almost miraculous escape. There on the bleak mountain-side she knelt, and poured out her heart to God. In answer, there came to her a feeling of safety, a sense of being guarded, which she never had before. With a distinctness which made them seem as if spoken, the inspired words came into her mind, " Fear not thou, for I am with thee : Be not dismayed ; for I am thy God : I will strengthen thee ; yea, I will help thee ; yea, I will uphold thee with the right hand of my righteousness."

" Oh !" she cried, stretching out her arms toward heaven, " Oh that God would take me home to mother now ! Why must I descend into this dark and stormy valley ?"

Again the voice whispered in the depths of her soul, " The Lord is thy keeper : The Lord shall preserve thee from all evil : He shall preserve thy soul." " Let not your heart be troubled, neither let it be afraid."

With a feeling of resignation and trust, to which she had long been a stranger, she set out on her journey of several miles through a rugged and unbroken wilderness. Her intimate knowledge of the mountains enabled her to go toward her home, even in the gathering darkness, with as much directness as the almost impassable region permitted ; but it was night before she descended the hills that sloped toward the cabin. She began to think that her strength would fail, and that after all she might perish ; but, in her weariness and loneliness, the thought brought peace instead of fear. Mechanically she tottered on, scarcely conscious from exhaustion, until she reached the valley where stood her home. Summoning all her failing energies she tried to gain its door, but in vain. The utmost limit of endurance had been reached, but, as her last effort, before sinking on the ground in unconsciousness she cried,

" Father ! Gula !"

CHAPTER XVIII.

"THE BLACK WITCH OF THE HIGHLANDS."

VERA'S absence had not caused much anxiety to the inmates of the cabin. They were both so wrapped up in their own strange fancies that they could think of little else, and it was not unusual for her to return from hunting expeditions after nightfall. They were so preoccupied that neither of them noticed that the light fowling-piece was in its accustomed place.

Throughout the entire day, Gula imagined she had been hearing voices, and even the winter's cold did not prevent her from leaving the door of her little kitchen open, that they might be more distinct. While busy in preparing as good a supper for Vera as a very meagre larder permitted, she would often go to the door, and listen intently, not for the footsteps of the young girl, but for the strange echoes that, in her disordered mind, came from her tropical home.

And she was thus listening, when Vera's cry reached her. In great excitement she said,

" Dare, dare, dat a voice sure. P'raps I'se gwine home to-night. I'se a coming," and she hobbled down the glen as fast as her age permitted, till her feet struck against the poor girl's unconscious body. Stooping down, she felt of the unexpected obstacle, and then, in a shrill scream, called,

" Mas'r Brown, come quick ! Missy Vera 'pears like she's dead."

The father hastened to the spot, and between them they bore her into the cabin.

" Is she dead ?" asked the man in a husky whisper.

" Dunno ; allers been afeard she'd git home afore me. De strong stuff in dis bottle did her mudder good ; I'll put a little in her mouf," and Gula moistened Vera's lips with the remnant of the brandy, and was comforted by seeing the spasmodic effort to swallow.

" She was a' most home," soliloquized Gula ; " and it's orful cruel in me to bring her back ; but I couldn't let her go afore me."

" O God ! if there is a God ! save my child !" cried the father in agony. " What have I become, to leave her so exposed ?" and he bent over her in remorseful terror.

Slowly Vera revived to consciousness, and was at last able to give them a smile of recognition.

" Where have you been ? What has happened ?" asked her father eagerly.

She shuddered, shook her head, and said faintly, " Not now. I can't tell you now."

At Gula's urgent request, she took a little food and some more of the brandy, and then sank into a deep sleep, which lasted until the sun was shining into the casement. On awaking, she found her father watching her with the most intense anxiety. In the hope of arousing him from his morbid condition, she told him the truth, and the last remnants of the man and parent flashed up in his soul.

His face became ashen in its hue, and again he exclaimed in agony, " Great God ! what have I become ?"

Then he seized his rifle, and started for the scene of Vera's peril, with the half-crazed hope of finding her assailants still there. After a time he returned with Vera's basket, and commenced restlessly pacing the cabin floor, muttering deep curses on the caitiffs who were beyond the reach of his vengeance.

" Father," said Vera piteously, " won't you take care of

us ? won't you be your old self, as I remember you when
a little child ?   It may be long before I am able to go out
again, and I ought not to go at all."

" I will, my child, I will," he replied.   " Would to God
I had never been born !"

" O father ! be a brave man.   Do as Mr. Saville wished,
and all will yet be well."

" I will, my child ; I will remove you and Gula to a
place of safety, and then join the army."

" Act now, father, act at once."

" I will—soon."

For a few days he made desperate efforts to throw off the
incubus that was crushing body and mind, and supplied the
household with abundance of game.

After a few days of perfect rest, Vera's healthful frame
quite recovered from its terrible strain ; but there remained
in her eyes a troubled, frightened expression.   Her mind
was constantly dwelling on the strange epithet that the
ruffians had applied to her.   Why did they call her the
" white witch of the Highlands ?" and what did they mean
by this term ?   A vague sense of danger oppressed her, and
a fear lest their seclusion was causing people to imagine
evil concerning them.

This surmise was not long in being verified, for spring
had scarcely opened, before an officer with a squad of men
marched to their door one morning.

" I wish to see a man named Brown," was the prompt
request.

Nerving himself for an ordeal that was terrible, her father
came to the door, and said haughtily,

" I am he."

" I am directed, sir, to inform you that you are suspected
of disloyalty to the American cause, and of being in the
employ of the enemy.   As there are no definite charges

against you, and as Mr. Saville once spoke in your favor, you are not to be arrested on this occasion. But your presence is no longer desired in the vicinity of the forts, and it is requested that you leave this region before the campaign opens. If after two weeks you are here and can give no satisfactory account of yourself, you will be arrested and put in confinement."

The terrified man could scarcely retain sufficient composure to bow in silent acquiescence ; but, as the officer was turning away, Vera exclaimed,

" Indeed, sir, we are loyal. You do my father injustice."

" Let him be prompt in proving it then," was the stern response ; then came the word of command, " Right about face ; march," and they were gone.

Vera thought that she recognized among the soldiers the malignant face of the wretch who had narrowly escaped drowning in his reckless pursuit of her upon the ice. She was right. At first, the ruffians had kept quiet, fearing lest Vera should report their conduct, and they be severely dealt with. But the man in question vowed vengeance, and was so besotted in his egotism and depravity as to feel that he had good cause to punish one who, in escaping his brutality, had involved him in great peril.

He was one of Captain Molly's satellites, and she had soon beguiled from him the story, but embellished and changed somewhat to suit their interests. The worst of villains do not like to portray themselves in their true colors.

" She is a witch, indade," concluded the irate ruffian ; " for nary a one that the divil didn't help could have walked right up straight rocks. But, by the holy poker, I'll pay her off for that drooning she guv me."

The story of Vera's scaling the precipice spread rapidly among the ignorant and superstitious members of the garrison, over whom Molly ruled, and became positive proof that the innocent maiden, as well as old Gula, was in close league with the Evil One.

"Let us go over and roast them out some day," was a proposal often made, and once or twice in danger of being carried out ; for the discipline of the fort was not severe, and the men were often permitted to be absent.

But Molly was shrewd enough to counsel prudence. Larry had cautioned her that Saville was the "very divil himself" when angry ; and she remembered his threat. Though she had not seen or heard anything of him for a long time, he might return. Besides, Molly, although capable of any amount of wicked gossip, had too much humanity to face its consequences. She liked to scatter firebrands and arrows recklessly, but did not enjoy seeing the wounds and suffering ; and there was woman enough in her nature to shrink from the deeds of cruelty and violence which she foresaw would occur, did the vindictive Barney lead a band of kindred spirits against the cabin. So she tried to satisfy his revenge by inducing him to throw out hints that "Brown was a Tory, a-watchin' the garrisons." This story the officers took up promptly, and Barney was asked for definite proof. But Molly had told him not to say anything with certainty, but to abound in suspicions ; so the authorities concluded that, as there had been considerable doubt about the man, they would compel him either to join the service, or to remove from a region where, if he were so inclined, he could be very useful to the enemy. Thus, the evil consequences, which even the dead wife had foreseen, occurred, and worse dangers threatened.

As the officer departed with his squad, Vera turned to her father with the purpose of entreating him to follow at once, and enlist in the army. But, after one glance, all hope died. It almost appeared as if he were shrinking and shriveling away. He tottered back to his dusky corner, as seemingly scarce able to walk. In a trembling whisper, he said,

" Vera, we must fly at once."

" Fly where ?" she answered desperately. " Are we birds, that we can take wing in a moment, and live without shelter ? O God ! is Thy mercy clean gone forever ?"

" There isn't any God," said her father with sudden and vindictive passion ; " there is only a devil. Witness my wife's grave yonder ; witness your unmerited suffering ; and, chief of all, witness myself. I dare not live—I dare not die. I have but one vile impulse, and that is to hide ; and hide I will, where no human eye shall see me again. I know of a wild gorge in these mountains that I believe untrodden by any foot save mine. Before your mother died, I built a hut there for a refuge, if the worst came to the worst. Last fall I repaired it, and made it stronger. No one knows of its existence, for this is the first that I have spoken of it. Come, we will go at once."

Vera sank into a chair, and sobbed as if her heart would break. As he saw her grief, he relented somewhat, and said,

" Well, we will not go till to-morrow. They gave us a little time."

" If we are to go, let us go at once," said Vera despairingly. " But is there no way out of this darkness, no escape from this terrible isolation which is destroying us all ? I fear I shall go mad myself."

" No," said her father, with the gloom of the most hopeless fatalism in his tone and manner ; " there is no escape, and there is darkness all the way on forever more. You are in the grip of the same awful destiny as myself. I am mad, and the worst of it is, I know that I am. I can see my mad self, and can see my former and nobler self when I was sane, and all day and all night I sit and compare the two.

I expect you will become like me, for I have been a curse to myself and all bound to me. But I will go where I can never see another soul, and the curse will die out with us.''

'' But, father, have you no pity for me ?''

'' Pity ! ᵀ pity you from the bottom of my heart. Don't I know that we are both in hell ? I shall pity you forever, but what good will that do ?''

'' Oh, hush !'' said Vera, shuddering. '' Say no more.''

Until late that night, she prayed and questioned God as to her duty. Would it not be better to go to the commander of the garrison, and, throwing herself on his mercy, declare that her father was no longer responsible for his actions ? And yet each time she had sought to make her way alone out into the world, she had been met by experiences that caused her womanly nature to shrink with inexpressible fear.

'' Is there only one true, kind man in the world ?'' she groaned in bitterness.

At last, she concluded that her father, in his present mood, would not remain near the dwellings of others ; and that, if she tried to compel him to do so, he would wander off by himself, and perish in the forest. She also saw the difficulty of accounting for his condition of mind, for, as he said, he was both sane and insane. It would become evident to all that his gloom, fear, and remorse had their dark source in guilt of some kind. He would not explain ; she could not ; and thus mystery and her twin sister, suspicion, would ever follow them with pointing fingers, till even she might be glad to hide in the depths of the mountains.

She recalled her mother's words in regard to her father : '' You will have to be his guardian and protector more truly than he yours. Be very tender and patient with him for my sake.''

'' I will go with him to his mountain-gorge,'' concluded

she, "although it is the same as being buried alive. Mr. Saville will never find me there, and I have now, in sad truth, lost my only friend."

Again a comforting and reassuring voice spoke in the depths of her soul, "Commit thy way unto the Lord ; trust also in Him, and He shall bring it to pass."

There sprang up a sudden hopefulness within her heart, that God, in His own time and way, would break down the barriers that rose between them and their own kind, and that He would guide Saville to their hidden retreat. An impression, which soon became a conviction, that it would be best and safest to leave all to Him, brought rest to her mind, and she slept until her father summoned her in the morning.

After an early meal, they made up two packages, containing tools, bedding, some food, and cooking utensils, and taking their guns, started for the secluded hut, which, after all, was not so distant as it was inaccessible, and apart from all the mountain roads and paths. It was their plan to spend two or three days in repairing and putting it in the best condition possible, before removing thither old Gula and the household furniture.

But, in their absence, the elements of evil were at work, and poor, pagan Gula had another experience with Christians, upon whose profane lips was continually the name of the God whom she had learned to associate with deeds of fiendish cruelty.

The ruffian, Barney, had accompanied the officer, and heard the order which would soon make the little cabin tenantless. But this did not satisfy his malignant spirit ; and so, one afternoon, when heated with liquor, he proposed to a few kindred villains that they should go and hurry the departure of the witches. By reason of their superstitious fears, the others were rather reluctant ; but he stimulated them up to the reckless point by fiery potations from a stolen bottle of rum. They doubted Captain Molly's acquiescence in their action, and so did not inform her ; but, on one pretext or another, obtained a brief leave of absence from their officers.

It was quite late in the afternoon when they reached the vicinity of the cabin. They approached warily, for Brown had the reputation of being savage and dangerous. At last they made a rush for the two doors, having already had experience of Vera's quickness in flight. But, to their surprise, not a soul was to be seen. They looked cautiously in every place where one could be concealed in the main room and kitchen, with their weapons ready, but there was no trace of their victims. Then Barney and two others of the most reckless of the gang went up the covered way to Vera's little room ; and beastly satyrs of Grecian myth, in the grotto of a nymph, could not have appeared more hide ous and devilish than these caitiffs in that refuge of maidenly purity and beauty. Again, in after days, with a gratitude beyond words, Vera thanked God that she was absent. Her filial loyalty to her father had brought unspeakable reward.

The ruffians were now convinced that the occupants of the cabin had fled, and with sacrilegious hands they destroyed, pillaged, and defaced, till their attention was diverted by a loud shout from one of their number who had ascended the ladder to peer into the little loft. Here he caught a glimpse of Gula, cowering in the remotest corner, and was now, in brutal glee, dragging her down to his companions, who with oaths and imprecations gathered around.

The aged negress, speechless and paralyzed with terror, was as limp and unresisting in their hands as if dead ; turning, as the only evidence of life, her wild, horror-dilated eyes from one to another of her persecutors, who were to her so many torturing fiends.

"Where is the other she-divil? where is the white witch o' the Highlands?" demanded Barney. "Speak, or we'll make ye swallow coals o' fire."

But Gula's unearthly stare was his only answer.

"Tie her to the tree there, or the divil may carry her off in spite o' us;" and they hustled the poor creature out, and did his bidding, Gula making no resistance, and uttering not a sound.

"Now take what ye want, and thin set fire to that divil's nest o' witches," continued Barney, who, by common consent, was leader in the outrage.

Gula's eyes dilated with increasing terror, as she saw the cabin speedily wrapped in flames. Then the demons gathered round her, and Barney commenced,

"Now, ye ould black hag o' Satan, tell me where the white witch is a-hidin', or I'll roast the flesh off yer bones."

But Gula only turned upon him her horror-stricken stare.

He seized a firebrand, and held it scorchingly near her hand. She writhed, but would not speak.

"Here, boys, git some dhry sticks, and put 'em around her feet. Ye'll see how blue she'll burn."

"Hold on, Barney," said the others; "don't let us go too far. Her looks'll haunt us all our days now."

With loud curses on their cowardice, the drunken wretch began to carry out his fiendish cruelty himself.

Gula at last seemed to realize that she might be near to death, which to her meant return to kindred and rude regality in her far-away home, and she suddenly broke the silence, thus far maintained, by a weird, shrill cry of ecstasy,

"De voices, de voices! I'se hear you plain. I'se a-comin' now, sure."

The ruffians started back aghast.

"What voices?" demanded Barney.

A piercing shriek from the hill west of them was the answer. Then the report of a rifle rang out, and Barney fell dead at his victim's feet, with a bullet through his cruel heart.

His companions turned in precipitate flight, but another yelled with pain as the contents of Vera's gun reached them.

Marking the course of their flight with blood, they reached their boat half dead from fright and bruises, and, crossing to the garrison, told a terrible story of Tory outrage. A strong party was sent over immediately to arrest Brown and the '' Tory horde'' that was declared to be with him ; but nothing was found save the smoking embers of the cabin, and the dead body of the ruffian Barney, which was brought over to the island and buried.

From what he saw, however, the officer in charge of the expedition suspected that there might be two sides to the story, as Barney and his companions were known to belong to that human scum which always exists in every army. Beyond some effort made to discover whether Brown still frequented his old haunts, nothing further was done, and the affair was soon forgotten in the excitement of the opening campaign.

CHAPTER XIX.

A DIRGE ENDING JOYOUSLY.

OUR story now passes over an interval of several months. The autumn winds of early September were again prophesying of winter among the Highlands ; but only in plaintive suggestion, for summer yet lingered in their mild breath.

As the sun was sinking low in the west, on a certain afternoon, a form, that could scarcely be recognized as that of Vera, were it not for the old wealth of golden hair—but uncovered now by the jaunty plumage of the snowy heron —might have been seen stealing through the defiles of the hills toward the river. A painful timidity characterized her movements, and she seemed to fear her own shadow. There were traces of suffering and almost famine on her sunburnt face, and in her deep blue eyes an expression akin to that of some helpless animal that had been hunted almost to the death. Her dress was in tatters, and would not much longer conceal her thin form. Instead of shoes, rudely constructed sandals of buckskin protected her feet. Her frame appeared shrunken and somewhat feeble, and yet, as if impelled by a powerful motive, she made her way rapidly, although furtively, along a path which no one save herself could follow.

As she reached the vicinity of her old home, her approach became more cautious and stealthy. She flitted, like some timid creature of the forest, from cover to cover, till she could look out unperceived on the little glen made dear by so many memories.

The first object that her eyes dwelt on was the grave of her mother, and she seemed to dread lest, among the sad changes occurring, it might also have disappeared. But the mound was untrampled, and the flowers she had planted near were still growing. As the glen seemed as lonely as her own life, she ventured from the thicket to the shade of the elm, where rose the grassy mound. A visit to this grave had become the poor child's best earthly solace, and the nearest approach to comforting companionship within her reach. There was no one in her dreary home to whom she could speak of the sorrows that were crushing out hope and life ; but here she could imagine, at least, that her mother listened to her as in the past.

Becoming satisfied that she was alone in the sacred place, her furtive, apprehensive manner passed away, and she gave herself wholly to the tender memories naturally inspired. Leaning her head on the grave, as she had upon her mother's bosom when a child, she spoke of past scenes in tones that would have touched the most callous. Her sentences were fragmentary, mere indices of passing thoughts. From them it would seem that her hope of meeting Saville again had almost perished, but that her recollection of his kindness was of such a character as to be in harmony with the sacred memories of her mother.

At last, with a weary sigh, she saw, from the deepening shadows in the glen, that night must be near. She clasped the cold earth of the mound in close embrace. She was indeed orphaned and alone, when the pressure of her heart against a grass-grown grave could give more comfort than aught else.

When about to rise, she heard footsteps, and she hastily stole into the thicket from which she had first issued, and which would cover her flight back to the hills. But, though almost fainting with alarm—such had become her weakness of mind and body—a faint hope stayed her fleet steps till she could obtain one glimpse of the intruder.

There was something in the distant outline of the tall form that was strangely familiar. But, as the stranger's rapid advance revealed his face, she sank upon the ground overwhelmed with her feelings. It was, indeed, the friend and brother whom she had mourned as lost, and he was apparently as unchanged as on the day she last saw him. Was his presence actual, or was it merely a vision of her overwrought and morbid mind? She scarcely dared to move or breathe, and feared lest the wild throbbing of her heart would break the illusion.

And yet he was so real, he could not be a phantom ; his step was not ghost-like, but struck the ground firmly.

Now she saw the expression of his face—the perplexity—the alarm, the trouble, and distress depicted there—as the desolation of the glen became apparent. He went to the stone step that had led to the threshold of the cabin, and peered into the charred ruins, as if he dreaded discovering there traces of its inmates. He next ascended hurriedly to the place where Vera's grotto-like apartment had been, but the scrutiny of the ashes gave no confirmation of the fear that apparently had risen in his mind.

He took off his hat, and passed his hand across his brow and eyes, as if all were to him a vision which he would gladly dispel. He looked up and down the glen till his eye rested on the elm under which was the grave, and he approached it rapidly, as if hoping to find there something that would lead to the discovery of those he sought.

" She must be living," he said aloud, " for here are the proofs of her care and taste. Indeed, from the marks upon the grass, I should think that some one had been here to-day."

Again he looked up and down the glen, in the hope of

:seeing something or some one that could explain the mystery. The poor girl, who was but a few feet away, seemed under a strange paralysis. She tried to speak, but, as if dreaming in very truth, though her lips moved, there was no sound.

But, as Saville sat down upon a rock, and, taking out his flute, commenced playing the same dirge which once before had summoned her to him and kept her heart from breaking, the stony spell that bound her was broken. Tears rushed to her eyes.

"' I know a bank,' " she faltered ; then, springing from her concealment, she knelt at his feet, as one might do who sought deliverance from some pressing danger.

"Vera !" he exclaimed, raising her up. "My friend, my little sister ! what has happened ? What has changed you so ?"

But, for some moments, her tears and sobs were his only answer. He gently seated her on a rock beside him, and held her hand, while stroking her head in gentle caresses, accompanied by equally tender and soothing words.

"My poor little sister, it is plain that much has happened, and that you have suffered deeply, since I saw you last."

"But thank God, thank God ! you are not dead—you have not forgotten me," she was able at last to say brokenly.

"You may indeed take all the comfort you can out of these facts," he replied cheeringly. "I never had a better prospect of living, and there was never less danger of my forgetting you. So cease your trembling, little one, and dry your tears. I am again stationed at Fort Montgomery, and can see you often, as in old times. Now tell me what has happened—no, first tell me where you live, for it is almost night, and we can talk on our way thither."

"Oh !" exclaimed Vera, "in the joy of seeing you, I have forgotten all else. The wretched little hut, which I cannot call home, is miles away. You can't go with me there. The path is too rough and tangled for aught save a mere creature of the forest, as I have become."

Then, for the first time conscious of her tattered and forlorn dress, and her bare and brier-torn ankles, she turned away with a burning blush, and said, in a low tone,

" I am glad night is near, that its darkness may cover me. I wonder at your kindness, for I looked into a mirroring pool on my way hither, and saw my poor, miserable self as you now see me. What must I seem to you, who have seen the best of the world ?"

" Vera," said Saville gravely, " did not your mother, when living, hope that I might become your friend ?"

" Yes," said Vera, with fast-falling tears.

" That hope has been fulfilled ; but, were I only a casual stranger, what else could I feel for you, in this place, and by this grave, but the deepest sympathy ? You may trust me then without fear or embarrassment, because of your ragged dress and bruised feet, which are to me the touching proofs of your misfortunes. There are no stronger claims than those of humanity, and unconsciously you assert these in a way to make them most sacred. I feel that you are committed to my charge, and that nature and all-controlling destiny constitute me your brother and guardian. So, rest assured, you shall lean upon my arm all the way to your mountain hiding-place, which, I fear, is little better than the nests of the birds, which are open to the sky."

" But the way is longer than you think."

" Will it seem shorter to you without me ? All the more reason for my going. Come, little sister ; I have a will of my own," and he drew her hand within his arm.

" I can take the more open paths, now that you are with me," she said, with sudden gladness in her tone.

" Yes, any you like. I will take care of you."

With a sigh of intense relief, she exclaimed, " Oh ! what a comfort it is not to be oppressed with fear every moment. Constant dread was becoming a habit of my mind, as it is with father. There are such cruel and terrible men in the world ; and we are so helpless, and are the objects of so much suspicion, that concealment and flight have become our only safety ;" and, with the simplicity of a child, she told him of her own and Gula's experience, and the burning of the cabin.

" When we saw the smoke," she said, " we thought it had caught fire by accident, and we ran, in the hope of saving something. But Gula's cry, and the horrible men's rough voices, soon led us to fear the worst. I was afraid, at first, that father would leave old Gula to her fate, for often he is so strangely timid. But, for a few moments, he seemed like an enraged lion. He shot the leading villain, and then, snatching my gun, fired again. Only their rapid flight kept him from attacking them single-handed. He seemed to think they were the same ruffians that tried to catch me ; and, from what old Gula said afterward, I am sure they were. Ever since, I have lived in a state of terror lest they should spring out upon me."

Her tragic story was often interrupted by Saville's exclamations of pity and anger ; and when she described her peril upon the ice, and in climbing the precipice, she felt his arm tremble beneath her hand.

" You shall be amply revenged," he said in a deep tone, as she concluded.

" Oh, no," she cried pleadingly ; " any effort to avenge me would only add to my pain and fear. Please make these dreadful men understand that father is loyal, and that Gula and I are not witches. How came they ever to imagine such a thing about two such inoffensive creatures ?"

" That's the cursed quality of superstition," he muttered.

"The less reason and cause, the more monstrous and bigoted the belief."

"You can never know all I have suffered of late," she said, finding much comfort in his strongly manifested sympathy. "We often do not have enough to eat, and I was beginning to hope I should die before winter came. Father is more gloomy and taciturn than ever, and I often find him looking at me with a strange pity and almost horror in his eyes, as if he were murdering me and could not help it. His looks haunt me. Old Gula, too, is growing more strange, and mumbles unceasingly of her unearthly voices. Still I could endure all this, were it not for my constant and unspeakable fear lest those wicked men find our hiding-place, or spring out at me when I am away alone among the mountains. When I heard your step this evening, I came near flying, without looking back (God saved me from that at least). I even wake out of my sleep, and imagine I hear them coming with their dreadful oaths. Are you sure you can keep them away?"

"Yes, Vera, sure. Poor child! I did not dream it possible that misfortune and wrong could so single you out."

"What you say," she continued, in an awed, frightened tone, "leads me to speak of the worst trouble of all. Mother's Bible was burned in the cabin, as was nearly everything else. I have tried to remember its teachings, but of late they seemed slipping from my mind. Indeed, I appeared sometimes to be forgetting everything. I felt as if I were dwindling to nothing in body and mind, and a great fear has at times chilled my heart lest death should be just becoming nothing. When we first came to our hiding-place, I felt that it was very doubtful whether I should ever see you or any one else again, and I gave up almost all hope of happiness in this life. But, while the world was so dark, the door of heaven seemed wide open, and mother standing in its light, waiting for me. For a long time this beautiful vision was ever before me, and I felt like a traveler who is going toward his home-light. But at last the open door, with its streaming rays, began to recede, and mother's form to grow dim ; and now they have gone so far away that they seem like that faint star just above yonder mountain. What does it mean ? Has God forgotten me ? Is He in truth taking mother far away into heaven, and am I becoming so much like the poor, timid little creatures of the woods, that I shall at last die like them, and become nothing ? I wish you could explain it all to me.''

" I can, my poor little friend, very readily. When one has been long under the influence of trouble and solitude, and especially when there has been a lack of nutritious food, the mind becomes morbid, and full of unnatural fancies, just as the night is full of strange, monstrous shadows, which all disappear when the sun rises. The sun has risen for you, and all these strange shadows upon your mind will soon pass away.''

" But are you sure that God never forgets any of His children, though they are weak and insignificant ? It is this fear that troubles me most.''

" Well, Vera, to tell you a truth, which you would have suspected long ago, if you had not been so innocent, I do not know much about God. I think you had better try to overcome all these morbid fancies, of which you have spoken, in a new and hopeful interest in your present life. I promise that I shall never forget you, and will try to make it certain that you shall never be so exposed to misfortune again.''

At first, Vera gave him a troubled, startled look, and was silent for some moments. Then he felt her hand tightening in its grasp upon his arm, as if the thought were in her mind, " If God is failing me, I must cling the closer to this friend, who is so near and sympathetic.''

To divert her mind, he told her of his experiences during his long absence, and how he had written to her, and had hoped that she knew about his life elsewhere, while he remained ignorant of hers. He explained how very uncertain letters were to arrive, even along the regular lines of travel. And yet his heart reproached him that he had, in some degree, forgotten her in his manifold duties and excitements, and that he had not made greater effort to learn of her welfare, and provide for her safety.

They at last reached a point where they must leave the comparatively open path for one that was narrow, precipitous, and often, to his eye, entirely blocked by rocks and tangled undergrowth. But she picked out a way for him, where, in the darkness, none appeared. Toward the last, however, her movements became slow and feeble.

" Let us rest awhile," he said ; " you are becoming too wearied to stand, almost."

" I am sorry to say, it is more than weariness, Mr. Saville. I have scarcely tasted food to day ; and the worst of it is, I fear that we shall have little, if anything, to offer you in the way of supper. I cannot tell you how it troubles me."

" And are you forgetting your own pangs of hunger and consequent weakness, in the fear that you may not have a supper for one who dined heartily a few hours ago ?" he asked, taking her hand.

" But I am accustomed to being hungry, and you are not."

" My poor little friend, I can scarcely realize it all. If you could spread a banquet before me, my heart would be too full to permit me to think of eating to-night." And the thought passed through his mind, " Can this maiden and my bigoted, selfish wife belong to the same world and race ?"

He was naturally generous and sympathetic, and his heart

overflowed with pity and tenderness for the lonely girl, whose thoughts had constantly followed him, while he had partially forgotten her.

He now insisted on her pointing out the way ; and going before, he lifted her down the rocks and steep places.

" It is so strange to be petted and taken care of," she said, with a low laugh, " that it must be all a dream."

" Thanks for that laugh," he cried ; " it is the first I have heard from you, but I shall be much mistaken if it is the last. If I can carry out my will, this is your last dark, miserable day."

" This day is no longer dark and miserable," she said promptly.

" How is that ?" he asked. " It is night, and you are both hnngry and weary."

" But comforted and happy," she added. " The only ache that I cannot endure is the heart-ache, and your coming has cured that."

Having at last descended into the wild, secluded valley, they were not long in reaching what Vera had called with truth " a wretched little hut."

CHAPTER XX.

GULA HEARS A VERITABLE VOICE.

WHEN Vera told Saville that they were near the little cabin, he asked why no light appeared.

" We live literally in darkness much of the time," she replied ; " for father will not permit a light, lest its rays reveal our hiding-place ; and I have been so timid, also, that I was well content to submit. Please wait here, and I will prepare father for the meeting."

" Is it possible," he thought, scanning the place by the light of the rising moon, " that this poor little hovel has been her only shelter for long months ? Even our soldiers' huts are better than this."

Vera noiselessly raised the latch, saying, at the same time, in a quiet tone, " It is I, father."

" I am very glad you have returned, for I was beginning to surmise horrible things. What has kept you ?"

" I met an old friend."

" Met an old friend ! Who ?"

" Your friend as truly as mine. Can you not think who he is ?"

" Has Mr. Saville returned, and is he indeed friendly ?" he asked eagerly.

" He is more friendly than ever ; he shall speak for himself. Mr. Saville !"

" O Vera ! you have not brought him to this, our only refuge ?" cried her father in great agitation. " I fear evil will come of it."

"No, Mr. Brown," said Saville, cordially taking his hand; "good and only good shall come of it. I am here as a friend to you both. Besides, I bring you cheering tidings, sir. We are making good our Declaration of Independence, which you heard over a year ago, and have now excellent prospects of final victory."

The fear-haunted man drew a long breath, and then said, "The deed has now been done, and, since you are here, we will treat you with the best courtesy we can; but I had hoped no living soul would ever discover this retreat."

"God has in mercy willed it otherwise, father."

"God forsooth!" he responded bitterly. "If I could hide forever from Him, I might hope for a little respite."

"We have not a chair to offer you," he continued, turning to Saville. "Will you accept of this rude bench?"

"I shall be most content in faring as you do," answered Saville, in the frank, cordial manner which always gives confidence. "And now, I pray you, sir, sit down with me, while I tell you of the progress of the war. Vera has related enough of your experience to fill me with the deepest sympathy for your misfortunes. At the same time, I clearly foresee brighter days in store for you both."

Before the exile was aware, Saville held him completely absorbed by his graphic descriptions of the battles that had occurred during his long absence. Vera, in the mean time, disappeared, and nothing was seen of old Gula.

At last the door of the hut was opened from without, and Vera called, "Come, Mr. Saville, to my banquet."

"Banquet!" he said, laughing. "If you and Gula have prepared a banquet to-night, I shall be ready, also, to believe you are witches, or good fairies, rather."

"Oh, I am so glad!" she exclaimed. "Everything has turned out better than I expected. Father, come with us."

To her surprise and joy, he who had seemed hopelessly

beyond even the desire of seeing or speaking to a fellow creature again, rose hesitatingly, and followed them.

Taking Saville's hand, with the freedom of a child, she led him to a grassy plot behind the cabin, where, in the moonlight, stood a rude table.

"I much feared," she said, "that we should have nothing to offer you to-night. As I told you once before, we are fed as the ravens are. I do not know whether they ever go supperless to bed, but we do sometimes. To-night, however, in honor of your coming, two young partridges considerately put their heads into my snares, and there they are awaiting you."

"Have you been out in the forest after them since your return?" asked Saville, still retaining her hand.

"Yes, but it wasn't very far."

"And have you not had anything to eat yet?"

"I eat before my guest?"

"Yes, or your guest will be most pained and unhappy. See, your hand trembles from weakness; your pulse is rapid, yet feeble, while mine is strong and even from generous living. Can you think that I, who dined heartily but a few hours since, would take the smallest part of those dainty morsels which you need to keep soul and body together? Do you and your father sit down upon this mossy rock, while I carve the birds, and help you," and he almost compelled them to do his bidding. Then lifting the light table, he placed it before them so that they could not well rise.

"Now you are my prisoners," he continued; "and only on the condition of your making a good supper, shall I permit you to escape."

"Hungry as I am, I cannot eat, unless you share the birds with us," persisted Vera, leaving the choice bits before her untasted.

"Was there ever such a queer little sister? If any pain were to be borne, you would want it all, I warrant you. Well, I'll take a wing."

"No, that may portend your sudden absence again."

"Where is Gula?" he asked abruptly.

"I'se here," said the old negress, stepping from the deep shadow of a rock.

"And right glad I am that you are still here," said Saville cordially. "I have heard how badly you were treated, but I am going to take care of you all now."

"Mas'r Brown fired little too quick, or I'd been home now. I would like to git home afore de cold winter come. Tink I will, for de voices is callin' po'ful strong lately."

"But our voices will call on you more strongly to stay with us; besides, I am going to bring a lively young colored boy to help you, when I come again. Vera," he said in a low tone, turning to the young girl, "be so kind as to let me give my portion to this poor old creature. When I come again, I will, in truth, be your submissive guest."

"Well," said Vera laughing, "I do not know much about the world; but I imagine that men always have their own way in it."

"You have indeed forgotten your Shakspeare if you think that. But I am much interested in your gypsy life. Where were these birds cooked so nicely?"

"We has a stone fireplace in de side ob de hill," said Gula, with a courtesy.

"Father has arranged it so that the smoke is carried off among the rocks, and in such a way that it cannot be seen by any one on the hills around us," added Vera; "and the cabin, you perceive, is quite hidden by evergreens."

It was, indeed, even from them, who were but a few feet away.

"A l this may answer in summer, but not in winter," said the young man decidedly.

"I doubt whether we could have survived the winter," Vera replied in a low tone.

"How quietly you speak those darkly suggestive words!"

"It was my best hope, till you came."

"Thank fortune, my coming was not delayed."

"I thank God," added Vera reverently.

"Don't mention that name," said her father irritably. "I have always heard it oftenest when my troubles thickened." Then to Saville, "You spoke of bringing your colored servant. I fear it will not be safe, sir."

"I will give you my personal pledge that it is ; and when you come to know the boy, you will fear no harm from him. So I trust you will leave all to me, for I can provide for your safety more surely than you can yourself."

Mr. Brown acquiesced so far as to be silent.

Saville had seen much of the world, but the picture made by that wild mountain-gorge and the little group before him left an ineffaceable impression upon his memory. Rugged, rocky steeps rose on either side, one shimmering in the moonlight, and the other lying in the deepest shadow. Glades and vistas opened here and there, with strange effect, among the giant trees of the valley. The closely ranked cedars and hemlocks concealed every vestige of the little log hut, and the inmates, as they then appeared, were so unlike ordinary people, that he felt that they and the whole scene were more like a creation of the fancy than a part of the real world. But to him, who was weary of the platitudes and hollowness of conventional life, the picture had an unspeakable attraction.

Old Gula stood a little back from her master and mistress, leaning her tall, gaunt form, that was feeble from age and lack of food, against one of the granite boulders that were scattered thickly at the base of the mountain. Her wrinkled features formed as elfish and unearthly a visage as could well be imagined.

The unbroken rays of the moon, as they shone full on Vera's father, only made more evident what a wreck he had become. His face was haggard, his hair unkempt, and his grizzled beard had grown to enormous proportions. At times, when Saville was speaking to him, he had almost the bearing of a finished gentleman ; a little later, he wore the look of a frightened animal, furtively devouring its food.

Although Saville, with almost the appreciation of an artist, marked the other features and accessories of the picture, his eyes constantly reverted to Vera with increasing interest. Having finished the repast, which, after all, was very meagre, she leaned her head upon her hand, and listened with such a wistful, intent expression in her face, that it was difficult for him to dwell merely on the details of a past campaign. He wished to comfort and reassure her.

He now had opportunity to note the changes that had taken place in her appearance, and saw, with boding anxiety, how frail and thin she was. Her sun-browned face was very pale in the moonlight, and more suggestive of spirit than of flesh and blood. To his kindled fancy, her wealth of unconfined hair grew into a halo, and the pure, beautiful face beneath resembled portraits of saints that he had seen in picture galleries abroad, and he thought,

" If the world would only worship such saints—lovely, unselfish, and living women—there would be more hope for humanity."

But the night was passing, and he rose to depart.

" You will not think of returning before the break of day ?" remonstrated Vera.

" Yes ; I have lingered too long already ; I must be at my post in the morning, and I have much to do during the day. I shall return to-morrow evening about the same hour I came to-night. And now, sir, I shall ask your kindness to guide me back to the open path.''

'' I can lead you by a much nearer way to Fort Montgomery,'' said Mr. Brown, rising promptly ; '' and to-night I feel like taking the walk.''

'' I will not say good by,'' said Vera, in parting, '' lest it be followed by another long and dreary absence.''

Her father guided their guest for several miles, and left him only when the path became so plain as to be easily followed. Saville was greatly pleased that his visit had so aroused the unhappy man, and, during their walk, continued to do his best to kindle in his mind a healthful interest in the outer world. He even obtained from him a promise that he would come with Vera, at sunset the following evening, to the place where they parted.

During the remainder of his walk to the fort, Saville's mind was very active in trying to solve the problems presented by the peculiar character and situation of the family. It was clearly his first duty to supply them with food and clothing. He also resolved, at the earliest opportunity, to assure the military authorities of Mr. Brown's loyalty to the American cause, and thus preserve the family from further molestation, because suspected of being Tories. He also determined that if Larry and his wife, Molly, had aught to do with the outrages that had been committed against the family, he would make them suffer to the extent of his ability. Vera, fearing that it might lead to a bloody quarrel, had not told him of the insult received at Fort Constitution, when she crossed thither to learn what had become of him.

Early the following morning, he sought an interview with James Clinton, who now commanded the forts, and who, several months previous, had been promoted to the rank of

General.   Saville, also, on the ground of merit, had recently been commissioned captain in the engineer department.

It was impossible for the young man to be a cool advocate, or to be satisfied with halfway measures, and he soon quite enlisted General Clinton's sympathies in behalf of his *proteges.*   His request for a brief leave of absence was readily granted, and full protection for the family promised.

His next step was to secure a boat in which to visit Peek-skill, that he might obtain the articles of apparel and comfort which both Vera and her father greatly needed ; and therefore he summoned the colored servant whom he had lately taken into his employ, and who thus far had proved a bundle of contradictions, a human riddle, that his master had been unable to solve.

He was a genuine African in features and manner, and of that uncertain age which made it doubtful whether he was man or boy.   He had presented himself at Saville's tent on the morning after his arrival, asking for service.

" Where do you come from ?" Saville asked.

" From nowhar in 'ticklar," was the indefinite response.

" What is your name ?"

" Mas'r kin call me what he likes."

" Haven't you any name ?"

" I'se had a sight o' names ; jes' as liv hab annoder.   I'll answer quicker'n lightnin' to any name you gub me, if you'se ony take me."

" Well, who are you, any way ?"

" I doesn't jes' know."

" What are you doing in this region ?"

" I'se a-lookin' for somebody."

" And somebody is looking for you, I imagine.   You have run away.   Where is your master ?"

" Dar he is, I'se a-hopin'," said this most indefinite of human atoms, at the same time ducking his head toward

Saville. " Jes' guv me a chance, and you'se 'll see I knows a heap more 'bout some oder tings dan I does 'bout my-self."

" Very well," said Saville carelessly. " I will keep you till you are claimed, or till I find you will not answer my purpose."

At this, the boy had ducked again, and pulled a little horn of wool that he had seemingly coaxed over his fore-head for polite or politic uses.

" Now, if mas'r 'll jes' guv me a handle, I'se 'll begin to be use'l right straight."

" ' A handle ! ' "

" Yeh, sumpen to call and send me by."

" Oh ! a name. Any one of your old ones will answer. "

" If mas'r please, I'd rudder he guv me a new un."

" Bless me ! I don't know what to call you, unless I take the mathematician's terms for an unknown quantity, and name you X Y Z."

" Dat'll suit kerzackly," was the delighted response. " ' Ekswyze.' I neber had as big a name as dat afore."

" But I shall call you X for short," said Saville, laugh-ing. " Now let me see what you can do."

The boy, even in a few hours, proved his ability to serve well, if he so chose, and now was on hand, ready to do his master's bidding with alacrity.

" Find me a small sail-boat, that can be rowed if the wind is contrary, and be ready to go with me to Peekskill in half an hour.'

Within less time, the boy reported that all was ready, and a favorable breeze soor. enabled them to reach the store of Daniel Birdsall. From his meagre stock, Saville made the best selection he could. half smiling, half frowning over the coarse material and stout shoes he was compelled to buy for Vera's wear.

"They will at least keep her warm," he thought, "and I have no fears but that, by some form of woman's magic, she will conjure this dark stuff into a tasteful dress. Perhaps I may do better another time in the stores up the river."

He also purchased an abundance of ammunition, and such provisions as the place furnished. Making all into two stout bundles, he returned, landing considerably above the fort, as he did not wish to be followed by curious eyes.

"Now, X, take the boat back, and return as soon as possible. If any inquire where I am, say that I am shooting among the hills."

X speedily rejoined his master, at whose bidding he took up the heavier bundle, and followed without a jot of interest, apparently, as to their destination.

"I am glad that you have sense enough to hold your tongue," said Saville. "For a time, you may be able to serve me best by serving others. I have friends back in the mountains, with whom I may leave you ; and if there is anything about them that seems strange, think what you please, but never speak of what you see and hear to any one. If you do, I have the means of making you wish you had bitten your tongue off first."

"Mas'r Saville'll find out by-and-by dat I'se po'ful good at knowin' nuffin dat's nobody's business."

"Yes," laughed Saville ; "you have given me a proof of that already. I think you may be just the boy I want."

The sun appeared like a great beacon-fire on the summit of a western mountain, as they reached the place where Mr. Brown had promised to meet them with Vera ; but there was not a trace of their presence.

"They have not arrived yet," thought Saville, "but it is time they were near. I will give our old signal, and Vera may answer ;" and he played the familiar air.

Almost immediately a powerful yet bird-like voice answered, from a neighboring thicket,

"I know a bank whereon the wild thyme blows."

"Gosh! what's dat?" said X, starting up in great alarm.

"That is your future mistress, X; don't run away till you see her."

As Vera stepped forth with her father, her strange appearance and remarkable beauty so impressed poor X that he muttered,

"I knowed any critter wid a voice like dat mus' be a speret from one place or t'oder. Tink she ain't from t'oder, dough ; for dat ar singin' was hebbenly, sure 'nuff. But I doesn't like de looks ob de ole man."

X soon gained his stolid composure, however, and was able to pull his little woolly horn with his wonted nonchalance, when introduced with his big bundle.

Saville greeted his friends with the utmost cordiality, and sought by his manner to banish their timidity. Hope and happiness had already wrought a marvelous change in Vera, and Saville, as of old, found himself wondering at her beauty.

"What have you here?" she asked, with childlike curiosity and vivacity.

"Well, in the first place, this is X Y Z. If you can find out any more about him, you will accomplish more than I have done. As for these bundles, we will open them at the cabin. If you will spread a banquet for me again to-night, you will find that I shall need no urging to partake of it."

"I have nothing better than a few more birds," said Vera ruefully.

"What could be better, my quaint Ariel? Come, moonlight will not satisfy me to-night."

The moon was just rising when they reached the cabin. X sat down with his bundle where he was bidden, and,

wearied with the fatigue of the day, was inclined to go immediately to sleep, when a name, uttered by Saville, aroused
him thoroughly.

"Gula," Saville had called, "come and see what I have
brought you."

"Gula!" repeated X. "What Gula is dis?" and he
strained his eyes toward the dark recess among the rocks
where glowed a few live coals. After a moment, he could
endure his suspense no longer, and said,

"Mas'r Saville, shall I bring de tings dar?"

"What voice is dat?" cried Gula in her shrillest and
most excited tones. And she rushed to the spot where
X was standing in trembling expectancy.

"Who is you? What is your name?" she asked eagerly.

"De name Mas'r Saville guv me is Ekswyze," said X
mechanically.

"No! no! no!" cried Gula, more shrill and excited
than ever. "What name did you'se mudder gib you when
you'se was a little chile?"

"Tascar."

With a wild cry Gula threw her arms around the boy, exclaiming, "I'se your mudder! I'se called you Tascar
when you was a baby, arter one I lubbed in de warm sun-
land. Oh! my po', ole, dead heart jes' seem as if it had
riz right up out ob de grave."

All gathered round Gula, overflowing with sympathy and
congratulations, and the moon, rising above the eastern
Highlands, enabled the mother to see the features of her
long-lost son. Every moment or two she would cry out,

"Yeh, yeh, it is my little Tascar, sure 'nuff."

"I knowed I'd find you, mudder," said the boy delight-
edly. "Dey couldn't keep me long down dar when dey
sole me 'way from you. I came back to whar you used to
be, and foun' you had run up dis way (lame Tom to'e me).

De world is po'ful big place, but I knowed I'd find you if I only looked long 'nuff.''

"You are now no longer an unknown quantity, so we will call you Tascar after this," said Saville, laughing.

"And now, Gula," added Vera, "you have at last heard a real voice, and I hope it will satisfy you, so that you will not listen any more for those strange, unearthly voices that you thought were calling you away from us. I suppose Tascar is hungry, like the rest of us ; so you may take him into your rocky kitchen, and let him help you get our supper. Mr. Saville has generously brought us a great many things.

"See, Mr. Saville," she continued, taking his arm, and leading him a little apart ; "see what a difference your coming has made to us all. Old Gula has found her son ; and father has changed so much for the better, I scarcely know him."

"And you ?" he asked gently.

"Ah ! Mr. Saville, you have never known what it was to have but one friend, one hope, in the world. When I first heard your steps, I was lying on mother's grave, and praying that I might speedily sleep beside her. Surely God sent you to us."

"Think so, little one, if it does you any good."

"But do you not think so ?"

"All I know is that I have come, and very glad I am that it was not too late."

"I wish you could explain to me abou God, and make Him seem near to me again."

"I cannot, Vera ; let us change the subject," Saville replied, a little abruptly.

She sighed, but soon gave herself up to thorough enjoyment of the happiest hour that had ever yet come into her brief and shadowed life.

CHAPTER XXI.

CAMP FIRES AND SUBTLER FLAMES.

NOT very long after their bountiful supper, Saville said,

"I had but little sleep last night, and have taken many steps to-day ; so, with your permission, I will seek a resting-place."

"I am sorry that we have scarcely anything better than the cabin floor to offer you," said Vera ruefully.

"You forget that I am a soldier, and that at this time of the year I ask no better bed than the greensward."

The cabin, like the larger one near West Point, had been constructed with a small loft. Into this Vera crept, but for a long time was too happy for sleep.

Saville took the blanket that Tascar had brought at his bidding, and, throwing himself under a wide-spreading hemlock, slept as only the strong and weary can sleep. Gula and her son dozed and crooned in their rocky recess, till the dawn aroused them to preparations for breakfast. Even the poor, remorseful exile rested with an unwonted sense of security.

The next morning, Saville tried to induce Mr. Brown to permit him to find them a better home nearer the fort, but found that any proposition of the kind would not be entertained.

"I have a feeling that I am safe here, and nowhere else," he said. "If you think best, Vera and Gula can go, but I shall remain."

. " I shall not leave you, father," said Vera, quietly.

" Well," said Saville, cheerily but firmly, " then we must make you all as comfortable here as we can. A new cabin, as large as the old one that was burned, must be built."

" But that will attract attention," remonstrated Mr. Brown.

" Suppose it does. I have satisfied General Clinton that you are loyal to our cause, and he has promised you and your family full protection."

" Does General Clinton know anything of me and my whereabouts ?" cried the man, starting up in great alarm.

" Yes, sir ; and if he had only known before what I told him yesterday, you would not have been molested in your old home. Can you not see, Mr. Brown, that nothing so draws attention and suspicion as your effort to hide from every one ? At the time I was so hastily ordered away from this region, I yielded to your judgment, and did not say much concerning you, not having your permission. But now, for Vera's sake, as well as your own, I can allow no doubt to exist as to the fact of your being heartily on our side. In respect to anything else, no one seeks to know aught. I can promise you all perfect safety, if you will do just what I ask."

The exile's brow contracted darkly, but he would not meet Saville's eye.

" Mr. Brown," said Saville, in a low, meaning tone.

The man now gave him a startled, apprehensive look.

" I can promise you perfect safety, if you do just what I ask," Saville continued, in the same low, significant voice.

" I will, I will," was the eager reply.

" There's my hand in pledge."

Mr. Brown seized it like a drowning man, and from that hour became Saville's slave.

Vera watched this strange interview with a beating heart, and, at its close, felt as never before, even that her destiny also was controlled by the young stranger, whom Providence had sent, as she believed, to rescue both herself and her father from the hopeless and helpless condition into which they had drifted.

With characteristic energy and promptness, Saville set about the tasks made necessary by the decision to remain in the secluded glen.   He decided that the little hut already built should be preserved for Gula and her son ; and the plan of a much larger cabin, for the use of Vera and her father, was marked out adjoining it.

" I also mean to have a little nook myself," he said.

" It will all be yours," Vera added promptly.

He looked at her so earnestly that the blood came into her face, though why, she did not know.   After a moment, he said, half to her, and half in soliloquy,

" I cannot tell why it is, but this place already seems to me more like a home than any I have yet known."

" I do not understand how *you* can feel so," said Vera, looking frankly into his face.   " It will, in truth, be home to me ; because containing, when you are here, all whom I love."

Again he gave her an earnest look, as he said,

" Nature is a rare teacher, my little friend ; and she has taught you a truth which we sometimes forget, to our sorrow.   Only the places which contain those whom we love can be homes."

" And it is your love for us," exclaimed Vera, openly and joyously, as if she had solved the mystery, " that makes this forbidding place seem homelike."

" That is not bad logic," he replied, laughing ; " though your pronoun is rather too general."

" How strange it is," said Vera, musingly, " that we

should have met as we did, and that you should have become my brother in very truth ! Do such things often happen in the world ?"

" I am afraid not," he replied, shaking his head.

" Then I have been specially favored, when I have been almost repining at my lot."

" I certainly have been very fortunate in finding such a sweet, wild flower in this wilderness of a world. But come ; this is not preparing for the cold storms of winter, which, unfortunately, are near. You must ply the needle, and bring home the game, while your father and Tascar do the heavy work. Ye gods ! how I would like to stay here and help you ! I have brought plenty of powder and shot for your gun."

" But will it be safe to have the report of fire-arms heard here ?"

" Certainly ; the old policy of hiding and concealment is past ; and as soon as I can, I shall find you a home where you can have good, kind neighbors. Bring your gun, and let me see if you can hit that gray squirrel in yonder tall tree."

She complied, with the joyousness of a child, and was soon within range with her light fowling-piece.

" Now, quick ! before he moves," cried Saville.

Her merry laugh rang out, as she threw pebbles at the little creature, till, thoroughly alarmed, it ran to the topmost boughs. Then, as it was in the act of springing to another tree, she fired, and it fell dead at her feet.

" I take off my hat to you," cried Saville. " You excel Diana herself."

The morning passed all too quickly, and, after an early dinner, Saville returned to the fort, taking Tascar, that he might send back by him tools and other needed articles.

During the week following, Saville pleaded, with justice, that he had scarcely had a respite from duty since joining the service, and obtained leave to absent himself for several days. He started ostensibly upon a hunting excursion in the mountains, but took the shortest path to the secluded valley, which was beginning to have for him peculiar attractions.

The days passed like enchantment. Under the new and happier conditions of her life, Vera appeared to grow hourly in beauty and fascination. The recuperative power of nature was in her mind and body. She was like a sunny bank, that a few warm spring days change from wintry bareness to fragrant bloom.

Her feeling for Saville was the frank, undisguised affection of a sister ; or, perhaps more truly, the strong, innocent love of a child, that gives its heart wholly for the time to those who win it.

The woman in Vera was still unawakened, though, at times, there was an intensity in Saville's gaze that quickened her pulse a little, and mantled her cheek with a richer hue than even restored vigor was giving it again.

As for Saville, he was self-deceived. We have already seen that he had a faculty for illusion, and this was especially true in the line of his favorite theories. As he had once imagined his transient passion for a most unworthy object to be the precursor of lasting and conjugal affection, so now he regarded the pure flame of love, which was kindling in his heart for Vera, as a lofty kind of friendship, resulting from the peculiar accord of their two natures. He felt that he was in all respects ennobled and made better by her society. Unconsciously she stimulated every good quality he possessed into greater vigor. She was so pure and innocent herself that his passion slept in her presence, while his higher faculties of mind and heart were awakened into aspirations that were as thrillingly delightful as they were foreign to all his former experience.

Moreover, his conscience commended the part he was acting toward her. The circumstances of their acquaintance had been such, that every generous, sympathetic trait he possessed was enlisted in her behalf. He regarded himself as a disciple of nature and an apostle of humanity. In his view, nature had been her teacher, and had formed her character; and the result confirmed his theory that all should be guided by nature's teachings. In their warm and growing friendship, were not they both following the strong and natural impulses of their hearts?

As one devoted to the interests of humanity, he would consider himself most false, did he leave this innocent maiden to the perils of her peculiar isolated condition, and he honestly desired to obtain for her a safe and recognized position in society, as soon as possible.

But the spell of her beauty grew daily upon him; the touch of her hand was acquiring subtle power to thrill every nerve and fiber of his body; the tones of her voice kept repeating themselves for long hours in his heart; and before his visit was over, even the man of theories and illusions was perplexed at certain peculiarities in his platonic friendship.

But the woman in Vera still slumbered, and she returned his affection with the same frank innocence as at first.

After his visit to the romantic glen, life at the fort was to Saville very " weary, stale, flat, and unprofitable." Not even the fact that the enemy might soon make a demonstration up the river, could greatly divert his thoughts at first, and only as the tidings from the armies, under both Washington and Gates grew full of exciting interest, and the prospect that the British forces in New York would seek to force their way through the Highlands became quite certain, did his old military ardor rekindle. As all seemed quiet on Saturday evening, the 4th of October, he obtained permission to be absent from the fort during the Sabbath. The moment the duties of the day were over, he was on his way to the secluded valley, which now shut in his thoughts from the outer world almost as completely as it immured the exiles who had found a refuge there.

His coming was a glad surprise to Vera, and there were evidences of deeper feeling in her welcome than she had ever yet manifested.

" You are not going away again from this region ?" she asked eagerly.

" Not soon, that I am aware. Why ?"

" I have had such a dreary foreboding of evil of some kind, and last night I dreamed———" and she suddenly covered her face with her hands, and burst into tears.

" Why, Vera, this is unlike you : are you well ?"

" Yes, yes ; but it was such a terrible dream !"

" Tell me it, and I will explain it away."

" I dreamed that there had been a battle, and that you were left wounded and dying on the ground, and I could not find you," she said, in a low, shuddering tone, with tears starting afresh. " Is there prospect of a battle ?"

" No special prospect—no more than there has been for several days past ; but a soldier cannot look for anything else."

" I wish I did not feel so, " said Vera.

" Come, cheer up, my little friend. Dreams go by contraries. Never shed tears over troubles that may not come ;" and he exerted himself to his utmost to banish her gloomy fears.

The new log cabin, at which he also had labored during his visit, was now nearly complete, and he kindled a genial fire in its ample chimney-place.

He took a genuine interest in all that had been done in his absence, and praised the results of each one's labor. But Vera noted with pleasure that he lingered longest over her handiwork. Never before had he been so kind or so thoughtful of her. His mere tones and glances were like caresses. But all this only made her heart more full, for she could not cast off the miserable presentiment with which she had risen that morning. For his sake, however, she disguised her feelings.

After dinner, the following day, they took a long walk together, and she accompanied him well on his way back to the fort.

As they were parting, she said, as she clung to his hand,

"Promise me one thing—if there is a battle—that you will not needlessly or recklessly expose yourself. What would become of us if you were—if you were—oh! m' heart almost breaks even at the thought! If you have any pity or love for me, grant what I ask."

"'If I have any love for you,' Vera? I hardly dare trust my heart to answer. Well, well, little sister, I will be as prudent as a soldier can be with honor. I must say good-by at once, or I may be tempted not to go at all," and for the first time he stooped down and kissed her forehead.

She watched his receding figure as long as it was visible, and then returned to the cabin, with an increasing weight upon her heart.

By the time he reached the vicinity of the fort, the camp fires were lighted, and around these the men were gathered, cooking the evening meal. To divert his thoughts, he wandered aimlessly here and there, watching the strange effects of light and shadow among the rocks and evergreens, and the picturesqueness of the bearded men as they passed to and fro between the fires. Even the coarse rations of the soldiery gave forth a savory odor in the open air.   From all sides came the cheerful hum of voices, and from many groups, the sound of laughter, or the notes of a rollicking song.

" This scene has more the air of a gypsy encampment than the stern aspect of war," he thought.   " I wish Vera could see it, for it would quite allay her fears.   What does that singing mean yonder ?" and he made his way to a large fire, around which numbers were increasing continually."

" Oh ! it's a religious meeting.   There is Parson Gano ! How dearly Vera would love to hear his pious jargon, and would swallow it all, poor child, as undoubted truth ! Still, I am glad to note that she speaks less and less of these things, and think she has a native strength of mind which will enable her to outgrow her superstitious trammels. Well, Gano is a good, brave fellow, if he is teaching solemn nonsense ; and out of curiosity I'll stay, and hear what he has to say."   And he sat down under the shadow of a tree, and watched the scene, as one might look on some heathenish incantation.

The throng around the fire grew large, for the preacher was a popular speaker.   Officers mingled with the men, as they would do in the plain meeting-houses in their distant village homes ; and Saville could not help noting that the serious faces lighted up by the glare of the central fire, were, in the main, manly, self-respecting and intelligent.

" How is it," he asked himself, " that sane and even very clever people can keep up with so much pains this old-fashioned mummery of religion ?   *Cui bono?*   What is the good of it all ?   Here we are living in a world of inexorable law and destiny, and yet multitudes are praying to an old Hebrew divinity, that never had any existence, as if they expected practical help !   Could anything be more absurd ?

The idea of my getting down on my knees, and praying to one of Homer's demi-gods !   What is it in men that makes them so credulous ?''

Here he suspended his soliloquy to listen to the hymn which the chaplain gave out before his sermon.   The voices that sang it were untrained and rough, and the harmony not very smooth, and yet the critical listener admitted to himself that there was a certain element in the music which made it differ from a mere performance.

'' Human action, however absurd and unreasonable, is always impressive when earnest,'' he philosophized ; '' but, after all, what is the secret spring in man which leads to this folly ?''

Though not aware of it at first, he was answered by the text, which was now announced :

'' Jesus saith unto her, I am the resurrection and the life ; he that believeth in me, though he were dead, yet shall he live ;

'' And whosoever liveth and believeth in me shall never die.   Believest thou this ?''

'' No, '' was Saville's decided mental response.   '' That Jesus said this ' unto *her*,' is most appropriate, for it was an assertion fit to be addressed only to a credulous woman. ''

'' The Being who uttered these remarkable words, '' began the chaplain, simply standing up before the fire, and talking in a familiar and fatherly way to his audience, '' had the power to make them good ; and, therefore, we may take to our hearts all the hope and encouragement they contain. ''

'' That is where we differ, '' thought Saville, rising and shrugging his shoulders.   '' Why had the man, Jesus, such power, more than other enthusiasts of the past ?   That is the way with all these teachers of religion.   They first assume what is contrary to reason, and, as a matter of course, their conclusions are absurd, and often monstrous.   There is no use of my wasting more time here." But, as he was moving away, the preacher's words again caught his attention.

"To-night," said Chaplain Gano, "the scenes, even within and around these military forts, are peaceful, rather than warlike. The sky is cloudless, and there are the stars looking down as steadily as the eyes of God. Only the insects' chirp is heard in the dark valleys and on the steeps around us. The Sabbath stillness is broken by no ruder sounds than the profane mirth and songs which sometimes disturb our worship. To the ear of heaven, though, ribald words and laughter make harsher discord than the wildest din of battle, where freemen are warring for their rights. Still, there is nothing apparent to man, in the scenes about us to-night, to awaken the emotion of fear, even in the breasts of the fearful.

"But, what shall be on the morrow? Such is our uncertain tenure of earthly life, we could not ask this question in our peaceful homes without misgivings. But, how much it means to the soldiery! Only by killing many of us, do our enemies hope to put their feet again upon our necks. Many of us must be slain before our righteous cause can triumph. A few years, perhaps but a few days—do not think I am talking wildly when I say, but a few hours— may elapse before these warm, living bodies of ours become like the clods beneath our feet."

A foreboding recollection of Vera's dream came into Saville's mind.

"Young man," continued the chaplain more earnestly, leveling his long finger at a careless young fellow, who was whispering to a comrade on the opposite side of the fire, "I have no doubt that you are a brave soldier. Alas! you seem so bold that you are willing to defy God as well as man. When the foe attacks these forts, you will try to do your duty. But do you not realize that this very duty may cause your vigorous young body to be racked with dying pains? If I could tell you that to-morrow evening you would be lying dead somewhere in the cold starlight, what ought you to do now? What ought you—and you—and you—to do?" he asked solemnly, sweeping his finger around the entire circle. "What *ought* we all to do?

"Ought? How great the privilege, rather, of creatures like ourselves—weak and ready to perish at all times, now hourly exposed to peril—how great is the privilege of heed ing the Divine Saviour as He cries, 'I am the resurrection and the life.' If we trust and fear the One who spake these words, we have naught else to fear. The bullet that pierces us may be but God's swift messenger to summon us home. Suppose our mangled bodies do strew these rugged hill-sides and rocky forts! The cruel foe cannot so trample them out of shape, nor time so destroy them, nor the winds so scatter and dissipate them, but that He, who declared, 'I am the resurrection,' can raise them up, no longer dead and defaced, but fashioned like unto His glorious body; and so shall we be ever with the Lord. Then why live another hour, why go into desperate battle, without this precious Friend?

"Comrades in peril! I have not sought to work upon your fears to-night, but rather to lead you to accept a faith which makes even cowards brave, and strong men lions for the right. We have reason to think that we shall soon meet the enemy; but there is no foe on earth, or in hell beneath, that can strike a fatal blow at the honest Christ-believer and follower."

To Saville's surprise, the preacher had kept him a listener until the close of his exhortation. Then with a shrug, he strode away into the darkness saying, "Here, I suppose, is the secret of it all. Men know they must die; these poor fellows are aware that they may be knocked on the head within a few days. They all want to live after they are dead (as if the very idea were not absurd), and they give a ready hearing to anybody who holds out the hope that they may. Well, I wouldn't mind an eternal Elysium myself, if I could have the fashioning of it. One thing is certain—Vera would share it with me."

As he was threading his way among the camp-fires, toward his quarters, he heard his own name mentioned, and naturally paused to learn in what connection it was used. The voice came from beyond a clump of cedars to his right, and, looking through it, he saw, just below a ledge of rock, a circle of visages, differing widely in character from those gathered round the chaplain's fire. The physiognomy of Larry, his old servant, was the type of the majority on which the flames were flickering, although the expression of many was still more unpromising. But the bold, handsome face of his wife, "Captain Molly," would have received the first attention, even if she had not been speaking.

" Is it where yer ould masther, Saville, does be goin' out in the woods that ye're askin', Larry ?"

" Yees."

" Well, I'm a-thinkin', should ye follow his trail, ye'd foind the White Witch o' the Highlands."

" It's a long day since she's been seen or heard on."

" He's found her, I warrant ye ; an' moighty glad I am we had nothin' to do wid the diviltry when Barneyw as shot. He questioned me close, an' if I'd been a-lyin', I fear he'd a-cotched me. Wherever this gal o' his'n is, folks as don't want their heads broke ud better let her alone."

" But what would his wife say to his galivantin' off in the mountings ?" asked Larry.

" Why should he care ?" said Molly carelessly. " If

what ye tell me is thrue, he's got a divil for a wife, and may well look for a betther one.''

'' 'Cordin' to that,'' snickered Larry, ''it's me that shud go galivantin' off in the mountings too.''

A loud laugh followed this sally.

'' Thry it once,'' cried Molly, ''an' ye'll foind that the divil will be arther ye in a way ye'll not forgit.''

'' Now Molly, me darlint, ye knows I was only a-givin' ye a poke in the ribs in sport, so ye needn't guv me any in good earnest. My ould masther can have the White Witch o' the Highlands, and the Black Witch, too, for all o' me.''

Saville stayed to hear no more of their low talk, but hastened on, his cheeks tingling that his name had been coupled with that of the maiden under such circumstances.

He sat down in his tent in no enviable mood, and, for the first time, permitted his mind to dwell on the consequences of his growing intimacy with Vera. After all, would his brother officers, would the world, take a more charitable view than that which he had just heard expressed? He might assert that his love for Vera was friendship, brotherly affection; but he plainly foresaw society's shrug of incredulity. From the depths of his heart, also, a question was beginning to arise.

'' Is your love for Vera fraternal or platonic only?'' And he found that he could not give a prompt and positive answer. Then the pledge he had made on the memorable Sabbath evening, when he sacrificed all ties to his patriotism, rose up before him like a spectre.

'' I shall be loyal to the name of wife, though the reality I never had.''

'' Curses on the priest-ridden, law-marred world!'' he muttered, '' wherein every natural impulse is thwarted. If I continue to act the part of a brother toward Vera, society will point its finger toward us both in scoffing unbelief, and imagine the worst. If, because she is so truly lovable, I come to love her more warmly, and seek for some honorable solution of the problem, society will heartlessly tell me that there is none, in this prudish land, save open shame. I shall be informed that the combination of woman, devil, and bigot, in New York, is my wife ; that the mummery in the church made us one, when we have nothing in common except our hate ; and that it is foul sin for me to think of another. Where is men's reason ? Why, even the instinct of this coarse, untutored Irish woman hit upon a better philosophy. And yet so it is, and so it will be until the broad and rational principles which are revolutionizing France are accepted and acted upon here. Oh ! that we had a Voltaire and a Rousseau to break the chains of the past, and teach that the impulses of the heart are right ! But now, all my pure and ennobling affection for Vera, and her snow-white love for me, will be jumbled in the same category as the infidelity of this woman, Molly, to her husband.''

Further bitter musings were interrupted by the appearance of an orderly, with the message that his presence was required at once at headquarters.

CHAPTER XXII.

THE STORMING OF THE FORTS.

ON reaching the tent of General James Clinton, Saville found all the leading officers of the garrison already assembled, and was informed that the enemy were advancing up the river, and had already landed large forces at Tarrytown and Verplanck's Point. He also found that Governor Clinton had just arrived, with a considerable reinforcement of militia. After giving such directions as were deemed necessary, Governor Clinton said,

" The enemy will probably strike Putnam at Peekskill first, but we shall have our own share of fighting, no doubt, and may have to do the most of it. It is well known to you, gentlemen, that the garrisons are not as strong as we could wish. We must double our strength by doubling our courage and efforts. I shall expect every man to do his whole duty. I request that the engineer officers do all in their power to strengthen the unfinished portions of the works. "

Throughout the remainder of the night, the din of labor resounded, and only toward the break of day was Saville able to get a little sleep.

On awakening, he immediately repaired to the governor's tent for instructions, and had scarcely reached the place, when Major Logan, who had been sent with one hundred men on a scouting expedition beyond the Dunderberg, returned, with the startling information that about forty boats, crowded with British troops, had landed near Stony Point.

Saville, having no special command, was willing to do anything which promised active and exciting service ; he therefore volunteered to go on a reconnoissance. Governor Clinton, who had learned his value in such employment on a previous occasion, at once accepted his offer, and gave him, as a support, a lieutenant and thirty men.

Saville and his party proceeded rapidly along the mountain-road leading from Fort Clinton to Haverstraw, and, when between three and four miles out, suddenly met the vanguard of the English forces, upon the rapid and stealthy march which had, as its object, the surprise of the forts.

The small American detachment was peremptorily summoned to surrender.

"Give 'em a volley as our answer," said Saville ; and the wooded defile was at once filled with the preliminary echoes of the mighty uproar soon to rage among the Highlands.

Under the cover of their fire, the scouting party retreated rapidly to a new point of observation, fortunately none being wounded by the return fire of the enemy.

After some further skirmishing, in which the numbers and purposes of the attacking force became more apparent Saville retreated rapidly, without the loss of a man, and reported. In the mean time, patrols had brought word that the enemy were also advancing around Bear Mountain, to the rear of Fort Montgomery.

"Putnam has been outwitted," said Governor Clinton, "and we've got to take all the blows. Well, I believe in giving even the devil his due ; and, in my opinion, Sir Henry Clinton has executed a magnificent piece of strategy. He really does honor to the name, and I am quite inclined to claim relationship. We must see to it, James, that we prove that the American branch of the family has not degenerated " and the brothers smiled grimly and significantly.

Before many hours passed, Sir Henry himself would have been among the first to admit the sturdiness of the colonial stock.

"It is now past noon," said General James Clinton, "and yet we hear nothing from Putnam. It's very strange!"

"I will send a messenger at once to him," said his brother, and a man by the name of Waterbury was dispatched.

"I hope that fellow can be depended upon, for I did not like his looks overmuch," said James Clinton. "The firing is growing sharp out on the Bear Mountain road, and we must have reinforcements soon, if they are to be of any service. There! the firing has commenced at the abatis, where the road passes Sinnipink Pond. I will return to Fort Clinton at once, and do my utmost to carry out the measures we have concerted."

"God be with you, brother! Hit hard and often, and remember, we won't lower the flag while we have a foot of ground to fight on! How many men did you say were at the abatis by the pond?"

"Over a hundred."

"Let them hold the point obstinately. Time is worth everything to us now. Troops from Putnam must be here soon. Farewell."

"Saville," continued the governor, "as you have no command, you can serve me best by acting as an *aide*. Colonels Bruyn and M'Claghrey are out on the Orange Furnace road with sixty men. Tell Colonel Livingston to detach thirty more to their support. Take that horse yonder, ride out, learn what you can, and report as soon as possible."

Saville urged the poor beast at a tremendous pace up the rocky way; but, by the time he reached the point of conflict, the advance skirmishers of the small American force had been driven in, and Colonel Campbell, with the assaulting column, was pressing on as rapidly as the narrow road, leading through a wild, rugged pass, permitted. The enemy paused a moment, as a brass field-piece sent a ball plowing into their ranks, and then, with the courage and steadiness of trained soldiers, filed off, on either side of the road, into the partial shelter of the wooded hill-sides, and pressed on as before, in the face of a brisk fire of small-arms. Their advance was so rapid, and the road so rough and impracticable, that it was found impossible to extricate the field-piece, and it was therefore spiked and abandoned.

With these tidings, Saville returned to the fort. But, while present at the affray over the field-piece, his attention had been caught by the occasional report of a single rifle from a shaggy hill-side, along which he knew the enemy must be advancing, and he correctly surmised that it was the exile, striking at the power he so greatly dreaded. Vera's dream and presentiment flashed into his mind, and he muttered,

" Poor child ! this firing no doubt causes her to imagine that all her forebodings of evil will come true. I hope I shall live to laugh her out of such fancies for the future."

On his way back to the fort, he had observed that Colonel Lamb had posted himself in a commanding position, with a twelve pounder ; and the veteran had grimly remarked that they would hear from him soon.

" Return, and request Colonel Lamb to hold the enemy in check as long as possible. Then cross to Fort Clinton, and bring me word how things are going there. Good God ! Why doesn't Putnam send me help ?" said Governor Clinton, who was chafing like a lion in the toils.

Saville made the fire fly along the flinty road, and soon regained the crest of the hill upon which Colonel Lamb had posted himself with his formidable twelve pounder. The advance party, under Colonel Bruyn, were marching around to the rear of the gun, within supporting distance. As soon as the head of the English column showed itself, Lamb opened with the precision of aim for which he was famous, and his quick firing, with the havoc which it made, once again, and more decidedly, checked the hostile advance.

The sharp-shooters under Colonel Bruyn were seeking stations among the trees and rocks, from which to gall the enemy with small-arms, and aid in maintaining the position, when, unfortunately, the cannon with which Colonel Lamb was doing so much execution burst. The British troops, with a loud huzza, rushed forward, and the Americans retreated, fighting, to the fort.

When Saville reached Fort Clinton, the abatis at Lake Sinnipink had been carried, and such of its defenders as had not been killed and disabled were retreating rapidly, with the enemy close upon them.

Coolly walking the parapet of the fort, with the bullets already whistling round him, was the tall form of Chaplain Gano ; and his intrepid bearing had an excellent influence on the militia, most of whom were now, for the first time, to face the dreaded Hessians, who were, to many of the simple rustics of that day, monsters rather than men. Fearful stories concerning them were rife, the mildest of which being that, as they were unacquainted with the English tongue, they neither understood nor heeded offers of surrender or cries for mercy ; but bayoneted indiscriminately all who fell into their hands.

The survivors of the conflict at the abatis brought word that these terrible Hessians were advancing in vast numbers, at which poor Larry so quaked that he could scarcely serve his gun, and not a few others wished themselves safe in their humble homes. But "Captain Molly" rallied the spirits and courage of those near her, by springing on the rampart, and calling, in her shrillest tones,

"Come on, Hessians or Red-coats; we'll trate ye all the same, and'll put more bullets an' balls intil yees than ye'll loike for supper."

"Och! Molly, me darlint, get down," cried Larry. "What wud we all do an' ye shud sthop a Hessian bullit?"

But Molly recklessly kept her exposed position, gesticulating and firing volleys of epithets toward the advancing foe, until ordered down by one of the officers. She then descended, amid the loud huzzas and laughter of scores of poor fellows whose voices would soon be hushed.

Having received such message as General James Clinton desired to send to his brother, Saville galloped back to Fort Montgomery, and barely escaped being intercepted by the environing forces.

It was now four o'clock, and both the forts were fairly invested. The two brave men who commanded them were still hoping for aid from Putnam, and determined to make as obstinate a resistance as their inadequate forces permitted.

The enemy gave but brief respite, and, after a rapid disposition of the assaulting columns, pushed forward to the attack. By the aid of his glass, Saville could see his old acquaintance, Colonel Beverly Robinson, leading forward many neighbors and fellow townsmen whom he knew.

It was evident that the enemy did not calculate upon a very stubborn resistance, and hoped to carry the works by a simultaneous attack. Therefore they advanced confidently, and in imposing military array, expecting to awe and intimidate the rustic soldiery opposed to them. But the terrific and well-directed fire, both of cannon and small-arms, that circled around the ramparts of both the forts, soon taught them their error, and showed that the keys of the Highlands could be won only by a bloody battle.

Again and again they advanced to the charge, but only to be repulsed and driven back, strewing the broken and rocky region with their dead and wounded.

An hour passed—an hour of bloody, obstinate fighting, on both sides—in which many souls, hot with wrath, mad with excitement, passed away from the scene of conflict.

But, to the scanty garrison, the loss of men was a far more serious matter than to the full battalions of the enemy. The lines of Fort Montgomery were extensive, and but partially finished ; and Governor Clinton was able to repulse all attacks thus far only by good generalship and the indomitable spirit of his men.

The British officers, however, had by this time gauged quite correctly the forces opposed to them, and were satisfied that they could eventually carry the works by the mere weight of numbers. In order to save himself further loss, Sir Henry Clinton ordered a brief cessation of hostilities, and sent in a flag of truce, with the dire threat that, unless both the garrisons surrendered within five minutes, he would put all to the sword.

Lieutenant-Colonel Livingston was ordered to receive the flag, and instructed to inform Sir Henry Clinton that the Americans would defend the forts to the very last extremity.

" This putting everybody to the sword is a game that two can play at," remarked the governor grimly. He still had hopes that a reinforcement from Peekskill might arrive at any moment, and felt sure that if he could maintain the position until the following day, he would certainly receive relief.

Having defiantly refused to capitulate, nothing now remained for the garrisons but the most desperate resistance. As the men in Fort Clinton saw the flag retire from the open space where the parley had been held, they set their teeth, and many faces grew white and stern with the determination to sell life dearly.

The October day was drawing to a close. The sky was overcast with clouds, as if heaven, offended at the rude clamor of earthly passion, were frowning upon the scene.

As the flag disappeared within the hostile ranks, there was, for a few moments, an awful lull and suspense. The echoes of the preceding strife had died away, and there was now an ominous and oppressive silence, broken only by the groans of the wounded and dying. Then, from the environing foe, came a hoarse and increasing murmur of rage. Commands and orders were given rapidly, and the storm of war broke forth more vehemently than before.

The British ships, under Admiral Hotham, had now come up within range, and commenced bombarding the forts and the American vessels that were anchored above the chain and *chevaux-de-frise*, which had been stretched across the river for the purpose of obstructing navigation. The conflict was thus raging upon the water as well as on the shore, the heavy guns of each party adding greatly to the fearful uproar resounding among the mountains.

The sun was setting behind obscuring clouds, and, in the early and deepening gloom, the flashes from the firelocks and cannon grew more lurid and distinct, increasing the terrors of the scene. The garrison of Fort Montgomery, thinned by the strife which had already occurred, and compelled to defend works far too extensive and imperfect, considering its scanty number, was fighting heroically, and had thus far repulsed the most determined assaults. But the governor's forces were inadequate, and the enemy were gaining and holding positions, in the broken region in the rear of the fort, that were menacingly near the American lines.

At one of these threatened points, Saville, who was sweeping the field with his glass, saw a heavy massing of British grenadiers, and he directed the governor's attention thither. Lord Rawdon was preparing for his memorable charge, which, with the supporting attacks all along the line, decided the fate of the day. As a chivalric volunteer, at his side was his friend, the Count Gabrouski, a Polish aide-de-camp of Sir Henry Clinton.

The governor, for a moment, scanned, with a heavy frown, this thunderbolt, whose shock he must soon sustain, and then made such disposition to receive it as was possible in the brief time allowed him.

"If we do not repulse this attack, and the worst comes to the worst," he said to Saville, "cross to Fort Clinton, by the foot-path, and tell my brother not to surrender, but cut his way out among the hills. The darkness will favor this."

Slowly and steadily at first, but with increasing speed, the assaulting column advanced through the gloom, becoming every second more distinct and terrible. Cannon and musket balls made gaps, but the ranks closed up, leaving no more trace than the smooth surface of a smitten lake. The foremost fell. The point of this human entering wedge appeared to crumble, as it reached the fort. The tall Polish count seemed at one moment a Homeric demi-god, as he was about to spring across the fosse upon the rampart. A second later, he was a weak, dying man, with only strength to gasp, to the grenadier who bent over him,

"Take this sword to Lord Rawdon, and tell him the owner died like a soldier."

The American resistance was as vain as it was heroic. The assaulting column, like a black river, flowed steadily on, and by its enormous weight alone pressed everything back.

"To my brother, quick, with my message," cried the governor to Saville; and by the time Saville extricated himself from the fort, a hand-to-hand *mêlée* had commenced.

In his swift transit across the deep ravine, Vera's dream

again occurred to him, with an ominous significance, and
his face grew white and rigid, with the determination un-
waveringly to meet the worst.   But as, in this moment of
solitude and respite from the mad excitement of battle, he
realized his danger, and therefore hers, in her isolation, his
heart sickened.

When he entered Fort Clinton, the situation was as desperate as it had been at Fort Montgomery at the moment of
his departure.   All was confusion.   In the increasing darkness, he could not discover General Clinton.   At several
points, the enemy seemed pouring over the ramparts.
Shouts, yells, curses, groans, the clangor of weapons, and
crash of musketry deafened and bewildered him.   He also
noted, as proof that the enemy were taking the fort, that all
firing of cannon had ceased on the part of the Americans.
Suddenly he heard, above the uproar, a shrill voice, which
he knew to be " Captain Molly's," crying,

" Back, ye spalpeen !   Fire the gun."

" Here, at least," he thought, " must be enough of our
troops to form a rallying-point," and drawing his sword, he
rushed toward the place from whence came the voice.   Fugitives rushed against him ; a second later he saw Larry break
from the grasp of his wife, throw down his lighted match,
and fly.

" Divil a sthep will I rin, till that gun's fired," cried
Molly, seizing the match ; and, in the faces of the enemy,
who were climbing the rampart, she touched off the las*
cannon that was discharged in Fort Clinton.

All this passed in a very few seconds.   With a wild Irish
whoop of exultation, Molly turned to escape, when a Hessian lieutenant laid his iron grasp upon her, and raised his
heavy saber to strike.

" Wretch I would you kill a woman ?" cried Saville, and
he ran the man through the body.

"The Holy Vargin bless ye ! Misther Saville," ejaculated Molly, springing away like a deer, the moment the grasp on her arm relaxed. But, looking back as she ran, she saw Saville fall, from a savage bayonet thrust in his breast. Then, the human wave that was surging into the fort swept over him. Under the cover of darkness, she leaped the parapet on the opposite side, scrambled down the steep bank into the ravine of Poplopen Creek, and escaped with many other fugitives, among whom was General James Clinton, wounded, but indomitable in his purpose not to fall into the enemy's hands.

Governor Clinton was also among the last to leave Fort Montgomery. On reaching the shore of the river, he saw a boat pushing away, and hailed it. The officer in charge knew his voice, and caused the boat to return. But it was found to be already loaded to the gunwale, and the governor would not endanger the safety of its occupants by entering it. The loyal officer generously offered to give up his place, but the governor, equally generous, would not listen to this. The enemy were pressing closely, and it was agreed to try the experiment of adding the weight of one more, and, to the joy of all, the boat was still above the water's edge. The perilous transit was made in safety, and on the further shore were found five hundred men, whom the bewildered Putnam had at last sent, but too late to be of any service.

The man Waterbury, whom the governor had dispatched to Peekskill, had treacherously delayed his departure, and, on the following day, deserted to the enemy.

On the capture of the forts, the American vessels above the *chevaux-de-frise* slipped their cables, and tried to escape up the river ; but the wind was adverse, and their crews, to avoid capture, set them on fire, and abandoned them. Then followed scenes that were weird and awful in the extreme, forming an appropriate close to the bloody drama of the day. By reason of the clouds, night had come on suddenly, and was very dark. When the torches were applied to the ships, every sail was set, the cannon were loaded, and there was an abundance of ammunition in the magazines. In a few moments, they became pyramids of fire, as the flames, fanned by the gale, leaped from deck to mast-head. The rugged, precipitous shores were lighted up as with the glare of noon, and the neighboring mountains seemed like a group of giants standing around their mighty camp-fires.

As the flames reached the heavy guns, they were discharged, not as in battle, but irregularly, fitfully, as if some capricious demon were directing all in accordance with its mad impulses.

The region where the vessels were drifting has ever been famous for its echoes, and, from the first, the clamor of the strife had been repeated and augmented, until it might have seemed that the combatants were innumerable. But when the fire reached the magazines of the ships, volcanic explosions followed, at which even the granite hills appeared to tremble, and it seemed as if the deep reverberations never would cease. Old Gula, cowering in her rocky niche, muttered,

" Dat's de mos' awful voice I'se eber heard. I'se afeared on't."

The burning wrecks were at last quenched beneath the water. After all, the passions of men cannot long disturb nature's deep repose, and soon silence and night held undisputed sway on the river, and among the mountains.

CHAPTER XXIII.

THE WIFE'S QUEST AMONG THE DEAD.

FOR a long time, lights had glanced hither and thither on the battle-field and within the forts, and, to one eager watcher in the distance, their movements had seemed as erratic and meaningless as the glimmer of fireflies in June. The surgeons, with their assistants, were gathering up the wounded, and conveying them to points where they could receive such attention as the hour and place permitted.

At last, Fort Clinton was deserted by all except an occasional sentinel, and those who still lay within its walls were very quiet.

At an early hour in the evening, its parapet was crossed by two British officers, one of whom carried a lantern, and seemed bent on an eager quest.

" I say, Vennam," asked his companion, " why are you so anxious to find this Saville ?"

" For the sake of his wife."

" Nonsense ! His wife will shed no tears if you find him with a bullet through his head. If all is true that I have heard, she hates him like sin."

" Far more than sin, *mon ami,*" and the lantern that he held down that he might peer into a dead man's face, revealed the traces of recklessness and dissipation in his own. " Indeed, I scarcely think she hates sin at all. You are right, however, in one respect. No tears will be shed, if I can find him in the condition of this carrion here, unless they are tears of joy. Still, for her sake, I am looking for her husband ; and, I may add, for my own. Knowing how glad she would be to find him here, snoozing quietly in the eternal sleep of which he prates, I, as her proxy, am looking for him, as I promised. He is not among the wounded or prisoners, as far as I can learn ; if I cannot find him among the dead, he must have escaped, and we shall have reason to curse our luck."

" Well, if you find him here, and food for the crows, what then ?"

" Then I invite you to my wedding."

" Wedding, indeed ! I doubt that ! You are not one to trammel yourself with a wife."

" I confess I have had prejudices against the holy state of matrimony, but any other relation with my present lovely charmer would involve half a dozen duels, and with good shots. I wouldn't have a ghost of a chance in running the gauntlet, and so I must emulate the example of the good King David, and get her husband out of the way. I snatched a musket and fired at him twice to-day, but for once the devil did not help his own."

" By St. George ! Vennam, I should think the devil would be afraid of you."

" Ha ! ha ! ha !" was the reckless response. " Julie Saville Ashburton is not, and she is the most magnificent creature I've ever seen, and I've been something of a connoisseur in several lands. Besides, she's an heiress, which, to a man of my tastes, is no small consideration."

" By St. George ! Vennam, this turning up of dead men's faces is grim business. I'm getting sick of it."

" Well, well ! you are not playing for the stake that I am, so I don't wonder. Perhaps I may find him in the morning. Hold ! who is that lying behind yonder big Hessian ? That's an officer's uniform. O ye Plutonian gods ! here he is ! dead, too, as the immortal Cæsar. That bayonet-thrust would have killed an ox. Here's to thee, Julie, and our wedding-bells ;'' and, drawing a flask of wine from his pocket, he drank deeply, and then passed it to his companion.

" And will the bells be rung soon ?''

" Ay, that much we shall make her proud relations yield. Up to a certain point, she always has her own way. A soldier's life is too uncertain to wait upon the slow forms of decorous custom. Besides, in this case, there will be no ' funeral baked meats ' to grow cold. There, I'll take his sword, if I can withdraw it from this beastly Hessian, and that will be proof positive that I saw him dead. Farewell, now, most accommodating of husbands ! your sleep may be as ' eternal ' as you like ;'' and the human ghoul, who had been feasting his eyes on the dead, disappeared, in the darkness, toward Fort Montgomery.

CHAPTER XXIV.

VERA'S SEARCH AMONG THE DEAD.

THE Sunday evening following the departure of Saville
had been to Vera one of peculiar sadness and depression. " If I only had my dear old Bible," she thought,
" and could turn to some of God's promises, perhaps they
would comfort and reassure me ; but, in a way that I cannot understand, they have grown vague, and He seems far
off."

Still, she again and again tried to lift her heart to heaven
in prayer ; but the image of Saville would enter, and absorb
every thought, and the presentiment of some evil or danger
weighed down her spirits with increasing despondency.

The night passed mainly in sleepless imaginings of what
might happen ; but, with the light of Monday morning, she
tried to throw off the incubus, and busy herself with the tasks
which she knew were pleasing to him.

She noted that her father appeared restless, and that he at
last took his rifle, and disappeared among the hills.

About the middle of the forenoon she thought she heard,
faint and far away, the report of fire-arms, but tried to
ascribe the impression to her over-wrought and anxious
state.   But when the skirmishing commenced on the Orange
Furnace road, and there was no longer room for doubt, her
heart sank, with such an overwhelming foreboding of evil,
that she almost fainted.

But her native vigor and her strong affection for Saville
soon banished all weakness.   If her presentiment had any

foundation, it might be that even her hand could reach and minister to him.   While Vera had inherited her mother's gentleness, she also had her readiness to suffer anything for the sake of one she loved.

Summoning Tascar, she bade him prepare at once to accompany her toward Fort Montgomery.

"Take a small ax, some food, and materials for kindling a fire," she said.

At the same time she herself took some bandages, a flask of brandy that Saville had brought, and (what seemed a strange act in so gentle a maiden) she also concealed, in the folds of her dress, a keen-bladed hunting-knife.

"God grant I may have no use for this!" she sighed; "but I have been taught what some men are."

By the time that the first report of the field-piece was echoing through the mountains, they were on their way.

With a boldness which greatly taxed poor Tascar's courage, she approached so near the fort, that two or three half-spent cannon balls splintered the rocks a little below her hidden outlook.   Her eyes dilated with horror, as she watched the bloody conflict that was taking place almost at her feet.   Her keen eyesight enabled her to see men falling within the fort, as the strong north wind swept aside the smoke.   At times she could scarcely resist the wild impulse to rush through the ranks of the intervening enemy, and assure herself that Saville was not among those who lay motionless within the ramparts, or who were being carried to a more sheltered position.   Soon all became dusky and obscure in the early descending night.   The lurid flashes grew more distinct, and these indicated that the besiegers were drawing continually nearer the besieged.   As the lines of fire drew nearer and nearer, she pressed her hands upon her throbbing heart.   Then there came a great shout.   With lips parted, and eyes wild with terror, she sprang to the edge of the cliff. A dark mass was entering the fort. The flashes became intermingled, irregular ; they receded toward the river and the northeast side of the fort, and at last ceased.

She sat down, and covered her face with her hands, as she moaned shudderingly,

" He is lying yonder, bleeding or dying. I feel it—I know it ! O Tascar ! what shall we do ? "

But the poor boy could give no advice in this emergency.

Voices approached, and soon a stream of fugitives escaping to the mountains began to pass near where they had posted themselves.

" Quick, Tascar ! " said Vera. " Let us go to the edge of the path. You ask for Mr. Saville, and say you are his servant. I will hide within hearing."

This plan was at once carried out.

" O God ! grant that he may be among these who have survived," she sighed.

In response to Tascar's eager questions, several replied that they had seen Saville during the fight, but did not know where he was now.

The last weary and wounded straggler seemingly had passed, and Vera's hope was dying, when another step was heard, and a woman's voice was heard complaining.

" I hope poor Larry's aloive. I've tried so long to foind him, I've got ahint all the rest."

" O Captain Molly ! " began Tascar.

" Och ! ye spalpeen ; how ye stharted me. Me nerves is all shuck up ! "

" But, hab you seen Mas'r Saville ? "

" Is ye the little nig he had a few days, and thin sent off in the mountings ? "

" Yeh ; and I wants to find him po'ful bad."

" I'm sorry to tell ye, I'm afeard ye won't. God rest his sowl ! "

With a wild cry, Vera sprang out, and grasped the wom-an's arm.

" Speak ; what do you mean ?" she demanded.

" Holy Vargin !" gasped Molly. " I thought yees was a cat o' the mountings. Be ye the one they call the white witch ?"

" No ; I'm a poor, orphaned girl ; and Mr. Saville was my brother—my only friend. Tell me, have you seen him ?"

" Now, bless the poor young crather's heart, what kin I tell her ?" gröaned Molly, turning away and beginning to sob.

" You have told me all," said Vera, feeling as if turning into stone. " He is dead."

" I'm afeard he is, unless the saints has kept him aloive for the good turn he did for sich a poor wicked divil as I be. He saved me life—he kilt the big Hessian as was killin' me—ochone, ochone !" and Molly, in the exuber-ance of her feeling, sat down, and rocking herself back and forth, uttered a wild Irish wail of sorrow.

Vera's face grew almost as rigid as the granite on which she stood. After a few moments she said,

" You say he saved your life ?"

" He did, ochone ! he did, God rest his sowl !"

" If any one had saved my life," continued Vera, in a tone that was almost taunting, " I would not sit down and weakly whine about him."

" Now what do ye mane by that ?" cried Molly, starting up, and dashing away her tears.

" I mean that if he saved your life, you ought to be will-ing to try to save his. You are a strong woman, and have lived among soldiers ; but I will see if you are as brave as a timid young girl. Will you go with me, and bring him away, dead or alive ?"

"Faix an' I will," cried Molly sturdily. "I loikes this betther'n cryin' about him. Besides, I know jist where to look for him. It was behint Larry's gun he fell, and I could go there wid me eyes blinded. What's more, no gal, nor man nayther, dares do what Molly O'Flarharty darsent."

But Captain Molly's heroic fire was suddenly quenched for a few moments ; for Vera threw herself upon her neck, with sobs that caused the young girl's slight frame to quiver almost convulsively.

"Ye poor little tender-hearted crather," said Molly, crying in sympathy ; "yees jist as human as I be ; and I, like a pig-headed fool, was a-thinkin' ye was a witch ! Yees isn't able to go on any sich dare-divil irrend as snatchin' a body out o' the jaws of that orful baste they call the British lion."

"Wait a moment," said Vera, growing calm. "I shall be the better for these tears. I am, indeed, but a weak child ; but for Mr. Saville I could die a thousand deaths. Come."

"Well," said Molly, with a shrug, "it's only honest in me to risk one life for him, afther what he did for me. So I'm wid ye."

"You hab been kind to my ole mudder," said Tascar, "and I'll go wid you, too. Mas'r Saville is po'ful heavy, and'll take a sight ob liftin'."

"We must wait a bit," said Molly, "till them Britishers git the wounded gathered in. That's what they are doin' now where them lights is movin' 'round."

"But they will carry him off to die somewhere else," cried Vera, in great distress.

"No, child ; if they carry him off, the docthers'll take care of him. So, if we doesn't find him by the gun, ye kin comfort yer heart wid the thought that he's doin' well somewhere. If we shud go down there now, before they all git aslape, they wud treat us moighty oncivil."

" You are right," said Vera. " But it is desperately hard to wait."

" We hain't ready to go yit," continued Molly. " We must thry to rig up sumthin' to carry him on, or else I'll have to stale a stretcher down there, and that may be risky."

" I know what you mean," said Vera, catching the thought quick as light. " With Tascar's help, I can soon make one. Tascar, cut two long straight poles."

While the boy was obeying, Vera drew her hunting knife, and feeling around among the copse-wood, selected tough and very slender young saplings. Having secured a sufficient number, she twisted them back and forth across the poles, and secured them in their places with some fibrous bark, which she was not long in discovering. Never did her thorough wood-craft serve a better purpose than in this emergency.

" Ye're a moighty handy little thing," said Molly. " When did ye learn all these things ?"

" My heart would teach my hands to do anything that is needful to-night. Can we not go now ?"

" Not jist yet. Sit down and rest yerself. "

" As if I could rest ! Oh ! do let us go. It will be a comfort to get a few inches nearer. What a wild night it promises to be ! ' The bleak winds do sorely ruffle.' "

" All the betther for us ! There'll not be so many abroad. They're gittin' quiet, an' I think we may stale up a bit toward the place now. We've got to take quite a woide turn, anyhow, to git around the creek, for they'll have guards at the bridges. I know a place down here on the right, where we kin git over."

The strangely assorted group now started on their most perilous adventure, Molly leading, because familiar with the region, and Tascar bringing up the rear with the rude but strong stretcher which Vera had improvised. Molly's early years had made her perfectly familiar with the wild mountain region through which they must find a path, and she threaded her way quite as readily as Vera would have done in her own haunts.

"I've fished up and down this creek often enough to know every inch of it," said Molly, who was now as eager to serve Vera as she had once been to get her into trouble, for being so "stuck up an' oncivil loike;" and she was not long in leading her little party to a place where the shallow stream could be easily crossed. Then they ascended the further bank by a slanting path that led toward Fort Clinton.

"We must git well up on the hill," said Molly, "for they won't be a-lookin' for anybody on the mounting sides, and thin we kin crape intil the fort right by Larry's gun. Ochone, Larry, me darlint! I've been kind o' rough on ye sometoimes, an' if we both git through this wild night's work, I'll thry to be more aisy on ye. I tell you what 'tis, Miss Brown, when ye're ''twixt the divil an' the dape say,' as I've heerd some o' the sailor sogers spake, ye think on ivery oncivil thing ye iver said or did. May all the saints be wid us ! Faix, an' they ought to be !" she concluded, with sudden emphasis. "Ain't we a-thryin' to do as good a job as they iver did ?"

By this time Molly had reached the end of her theology, and exhausted her sentiment ; but her practical energies and shrewdness seemed inexhaustible. With firm yet stealthy tread, she led them down into the neighborhood of the fort, and her familiarity with military life enabled her to suspect just where guards and sentinels would be placed.

"Their fires show that they're down toward the river, loike," she whispered ; "an' that's good for us, too. If they git aither us, we must cut roight back on the path we come, as no one could foller it who didn't know it. Now step loight, an' keep yer mouths shut, for we're gittin' ticklish near."

Fortunately, the early part of the night was so dark that they must have stumbled immediately upon some one to be observed. As they approached quite near the fort, they heard a sentinel walking his beat. As his steps receded they slipped by, and sprang down into the ditch under the parapet, and then crouched a few moments, scarcely daring to breathe.

"Give me yer knife," whispered Molly. "I've stuck many a pig in my day, an' I'll stick a Hessian—yes, two or three on 'em—afore they'll git sich a holt on me as that big feller had as is lyin' dead over there."

Vera shuddered, but complied.

"Now," continued Molly, slowly rising, "let me git my bearin's, so we kin climb in jist beside Larry's gun."

The dark outline of the mountain soon satisfied her how to proceed, and she said, "Come around this way a bit."

Stumbling, with thrills of horror, over the dead that lay in the fosse, Vera followed. Suddenly Molly whispered,

"Hist, down!"

Footsteps approached, but died away again.

"Now wait a bit where ye are. I think this is the gun, and kin tell soon as I fale of it. Ah! ye ould bulldog, this is ye, thrue anuff. I made ye bite 'em the last toime, didn't I, ye good ould baste?"

Vera was at her side instantly, whispering, "Was it here he fell? Oh! quick, quick! I cannot endure this suspense a moment longer."

"Not too fast, or we may spoil iverythin' yit. I'll cloimb up this side o' the gun, an ye on that side. Let the bhoy bide down here till we call him Aisy loike, now," she cautioned, as Vera, with a bound, was up beside the cannon. "Let us look over and listen."

CHAPTER XXV.

THE WOMAN IN VERA AWAKES.

IN falling, Saville was not so stunned but that he had sufficient presence of mind to make the huge Hessian he had killed a sort of rampart against the thronging enemy, and the man who had bayoneted him was carried forward with the impetuous advance of the victors. He was well content to be somewhat trampled, instead of receiving another thrust which would pin him to the earth.

Almost his first thought was, " Vera's dream comes true I am desperately wounded, perhaps dying ; and she, poor child, in sad truth, can never find me here.''

As the rush of battle swept away elsewhere, so that he could venture to move, he tried, by feeling, to learn the nature of his wound, and found, with a thrill of hope, that a thick memorandum-book in his breast-pocket had caused the bayonet to glance from his vitals into his shoulder, inflicting what seemed only a flesh wound.

He soon became aware, however, that it was a deep one, and that he was losing blood rapidly. His main hope now was, that he might not become unconscious before the surgeons gathered up the wounded ; and yet he now dared show no sign of life, or assume any position that would attract notice ; for the brutal Hessian soldiery were raging around the fort, often striking down the wounded who begged for mercy ; so he turned over upon his face, and thus passed for one of the dead. When it became evident to the British officers that all resistance was over, they called off the "dogs of war," and soon none were left near Saville except those as helpless as himself. He now ventured to turn over again, and then tried to sit up, but found himself too weak.

Not far away, he heard a wounded man repeating to himself the text the chaplain had chosen the previous evening :

"I am the resurrection and the life ; he that believeth in me, though he were dead, yet shall he live :

"And whosoever liveth and believeth in me shall never die."

"Poor fellow !" thought Saville ; "believing that, he can die easily, and, after ceasing to be, can have no disappointment over his illusion. And yet, situated as we are, one might well wish that it were all true. Oh ! that a surgeon would come."

The surgeon was coming, but his blood and strength were ebbing fast. In the fierce excitement of the day, he had eaten scarcely anything ; and this abstinence, together with his previous night of toil and the loss of blood, made a fearful drain upon his vital powers. When, a little later, the light of a lantern was carelessly flashed upon his pallid face, the man who held it muttered, "He's done for," and passed on to those giving signs of life.

The deep swoon lasted while his wife's lover feasted his murderous eyes upon him.

Had Vera's prayers received no answer ? Why had he seemed like the dead, when a man stood over him who would have stamped out the faintest apparent spark of life ? Why does he revive again, now that Vera is stealing toward the fort ?

Slowly he became conscious of what had happened, of his desperate situation. He felt that the deep sighs that heaved his breast caused the slight remnant of his blood to ooze more rapidly.   He was now sure that he would die.

"Poor mother!" he groaned.   "Dear, kind mother! you will have a dreary old age."

A light step was gliding swiftly toward him.

"O Vera!" he murmured ;   "my more than sister, my heart's true mate!   How can I enter on my long, dreamless sleep, and leave you waking and suffering?"

She knelt beside him, sobbing.

"Theron, I have found you!   Thank God!"

"Is this real?" he said, in a husky voice.

"It is—feel my warm hand ; it's strong as a man's to rescue you!   There are others here to help.   Courage! O God! spare him, spare him, or let me die also!"

"Hist, aisy now," warned Molly.   "Kape all yees perty sayins till we're out o' this divil's nest o' Hessians.   Give him some brandy, while I call the bhoy wid the sthretcher."

As Vera put the flask to his lips, she whispered,

"You will live ; you will not die, and break my heart?"

"If mind has any power over matter, I *will* live," he said doggedly, "and more for your sake than my own. From henceforth my life is yours, my peerless Vera.   How, in the name of wonder, have you reached me?"

"Don't speak now.   Save every atom of strength.   Lay the stretcher here, Tascar.   Lift him gently now with me." And, as if endowed with tenfold her usual power, she put her arms under his shoulders, and lifted him on the green boughs that she had twined for the purpose.

"You are an angel of mercy," said Saville.

"Hush!   Now, Molly!"

"Git out o' the way, ye bloody spalpeen!" snarled Molly, giving the poor Hessian whom Saville had slain a contemptuous push with her foot.   "I'm glad ye got yer desarts."

With some difficulty they made their way over the parapet and fosse with their burden, and then started rapidly for the hills. When a little beyond the sentinel, Tascar stepped on a dry stick, which cracked sharply.

"Who goes there?" challenged the sentinel instantly.

"Whist! let the stretcher down a minute. If he comes to see, I'll fix him;" and she went back a few feet, and crouched like a panther at the side of the path.

As there were no further sounds, the man evidently thought that it was some animal in the woods, and continued walking his beat.

With throbbing hearts and stealthy tread, they again pressed on, Molly following, with the hunting-knife, as a sort of rear-guard; and they soon breathed freer, with a growing sense of security.

"Let me spell ye now," said Molly to Vera. "I've got a stronger back, if not a stouther heart, than yees."

They were not very long in reaching the place where the ax, provisions, and material for kindling a fire had been left. Vera took up these, and for an hour they toiled on, with frequent rests. Saville often essayed to speak, but Vera enjoined silence, and, when he grew faint, she put the flask to his lips.

At last they found a secluded place, quite out of the course that any of the fugitives would take, and hidden from the enemy in the forts by intervening hills. A brook ran near, and Saville's thirst was growing very painful. Vera thought they might venture to rest here, and kindle a fire. They were all desperately weary, and in need of food. Saville, also, was growing so weak that he might again become unconscious. Vera asked Molly to help Tascar gather dry wood, saying that she would wait on Mr. Saville, for she esteemed this so great a privilege that she was unwilling to share it.

"Never was there such music, excepting your voice, Vera, as the babble of that brook," said Saville feebly. "I have heard of the thirst of the wounded, but did not know what it was before."

Taking a cup from the bundle she had carried Vera soon placed a cool draught to his lips. He held her hand, as he drank eagerly.

"Oh! that gives me life," he said. "Did you mutter any potent words over this cup?"

"My every breath is a prayer for you," she said.

"It seems to me that you are answering your own prayers, my sweet divinity. I shall worship you while I have breath to pray or praise."

"Your mind is wandering, Mr. Saville."

"Never from you."

"Hush! you must not talk."

"Like all other devotees, I find it easier to worship than to obey."

"Please don't speak in this manner, Mr. Saville. I am so grateful to God for having spared you that your words pain me."

"And I am so grateful to you that I can scarcely find words that mean enough. May I live to show you how I feel! Do not call me Mr. Saville any more."

"Do you not think I had better try to dress your wound by the light of the fire, Theron?"

"Yes, do; your very touch is healing."

She took out her bandages, and bade Tascar heap light wood on the fire. Then, laying her sharp hunting-knife within reach, she set about her delicate and difficult task. But her beautiful face, as she bent over him, revealed only the deepest solicitude for him, and not a particle of embarrassing self-consciousness. She first took from his pocket the torn and deeply indented little memorandum-book.

"Theron," she exclaimed, "this saved your life!"

"I think it did. It was fortunate that it was in that pocket instead of the other."

"Fortunate! Oh! why do you use such meaningless words? It was so much more than fortunate! Will you give the book to me?"

"Yes."

She pressed her lips upon it, and hid it in her bosom.

Then Molly and Tascar were surprised to hear Saville's audible laugh, but tears were in Vera's eyes.

"Alack!" she sighed, dashing them away; "I am a foolish child, and not equal to this work. I must cut your coat, Theron."

"Yes," said he; "pass your knife up my sleeve; cut all away around my throat. It will not do for me to move much. I can direct you somewhat, for I know a little of surgery. On entering the service I foresaw wounds, but no such blissful experience as this."

"Only speak in directing me," said Vera, deftly doing his bidding. "Oh! what an awful gash!" and for a moment she covered her face with her hands.

"I tell you I am going to live, Vera. I feel it in every nerve and fiber of my body. How does the cut run?"

"Across the upper part of your breast, into your shoulder."

"You see it is a flesh wound merely. Remove only the clots of blood that prevent you from pressing the sides of the cut together. Now bandage as tightly as you can around my shoulder. There, that is right. How infinitely different your touch is from that of a half-drunk British surgeon! Suppose that in your place, my dainty Ariel, my ministering spirit, a broad-faced Hessian butcher were bending over me, bungling away with fingers as hard as his heart! That will do. Now cover all up well, so there may be no danger of my taking cold, and then rest yourself."

" I will rest when you are out of danger.   You must take some food now."

" Not much.   We must run no risk of inflammation."

Again she brought water from the brook, and dipping the hard, dry bread into it, fed him as she would a child.   She saw that his head did not rest comfortably, and so she lifted it gently into her lap.   But, as she did so, there came a warmer glow into her face than the ruddy firelight warranted.

" I will waken you," she said, " when it is time to re-sume our journey home."

" Home !   How sweet that word sounds, as you speak it !"

" Hush ! hush !"

" Well, then, good-night, Vera.   This is not the dream-less sleep that I was dreading in Fort Clinton."   And almost instantly he sank into quiet slumber.

Molly and Tascar, as soon as they found that they could do nothing more to serve Vera, had thrown themselves down by the fire, and were soon in deep oblivion.   But the young girl, with eyes as clear and steady as the stars which now shone brightly, watched through the silent hours.

She had never had less inclination to sleep.   There was a strange, delicious tumult in her heart.   She thought it was gladness and gratitude for Saville's escape.   She thought it was hope for the future.   She would understand, by-and-by, that it was far more.   A hand was on the door of the inner chamber of her heart.   Its silence was broken by a voice whose echoes would never cease.   During the agony, the fear, the awful suspense, of that eventful day, Vera had ceased to be a child, and had become a woman—strong to act and to suffer.   And now that the man, on whom she had leaned as might a younger sister, and whom she regarded as a superior being, far beyond and above her, had become utterly helpless—dependent on her for existence—woman-like, she began to love him as only a woman could love, and with the same spirit of self sacrifice and self-forgetful. ness which had been the characteristic of her mother.

Innocent love is happiness ; it brings its own reward ; and the more unselfish it is, the more profoundly it satisfies.

The world began to grow more beautiful to Vera, even on that chill autumn night, and the sounds of nature to make sweet chords with the new and mysterious impulses of her heart. The brook sang to her as of old, when she was a child ; but now with richer, deeper meanings ; the chirp of the crickets seemed cheery and companionable ; the light of the stars grew kindly and sympathetic. A stag, attracted by the fire, came and stood in the outer circle of light, and gazed at her a moment with his large, wistful, questioning eyes. With something of her old mirthfulness, she shook her finger at him, as if he were an unruly child, that might disturb the sleeper over whom she was watching, and the timid creature bounded away.

The hours passed swiftly, with strange, happy thoughts and fancies flashing up in her mind, as little understood as the mysterious aurora that was illuminating the northern sky.

The young girl was consciously puzzled by the fact that she was beginning to look forward to Saville's awakening with something like shyness and embarrassment ; her heart fluttered at the very thought. Heretofore, she had lifted her eyes and face to his with no more self-consciousness than that of a flower opening to the morning sun. And. yet, that which she half dreaded she anticipated with a new and vague delight.

Her finger often sought his pulse, and her confidence increased, as she found that it was quiet and even, though feeble.

As dawn began to tinge the eastern horizon, he seemed to grow uneasy. His brow contracted heavily, and, bending down, she heard him mutter,

"Stand aside ; your power to curse my life has gone."

Then, after a little, his face became calm and quiet for a while. But soon another painful dream disturbed him, and from broken words and sentences it was evident that he was living over the terrible scenes in Fort Clinton. Suddenly he said, quite plainly,

"Vera, my heart's true mate, how can I leave——" and he started up, and looked wildly around for a moment.

"Theron," said Vera gently, "it's only a dream ; and dreams, you told me, ' go by contraries.' "

He looked at her earnestly a moment, and then asked, "What has happened ?"

"I dreamt that you would be wounded, and alas ! it came true. I also dreamt that I could not find you ; but, thank God ! the contrary was true."

"Oh, yes ; it all comes back to me now. You found me dying in the fort."

"But you promised to live," said Vera, with a sudden chill of fear.

"Did I ? My head is confused. Will you please give me a little water ?"

Trembling with apprehension, she hastened to the stream, and returned with the cool and refreshing water. This awakening was so different from what she expected.

After taking the water he seemed better, and his eyes sought hers wistfully and questioningly.

"I am very weak," he said ; "you must be patient with me."

"O Theron ! live ! live ! that is all I ask !"

"I feel that I shall, Vera ; but it may be long before I am well. You were holding my head when I awoke."

"Let me support it again," she said blushing, and she lifted his head into her lap.

"I want to see your face."

"No, no," she answered hastily ; "look at the beautiful dawn yonder."

"Your face is to me more beautiful and more full of hope than the morning. Are you sure that you are well ? I have had such painful dreams. Please let me see you and reassure myself."

She moved so as to comply with his wish, and as he fixed his eyes eagerly upon her face, it drooped, and a warmer light stole into it than glowed in the eastern sky.

"I do see the dawn in your face," he said, "and it grows more lovely every moment. Have you been watching over me all the long night ?"

"It has not seemed long," she faltered.

"Vera !"

She raised her eyes timidly to his, but they soon fell again before his ardent gaze.

"Vera, your face contains the true elixir of life, I shall get well, never fear !"

"O Theron ! I am so glad—so very happy. But if you cannot sleep any more, had we not better try to get home ?"

"Yes," he replied, in a voice of deep content ; "take me home."

She was glad to escape. Arousing Tascar and Molly, they were soon on their way to the secluded mountain gorge, in which was the rude cabin, which, to Saville, promised to be a haven of rest such as he had never known before.

CHAPTER XXVI.

VERA'S ONLY CRIME.

AFTER a toilsome, difficult journey, during which Saville's wound became very painful, they reached the cabin. Old Gula met them with a scared expression on her wrinkled face, but was overjoyed at finding Tascar and Vera safe.

"I'se had an orful time," she said. "Strange, loud voices, speakin' among de hills, an' I didn't know what dey mean. Den Mas'r Brown come home wild and drefful, a-cryin' dat all was lost. Den he sat a long time like a stun. All on a sudden he ask, 'Whare's Vera?' I telled him dat you took Tascar, and went away yesterday mornin'. And he began to go on orfully agin, and took de big gun and went arter you."

"Well," said Vera, with a sigh, "if he does not come soon, I will try to find him. Mr. Saville has been badly wounded, and we must all do our best for him. You get us some breakfast. Tascar, make a fire on the hearth in the cabin, and then help your mother. Molly, will you help me carry Mr. Saville in?"

They laid him down on the cabin floor, and Vera brought a pillow, saying, as she placed it under his head, "You are at home, Theron," and was well rewarded by his contented smile.

One end of the cabin had been partitioned off into two apartments. In one of these a couch was prepared for

Saville ; but, as they were about to carry him thither, Mr. Brown entered in strong excitement, exclaiming,

"Great God ! Vera. What does this mean ?"

"Hush, father !"

"Are you bent on my destruction ? Why have you brought this strange woman here ?"

"I'm not so moighty strange," snapped Molly.

"Mr. Brown," said Saville, in his old, significant tone.

The exile turned tremblingly to him.

"You are safe, as I told you, just as long as you do exactly as I direct. Sit down there and rest, and all will be well."

The man obeyed, but was evidently dissatisfied, and under great perturbation.

Before the day was over, both Vera and Saville were satisfied that the services of a surgeon would be required. Molly was anxious to depart, that she might find her husband, Larry. Vera therefore decided, without consulting her father, to send Tascar with her across the mountains to New Windsor. Molly thought that all who had escaped from the forts would probably be in that region, and said that she knew the way well, after she got down near to the river ; so it was arranged that they should go early the next morning.

Saville slept a great deal of the time, and seemed strengthened by the nourishing broth which Gula made for him. His deep content, and the anticipation of Vera's society and care, did more than anything else to forward recovery.

The next morning. Molly and Tascar departed. Vera accompanied them, and directed the boy to blaze the trees until the path became plain. Molly did not tell Vera that she had learned from her husband a great deal about Saville's previous life, nor did she hint that he had a wife living in New York. The redoubtable "captain's" ideas concerning morals were rather confused, at best ; but, in this case, she acted in accordance with such light as she had, and her reasoning was simple, if not correct. Saville had saved her life ; and, whether he was right or wrong, she was in honor bound not to put a straw in his way ; and, from what Larry had told her about Saville's wife, she felt that no one had a truer right than he to find a better one.

Toward the close of the following day Tascar returned, and, to Vera's great joy, was accompanied by her old acquaintance, Surgeon Jasper. He pronounced Saville's wound severe, but not dangerous, if he had good care and nursing ; ''and that, I know, he will get,'' he added, with a glance that brought the rich color into Vera's face, which, for some reason that she could not understand, was now so ready to come and go.

'' I am here, prepared to stay a few days,'' said the kind surgeon ; ''and when I leave, good living and sleep will be all that are needed, I think.''

'' How can I repay you ?'' exclaimed Vera, taking his hand.

''No occasion for thanks,'' was the brusque reply. '' This is my business, and we can't afford to lose such good soldiers as Saville.''

Her father chafed greatly, at first, when he found that another stranger had learned of his hiding-place, but the man was so genial and frank, and the fact that he had been at the bedside of Vera's mother partially reconciled the exile to his presence. The surgeon, also, raised his hopes that the American cause was not hopelessly lost, as he had believed on the capture of the forts.

Under skilled treatment, Saville's wound healed rapidly, and he was soon able to sit up before the fire on the ample hearth of the cabin. The genial surgeon was the life of the party during the long autumn evenings, and to Vera these hours were ever remembered as among the happiest of her life.

Whenever it was possible, she found Saville's eyes following her with an expression that warmed her very soul ; but she, in her innocence, imagined that his rapid recovery was the cause of the springs of joy welling up in her heart.

But, as Saville grew stronger, he often fell into gloomy fits of musing, which perplexed and distressed her. She also noted a troubled expression on the surgeon's face, as some little act on the part of Saville suggested that his feelings were warmer than gratitude or friendship inspired.

Jasper knew that Saville had a wife, and, moreover, that she was a wife only in name. He felt that Vera was too fine a girl to be trifled with ; but as she was situated, the man to whom she had unconsciously given her heart might do more to make than mar her happiness. At any rate, the surgeon, who was a man of the world, concluded that it was not his business to interfere, and so at last took his departure in his wonted jovial manner.

" I suppose you won't thank me, Saville," he said, " for taking you away from this fairies' bower ; but I shall report to the governor that you will be fit for duty in a month."

" I shall not forget that I am a soldier," said the young man, flushing ; " and you may see me in less time."

After the surgeon's departure, Saville's moody fits did not cease, but rather increased. While he was exceedingly kind and gentle, Vera saw that he was passing under some kind of restraint ; his eyes did not seek hers with the old, frank, ardent expression ; and, at times, she observed him regarding her furtively, and with such a sad, wistful look, that she began to shed tears in secret, though, with womanly instinct, she tried to appear cheerful, and blind to all changes in him.

But when his growing distress of mind began to retard his

recovery, she felt that she could endure it no longer.   One
day, when he scarcely tasted some delicate birds which she
had shot for him, she burst into tears, and said,

"Theron, what is the matter?   I can shut my eyes to
the truth no longer.   Something is preying upon your mind.
You have a deeper wound than that which Surgeon Jasper
healed.   For the last few days, you have failed, rather than
gained, in health."

He grew very pale, and did not immediately answer.

"I do not ask to know the cause of your trouble," she
continued ; "for you would tell me if you thought best ;
but I cannot endure to see you suffer.   If there is anything
that a poor, friendless young girl like myself can do, I pray
you, speak plainly.   Believe me, I would think any self-
sacrifice that would serve you a privilege."

"Any sacrifice, Vera?"

"Any, any that you can ask," she replied eagerly.

But, looking into her pure, innocent face, and rem m-
bering how totally ignorant she was of the world's harsh
judgment, his own manhood rose up to defend her.

He took both of her hands in his, and said, very gently,
"I believe you, my dearest sister ; you are unselfishness
itself.   But no cruel self-sacrifice on your part would help
me.   Some day I will tell you what is troubling me.   I cannot now.   The miserable and misgoverned world, of which
you know so little, often brings to those who must be out
in it many hard problems to solve.   Rest assured, if I need
your help, I will ask it, and would rather have it than that
of any other living being.   Now take your gun, and get me
some more birds, and at supper I will try to do better."

She saw that he wished to be alone, and so, sorely perplexed and heavy-hearted, she complied.

After she was gone, Saville grappled with the strongest
temptation which life had yet brought him.   In the eye of

the law, he had a wife, and could not marry Vera, and yet he loved her with the whole intensity of his nature. From the hour, also, when she blushed under his searching glance in the early dawn, at the time of their bivouac in the mountains, he had thought she was learning to give him a warmer affection than that of a sister. In his weakness and inability to think connectedly, this hope had filled him with a sort of delirium of happiness ; but he had soon commenced asking himself how this mutual regard must end.

With his French education, and as an honest adherent to the creed that the impulses of nature should be man's only law, he required no priestly sanction to his love ; but could have said to Vera, in all sincerity, '' My heart claims you ; my reason approves the choice. I cannot help my past folly, but know that I am acting wisely now. I will ever be your true lover. I will be such a husband as love can make me, and such as mere form and law cannot.''

While all this was true, he also clearly saw that Vera in remembrance of her mother's teaching and example, and with her faith in the Bible, and in the Being whose will she believed that book revealed, would not look upon any such relation in the light in which it appeared to him. Although the young girl had proved her readiness to sacrifice her life for him, there had always been something in her words and manner which led him to doubt greatly whether he could induce her to violate her conscience, even though that which he asked seemed perfectly right to him.

In justice to Saville, it should be said, that though he regarded her faith as an utter delusion, he would not wish her to do anything which she thought wrong ; and, although he could honestly declare his love, he felt that it would be a base thing to ask her to reward it, since she could not do so without great moral wrong to herself.

There were, besides, other very important considerations.

He had always promised Vera, and had sincerely proposed to secure for her, a recognized and respected place in society. If she listened to his suit, this would be impossible.

She was defenseless, friendless, more than orphaned. She trusted him implicitly, and, as a man of honor, he found that he could come to but one conclusion. He must be true to her interests, at any and every cost to himself.

"Am I equal to this?" he groaned, and he strode up and down the little cabin in such agony, that great beaded drops came out upon his forehead.

At last he sat down, and covered his face with his hands, while his mind went rapidly over the past. In imagination, he saw the timid maiden venturing down into the dark fort, where on every side a fate worse than death threatened, that she might rescue him.

"I am a base wretch to hesitate," he cried ; "but would that I had died there, rather than have lived to suffer this ! She shall not surpass me in self sacrifice, however. I will place her as high in society as a brother's love can raise her, and then, if the burden grows too heavy, I can soon enter on the dreamless sleep from which she recalled me. O hating and hateful wife ! even your malignity would be satisfied if you could see me now."

Vera returned empty-handed. "My hand trembled so that I could not shoot," she said. "I am very sorry."

"Never mind, little sister ; I am better now, and do not need anything," he said soothingly, for he saw that her heart was full.

"Better !" she cried, with tears starting to her eyes. "You are but the ghost of your old self. I never saw you so pale, and you look years older than when I left you an hour ago."

"You are tired and depressed, Vera. Come and sit down by me on your low bench, and see if I cannot cheer you."

She gave him a wistful, questioning look, which he found it hard to meet.

Making a strong effort at self-control, she complied with his wish, and for a few moments neither spoke. Again and again she would look at him, with the same childlike, questioning manner.

" What is it, little sister ?" he at last asked.

For some reason, this term, which had once seemed so sweet and endearing, but which of late he had seldom employed, now chilled her heart with fear. His face, though very kind, had a strong, resolved expression. She felt as if a viewless but impassable barrier were growing up between them. While at her side, and holding her hand, he still seemed far off and receding. He called her his " dear little sister," and yet she would rather that he should say simply, Vera, in the tone in which he had spoken her name, when, after her night's watch, she had raised her downcast eyes to his. She neither understood herself nor him, but her heart craved for more than mere brotherly affection ; and now that he sought to manifest only this, he rudely jarred the deepest and most sensitive chord of her being. When he again asked, in a gentle, soothing tone, as he might speak to a child, " Tell me what troubles you, sister Vera. Speak as frankly as if I were indeed your brother," she bowed her head upon his knee, and sobbed as if her heart would break.

" I don't know what is the matter," she faltered. " It seems as if you were miles away from me, and that something dreadful is going to happen."

A spasm of pain crossed his face, for he interpreted her feelings far better than she could herself ; and he learned, as never before, how penetrating a loving woman's intuitions often are.

Suddenly she asked, " Are you going to leave me, Theron ?"

He had about decided to tell her the whole truth, and show the necessity of his course, when her father entered the cabin. Before doing so, he had marked his daughter's attitude and distress, also Saville's caresses as he stroked her bowed head. He said nothing, however, but sat down in his accustomed place, with the deepest gloom lowering upon his haggard face.

Vera was about to move hastily away, but Saville retained her at his side, saying,

"No, Vera ; no one has a better right here than you."

For a little time they all remained silent. Vera made desperate efforts to gain the mastery of her feelings, though with but partial success ; for she felt that some blow was impending, which she could not avoid, and yet from which she shrank in sickening dread.

At last Saville began, in a quiet, steady voice,

"Mr. Brown, I have so far recovered from my wound that I ought soon to report for duty again. I feel that it would be very wrong to leave you here in this remote and lonely place. I tremble as I think of what might happen in case of sickness or accident. Moreover, the country is filled with lawless, reckless men, as you have learned, to your sorrow."

The exile sprang up, and commenced pacing the room in great excitement, but Saville continued firmly,

"You owe it to Vera to place her in a more secure position. This wild mountain gorge is no place for her. She is fitted to shine among the highest and best, and I think I can say, without boasting, that I have the influence to place her there. All that——"

A harsh, bitter laugh interrupted him, and her father said,

"Mr. Saville, you are unequaled at sarcasm."

The young man rose and faced the speaker, and Vera,

also, stood tremblingly at his side. "I mean every word
I say. I can——" he began earnestly.

"Mr. Saville," again interrupted the exile, "your words
are worse than useless. It is time you learned the truth.
For the sake of the past, in memory of what my daughter
braved in your behalf, you will at least leave us unmolested,
after you learn who and what we are. Blinded as I am by
remorse and fear, I have still marked your growing affection
for Vera ; and though I am but a wreck—a miserable frag-
ment of a man—I have still some sense of honor and justice
left. You are a gentleman, sir. I knew that from the
first ; and it is not right that you should associate with
such as we are any longer."

"You are talking wildly, sir. You are not yourself."
Saville answered soothingly.

"I am speaking terrible truth," continued the unhappy
man. "Whatever else has failed in me, memory has not,
and it is my hourly and relentless scourge. But enough of
this. It is sufficient to say that we are outcasts. A curse is
resting on us, which must die with us. This is no place for
you, and you will bear me witness, that I never sought to
draw you within the deadly shade of my destiny. I have
but one favor to ask—that you leave us to perish as remote
from human knowledge as possible."

"I cannot do this," cried Saville, quite off his guard.
"Why are you outcasts ? What crime has this innocent
maiden committed, that I should heartlessly leave her to so
horrible a fate ?"

"What crime has she committed ? The same as that of
her poor, fond mother, the crime of belonging to me, and
of being a part of me. Would you ally yourself—would
you even associate—with the daughter of one of the worst
criminals on the face of the earth ?"

With a faint cry, Vera fell to the floor, as if struck down

by a resistless blow.   Saville instantly lifted her up, say·
ing,

"Don't grieve so, darling. He charges you with nc
fault, only misfortune."

Her father looked at him in great surprise for a moment,
and then said,

"Well, since you differ so greatly from the rest of the
world, you may take her away, where her relation to me
may never be known. If she could escape from under the
curse which crushed her mother, I would esteem it a boundless favor. For me there is no hope."

"Will you go with me, Vera?" asked Saville gently,
pressing her closer to his heart.

"Go, Vera, go, since he is willing to take you," said her
father earnestly. "The thought that you were safe and
happy would render the miserable remnant of my life more
endurable."

Vera's sobs ceased speedily, and she became very quiet.
After a moment or two, she raised her head from Saville's
shoulder, and said distinctly,

"No, I will not leave you. You are my father, and my
dying mother commended you to my care."

"O God!" exclaimed her father, "that I should have
brought down the curse on two such hearts! My punishment is greater than I can bear."

"Theron," continued Vera, drawing away from him,
and trying to steady herself in her weakness and strong emotion, "the blow has fallen ; I have felt it coming all day.
We must indeed part ; there is no help for it, for my duty
is here. You must leave us to our fate ; for, as father says,
you cannot continue to associate with such as we are."

"Leave you!" he cried, drawing her closely to his side,
and looking down into her pale face with an honest, manly
flush of indignation on his. "May every plague in nature

fall on my dishonored head if I do ! You are rightly called ' Vera,' for a truer heart than yours never beat ; and I am not such a fool as to lose it. I shall not ask her to leave you, sir," he said, addressing her father. "But I charge you, by the memory of your dead wife, and as you value your safety, to place no obstacle in my way, as I seek to make her happy in this, her mountain home."

"Theron," said Vera, in a low, thrilling tone, that he never forgot, "I did not know that there was so noble a man in all the world."

"Give me no credit," he replied. "To very few does there come such a chance for happiness as I have found in you. Come with me out under the starlight, for I have much to say to you."

Before leaving the cabin, however, he turned to her father, who sat with his face buried in his hands, and said,

"I know not, and will never seek to know, what you have done, and I believe that your remorse is greater than your crime ; but, as the father of this dear and innocent maiden, I shall always treat you with respect. You have acted honorably to-night, and I honor you for it. I take my present course deliberately, and with my eyes fully open."

"I fear that you will have cause for regret ; and yet, for Vera's sake, I hope it may be for the best."

"I will never leave you, father," said his daughter, ten derly putting her arms around his neck, and kissing him.

Tears came into the poor man's eyes, and he said huskily,

"I am not worthy of this. Go, go ; it pains me !"

Saville, in the impulse of his strong love and excitement, had decided to tell Vera just how he was situated, believing that, in view of the circumstances, she would accept of his life long devotion, though unsanctioned by any formal rites ; but her first glad and natural utterance, as they stepped out into the quiet night, checked the words upon his lips.

"Thank God!" she cried; "thank God! How good my Heavenly Father has been to me! Oh! that I could tell mother how happy I am!"

Saville was silent. It was his turn to experience a prophetic chill of dread. What had that old Hebrew divinity, at whom he had scoffed so many years, to do with his happiness or hers? But now He rose up before him like a grim, remorseless idol, to which the maiden at his side, so gentle and loving, and yet so strong, might sacrifice both herself and him.

Prudence whispered, "You had better not tell her to-night, you have too much at stake; wait." And so, instead of telling her the sad story of his past blindness and folly, with their consequences, he led her thoughts away from every painful theme, resolving that they both should have one happy hour, whatever might be on the morrow. And yet, remembering the only relation he could offer, he did not dare speak frankly of his love, and could only comfort her with the general assurance that he would never leave her to the desolation which her father's language had so awfully described. He spoke of their old, happy trysts, and promised that they should be continued as often as his duties permitted. Thus, while he did not openly and formally declare his love, it so pervaded his tone and manner as to abundantly satisfy Vera, whose quick intuitions scarcely needed words.

CHAPTER XXVII.

VERA MUST BECOME AN ATHEIST.

THAT night Saville slept but little. He had thought that he had settled, in the afternoon, the question of his future relation to Vera ; but the strange, unexpected events of the evening, after her father's return, had given the problem, in his view, an entirely new aspect. The future he had proposed for the maiden—the chance for a happy life under its ordinary and normal conditions in society— seemed utterly blotted out and rendered impossible, and through no fault or weakness of his.

Saville was full of generous and noble impulses, and Vera's fidelity to her father excited his boundless admiration and respect, and greatly increased his affection for her. In con- trasting the faithful girl with his selfish and malicious wife, he could scarcely believe that they both belonged to the same race.

But, as he saw that Vera's beauty of character equaled that of her form and features, the more unspeakable became his reluctance to attempt any such self-sacrifice as he had re- solved upon in the afternoon. Nor did it now seem neces- sary, or even right, that he should. Every avenue into the world was closed against her, and she looked to him alone for happiness.

The fact of her love was most apparent ; and she, no more than himself, could be satisfied with the fiction of fraternal affection.

But one thing now stood in the way of their happiness, and that was what he regarded as her superstitious faith. Holding her present belief, what he must propose would seem wrong, and only by teaching her his own philosophy could he make it appear otherwise. But even if this were possible, he had promised, at her mother's grave, on the day of burial, that he would never do aught to shake the child's confidence in that mother's teachings, or lead from the course which the parent would approve. Did not that pledge prove as insuperable a bar as his wretched marriage? And he cursed his destiny as the most cruel that had ever fallen to the lot of man.

But as, in the long, wakeful hours, he sought some solution of the problem, this thought occurred: When he made that promise, he had foreseen no such emergency as this. Should he be more loyal to his own hasty pledge than to her whose welfare now wholly depended upon him? In breaking the promise, he would only be more true to her. He believed that her mother was only a memory. She was dead; she had ceased to exist. He was a strong, living friend.

As long as the religious delusion which the mother had taught her child had been a comfort and a support, it was right and kind not to disturb it. But should he permit this delusion—this old, antiquated superstition, from which the advanced thinkers of the world were fast freeing themselves —to stand in the way of actual and priceless advantages? Both Vera and himself would soon cease to exist, and the opportunity for enjoyment would pass away forever. Why, then, let an imaginary spectre in the path, that a bold approach and scrutiny would dissipate, prevent a lifetime of happiness? Was he not even under sacred obligations to take the trammels from her mind, when they would cause such remediless loss?

The honest theorist believed that duty coincided with inclination, and starting with this premise, there was no other
conclusion possible.

But the question which troubled him most was, Could he
do this? He had been shown how much the word duty
meant to Vera. Her faith was simple and absolute, and
having been taught by her mother, was most dear and sacred.
He foresaw that the task would be exceedingly difficult, and
yet there seemed no other course.

He resolved to attempt it as the only way out of his cruel
dilemma ; and it was a habit of his mind, when he had
reasoned a thing out to his satisfaction, to rest firmly in the
conclusion. It was not in his nature to be ever looking
back with doubts and misgivings. He had no fears but that
he could make a home in that secluded mountain region,
after the war was over, which would contain more of the
elements of happiness than he could find elsewhere. And
if she were willing, he was perfectly ready to proclaim to the
world that the impulses of nature are the only true and bind-
ing laws, and to support his creed by his open example. He
knew that his proud, conservative mother would never approve
of his course, but this was too near and personal a question
to be decided by her prejudices. He therefore decided to
conceal the fact of his marriage from the maiden, as much
for her sake as his own. For, if she learned of it prema-
turely, before receiving the enlightenment of mind which he
hoped to bring by his teaching, she, in her strong superstition, might destroy, not only his happiness, but her own.

Having settled upon his course, he fell into a refreshing
slumber, which lasted till late in the following morning,
when he was awakened by the report of Vera's gun. On
going out, she met him joyously, exclaiming,

" My aim is truer to-day. See what a royal dinner you
are to have !"

" I will come to your banquet, Queen Esther."

" You might do worse. And I'm glad you have no hateful Haman to bring with you." Then she added musingly, " How often I have read that story. Do you know that I think some of those old Bible tales are very strange?"

" Little wonder," he replied, with an expressive shrug.

' But I believe them," she said stoutly.

' I do not doubt it," he replied laughing ; " even to the acceptance of that marvelous, long-eared beast which was wiser than the prophet, and spoke his master's vernacular. There, forgive me ! I did not mean to pain your dear, credulous heart. You must remember, in charity to me, how these stories sound to a man. I hope you feel as well and happy as I do this morning. But I need not ask, when I see the tints of these October leaves in your cheeks."

" Here is one that is brown, and here another, yellow and green," replied Vera, in like playful spirit, permitting the cloud to pass from her brow.

" And here is one as beautiful as that dawn which I saw reflected in your face after the night you so patiently watched over me. Was that rich color only the reflection of the sky, Vera?"

" You had just waked up, and could not see anything plainly. But a busy housekeeper must not stand idling here. Come and see what Gula has for breakfast."

The day passed like a happy dream to them both. With a shy, maidenly reserve, Vera checked any open expression or manifestation of the love she was content to see in his face and catch in his tones, while the garish light of day lasted. But when they again walked out in the starlight, Saville would be put off no longer, and he asked,

" Vera, do you know why it was impossible for me to leave you?"

" You said, yesterday afternoon, that I was your dear sis-
er," she faltered.

" That is an endearing term ; but did it satisfy you ?"

She was silent, and he felt her hand tremble on his arm.

" I do not think it did. Your wistful eyes, unconsciously
to yourself, pleaded for something more—some dearer term.
Am I not right ?"

" Do you remember what you were saying when I found
you in Fort Clinton ?" she asked in a low tone.

" Tell me what I said."

" I would rather that you remembered."

" I was thinking of you, Vera. I supposed they would
be my last waking thoughts, and I said, ' My more than
sister, my heart's true mate.' Were not those my words ?"

" Yes ; and they have made sweet echoes in my ears ever
since, though I did not till last night understand all they
meant."

" Have they not made echoes in your heart also ? Have
you not found your own true mate ?"

" ' Thou knowest,' Theron, ' the mask of night is on my
face ; else would a maiden blush' tell you all. I cannot
add, with Juliet,

> If thou think'st I am too quickly won,
> I'll frown, and be perverse, and say thee nay ;

for you know well, already, that I am wholly yours. Indeed, if my heart had been as cold toward you yesterday as
it was tender, I could not fail of being won by your generous—O Theron ! your course toward me, who am so
poor, friendless, and shadowed with evil and shame, over-
whelms me with gratitude."

" Any other course would bring me life-long wretchedness. Now what cause have you for gratitude ?"

" More cause, since what you give is not an alms ; for
though I should perish without your love, I could not take

it as a charity. But are you sure you will never regret your action? My heart misgives me when I think of it; the world can offer you so much! You might easily win one who is dowered with wealth, rank, and beauty, instead of poor me, who am heiress only of a curse.''

Saville thought, with a mental oath of execration, how he had won such a one as she described; but, with the purpose of banishing all such misgivings on her part, he said,

'' If I were an ambitious boy who had never seen the world, there might, possibly, be some ground for your fears; but from my youth I have been out in the world, and know much about it; and never, in my happiest moments there, did I experience half the content I found in your companionship, even when I was first learning to know your worth, as we talked together on the height back of your old home, near West Point. Now that I have come to love you, now that I justly honor you above all other women, can you imagine I could ever think of another? It is because I have seen the world, and know what it contains, and how little it can do for me, that I prize you far beyond it all; and it is because you are so innocent and unworldly that you do not know your own value. If I had met you in society, I should have had scores of rivals.''

'' Now I fear you are flattering me,'' she said laughing; '' but you would have had no cause for fear. I shall come to believe in my value only as I can make you happy.''

'' Then I fear you will grow vain, indeed, for you will find that your power is unbounded in this respect.''

'' O Theron! if I could induce you to accept of my faith, what you say would eventually be true. I cannot help telling you now, at the commencement of our new and happy life, that I can never rest—never be satisfied—till mother's favorite words from the Bible, ' Let not your heart be troubled, neither let it be afraid,' mean to you what they did to her and do to me. For some reason, God had seemed afar off, and I was losing my faith in His goodness and mercy ; but, from the time He enabled me to find you in the fort, I have felt differently, and now I cannot thank and love Him enough.''

Saville was dismayed. This was reversing matters, and the one he proposed to win over to atheism was fully bent on leading him to become a Christian.

After a moment she added, '' I miss my Bible so much. Won't you get me another, Theron ?''

'' I cannot,'' he said, a little abruptly ; and then continued. very gently, '' We must agree to dismiss this subject, Vera, darling. The Bible is not to me what it is to you, and it never can be. Great as my faults are, I try to be honest ; and with you I cannot help being sincere. If you regarded the Bible as a result of human genius, like the plays of Shakespeare, I would get you one. But I cannot aid you in making its unnatural teaching and stories the law of your conscience.''

'' O Theron !'' exclaimed Vera, bursting into tears, and hiding her face upon his shoulder.

'' I knew what I said would pain you, darling, but I could not help it. Would you have me act the part of a hypocrite ? I am just as sincere as you are. You have told me your views and faith, and I tell you mine. As you believe in the Bible, I believe in man and nature ; and I see in you her most perfect work.''

'' But God is the author of both man and nature,'' said Vera eagerly.

'' I see no proof of it, and much to the contrary,'' answered Saville decidedly. '' Moreover, the great and wise of the world, who do their own thinking, hold the same views that I do. As the subject has come up between us, I could not help being honest with you, as I ever shall be ; but do not let us dwell on it any longer now."

Vera sighed deeply, but said only, " I cannot understand how any one can be so good and noble as you are and not believe in the Bible.   I never even dreamed that it could be otherwise than true, and to doubt it seems impossible.   And yet I know you are as sincere as I am."

" And thus you prove that you are no bigot, darling ; for, as a general thing, the devotees of all the various religions of the world are prone to regard those who cannot think just as they do as willful, wicked wretches, who ought to be knocked promptly on the head.   If you can't convert me, I am sure you will not put me to torture, will you, dear ?"

" If I did, I should torture myself most.   But, Theron, this is too sad a subject for me to jest about.   I shall never cease to hope that you will some day think as I do.   God can incline your heart toward Him as easily as He bends the tops of yonder trees."

" Now, Vera, darling, that is the wind which is bending the treetops.   Let us drop this subject for the present.   We have both been honest with each other, and we could not be otherwise.   There is so much on which we lovingly and heartily agree, why dwell on the one thing wherein we differ ?"   And he strove, with all a lover's zeal, to banish her sad thoughts.   She loved him too well to permit him to see that he failed.   Indeed he did not fail.   The cup of happiness which he placed to her lips filled her with a strange delight, even while she remained conscious that it contained one bitter dreg.

The following days passed all too quickly for them both. It was part of Saville's scheme to enchain her affections, so that she could not take any other course, when the test came, than that which he proposed ; and it would seem that he was succeeding beyond his hopes.   Her capability of

loving ~as large, and she had but few other ties and interests to draw her thoughts from him. His mind was culti-
vated, versatile, ever full of bright, fresh thoughts ; and thus
his society was to her like a sweet, exhilarating wine. But
that which weighed more with her than all else was the ever-
present memory of his devoted loyalty to her, when she
knew that the great majority of the world would have shrunk
away. She looked forward to their parting with inexpressible dread, and the remembrance of the constant dangers
to which as a soldier he must be exposed, gave to her affection a tenderness, which only those who hold their heart-
idols in uncertain tenure can understand.

During the latter part of his stay, Saville wasted no hours
in love-idyls ; but was busy, in every possible way, in providing for her security and comfort during the coming winter. He sent Tascar repeatedly across the mountains for
such things as were needed, and also employed him in con
structing a secure though hidden bridle-path down into the
glen. He induced Mr. Brown to aid him in building sub-
stantial shelter for a horse, two or three cows, and some
poultry. On the margin of a neighboring pond there was
still forage which might be cut, which, with the grain that
he intended to send, would be sufficient provision until
spring again brought its abundant supply.

Vera amused Saville one day by her spirit of independence.

" We cannot receive all this," she said, " without making some return."

" Give me a kiss, and I am amply repaid," he answered.

" I am in earnest," she continued. " Is there not some
way in which I can earn money ?"

" Yes, you have only to do as I ask, and you shall receive
the greater part of my pay."

"But something tells me that this is not right, Theron; at least, not yet."

He knew that she meant not until they were married. But, feeling that he could never have a better right than now, he tried to satisfy her by saying,

"Since I am yours, body and soul, can I not share that with you which I value only as it can minister to your comfort? This is the beginning of our future home, and you are doing more to make it homelike than I can."

"Oh dear!" she cried, half pouting, half laughing; "do men always have their own way?"

"No, my fairy queen. I will one day be your slave."

"Why not add that you will take the part of Caliban, and that I will call 'What, ho! slave! Caliban! make our fire; fetch in our wood.' Oh! but you will be 'a brave monster,' Theron!"

"Now I think of it, I will be Prospero, and you 'my quaint Ariel.' But I will never give thee thy freedom."

"Indeed! this is reversing the order; and yet I think you are nearer right now. I am 'to answer thy best pleasure,' and do 'thy strong bidding.' Your pet name of Ariel always makes me laugh, however, for you forget that the spirit says, 'To thy strong bidding task Ariel, and all *his* quality.' Tascar must be your Ariel, and I will be——"

"My heart's true mate. Come, there is Gula summoning us to supper;" and with a glance that gave the confiding girl more assurance than could any words, he led her within the cabin that he already called "home," and to which their united labors were fast giving a homelike and inviting character.

The parting which soon came was a sore trial to Vera, though, woman-like, she sought to hide from her lover how deeply she was pained. She comforted herself with his assurance, however, that in all probability he would not be far away, and that he could often visit her.

CHAPTER XXVIII.

A HASTY MARRIAGE.

ON reaching the headquarters of the force defending the Highlands, Saville received a warm welcome from his old associates and acquaintances. And yet he could not help noting something in their manner which both puzzled and annoyed him. He, at first, suspected that Surgeon Jasper had gossiped concerning his fair hostess and nurse ; and, therefore, drew him aside, with the intention of teaching him and others a severe lesson, in case his surmise proved correct. In matters personal to himself Saville was one to resent promptly, even to the extent of a bloody quarrel, anything which he regarded as an unwarrantable interference or liberty.

" Jasper," he said, " I cannot believe that you could have so far forgotten the confidential relations which you, as my medical adviser, sustained to me, as to babble of anything you saw or surmised when attending me in the mountains ; and yet what does the peculiar manner of my old acquaintances mean ? Why do they turn and look after me, and say something that is not designed for my ears ?"

" You are right, Saville. I am not capable of breaking professional silence, even if I had no friendly regard for you. Come to my quarters."

On reaching them, the surgeon fastened the door, and took out a New York paper.

" Read that," he said.

"Mother?" asked Saville, turning pale.

"No, no! Read!"

With a frown black as night, Saville read :

"Married, on the 12th of October, Captain Henry Vennam, of H. R. M. Service, to Mrs. Julia Ashburton Saville, widow of the late Captain Saville, who was killed during the storming of the forts in the Highlands on the Hudson. It is well known that Mrs. Saville had no sympathy with her husband, in his unnatural rebellion against her king, and that her loyal hostility to his disloyalty long ago led to a formal separation. This fact fully accounts for the seeming haste with which she has honored with her hand the brave and accomplished officer who this day leads her to the altar."

With a deep imprecation, Saville crushed the paper in his hand, and then sat motionless, with contracting brows, like one trying to think his way out of some unexpected emer gency.

"From one of our spies who has since come in," said the surgeon, "we have learned the additional fact, that this fellow, Vennam, found you himself in the fort, and brought away your sword as proof of your death. It is well he did not use it to let out what little life you had left."

"I have no doubt that he would, and with her full approval, if he had supposed I was alive," said Saville abstractedly.

"That's a harsh accusation to bring against your wife."

"Curse her!" cried Saville, starting up in great agitation. "That is the most infernal part of this whole shameful business! She is still my wife. If I were only rid of her forever, I could forgive the insult of her indecent haste in seeking the altar with another man. But the law still binds me to her, as fiendish cruelty once chained criminals to a putrefying corpse."

"It's only too true, Saville. Her marriage with that officer was only an empty form. Will she remain with him, do you think ? She must have heard that you are alive by this time."

"I don't know," said Saville desperately. "She is none too good. If she would only break her neck before she breaks my heart !"

"Well, Saville, pardon me for saying it ; but I think you will find both comfort and revenge in yonder mountains."

"Jasper," said Saville gravely, "you are my friend ; but touch lightly on that subject. If I were free to marry that innocent maiden, who, you know well, is unrivaled in all that can win respect and love, I would esteem it more than the best gift of the world. She saved my life when that vile thing the law calls my wife was waiting with murderous eagerness to hear of my death."

"I admit that you cannot legally marry your wild flower ; but you know what men do every day, and without a tithe of your excuse. She is evidently the daughter of a criminal, and can never hope for any better future than you can offer."

"The honest love and devoted, lifelong loyalty which I would offer I believe to be right and honorable. Do you suppose that I could ask that true, pure girl, to whom I owe so much, to do anything that I regarded as base, or even wrong ? That she is friendless and defenseless ; that her father, who should be her natural protector, has only darkened her life by some evil deed, all make it more imperative that I, as a man of honor, should be faithful to her interests. I do most sincerely believe that I have a right to offer her my love ; but, with her faith and training, I fear that I can never make it appear so to her, when she comes to know of that woman in New York."

"Well," said the surgeon, with a shrug, "I am neither Christian nor philosopher. I take the world as I find it, and try to have as comfortable a time as I can every day, hoping that the good luck which I have always had here will follow me into the next life, if there is any.''

'' Well added,'' replied Saville bitterly ; '' ' if there is any ! ' If men used their reason, and believed what they saw, they would know there is not. This life would be abundantly sufficient, and in the main happy, did not super-stition and the monstrous laws it has spawned curse and thwart us on every side. But, farewell, my friend ; I have much to think of, and I will inflict my ill-starred affairs on you no longer. Let all that has passed between us be buried where no gossip-monger can ever rake it up.''

After carefully considering the act of his wife in all its aspects, Saville concluded that it would be to his advantage. The haste of her marriage, which she had intended as an indignity to his memory, would react against herself, and involve more shame to her than to him. His hate was grat-ified at the thought of her intense mortification and disap-pointment when learning that he was still living. She must either separate instantly from the man for whom she had a passion—of love she was not capable—or else be disgraced for life. At best, even her own party would be far more in-clined toward censure than to entertain charity or sympathy.

He also felt utterly absolved from what he regarded as his rash promise to be loyal to the mere name of wife.

But the consideration which weighed most with him was the belief that Vera, in view of her act, could be made to feel that in reality he had no wife, that she had forfeited every claim, and so might be more surely led to accept of Saville as her lover, since he could not be her husband.

The fact that a certain amount of the odium of his wife's course would cling to him in the world's estimation, and that he would always be known as the husband of the woman who was in such haste to marry another that she could not wait till assured of his burial, made a secluded mountain home, with Vera, seem all the more truly a refuge.

Thus, every hope for the future came to rest, more completely than before, on the success of his scheme of teaching Vera that man was a law unto himself, and that there was no external power that had a right to set in judgment on his actions.

A day or two thereafter, a paper came through the lines, from New York, containing the following item :

"TRUTH STRANGER THAN FICTION.—Captain Saville, whom all supposed killed at Fort Clinton, is alive. It is said that he was taken from the fort, late at night, by some people whom he had befriended, and carried back in the mountains ; and that, though very severely wounded, he is rapidly recovering. These facts are so well authenticated that his wife has left Captain Vennam's quarters, and returned to her relatives. It is said that they are deeply incensed against the unfortunate officer, who rather deserves sympathy, since he has become, in a certain sense, a widower. There seems to have been strange blundering in the case somewhere. Perhaps the eyes of the gallant captain were still blinded with the smoke of battle, when he supposed that he saw Saville dead. There may be new developments in the comedy, or tragedy, whichever it may prove, before many days."

Saville smiled grimly as he read it, and then tossed it contemptuously aside.

CHAPTER XXIX.

SEEMING SUCCESS.

LATER in the day, Saville received a document which he read with keen delight. It was a leave of absence from his commanding officer, in which he was complimented on his behavior in the recent battle, and congratulated upon his remarkable escape. "The campaign is over," the writer went on to say, "and it is not yet fully decided just where, in the Highlands, the future works will be erected. Surgeon Jasper also informs me that, in your zeal for the service, you have reported for duty rather sooner than the condition of your wound warrants. You are therefore requested to leave your address at these headquarters, and are permitted to be absent until notified."

"Jasper, this is your work," said Saville, entering the surgeon's quarters.

"Well, suppose it is ; what have you got to say about it ?" replied Jasper, lifting his broad, good-natured face to the speaker.

"I say this, from the bottom of my heart, *mon ami*, may you never have to take any of your own medicine !"

"Amen !" cried the surgeon. "I was never wished better luck than that. But hold on, you are not through with me yet. I jogged the general's elbow only that I might get a chance to jockey you on a horse. I've a beast that's a little too skittish for one of my weight and temperament, and it occurred to me that if I gave you a chance to make a quick journey, you would buy him."

"Name your price ; charge what you please ; I'm wholly at your mercy," laughed Saville.

"That is the condition in which I always like to get a patient, for I can then bleed him to my own satisfaction. But if you were not my friend, Saville, I would charge you twice as much as I am going to ask."

The bargain was soon made, nor did Saville regret it, when, on the following short November day, the fleet animal carried him safely to the mountain gorge that he hoped would henceforth be the Mecca of all his pilgrimages.

He did not go clattering down the bridle path ; but, tying his horse some distance away, stole up to the cabin unperceived, and looked in at the window. How vividly, in after years, he remembered the picture he then saw ! Vera sat alone, on one side of the ample hearth ; her work had fallen on the floor at her side, and her hands were crossed upon her lap. She was looking intently into the fire, as if she saw more there than the rising and falling flames, which now illumined her face until its beauty seemed scarcely earthly, and again left it in shadow that suggested almost equal loveliness.

Her revery soon ended with a happy smile ; she picked up her work, and seemed chiding her idle hands ; then, in obedience to another impulse, she dropped it again, and her rich, powerful voice gave the old refrain,

"I know a bank whereon the wild thyme blows."

She had scarcely sung the line before Saville was accompanying her on his flute. She stopped abruptly, and sprang up, with hope and fear both depicted on her face. Was the echo real, or a ghostly omen of evil ? She darted to the door, and Saville took her into his arms.

How fondly she ever dwelt on the halcyon days that followed ! They hunted and rambled together among the hills that love made beautiful, even in bleak November ; and when the storms of early winter roared in the wooded heights above the cabin, the roar of the crackling flames up the wide chimney was louder, and the sound of their merry voices often louder still.   Their mirthfulness, at times, relaxed even the gloomy face of the poor exile, and he appeared to enjoy a pale reflection of their happiness.

Saville also sought to make the most of the opportunity which this visit gave, by commencing to give Vera a culture which would make her more companionable in future years. He gave her lessons in drawing and music, and found her a most apt scholar in these branches.   He also taught her how to express herself correctly in writing, and in the evening she usually read aloud to him for an hour or more.

He succeeded in obtaining quite a library for her.   Learning that among the effects of a wealthy Tory, whose property had been confiscated, there was a large number of books, he went to see them, and found that he could buy them all for a small sum.   He did not wish them all, but only such as would serve his purpose, and give Vera general culture and knowledge, without strengthening her faith.   To his joy, he found that the library was quite rich, for that day, in history, travels, biography, and even philosophy.   It also contained some of the Latin classics, a translation of Homer, and the " Plays of William Shakspeare," which he knew to be so dear to Vera's heart.   He and Tascar, who accompanied him, were quite well laden on their return ;   and Vera, at first, was wild with delight over these treasures.   She looked hastily and eagerly through the collection, and then sighed deeply.

" What does that mean ?" asked Saville.

" There is no Bible here," she replied in a low tone.

" No, Vera," he said gravely, and almost sternly ; for he was beginning to regard this book with bitter hostility, as the possible cause, in his view, of wretchedness to them both.

Tears came into the sensitive girl's eyes ; but he kissed them away, and sought, with his usual success, to divert her thoughts from the subject he most dreaded. He believed that he could educate her mind above and beyond her superstition, and thus enable her gradually and naturally to outgrow it, as he supposed that he had. In this effort, he made history and books of travel his chief allies, thinking that they were best suited to the simplicity and childlike character of her mind. He skillfully, yet unobtrusively, caused her to see that other peoples and races were as devoted to their multifarious religions as she was to hers. He placed before her, though in no argumentative way that would awaken opposition, the absurd, cruel, and monstrous acts of those who had professed to be Christians. He supplemented what he read with graphic descriptions. The old Greeks and Romans were made to live again, and she was shown that their mythology, which lasted for centuries, was now in truth only a myth, and that, as the people grew wiser, they lost faith in their gods.

Vera was not slow in drawing the inference, and clouds of doubt began to darken her mind ; but it seemed so dreadful to question her mother's faith, that she fought against her unbelief earnestly, though secretly ; for she knew that she could obtain no help from Saville. These doubts, however, became a low, jarring discord in the sweet harmony of her life.

But his personal influence had a still stronger effect than his suggestion of abstract thought, and of facts adverse to her faith. He one day obtained quite a clear glimpse of the silent workings of her mind ; for, coming in unexpectedly, he found her in tears. To his gentle but eager questioning, she sobbed,

" O Theron ! you are pushing God, and all relating to Him, out of my heart and thoughts, and I am beginning to worship only you.   My conscience tells me that it is not right, and that evil will come of it."

"Well, Vera, darling," he said, "this is scarcely more than fair, since you fill every nook and corner of my heart, and I have long worshiped you only."

She shook her head with a new rush of tears ; but he comforted her with many reassuring words, and she loved him too well to be willing to cloud his face with her trouble. Her conscious effort to resist his personal influence grew less and less, and he seemingly took sole possession of her heart.

As she was situated, she was scarcely to be blamed, for he had proved such a true and helpful friend ; he had made such an infinite difference in her life, and was so genuinely human, so sympathetic in all respects, save the one on which they differed, that her own humanity found in him everything it craved.   Even in his skepticism, she was compelled to respect him for his evident sincerity.

Still, she did not lose her faith in God, nor did she often neglect the form of devotion ; but she permitted Saville's image to crowd Him almost wholly from her heart and thoughts.

Saville occasionally sent Tascar with a note of inquiry to Surgeon Jasper, and thus kept himself posted in regard to public affairs.   During the latter part of January, he was ordered to report to Lieutenant-Colonel Radière, and found, to his great satisfaction, that his services would be required at West Point, from which place he could ride "home" in comparatively brief time.   The winter and spring passed rapidly away.   His hopes continually grew stronger, that his effort to teach Vera to eventually feel and think as he did, would be crowned with success, and he was even more sure that he had made himself so necessary to her very existence that she could never give him up, even though her conscience at first might be arrayed against him.

CHAPTER XXX.

A MASTER MIND AND WILL.

EARLY in the summer, Saville received instructions to go to the main army under General Washington, and thence to Philadelphia (which had recently been evacuated by the British troops), upon business connected with the Engineer Department.

On his way he stopped at the cabin, to inform Vera of his journey, but assured her of his speedy return. She grew pale at the thought of the possible perils which he might encounter, but he promised more caution than it was in his nature to practice, and also said, with a significant glance, that awakened a curiosity which he would not then satisfy, that he would bring her something from Philadelphia.

He reached General Washington's headquarters on the eve of the memorable battle of Monmouth. Though jaded and worn by his ride, he readily accepted Lafayette's invitation to act as his aid, his services being specially valuable at this time, from his familiarity with both French and English.

The command of the extreme advance, upon which would devolve the important task of first attacking the enemy preliminary to a general engagement, would properly fall to General Lee, who was second to Washington in rank. But Lafayette, ever coveting the post of danger, eagerly sought to be intrusted with this duty. As General Lee had been from the first strenuously opposed to the battle, and, indeed, to any interference with the British line of march through New Jersey, Washington was more than ready to comply, if that officer would waive his right to lead in person. This General Lee did unhesitatingly, saying to the Marquis, that he was only too glad to be relieved from all responsibility in carrying out measures which were destined to fail.

Lafayette, therefore, early on the morning of the 27th of June, advanced with a large force toward the enemy. The British troops were commanded by Sir Henry Clinton, who, perceiving that a battle must be fought, made his dispositions accordingly, moving his baggage forward on his line of march, but retaining the flower of his army in the rear to repel the approaching Americans. In the mean time, General Lee changed his mind, and requested Washington to give him the leadership of the advance which he had just relinquished. Indeed, as a matter of military etiquette, he almost claimed it as his right. Although Lee had been bitterly opposed to Washington's plan of battle, the latter still believed the crotchety general would do his duty as an officer, but did not know how to satisfy his punctilious claims without wounding Lafayette. Learning, however, that the British forces immediately before the Marquis were being rapidly increased, he dispatched two additional brigades to the front, under command of Lee, who, as senior officer on the field, would, as a matter of course, outrank all others. But Washington's friendship for Lafayette also led him to write him a note of explanation.

That sultry Saturday night was one of deep anxiety to both parties. The British general was encumbered with an enormous amount of baggage. Washington was about to assail the disciplined troops, whom Lee said it was madness to attack in their present force and strong position.

None who were burdened with responsibility slept, and even Saville, though very weary, was kept awake by the thought, that in a very few hours he might enter on the dreamless sleep which his love now made him dread unspeakably ; and that, should desperate wounds leave him helpless on the field, Vera was too far away to seek him again.

At midnight there was a stir and the heavy tread of men. Washington, who has been characterized as over-cautious, was so resolutely bent on fighting Clinton, that he had sent orders for a large detachment to move up close to the enemy's lines, and to hold the British general in check, should he attempt to decamp in the darkness.

At daylight, expresses galloped to Lee and to Washington with the tidings that the enemy were moving. The chief put the main army into motion instantly, and gave orders that the men should throw aside blankets and every impeding weight. Lee remained inert until positive orders spurred him into action. He then advanced, it is true, but languidly, very cautiously, without definite purpose, and without concert with his supporting generals.

By his direction, General Wayne gained a position where he was certain he could deal the enemy a tremendous blow , but was checked in the very act of striking, that Lee himself might carry out a brilliant piece of strategy, which ended, however, in a feeble and purposeless demonstration.

Lafayette saw an opportunity to gain the rear of a body of the enemy marching against them, and spurred to Lee, that he might obtain permission to make the attempt.

" Sir," was the reply, " you do not know British soldiers ; we cannot stand against them ; we shall certainly be driven back at first, and we must be cautious."

" It may be so, General," Lafayette replied ; " but British soldiers have been beaten, and they may be again ; at any rate, I am disposed to make the trial."

Lee then gave Lafayette permission to carry out his plan

in part. A little later, one of Washington's aids arrived upon the field in quest of information, and the marquis sent back emphatic word to his chief that his presence was needed.

Before the halfway measure which Lee proposed could be carried out, the permission was recalled, and the gallant Frenchman was ordered to fall back, though why he could not tell. He chafed like a chained lion, and now felt that the man whom he must obey was either a traitor or a coward.

Saville was deeply chagrined ; for Lee, from his outspoken skepticism and innovating tendencies, was one of his heroes.

This hesitation, this marching and countermarching, and cautious feeling around, gave Sir Henry Clinton just the time he needed. His immense train of baggage was well out of the way, guarded by a strong force under General Knyphausen, so he now decidedly took the initiative, by hurling the bulk of his army, under Lord Cornwallis, against the dilatory Americans, who had been wasting their time and strength in purposeless skirmishing.

The whole advance guard of the army under Lee was soon falling back, some with orders and some without, and it was not long before the retrograde movement developed into a disgraceful retreat As the enemy pressed faster and nearer, panic seized upon the Continental forces, and all the awful consequences followed inevitably. The day was intensely hot, and the unclouded sun smote many a poor fellow to the earth in surer death than the thickly-flying bullets. The already wearied men sank ankle-deep into the yielding sand, and those who, through feebleness, wounds, or fatigue, fell in the way, were trampled by the strong in their reckless flight.

And yet Washington knew nothing of all this. There had been no indications of heavy fighting in his front. To all the wretched blunders of that morning Lee added the most unpardonable, when he failed to inform his chief that he was falling back ; for he thereby endangered the entire army.

The first intimation that Washington received of what had occurred was the appearance of breathless, terror-stricken fugitives. With rare presence of mind, he ordered them under arrest, lest they should communicate their tidings to the main body of the army, which was advancing to Lee's support ; for there is no contagion so mysterious and awfully rapid in its transmission as that of a panic.

Still hoping that the report was unfounded, he sprang upon his horse, and spurred toward the front ; but the increasing stream of fugitives, and then the heads of the retreating columns, soon convinced him that the disaster which he believed impossible had taken place. He asked several officers in the retreating column what it all meant. No one knew. One smiled significantly, another was angry, while a third declared, with an oath, that "they were flying from a shadow."

Washington was ever slow to suspect others of evil, but the thought now flashed into his mind that Lee was making good his predictions of defeat, by his own cowardly or treacherous action. He stopped to ask no more questions, but, ordering the commander of the first division to form his men on the first rising ground, he, with his staff, swept across the causeway, past the disorderly fugitives, his anger kindling as he rode. The frown upon his brow grew black as night, and by the time he reached Lee, who was leading the retreat of the second division, his appearance was terrible. Saville, who rode near, with Lafayette, was deeply awed, and, were not the proof before him, could not have believed that a human face could become so powerful in its indignation.

" What is the meaning of all this, sir ?" Washington demanded, in a tone that was stern even to fierceness.

" Sir—sir," stammered Lee, at first overwhelmed by Washington's manner.

" I desire to know the meaning of this disorder and confusion," was again demanded, and with still greater vehemence.

" You know that the attack was contrary to my advice and opinion—" Lee began.

" You should not have undertaken the command, unless you intended to carry it through."

Lee's irascible spirit was now stung to rage, and he made an angry reply, which drew from Washington still sharper expressions. For a moment, the incensed generals confronted each other, like two thunder-clouds that are flashing their lightnings back and forth, as if within the dark folds of each there was a vindictive will.

Lee sought to give a hurried explanation, which ended with the assertion that the ground was unfavorable, and that he was not disposed to beard the whole British army with troops in such a situation.

" I have certain information," rejoined Washington, " that it was merely a strong covering party."

" That may be ; but it was stronger than mine, and I did not think proper to run such a risk."

" I am very sorry," was the reply, " that you undertook the command, unless you meant to fight the enemy."

" I did not think it prudent to bring on a general engagement."

" Whatever your opinion may have been," answered Washington disdainfully, " I expected my orders would have been obeyed."

All this had passed with inconceivable rapidity, and, as it were, in flashes, and yet too much time had been wasted, for the enemy were but a few minutes' march away from them. Casting Lee aside, as he might a broken reed, Washington ordered that the head of the second division, instead of continuing its retreat, should form instantly in line of battle. Then, wheeling his horse, he dashed to the rear of the American column, and toward the advancing enemy, who were now close upon the confused and disordered remnant of Lee's troops.

Until Washington appeared, the poor fellows were in sore straits. Their retreat had been checked ; they were standing helplessly in the road, artillery and infantry huddled together. No one knew what to do, or how the miserable blundering of the day would end. Only one thing was definite and certain—the solid columns of their pursuers were now almost upon them. They were on the eve of a headlong and disastrous flight, when Washington, with his staff, galloped up, and his presence and inspiring mien sent an electric thrill of hope and courage to every fainting heart. The great master mind, aroused to its highest degree of power, seemed to lay a resistless grasp upon the whole chaotic mass. It appeared but a moment before Colonel Oswald's guns were posted on a neighboring eminence, were unlimbered, and were pouring well-directed shots into the advancing foe. Two other batteries galloped off to the left, and taking position in the covert of woods, were soon adding their tremendous echoes to the deepening uproar of battle. In the mean time, and under a perfect storm of bullets and cannon balls, the intrepid chief formed the regiments of Colonels Stewart and Ramsay in line, and enabled them to reply to the destructive volleys they were receiving. He seemed to bear the same charmed life that had excited the superstitious wonder of the savages on Braddock's disastrous field in the old French and Indian war. Within a space of time so brief as to appear incredible, he had rallied into battle array fugitives that, a few moments before, were bent only on flight, and the impetuous advance of the enemy was checked.

Having made all the arrangements within his power, this born commander of men did a still greater thing : he controlled himself.   Riding back to Lee, in calmer mood, he asked,

"Will you retain the command on this height or not ? If you will, I will return to the main body, and have it formed on the next height."

"It is equal to me where I command," replied Lee.

"I expect you will take proper means for checking the enemy," said Washington.

"Your orders shall be obeyed ; and I shall not be the first to leave the ground."

Availing himself of the respite which his own masterly action had secured, Washington spurred back to the main army, which, under his rapid orders, soon bristled along the next height.

But he had left something of his own iron will among those who were now sustaining the enemy's attack.   His clarion voice, which had resounded above the din, was still echoing in their hearts, and the grand excitement which had animated his face made a hero of every soldier in the little force which the enemy's bullets were fast thinning.

They maintained their position gallantly for some little time, and when, at last, the left wing gave way, pushed back by the weight of numbers, and emerged on the further side of the woods toward Washington, both of the contending parties seemed intermingled in a hand-to-hand *mêlée*.

The enemy next attacked Varnum's brigade, posted near the causeway, across which the Americans must retreat, and here the conflict raged severely for some time.

As Saville was carrying an order across the field to a battery that was doing effective service, he was hailed by a familiar voice, and turning, saw his old acquaintance, Captain Molly, coming toward him with a bucket of water.

" The Holy Vargin bless ye, Misther Saville !" she cried. " I fale safe, now I know that ye're around."

" Ah, Molly, my brave girl ! is that you ?" he replied. " What are you doing here ?"

" Faix, sur, while Larry is givin' the Red-coats fire, I'm givin' him wather."

" Can you spare me a drop ? for I'm half perished with thirst in this infernal heat and dust."

" Take all ye want, and welcome. What are a few dhraps of wather, when ye spilt yer blood for me ?"

" Molly, you are a jewel ! What did you do for me ? Larry may well be proud of you."

" Och ! poor man ! I'm better to him now——"

A cannon ball was whizzing toward them ; a second later, Larry was a bleeding corpse beside his gun.

Molly saw him fall as she turned. With a wild shriek she dropped her pail, rushed to his side, and throwing herself upon his mangled form, gave utterance to loud cries of grief.

The officer in charge of the battery was about to withdraw the gun, as he now had no one competent to work it ; but Molly, obeying another impulse, sprang up, and dashing her tears right and left, cried,

" No, yer honor ! I'll take Larry's place, and it'll do me sore heart good to send some o' thim Red-coats, as killed him, to the divil ;" and she seized the rammer, and proved instantly that she had nerve and skill for the task. With her dark, piercing eyes ablaze with anger, and her disheveled hair flying about her inflamed face, she seemed a fury rather than a woman. When Saville left, the rapid discharges of the gun told how eagerly she was seeking to avenge the death of her husband.

The British cavalry, and a heavy body of infantry at last charged simultaneously, and broke the American ranks.

Lee ordered instant retreat, and, with Colonel Ogden's regiment, covered the passage of his men across the causeway.

Molly would not leave her husband's body, but lifting it on the gun, she tied it there, and then, by running, kept near to the retiring battery, the troops greeting her with acclamations as she passed.

The British forces promptly followed the hard-pressed Continentals over the causeway, anticipating a complete victory, and the battle speedily became general. But Washington was now upon his own ground, and supported by generals in whom he could trust implicitly. The enemy made successive attacks on his front, left and right, but were repelled. A tremendous cannonade was kept up on both sides, and seldom had the peace of the Sabbath been so rudely disturbed as on that sultry summer day.

General Wayne, whose headlong valor had justly earned him the sobriquet of " Mad Anthony," occupied an advanced position in an orchard, from which he maintained a brisk and galling fire on the British centre. He repeatedly repulsed the Royal Grenadiers, who sought to dislodge him. It soon began to appear that the success of the enemy's attack depended on driving him from his position.

Saville was directed by Lafayette to ride over to Wayne with a cheering message, to watch the struggle, and report to him its progress.

When Saville reached Wayne's advanced post, Colonel Moncton, who commanded the Royal Grenadiers, was deploying them in the open field, as for a quiet evening parade. It was evident that he was preparing for the stern and silent use of the bayonet, on which the British troops justly prided themselves.

When his men were in line, he made them a brief, stirring address, in which he appealed to every motive which could inspire an English soldier with unflinching courage. His voice was distinctly heard by those awaiting the assault, and at times even his words were intelligible. He next placed himself at their head, and led them in solid column against the Americans. They presented a truly magnificent sight in the warm, mellow light of the declining day. With the same firmness and steadiness that they would pass in review on some gala occasion, the poor fellows advanced toward the point where very many would meet wounds and death. So even and perfect was their step, as they marched shoulder to shoulder, that a cannon ball from an American battery en-filaded a whole platoon, knocking the muskets out of each man's hand ; but, with scarce a change in muscle, the ob-scure heroes strode on with their comrades, although un-armed. Moncton walked at their head, erect, stately, reso-lute, and his bearing was emulated by every officer in the column. Their silent progress was more impressive than if every step was accompanied by shouts and volleys. Their march was the very sublimity of courage, the perfect flower of discipline, and it seemed as if it must be resist-less.

They are now within a few rods of their equally silent, waiting foe ; and yet there is no hesitation, no change in the time of their strong, steady tramp. They are now so near that the opposing ranks can look into each other's be-grimed and heat-swollen faces. The same stern resolve char-acterizes the countenances of each dark array. To distant spectators the two clouds of war seem almost together ; the lightning flashes must come soon.

The American firelocks are leveled, not evenly, covering the whole advancing column, but concentrating on every officer visible. They are but a few yards away. Suddenly Moncton steps to the right, waves his sword aloft. and shouts,

" Charge !''

Wayne's signal is equally prompt. A volley from the whole length of his line rings out ; then, lowering their empty pieces, his men rush forward to meet the coming shock with answering bayonet thrust.

Moncton fell, and also almost every other British officer ; but his heroic column, stunned but for a moment, pressed on, and there was at once a desperate hand-to-hand conflict over the prostrate commander, one party seeking to retain, and the other to obtain his body. At last the Continentals secured the lifeless form of the gallant colonel, and carried it to the rear.

If the English courage was steady and unflinching, that of the Americans was reckless and enthusiastic. Gradually they pushed back the struggling and almost unofficered grenadiers, until, convinced that their assault had failed, they gave way. This practically decided the fate of the day. The sun was setting, and the British forces soon retired to the height whereon Washington had rallied Lee's disordered troops in the morning. Throughout the long twilight, something of the Sabbath's stillness settled down on a region that had, throughout the day, resounded with the horrid din of war. The battle-field, and the whole line of Lee's disastrous retreat, presented one strange feature. There were wounded and mangled bodies in abundance, but everywhere were found men dead or helpless, without a scratch upon their persons. The torrid sun had smote both parties as with the wrath of heaven.

Washington and his suite lay down under a broad oak, with the dead all around them, intending to renew the conflict with the light of the following morning ; but, while the Americans, from the fatigues of the day, were sunk in oblivion almost as deep as that of those whom the morning reveille could not awaken, Clinton stole away with his baffled army, leaving his severely wounded to the mercy of his foes. When, at daybreak, the advance was sounded, the Americans found only the deserted campaign ground.

It was a drawn battle ; but, if Lafayette had commanded the advance instead of Lee, and had Morgan, with his brave riflemen—who, but three miles distant, chafed all day without orders—attacked the enemy's rear, history might have given a different record.

CHAPTER XXXI.

THE REVELATION.

SAVILLE was naturally brave, but no man ever had a greater sense of gladness than he at having passed unscathed through the manifold perils of the day. Though wearied to the point of exhaustion, at the close of the battle, he sought Molly, as soon as his duties permitted, and tried to comfort the poor creature. He found her crooning and wailing by turns, at the side of her husband's body.

"Ah! Misther Saville," she said, "it's now I think on ivery oncivil word iver I spake to him. If I could only have him aloive once more, I'd be swater than honey all the toime. Faix, sur, Larry was a kind, dacent man, an' I'll niver git his loikes agin."

The story of Molly's action on the death of her husband had spread like wildfire through the army, and on the following morning General Greene presented her, all begrimed with powder and blood, to Washington, who, with words of praise and sympathy, conferred on her the commission of sergeant, while he afterward caused her name to be placed upon the list of half pay officers for life.

Saville saw that Larry had a soldier's burial, and then gave Molly the means of defraying her expenses back to her home in the Highlands, to which she soon returned. Immediately after her arrival thither, she went out to see Vera, to whom she related, with all the vividness of her demonstrative style, the events of the battle, enlarging upon her own loss, the dangers to which Saville had been exposed, and his kindness to her.

Her tidings, while in part reassuring, threw Vera into an agony of anxiety for the safety of her lover. Now, in his absence, she realized, as never before, how necessary he was to her very existence ; and again, with her old importunity, she besought Heaven in his behalf, though not with her old and simple faith ; and she watched for his return with almost sleepless vigilance.

In the mean time, Saville, finding that there was no further prospect of fighting, proceeded on his journey to Philadelphia, and, after attending to his official business, purchased a beautiful ring for Vera. Returning, he taxed his poor horse heavily, in his impatience to see again the one who grew dearer every day. The dangers he had passed through, and the uncertainty of life in that stormy period, made him feel that he could delay the consummation of his love no longer, and he half resolved to put his hopes to the test on his return. By rapid riding, he gained sufficient time to enable him to spend a day or two at the cabin, and still report as early as he was expected.

When he met Vera, he found that the knowledge of what he had passed through had preceeded him. Never before had her reception been so marked by a clinging tenderness, and he thought exultantly, "She cannot give me up." But she soon clouded his face and hopes by saying,

"O Theron ! God does answer prayer. It seems to me that I have entreated Him in your behalf even in my troubled dreams, as well as in every waking moment, and He *has* spared you to me."

"Is her faith still so unshaken in a mere name ?" he sadly asked himself. "Will it ever be otherwise ?"

After an early supper, he led her out to one of their favorite haunts upon the hill-side, and gave her the ring he had brought. He was pleased to see her unbounded delight and gratitude, and he said,

" When you no longer wish my love, you may return this ring to me."

" You will never receive it again," she answered, with tears in her eyes ; " for if I were dying, Theron, I could not give it back on that condition."

It proved a little too large, but she obviated this defect by drawing off the ring given by her mother, and then, putting Saville's gift in its place, she kept it there by the plain gold band which she had worn so long.

" That is the way it should be," she said ; " for I have felt from the first that I had mother's approval of my love." Then she added musingly, " How well I remember her words when she gave me this ring !"

" What were they, Vera ?"

She blushed deeply, for she had spoken half unconscious. ly, not realizing the nature of the explanation that must follow.

" Tell me her words," Saville again gently asked.

" They remind me that I have, in part, disobeyed them, Theron ; but I trusted you so completely, and all has happened so strangely and differently from what any one could have anticipated, that I could not do otherwise."

His curiosity and hope were now both aroused. Was the way opening for explanations that, in any event, must soon come ? So he said,

" I know you have acted right, darling. Were your mother living, she could have found no fault ; but what did she say when she gave the ring ?"

" I cannot hide anything from you, Theron," she said, turning away her face. " You must remembe the circumstances. Mother was leaving me alone and friendless. She feared I would be peculiarly unshielded. I would have been but for you.   Think of what I passed through in your long year of absence ! think of the condition in which you found me !   O Theron ! how much I owe to you.   Well, mother evidently feared I might meet with some one not so honorable as you are, and she made me promise that I would not permit caresses, even from one I loved, until he should wed me before God's minister with this ring.   I readily gave the promise, for I did not then know what love was.   But I could not keep it.   When you raised me from the floor, the night father spoke those dreadful words, I knew I could trust you.   I turned to you as instinctively as that climbing vine to yonder oak.   I could not help it, and I knew that all would be as mother wished in your own good time."

As she spoke he grew very pale, and, at her last words, buried his face in his hands with a deep groan.   It seemed, for the moment, as if the dead mother stood between him and her child.

" Theron !" she said in great alarm.

He did not answer.

" Theron, are you ill ?"

" Yes, yes, sick at heart ; my evil destiny will conquer yet."

" O Theron !" she pleaded, laying her hand on his shoulder ; " tell me your trouble.   You need dread no evil that I can avert."

" If that were only true," he answered, looking at her with a face so full of trouble that her tears started in sympathy.

" How can it be otherwise than true ?" she asked, beginning to dread, she knew not what.   " Can you think me so ungrateful that I will not make any sacrifice for you ?"

" You will never be ungrateful, Vera, and you have had, thus far, no more cause for gratitude than I have ; but I fear you cannot—mark, I do not say will not—I fear you cannot give up your superstition—your faith in what I am sure is all delusion—for my sake ; and yet you must, or else the chance for a happiness greater than I thought possible passes away from both. "

" Theron, your words are as dark as night. What can you mean ? Why are you so pale ?" cried Vera in great distress.

" I may as well tell you now, " he said, after a moment, " what I have been on the point of telling you before ; but I hesitated, as much for your sake as my own. I could no more endure the thought of your losing this happy future than of losing it myself ; and I hoped that in time, and under greater enlightenment of mind, you would outgrow the imaginary obstacles in the way. I too have broken the letter of a promise that I made you at your mother's grave. I said, in effect, that I would not try to lead you to forget or depart from her teachings ; nor would I, save in one respect, for her influence and that of nature have made you the sweetest, purest woman that ever breathed. But I could not be loyal to you and to your happiness and still keep that hasty pledge, for since that day our mutual love has grown till it absorbs us both, and in the wretched past an event occurred which would render the consummation of our love impossible, did I leave your baseless faith undisturbed. While it comforted you after your mother's death, I kept the promise. When, ere we were aware, we both began to 'ove each other in such a way that the terms brother and sister no longer meant the truth ; when your father's words taught me that this wilderness must continue to be your home, and that the position in society, which I that day had resolved you should have, became impossible, then I commenced trying to teach you what I firmly believe myself. I could sacrifice my own happiness ; I had decided to do so, and your quick intuition read my decision in my face. And yet how glad

I was that I saw, as I believed, a way in which we both could be happy by becoming one for life ! I then tried to undermine your delusion ; I sought to do it gently, that your old beliefs might pass away as clouds from the sky.''

Just then, in ominous contradiction of his words, the setting sun entered a dark cloud, and the gloom fell on the faces of both.

'' Vera, before I saw you I thought I had spoiled my life ; not by a crime, but by an act of folly. It is for you to decide whether my life is to be blighted by its consequences ; for your sake—not my own ; my pure, strong love needs no priestly sanction—for your sake, it cuts me to the heart to say it. I cannot, in truth, take you before a minister and wed you, with that ring. While my heart is free to love you, in the eye of our barbarous laws I am a married man.''

She started violently and became deathly pale, but she only moaned,

'' O Theron, Theron ! I should have known this before.''

'' Hear me, hear the whole wretched story, before you condemn me !'' he cried passionately. '' I could have brought a minister hither, and it might have been years before you learned the truth, if ever ; but no deceit shall ever sully my relations to you. When we were first acquainted, I did not tell you of my wife, because I never spoke of her to any one, not even to my mother. I was seeking to forget her hateful existence. When your father's words and your decision to remain with him prevented me from carrying out my self-sacrificing plan, then the thought came : Teach her the truth, show her how valueless are the forms and ceremonies which are based on falsehood.''

'' But they are right and true to me,'' said Vera sobbing.

'' They cannot continue to be so, darling, after you have calmly considered the proof to the contrary ; and when you come to know how cruelly I am placed, how utterly I am absolved from every bond save that which is purely legal, you will have pity ; you will see that I have a right to seek your love. "   And he told her the whole story of his marriage, softening no part that was to his own disadvantage ; he spoke with intense bitterness of his wife's recent and shameful marriage at the very time when he owed his life to Vera's tireless care ; " and this marriage,'' he said, '' was solemnized with all the forms that are called sacred.''

"And now, Vera,'' he concluded, '' how could I have acted otherwise ? I believe that this life is all.   It is all, '' he said earnestly ; '' everything in nature proves it.   We have before us but this brief life.   Alas ! in my calling, how uncertain it is ! Since our short day must pass swiftly at best, shall we waste our waking moments over delusions ? Shall we let what men imagined in the ignorant past stand in the way of real and practical happiness ?   Only obstacles created by the untaught minds of the superstitious are standing in our way.   Shall these unsubstantial spectres frighten us from a lifetime of deep content ?   In a little while we shall cease to be, and the chance for happiness is gone.''

But Vera drew another inference than that which he intended, and in a tone that pierced his heart she cried,

'' Then where is mother ?''

He was silent, for her distress was so great that it seemed a cruel thing to say that all that remained of one so dear was corrupting in a distant grave.   He never realized before how harsh and abrupt an end his creed gave to human life.   He tried to comfort himself with the thought that her intense grief would gradually pass away, and that realizing that she had in sad truth lost her mother, she would cling all the more closely to him as her only certain possession.

He endeavored to soothe her, but for a long time his efforts seemed utterly vain.   At last she grew calm enough to falter,

" I am in the dark, Theron.   It seems as if the mountain had opened at my feet.   I dare not move lest I fall into the gulf.   I don't know what's right, I don't know what's true ; my mind is confused, and my heart aches as if it would break   O mother ! are you indeed lost to me forever ?   If you should die, Theron, would I never see you again ? This is terrible, terrible.   Please take me home.   I cannot think.   Perhaps to morrow some light will come.   I am in thick darkness now.''

He could only comply with her request, and hope that time and thought would become his allies.   She told her father that she was not well, and shut herself up in her own little room ; but for hours her mind was so stunned and bewildered that it could not act coherently.

CHAPTER XXXII.

GROPING HER WAY.

THE night to Saville was one of sleepless anxiety. He felt that he was at the crisis of his life. Indeed, if Vera gave him back his ring, saying that, under the circumstances, she could not accept of his love, what would life be but a painful burden? The result of the council which he knew her to be holding with her own heart, and the mysterious faith which he had found so hard to overcome, might blast the hope upon which he built all his future. When she appeared, the following morning he scarcely dared lift his eyes to her pale face, lest he should there see the impress of a determination which he might not be able to overcome. But, instead of a strong resolve, he saw only irresolution and trouble, her mobile features revealing the deep disquietude and uncertainty of her mind. He also saw, from her greeting and wistful eyes, how tenaciously her heart clung to him. His manner was gentleness and sympathy itself, and while she evidently longed to receive it in her old, frank manner, as her right, she hesitated, as if it were forbidden and fraught with danger. Her restraint did not dishearten him, and he thought exultantly,

" She is mine. Her love will not permit her to give me up ; her old beliefs are shaken. Time, gentleness, and the truth shall be my strong allies, and to them she will surely yield."

Her father was too preoccupied to notice that anything

was amiss, and soon after the morning meal was over, departed on one of his lonely tramps into the forest.

Saville led Vera again to their old, secluded haunt on the hill-side, hoping that ere the day closed he might satisfy her mind sufficiently to secure an acquiescence in his plans, which, if at first hesitating and full of fear, would soon become hearty and decided.

" I learn by your face and manner, dearest," he said, " that you will not send me away a despairing and reckless man."

She shivered at these words, for they opened a new vista of difficulty and danger.

She sat down on a mossy rock and put her hands to her head, saying, in pathetic, childlike simplicity,

" I can't seem to think any more. I can only feel and suffer. My head is still all confused, and my heart is like lead."

" Let me think for you, Vera," he said, taking one of her cold, passive hands. " Let me assure you, also, that I do not consider my cause so desperate and my views so unsound that I must take advantage of your weakness, and urge you to a hasty decision. I wish to carry your reason and all pure, womanly feelings with me at every step."

" O Theron ! would to God I knew what is right, what is true ! And you say there is no God. I am bewildered and lost."

" The impulses of nature are right, Vera. The unerring instincts of our own hearts are true, if in each case our reason approves."

" The impulses of nature are right," she repeated slowly after him.

" Yes," he replied eagerly ; " and you, as nature's nearest and most perfect child, will soon see that I am correct. What we feel—what we think within our own breasts—that we know.   What we see and experience in nature without we also know ; but what else are we sure of ?   I am not asking you to peril your happiness on what some old, bigoted Jews wrote a millennium or two ago ; but to build it surely on what your own eyes, your own heart and reason, assure you of to-day.   I am here at your side ; I am loyal to you to my heart's core.   To the utmost extent of my ability you can depend upon me ; while I live———''

" Ah ! Theron, there is the terrible part of your belief— ' While you live.'   Do you not see that you are standing on a little point, with a black, rayless gulf all around you ? What if you should fall ?   What if you should die ?   Where could I find you ?''

" Dismiss these morbid fancies, dearest.   There is no need of supposing that I shall fall or die.   I have the pre-sentiment of a long and happy life with you, if I can only dissipate the clouds of superstition from your mind, and, after life is over, we shall sleep and not be conscious of our loss.   But now, long before that deep oblivion comes, to see a bliss beyond that of your fancied heaven, almost within our grasp, and yet to be denied—this is more than human fortitude can endure.   Let me teach you the truth from your own experience, and pardon the seeming egotism of my argument, for it is all for your sake as truly as my own. The evening you buried your mother you said I saved your heart from breaking.   The voice of living sympathy brought relief.   Your mother did not help you, simply because she could not.   She was sleeping, and even the voice of her child could not awaken her.   If you will calmly think of it, she has been lost to you from the moment she breathed her last, and all that she has been to you since has been due to your vivid memory and strong imagination.   At no time can you prove her presence or show that she gave you any practical help.''

"O Theron! I never felt so orphaned before," she sobbed.

"I know my words hurt you cruelly, darling, but they are necessary to your final health and happiness. When even your light touch bound up my wound, it caused me agony for the moment ; but I am here to-day because of that suffering. Go back with me to the time when I found you near your old desolated home. You were embracing the unresponsive mound beneath which your mother was sleeping, and the cold, unanswering silence was breaking your heart. You had become timidity itself, feeling justly that you had no protector. As soon as I appeared, you had a strong arm to lean upon. Has not your life improved since that day ? Has it not grown fuller, more complete and satisfying ?"

"I should have been dead but for your coming, Theron."

"That which is worse than death might have happened," he said shudderingly. "Think of the perils to which you were exposed before I came. I have been to the point of Butter Hill, where you escaped a fate too frightful to be imagined. As I pictured you climbing that awful precipice, I trembled and grew faint. Who helped you then ?"

"It seemed as if God helped me."

"But was there in fact any practical help save that which these little hands and feet gave, bruised and bleeding as they must have been ? Kindly nature held out a shrub here and there, and the granite rock, more merciful than your imagined deity, gave you a few crevices on which to step for a perilous moment. Your own weary feet carried you on that lonely, desperate journey home, and when your natural and human strength gave out, you fell. No one helped you, and, were it not for the accident of old Gula stumbling against your unconscious form, you would have perished within a few yards of your own door. And if, a little later, the ruffians had found you in the cabin, who would have saved you ? Who has saved thousands, equally helpless, from every outrage that incarnate fiends could perpetrate ? Poor, inoffensive Gula was rescued by a human hand. My life was saved by these dear hands. Tell me when and where any real and practical blessing came to our lives that was not brought by human hands, and prompted by human love.''

She turned and clung to him almost in terror, as she said,

'' Theron, is this arm, which death may at any moment paralyze, my only defense ?''

'' What have been the facts, darling ? Who has helped you ? Who rescued me when I should have soon died from my wound, as that thing which the law calls my wife devoutly wished ?''

'' There seems reason in what you say,'' she said ; '' and yet it is so contrary to all that I ever hoped or believed that I cannot grasp it,'' and her brow contracted for a few moments in deep thought.

He did not interrupt her, wishing to give his words time to make their impression.

At last she said slowly, '' I must try to feel my way out of this darkness, and come to some clear sense of what your words mean and involve. I shall have to trust you, Theron. You can easily deceive such an ignorant child as I am, but I know you will not. I have always lived in these mountains, and mother and the Bible have been my only teachers.''

'' You forget nature, Vera. I cannot help feeling that she has taught you more than all. It is her influence that makes you so docile and receptive. Your mind opens to the truth, like the flower buds to the rain and dew, whenever they fall.''

'' Alas ! the resemblance is too true. You might put

within the petals of the silly flowers that which would poison them, and they would know no better at first.''

'' And can you think I would try to poison your mind, Vera ?''

'' Not willingly and knowingly, Theron ; and yet I tremble at the thoughts you suggest, and fear they involve more to me than you realize. Besides, if you are right, so many must be mistaken ; at least I think so. I am so ignorant, and my life has been so remote from the world, that I distrust myself on every side. You say that the great and wise believe as you do ?''

Here Saville launched out with enthusiasm and sincerity. '' The learned men of France,'' he said, '' are the great thinkers of the world. They are rapidly emancipating their own nation, and their ideas are finding an increasing number of adherents in this country and England, especially among the educated classes. Only those who will not or cannot think for themselves hold to the old superstitions ; and in a generation or two more, all our barbarous laws will have to be remodeled in accordance with truth and reason. Men will evolve their laws from their own nature and needs, and hence they will cease to be mere arbitrary and irrational restraints. By following the impulses and teachings of nature, *we* may hasten forward that golden age. It was one of my dearest hopes that I might, in this new land, contribute much toward reorganizing society, and breaking the chains under which so many are groaning. Perhaps I have been made to feel how galling and unnatural they are that I might be fitted for the task.''

'' Who has arranged it so that you might be fitted for this task ?'' asked Vera innocently.

'' Well, destiny, nature, or perhaps I should more correctly say, it is a happy chance,'' answered Saville, some-what confused.

"It's all so strange and vague to me," said Vera despondently. "These questions are too deep for me. I cannot follow you. There seems nothing sure existing but yourself, and in a few hours you will be gone, and then comes the awful uncertainty whether you will ever return." After a few moments she added, with an averted face and burning blush, "As things are now, Theron, we cannot be truly married."

"Yes, Vera, it will be my only true marriage. Was that a true marriage which joined me temporarily to a woman whom I loathe and hate, though solemnized by every priestly and superstitious form? Nature joins our hands, hearts, and lives, and makes us one in reality."

"Would it be true marriage to your mother?" asked Vera, in a low tone.

"My mother holds to the old views," said Saville hesitatingly. "While we love each other dearly, we differ radically on many points. She does not approve of this war for liberty."

"It would not seem a true marriage to my mother, if she were living, Theron," continued Vera in the same low, troubled voice.

"Probably not Vera. With her prejudices and beliefs, the mere formal rite, which is impossible, would be essential. But your mother is dead, and I am here."

"The Bible would be against it, Theron."

"I suppose it would be. But, as the Bible is a mere expression of human opinion, we have a better right to our opinions in this more enlightened age."

"Would many people, in our own age, regard it as true marriage?"

"Not yet, I fear," he said sadly; "but they will in time. But what is the world to us? I am more than willing to share your seclusion among these beautiful mountains. As long as we know that we are doing right, what need we care what the world thinks ?''

'' If there is no God to whom we are responsible,'' she said in sudden recklessness, '' and if in a few days we shall cease to be, why need we care what is right ? It seems to me the words right and wrong have no meaning. The only question is, What do we want to do ? We must hastily snatch at whatever is within our reach, and make the most of it while we can.''

'' Now, Vera, darling, those words are not like your old self,'' he replied, with a slight accent of reproach. '' You have only to follow the instincts of your pure, womanly nature to do what is right and shun what is wrong.''

'' But your words are sweeping away all on which I based my motives and rules of action,'' she continued, in the same desperate tone. '' The Heavenly Father that I tried to please, as a dutiful child, is but a mere name. The mother, whose gentle teaching echoed His will, has ceased to exist. I am to live a few uncertain days, and then also become nothing. In accordance with all I have been taught to believe true, I have no right to sit here listening to your love. Neither your mother nor mine would believe it right, and, strange to say, I have a guilty fear in my own heart while doing so. I don't understand it. And yet, if you are not mistaken in what you have told me, why need I care ? You are here. I am sure of to-day. That is all.''

He was appalled at the reckless and unnatural expression of her face. Instead of the pure, gentle light which usually beamed from her deep blue eyes, it almost seemed as if a lurid flame were burning back of them. He asked himself, in wonder, Is this Vera ? But he only said, gently and soothingly,

'' The truth involves such great and radical changes in your belief that you are confused, darling. You will see everything calmly in its proper light by-and-by ; and, that you may, I will give you an abundance of time. ''

" ' Time !' '' she repeated, with a bitter laugh ; '' that is the only thing in which we need to practice economy.   In a few hours you will mount your horse and vanish like my other delusions.   What is sure, save this fleeting moment ?''

Then, in strong revulsion of feeling, she commenced weeping bitterly.

'' There is something wrong in all this, Theron,'' she sobbed.   '' I am frightened.   I tremble at myself, and am sore perplexed.   It seems as if I were falling down some black chasm, and even your hand could not reach me.   The impulses of nature, as you call them, and conscience are all at war.   I don't understand myself at all.   I only know that something is wrong, and that there must be a dreadful mistake somewhere.   Have pity on me and take me home.''

The man of theories was almost as greatly perplexed as herself, but he took comfort in the thought that she was unstrung by her strong emotions ; that her trust in her old beliefs had given way so suddenly that she was too bewildered to see the solid ground where he stood.   With soothing, gentle words he led her to the cabin.

'' I will go now,'' he said ; '' but shall return in a day or two, and then you will be able to see everything clearer, and you will be your old happy self.''

'' Theron; do not go,'' she said, with such sudden and passionate earnestness that he was surprised.   Then she added, almost instantly, in a tone of the deepest sadness, '' Yes, you must go, you must go.   Good-by,'' and she hastened to the seclusion of her own room.

He went away feeling that all was still in doubt.

'CHAPTER XXXIII.

STRONG TEMPTATION.

SEVERAL days passed before Saville's duties permitted him to be absent again.   To him they were desperately long, but to Vera they were interminable.   And yet she almost dreaded to see him, for she could not solve the questions of right and duty.   Her heart sided with him and his arguments with pleadings so strong that it seemed they would not be denied.   The doubts he had raised in her mind grew stronger as she dwelt upon them.

" If this life is all," she sighed again and again, " how unspeakably dreadful to lose this one chance of happiness ! But, even if I yield, will I be happy ?" she asked herself in prophetic dread.   " I have such a strange, guilty fear in giving up all my old belief, and doing what mother forbade. If I could only become his wife, as mother said, I should be the happiest, proudest woman that ever lived.   But now, although he is so true, I dare not trust him.   I dare not trust myself.   I feel that it is a leap into the dark.   Oh ! that I knew what was right ; oh ! that I knew what was true !

" And yet I cannot give him up.   It would now be a million-fold worse than death.   Can there be anything more dreadful in all the future even if the Bible is true ?   How much easier it would be to give him every drop of my heart's blood than to give him back this ring !   How strange it feels upon my finger !   It burns like a circlet of fire.   It can't be right.   Oh ! is it very wrong ?"

Thus, by turns, doubt, passion, fear, and love surged over her mind till she thought she would lose her reason.

Her old playmates, the flowers, began to look at her reproachfully, the notes of the birds to grow strangely plaintive, and the breathings of the winds among the trees were long drawn sighs, responsive to her own.

"It is just as mother said it would be," she moaned; "nature frowns upon me. It must be wrong. But if I am mistaken, if she were mistaken, if this is only a sick fancy of my disquieted mind—*oh! that I knew what was true and right.*"

One lovely afternoon, weary and torn by conflicting emotions, she went out to the old haunt on the hill-side. In her distress she threw herself upon the ground, and buried her burning face in the cool grass. How long, in her deep preoccupation, she lay there, she did not know, but at last a kind voice said,

"Vera."

"O Theron! have you come once more?"

"Yes, darling; I could not come before."

Then she became silent, and seemed under the most painful restraint. She was so unlike her former self that he sighed deeply.

She burst into tears as she said, "That is the way it is all ending; sighs, sighs, only sighs."

"Must it all end in sighs?" he asked very sadly.

"I fear that it will anyway. Theron, I get no light. I cannot give you up, and yet my heart forebodes evil till I tremble with dread."

"You are not well, Vera. Your hands are feverish, and your pulse rapid and uneven."

"It but faintly echoes the unrest of my heart. I have thought and thought till my head swam in a dizzy whirl. My love has been your ever present and eloquent advocate.

At times, I have been on the point of recklessly shutting my eyes, and of letting you lead me whither you would."

"My only wish, darling, is to lead you to deep content and lasting peace."

"How mockingly impossible that happy condition seems ! O Theron ! I don't understand myself at all. It seems but the other day, and I was a simple child ; now I am I know not what. My own feelings remind me of Shakspeare's tragedies, which I never half understood before. Even in my dreams I am walking on the crumbling edge of an abyss. Even if I yield, something tells me that I shall lose you. It can't be right, Theron, it can't be right, though your words and your unspeakable kindness to me make it seem so. I dare not think of your mother, much less of my own. Did my poor, dying mother have a prophetic insight into the future when she charged me, ' Be true to your God and your faith ; be true to my poor teachings and your own pure, womanly nature. Let the Bible guide you in all things, and then you will always have peace in your heart, and find sympathy in nature without. But rest assured, however wise and greatly to your advantage anything may seem, if your Bible is against it, do not hesitate ; turn away, for if will not end well. Keep thy heart with all diligence. When it troubles you, and your old playmates, the innocent flowers, look at you reproachfully, something will be wrong ' ? Theron, they do look at me reproachfully, and my heart is full of strange disquietude and fear. Mother said, ' Keep true, and our separation will be brief.' My feelings of late seem to rob me of the right of even remembering her. Half-forgotten sentences from her burned Bible come into my mind like lightning flashes. One of these is ever ringing in my ears I don't remember its connection, but the words are dreadful, and they too often express my condition. They are, ' A fearful looking for of judgment.' Then again I almost see the Saviour looking at me so reproachfully—just as He must have looked on Peter when he denied his Lord. And Shakspeare, too, which you say is one of the greatest books of the world, seems to echo the Bible. The writer must have understood the human heart, for he describes mine. He gives the experience of those who did wrong, and he portrays myself. But when I think of you and your devoted loyalty to me when any one else would have cast me off, I have not the heart to deny you anything. As for myself, I would rather die a thousand deaths than be separated from you. If I were only sure what was right—that is the only ground on which I can end this cruel conflict.''

'' And that is the only ground on which I wish you to end it,'' he said gently and soothingly, taking her hand.

But he was surprised at the intensity and far-reaching character of her thoughts and emotions. Were it not for the external shadows which had fallen so darkly on her life, she had seemed to him almost an emanation of the sunshine, a being akin to her companions, the flowers, and with no capabilities for the dark, passionate thoughts which were surging up in her mind. Was nature failing him who had been her disciple and votary? Her impulses in this, her child, were far from being satisfactory. In his strong delusion he then could not understand that it was Vera's very nearness to nature's heart that caused the deep unrest and dread as he sought to lead her into violation of the subtle laws which the Divine Author had caused to permeate all His work.

The eating of the forbidden fruit appeared a simple, harmless act in the mellow light of Eden ; but it broke the safe, harmonious control of God's will, and there has been jarring, deadly discord, ever since.

But, assured in his own theories, he reasoned with Vera

long and earnestly. He showed her how the mastery of a strong superstition is slow to yield to the light of truth. He explained how hard and gradual was the death of ancient faiths, which now have no credence whatever. He tried to make it clear that the transition from the habitual thought and belief of years must be stormy and full of misgivings.

She listened intently, honestly seeking light ; but when he was through, she shook her head sadly, saying,

" What you say seems true. I cannot answer you, I cannot refute your argument ; like a weak woman, I can only feel. You men think with your heads, Theron ; but I imagine that women think with their hearts."

" Well, Vera, both your head and heart will be satisfied in time. I feel sure that when I come again the clouds and mists will have disappeared. And it may be quite a long time before you see me, for this is a sort of farewell visit. The French fleet has arrived upon our coast, and officers are needed who are thoroughly conversant with both the French and English languages. I have been assigned to duty on General Sullivan's staff, and start for the East to-morrow."

Vera became very pale, and murmured, " Is God, seeing my weakness, sending you away, and into new and greater dangers ? This is the worst of it all, for, however I decide, you must suffer."

" No, Vera, only as *you* send me away shall I suffer, and you only have the power to blight my life. Without your love it would be an unendurable burden."

" You will never cease to have my love ; but, Theron, I have the dreadful presentiment that if I do wrong, I shall bring evil upon you, and that would be worse than anything that could happen to me."

" Well, darling, only time can cure you of these strange, wild fancies. I will fortify my heart with hope that when I come again, you will give me your old joyous and confident welcome.''

'' Must you go ?'' she asked passionately, a réckless light coming into her eyes.

'' Yes ''

She swayed for a moment like a reed shaken by the wind. She seemed about to throw herself into his arms, but turned away instead, and cowering to the earth, murmured,

'' May God have pity on us both.''

He lifted her up with a manner that was at once gentle, strong, and protecting, and, placing her hand on his arm, led her home.

'' Good-by, Vera,'' he said, pressing her hand only to his lips, in a way that was full of respect as well as of tenderness ; '' your healthful mind will soon recover, and be clear and strong when I come again.''

She did not trust herself to speak, but he never forgot the expression of her face.

CHAPTER XXXIV.

A STRANGER'S COUNSEL.

FOR several days thereafter Vera's distress was so great that even the self-absorbed inmates of the cabin noticed it ; but she satisfied them fully by saying that Mr. Saville had been ordered away, and it might be a long time before he returned.

But her spiritual conflict went on with increasing bitterness, until she grew almost desperate, and feeling that she must decide the question one way or the other, the thought occurred to her that perhaps at her mother's grave duty and truth might become clearer. Something might there make it known whether she was restrained, as Saville said, by the strong though shattered powers of an old superstition, or by the voices of truth and nature within her heart. So, one beautiful afternoon about the middle of July, she started, as some remorseful pilgrim might seek a shrine famous for its sacred powers.

But when she drew near the familiar place, unwonted sounds filled her with apprehension, and soon from a sheltered height she saw that the rocky hill back of the site of the old cabin was thronged with soldiers, under whose labors were rising the walls of a work afterward known as Fort Putnam. She could not descend into the valley without taking the risk of being seen by many eyes, and meeting those from whom she shrank with fearful memories. She hastily retraced her steps, weeping as she went, and feeling more than ever before that Saville's words were true—that she had indeed lost her mother, and that not even her grave would be left.

"Theron is right ; there is no hope, no protection for me but in him," she had almost concluded, when the sound of a horse's feet caused her to spring from the path and conceal herself in a thicket.

A tall, grave-looking officer soon appeared riding leisurely toward her. His face was so open and kindly in its expression, that Vera felt that she would have had no cause to fear him, even if he had discovered her.

A few steps beyond where she was hiding, a little stream fell into a rocky basin, sparkled a moment in the sunlight, and then stole on into the deep shade of the forest.

The stranger seemed pleased with the spot, for he reined up his horse, and, removing his hat, wiped his brow, and then looked around as if to assure himself that he was alone. Having dismounted, he drew a small silver cup from his pocket and drank from the rill. He then suffered his eager horse to dip his nose deeply into the water of the little pool.

"Ha ! Lion, that tastes good to us both, doesn't it ?" he said, stroking the mane of the beautiful animal. Then he slipped off the bridle, and permitted the horse to crop the grass that grew green and rank in the cool, moist spot.

Laying his hat on a rock near, the stranger sat down and took a small book from his pocket, which he quietly read for some little time, often moving his lips, and shaking his head with a slow, gentle emphasis, as if the words before him were full of deep, grave import.

Vera's tears dried upon her face as she watched him with increasing interest. "I wonder what he is reading," she thought. "It must be a good book, for it gives such a sweet, noble expression to his face. I could trust that man.

Oh ! that I dared ask counsel of him. Perhaps God has given me the chance. Be still, poor, foolish heart,'' she whispered, putting her hand to her side in her old, characteristic way. '' Why am I so timid ?''

But when, to her great surprise, the stranger laid the book down, and, kneeling beside it, commenced praying audibly to God, her hesitation vanished. Crossing the intervening space with silent tread, she knelt near, and her tears fell fast as his voice grew earnest and importunate. The burden upon his heart appeared to be his country's weal ; and in his earnest desire that all the blessings of liberty and good government might be secured, he quite forgot himself. As she listened to his strong pleadings, her own wavering faith began to revive. and she felt that a great living Presence was near to them both.

When the stranger rose, and saw the kneeling form of Vera, his surprise was very great, and he was almost resentful, at first, that his privacy had been intruded upon ; but a second's scrutiny of the bowed head and tearful face quite disarmed him.

'' What do you wish, my child ?'' he asked, a little coldly, however.

'' Pardon me,'' faltered Vera, rising. and putting her hand to her side. '' I—will you please forgive a poor child that would fain learn to pray also ?''

'' Surely I will,'' said the stranger kindly, becoming at once interested in one who appealed, by her modesty and unconscious grace, to both his taste and sympathy. '' Do not be so frightened, and tell me how you came here.''

'' I heard your horse's steps, and I was afraid and hid myself. But I was in sore trouble, sir ; and when I saw you kneel in prayer, I thought you might be willing to counsel one of the ' little ones ' of whom the Bible speaks.''

'' I shall be glad to advise you if I can ; but why not take counsel of the Bible itself? That is the best and surest guide."

" I have not any, sir ; it was burned," she said, her tears falling fast. Then she added eagerly, " Is the Bible a sure guide?"

" Certainly, my child. How came you to doubt it?"

" I have been told that a great many people are losing faith in it."

" I have not lost faith in it," said the stranger, with quiet emphasis. And he took up the little volume reverently, adding, " This book commends itself to my judgment and conscience more and more every day."

" Is that a Bible?" asked Vera eagerly, and he marked her wistful gaze. " Oh!" she added, again putting her hand to her side, " how long it is since I have seen one !"

" This is all very strange," said the stranger musingly. " Who are you, my child, and how came you to doubt the Bible?"

" My name is Vera Brown, sir. We are poor people, and live back among these mountains. My mother, who is dead, taught me to believe the Bible ; but it was burned in our old home by some bad men. I have not been able to get one since, and I am forgetting its teachings. And yet I have great reason now to remember them. I don't know what is right and true, but I must decide. When I saw you kneeling, I thought perhaps God had given me a chance to ask."

" Perhaps He did, my child. ' God is faithful ; He will not suffer you to be tempted above that ye are able.' "

" Oh ! I *have* been so tempted," said Vera, bursting into tears ; " and it seemed as if God had left me to struggle alone. I was told the Bible was not true."

" Who told you this?" asked the stranger, a flush of indignation rising to his face.

In painful embarrassment she faltered, " Father does not believe as mother did."

" Then remain true to your mother's teaching," was the decided response ; " and rest assured that anything which the Bible condemns will end only in wretchedness."

" That is what mother told me."

" Are you willing to be guided by the Bible ?" asked the stranger very gravely.

" I will try to be," faltered Vera, " as far as I can remember it."

" I will take away all excuse for failure. You shall have mine ;" and he placed the little book in her hands.

" May God bless you, sir, for this gift. I did not expect so much. Never did one need it more."

" Repay me by doing just as it bids you," said the stranger, with kindly interest kindling in his eyes.

" God help me to do so !" she replied in a low tone, but growing almost faint as she thought of all that obedience involved. " I have one question more," she began, but stopped in deep embarrassment.

" Well, my child, do not be afraid ; you may trust me."

" I was sure of that when I first saw you, sir."

" You were ? Well, that pleases me more than all the fine things I ever had said to me. But you are not making good your trust, and seem afraid to speak your mind."

" I have been told," continued Vera, " that the wise and great are the ones who doubt the Bible—people who are able to think for themselves—and that those who believe it do not or cannot think for themselves."

" That is always the arrogant way of these skeptics," he replied indignantly. " Those who do not at once accept their ever-shifting vagaries, are set down as fools or bigots." Then, looking at the timid maiden standing before him in almost trembling expectancy, his face relaxed, and he added smilingly, " I will try to satisfy your mind on this point also, and will be a trifle more confidential than I imagine you have been with me. *I* think for myself, and have to think for a great many others ; and though I may be neither ' wise ' nor ' great,' I am General Washington.''

Vera stepped back and bowed reverently.

" No, my child, no need of that,'' said Washington ; " bow only to the Being to whom we have both knelt, and on whom we are both alike dependent. Trust and obey Him, and all will be well. And now, good-by. If we ever meet again, I shall ask you if you have been true to the Book in which your mother taught you to believe.''

A sudden change came over the shrinking maiden, and, springing forward with the freedom and impetuosity of a child, she took his hand, saying,

" The God of the orphan bless your Excellency. You will lead our armies to victory. I know it. God will answer, through you, your own prayer.''

As Washington looked down into the beautiful, eager face turned to him, his eyes moistened, and he said, after a moment,

" Thank you, my child. Your words and manner strengthen me. You have helped me as I hope I have aided you. You have your burden to bear here in these lonely mountains, as truly as I have mine out in the troubled world. For aught I know yours may be the heavier. But God will sustain us both if we ask Him. Good-by,'' and he rode away toward West Point.

Vera afterward learned that his visit there was a transient one of inspection. In accordance with a habit to which, perhaps, the profoundest philosophy will ascribe the final success of the American arms, he had sought retirement in the forest that he might entreat the Almighty in behalf of the cause to which he was devoted.

CHAPTER XXXV.

THE PARTING.

VERA sat down on the rock which he had occupied, and, turning to the chapters that her mother's teachings had made most familiar, she read until the deepening twilight blurred the page. As she rose she exclaimed,

" It is true ; it proves itself. It meets my need as the light does my eye. My conscience echoes every word. O Theron, Theron ! we must indeed part !" and she bowed her head upon the little book, and wept until she was almost too exhausted to reach her home.

For several days following she did little else save read the Bible, and think long and deeply over its teachings. Every day deepened the conviction that its words were those of One who had the right to say to His earthly children, My will is your only true, safe law of action. The Bible's teachings and principles so commended themselves to her conscience and unperverted nature that she felt that she must doubt her own existence—doubt everything—or else take her old faith back into her heart with more than her old childlike trust ; with the strong and assured confidence, rather, of one who has tested a friend in a desperate emergency, and found him stanch and steadfast.

Thus the question of right and duty was brought clearly to an issue ; the question which she tried to put off in its full and final settlement until she had wholly satisfied her mind that her lover's views were faliacious.

She now felt perfectly sure that he was wrong ; and yet it was agony to come to the irrevocable decision which would doom herself to the old, lonely, and unprotected state, and, what was still worse, to darken his life with grief and perhaps despair.   What might he not do in his reckless unbelief ? In her intense affection she was almost ready to cast herself away, deliberately and consciously.   Were it not for that one word, duty, which meant so much to her, she might have been tempted to do so.   If she were sure that she alone would suffer all the evil consequences, her grateful love, her strong desire to make him happy at any cost to herself, might almost lead to the boundless self sacrifice.

" But it would not be right," she murmured ; " and as sure as there is a God, I can never make him happy by doing wrong."

She went out to their trysting-place on the hill-side, where she had been so sorely tempted, resolving that she would settle the question there once and forever.

Laying Washington's Bible on a rock beside her, she leaned her head upon it, and sighed,

" It's earth or heaven ; it's God or Theron ; it's a snatch at something forbidden, or a long, dark journey to my rest ; for, in giving him up, I banish the possibility of the faintest ray of happiness in this world.   O God ! help me, like a kind, strong Father ; direct and sustain thy helpless child. If I must decide against Theron, let no harm come to him."

Was it an audible voice that answered ?   The suggestion of inspired words that had helped her once before was so strong and vivid that they seemed as if spoken.

" Commit thy way unto the Lord ; trust also in Him ; and He shall bring it to pass."

As if directly addressed, she replied, with passionate earnestness,

"I will obey Thee; I will trust Thee; there is no other right or safe course for either Theron or myself."

In the solemn hush that followed, she felt as if a kind hand rested on her head in blessing. The guilty fear and disquietude fled from her heart like ill-omened shadows, and in their place came a deeper peace, a stronger sense of security than she had ever known before. Her mother's face, which had so long appeared averted in reproachful sorrow, was now beaming upon her in approving love.

"O God! I thank Thee," she cried, lifting her tearful face to heaven. "I will never doubt Thee again. Mother, dear mother, you are not lost to me. I am as sure you live as that I live."

If Saville had then come, her strong feeling and revived faith would have made the ordeal of parting less hard to endure; but week after week passed and still she did not hear from him. At last Tascar brought a letter, given him by Surgeon Jasper at West Point. It assured her of his continued safety, and every word breathed of the love and hope which she must disappoint. If it had contained the tidings of his death, she could have scarcely wept over it more often and bitterly. But she did not waver in her decision; and in the depths of her heart, far beneath all the tumultuous waves of her sorrow, the consciousness of peace and security remained. She was also gaining an assurance that God, in some way, would make her loyalty to duty result in winning her lover from his skepticism.

She did not dare to let her mind dwell on their meeting, his disappointment, and the inevitable parting that must follow; but her constant prayer was that she might be firm, and that he might not become reckless and desperate.

At last one September afternoon Saville came, and, as was his custom, stole into the glen that he might surprise her. From the hill-side in his descent he saw her seated on a ledge that projected from a rock lying near the cabin door. He silently approached and looked over the boulder. His eyes at first dwelt only on the maiden with an expression of the deepest affection ; then they fell on the page she was reading, and he saw that the book was the Bible.

He became very pale, and gave the little volume almost a scowl of hate. Instead of announcing his presence in some playful manner, as he had intended, he went directly around the rock into her presence, with the aspect of one who, feeling that he must face a dreadful crisis, will do it at once ; but she, in the strong, sudden impulse of her heart, sprang into his arms, as if it had been her right.

"I thank you, my true, loyal Vera ; I was dreading a different reception," he said, as if an infinite burden were lifted from his mind.

But her fast-falling tears, and the manner in which she extricated herself from his embrace, disappointed the hope which her impulsive reception had raised, and he almost despaired, as she said,

"Come with me, Theron ; let our farewell be where no eye can see us save that of our pitying God."

"Do not say ' our,' " he replied harshly.

"Yes, Theron, *our* God, though you may not believe Him now. I have found light that is unmistakable."

"Where have you found it ?"

"In this Bible."

"Curses——"

She put her hand to his lips.

"O Vera ! this is worse than the bitterness of death. Why did you not let me die in Fort Clinton ?"

"Theron, don't break my heart."

"Is it nothing that you are breaking mine ?"

"God pity us both," she sobbed, burying her face in her hands.

They had now reached the spot on the hill-side which had been their favorite trysting place and the scene of strong temptation, conflict, and victory. He seated her on a rock ; but, instead of being his old gentle self, he seemed to have become a man of stone. For some little time her emotion was so great that she could not speak ; he would not. At last, she asked brokenly,

"Theron, do you doubt my love ?"

"You listen to old bigots rather than to me."

"Is General Washington a bigot ?"

He was silent a moment, then said, "He has not thought on these things. He simply accepts what he is too indifferent to question."

"But he told me that he thought very deeply on these subjects."

"He told you ! Vera, you are talking wildly. Can it be that you have brooded so long over these wretched superstitions that your mind is becoming unsettled ?"

"No, Theron ; my mind never was so clear before. Only my heart is faint and pierced with sorrow because we must part. Look at the fly-leaf of this Bible."

He read, in the clear, unmistakable hand that he well knew, the name "*George Washington.*"

"He gave it to me himself," continued Vera.

"Am I dreaming ?" muttered Saville, in a low troubled tone.

"Theron," said Vera, laying her hand appealingly on his shoulder, "have pity ! be patient with me, and I will tell you all. You can never know what this effort is costing me. Going after you to Fort Clinton was nothing in comparison. You caused my faith to waver by your strong argument that all the practical help I ever had was human help —human only. I have had human help again ; but I have come to see that God helps us and speaks to us through creatures like ourselves. Even you will be inclined to admit that the fact that I have received personal counsel from General Washington is so strange as to be more than chance, and yet it is true.'' And she told him how it happened.

'' In asking his counsel I do not seek to know whether you mentioned my name,'' said Saville gloomily ; '' for I have not sought to tempt you to evil.''

'' Believe me, Theron, I never gave him—nor shall I ever give any one—a hint or clue of that which is between ourselves and our God. The truth of the Bible was the only question on which I needed light. That settles all the others. Theron, it is true ! I know it, as I know I exist ! I am not wise enough to answer your arguments ; but I have come to that point in which I am not so sure of anything as that the Bible is true.''

He buried his face in his hands, and fairly groaned in the agony of his disappointment.

'' Theron,'' said Vera, with a burning blush, '' you could not love such a woman as you have described your—your wife to be.''

'' Why stab me with that word ?'' he cried passionately.

'' Suppose I should become like her.''

'' Impossible.''

'' You do not understand a woman's heart. You have learned to love me as a simple, childlike girl, innocent if ignorant, gentle and loving, if not strong and wise. Could you love me if I became a reckless, passionate woman ? Pardon me that I speak so plainly, and, in this agony of parting, pass beyond maidenly reserve and delicacy. But, since we must part, I wish you to see the necessity. Theron, you are too good a man to love what I would become if I should turn my back on my faith, my mother's dying words, and my God. You know that I have been brought face to face with awful peril, and yet never have I so trembled at anything as I have at the dark abyss that seemed opening in my own soul. At one time, Theron, I was almost ready to lose my soul for your sake," she continued in a low tone ; "and were I sure now that I only would suffer, that my remediless loss would be your happiness, I should scarcely dare trust myself. But God in mercy has removed this temptation, and I have been shown that wrong on my part would eventually mean wretchedness on yours. There, Theron, I have shown you all my heart, and I appeal to your own noble manhood to protect me."

"My manhood is gone. I am utterly crushed and broken. Since to you it is a crime to keep my ring, give it to me and let me go. I can endure the torment of my loss no longer."

"O Theron, Theron !" Vera sobbed.

"If there is no help for it, give me the ring, and let me go before I become mad."

Slowly and reluctantly she drew off the two rings, as if the effort were almost beyond her power. He snatched his from her, and ground it into the earth under his heel.

She saw with terror that he was taking counsel of despair. Acting on an impulse to save him from himself, she again drew off her mother's ring, and seizing his hand, she pressed it, with difficulty, on his little finger.

"Theron," she said pleadingly, "if it is wrong, I cannot help it ; but I love you with my whole heart. Wear this priceless relic—my dead mother's wedding-ring—as token of my pledge that, since I cannot marry you, I will never marry any one else. Let its faint gleam ever remind you that if you raise this hand against yourself, you strike me a more fatal blow."

In answer to this appeal, his dry, darkly suggestive eyes for the first time moistened, and grew somewhat gentle in their expression.

"Vera," he said, pressing the ring to his lips, "you are stronger and braver than I ; you have more than human fortitude. Though I scarcely know whether to thank you or not, I believe your words and gift have again saved my life. Your promise, of which this ring is the token, holds out a glimmer of hope, and without hope who can live ? I can trust myself here no longer."

He took her in his arms one brief moment, then dashed away. A little later the sound of his horse's feet echoed from the opposite hill-side, but died quickly in the distance.

It was well for both that he did not see her weakness, her grief that was almost as despairing as his own, which followed his departure.

At last she crept home in the dusk, repeating over and over again, as her only comfort,

"Like as a father pitieth his children, so the Lord pitieth them that fear Him."

CHAPTER XXXVI.

SEEKING DEATH.

A YEAR had almost passed since the parting described in the previous chapter—a year of patient fidelity to duty on the part of Vera, a year that was clouded by the deepest melancholy and almost despair in the case of Saville. For a long time he had cherished faint hopes that her fortitude might fail ; that his arguments, from being more fully dwelt upon, would have their weight ; and, chief of all, that her loneliness* and love might overcome her resolution. While recognizing the truth that she was acting conscientiously and heroically, he still believed that the only obstacle in the way of their happiness was the tenacious hold of her old superstitions upon her mind. The fact that their mutual suffering seemed so unnecessary made him chafe all the more, and his mind and body were giving evidences of the bitterness of the long-continued ordeal. Perpetual gloom lowered upon his brow ; at times, fits of abstraction almost unfitted him for his duties, and again he would be reckless and inclined to dissipation.

To his old acquaintances, his wife's conduct accounted for his manner and actions ; but Surgeon Jasper knew of the deeper wound, and was often tempted to inform Vera of the disastrous results of Saville's disappointment. Indeed, he would have done so had not the young man charged him, almost harshly, " not to meddle. "

At first Saville had found some solace in sending Vera by

the hand of Tascar, such things as he thought might add to her comfort ; but she soon, in a brief letter, gently but firmly declined to receive his gifts, and entreated him to remember that they must accept their whole duty, and school their hearts into submission.

But there was this radical difference between them : while her suffering was the keener, because of the sensitiveness and delicacy of her nature, she was finding increasing strength and calmness from the Divine help that is ever given in answer to prayer.

He was unaided in his struggle, and, if he still believed that man was a law unto himself, he was learning by bitter experience that he is not sufficient in himself for life's emergencies. He had at last reached that desperate condition in which, though still restrained by Vera's words and the ring she had given him from any directly suicidal act, he was only too ready to throw away his life by reckless exposure in the first battle that occurred.

Vera learned of his growing despair and consequent dangerous moods in a rather peculiar way. In introducing Tascar to the secluded cabin, Saville had virtually provided for the household, for the boy proved the most ubiquitous, industrious personality that ever taxed earth, air, and water for the means of livelihood. He soon became as accurate a shot as Vera herself, and she had no more occasion to range the hills with her gun save as a pastime. His knowledge of the instincts and habits of game made escape from his cunningly prepared traps and snares very improbable. His good luck as a fisherman became almost unvarying, because he knew just when and where to go. He enlarged the garden which he had made the preceding year, and kept it green and flourishing by turning through it a brook that had its unfailing source deep in the mountains. He scoured the hills and valleys for wild fruits in their season, and these.

with the surplus of game, found a ready sale at the garrison of West Point.

Vera had thoroughly adopted Saville's plan of perfect openness, and would permit nothing that looked like guilty fear or desire for concealment. Thus, through her management and Tascar's able seconding, the little cabin was becoming a recognized base of supplies for several officers' messes ; and Saville had always been ready to buy everything that his quondam servant brought, whether he wanted it or not.

In answer to her father's questions concerning Saville's long-continued absence, Vera had said briefly,

"Circumstances are such that Mr. Saville cannot marry me, and since he cannot, it is best for us both that his visits should cease. Ask me no further. Let it satisfy you that he has acted toward me like an honorable man, as he is, and that he is still a true friend on whom I can call should I need him."

The exile turned gloomily away, satisfied that Saville at last realized the folly of allying himself to the daughter of one whom he knew to be a criminal ; but from that time his remorseful pity and tenderness for Vera increased.

Tascar's success as a huckster finally led to his acquaintance with a redoubtable negro by the name of Pompey, for whom the boy soon conceived a strong friendship, and a boundless admiration. Pompey was ostensibly following a like calling ; but, in supplying the British garrison at Stony Point, he brought away shining coin for his fruits and vegetables, instead of the depreciated Continental money which was paid chiefly at West Point. This fact alone gave the elder sable trader a marked pre-eminence.

But one day Pompey took Tascar into the depth of the forest, and, with great mystery and solemnity informed him,

"You' se a peart likely boy, and I'se 'bout to put you up

a peg higher.   I'se a-gwine to let you inter a deep 'spir-acy.''

"Where is dis deep hole, an' how deep'll I hab ter go in ?'' asked Tascar, in some trepidation from Pompey's words and manner.

"What a chile you is !'' said Pompey loftily.   "'Tain't a hole ; it's a 'spiracy agin de Red-coats.   Does you tink I goes down to de Britishers at Stony P'int to hawk berries ? My mas'r, Capting Lamb, doesn't need to sell berries ; I takes a heap mo' inter de fort dan I carries in my basket.''

"What does you take ?'' asked Tascar, agape with curi-osity.

"I takes dese two eyes.   I takes dese two ears.''

"Well, you doesn't sell 'em ?''

"What a chile you is !   I comes back wid my basket empty, but my head is chuck full, an' I tells mas'r all I sees an' hears, an' he tells a 'Merican ossifer, an' soon Gin'ral Washington hisself knows all *I* does.''   And at this point Pompey assumed an air of such mysterious importance that Tascar was deeply awed.

"P'raps *we'll* take dat ar British fort.   We're a-thinkin' ob it,'' continued Pompey, half in soliloquy.   "It 'pends werry largely on me.   Now it isn't 'comin' dat a man in my 'sponsible 'sition should be out berryin' all de time. I'se got to tink'' (with a suggestive tap on his forehead); "an' while I'se a prowidin' sumfin' dat you doesn't know nuffin' 'bout, an' what is called strogedy, you can pick de berries an' bring 'em to me, an' I'll gib you de shiners for 'em.   Your part ob de 'spiracy is to pick de berries an' keep your mouf shut, an' den some dark night you'll hear more'n you eber did in de daytime.''

Though Tascar's share in the dark conspiracy against the British garrison was rather humble, he was more than satis-fied, and was so elated with his secret and his importance that old Gula asked,

" What's de matter, chile ? • 'Pears like you'se a-bustin'
wid sumfin'."

But Tascar, by a mighty effort, was able to keep his
" mouf shut."

Vera also asked. " How is it you get coin of late for the
fruit ?"

" I gits it honest, Missy Vera," was all that the sable
sphinx would vouchsafe.

But one July midnight he roused them all by his wild and
excited cries.

" Dar ! dar !" he shouted, " Pompey's goin' fur de
Red-coats. I'se in de 'spiracy, an' mus' go to look arter
it," and he started southward, in spite of his mother's ex-
postulations.

The heavy jar of a brief cannonade, and the faint reports
of musketry, satisfied Vera and her father that a battle was
in progress. To the maiden these sounds suggested danger
to the one ever present in her thoughts, and, in the solemn
night, they were peculiarly ominous and depressing.

She soon learned how profoundly she had reason to dread
such evidences of battle, for one evening, a few days after
the capture of Stony Point, Tascar induced his great lu-
minary, Pompey, to come and beam on the inmates of the
cabin for an hour, and to relate the events of the assault, as
far as he saw and imagined them. Tascar was peculiarly
eager to bring about the recitation of this epic, not only that
he might, as one of the " 'spirators," reflect a few rays of
Pompey's glory ; but also that his master might learn of an
important American success, and that Vera might hear how
strangely Saville had acted. He introduced his friend as the
hero of the occasion, declaring excitedly,

" Does you believe. Mas'r Brown, Pompey tuk our folks
right into de fort, an' cotched 'bout a million Red-coats ?"

" Well," began Pompey, with a patronizing glance at Tascar, "I don't 'spcse dere was quite so many as dat, an' den you mus' know, Mas'r Brown, dat I had 'siderable help. From what dis yer peart boy hab told me, you'se 'ud like to know how 'twas done."

"We would indeed," said Vera, welcoming anything that beguiled her sad thoughts for an hour. Tascar had not told her that Pompey had aught to relate of Saville, for he was magnanimous enough to detract in no respect from the force and freshness of his friend's narration. He had hinted to Pompey that Mas'r Brown would be greatly pleased to hear any tidings of Saville ; but, with a little diplomacy of his own, said nothing of Vera's interest. He had not been a member of a " 'spiracy" for nothing, and could keep other secrets than those of Pompey to himself.

"Well, you see, Mas'r an' Missy Brown," Pompey continued, assuming a histrionic air and attitude, " it all begin in a 'spiracy, an' I was de big 'spirator. Dis yer chile was in de 'spiracy too" (and he laid a patronizing hand on Tascar's head), " an' his part was to pick de berries an' keep his mouf shut. He's a peart boy, an' a good 'spirator."

Tascar, in the exuberance of his delight at such high praise, stood on his head a moment, and then righted himself again in the attitude of an intensely eager listener.

Pompey complacently waited till the boy was through with his demonstration, as an orator or actor might yield a moment to an outburst of applause, and then proceeded :

" De 'spiracy rested on two tings : De British ossifers like strawberries, an' my mas'r an' Gin'ral Washington liked ter know what de Red-coats was up ter. I" (with an air of conscious power) " was able to guv bof parties what dey wanted. I tuck de berries inter de fort, an' I brought back eberyting I seed an' heerd, an' often my head was fuller when I come out dan my basket when I went in. Well, ter git in an' out I had ter hab what dey call a countysign—a

sort ob sayin' or word dat is like a key dat unlocks de do'.
It's a mighty quar ting, de countysign is; it jes' makes
'em big grannydeers like suckin' lambs, when, if you habn't
any countysign, dey'd spit you on de p'int ob dare bayonets.

"Well, I'se had allers carried de berries to de Red-coats in
de daytime; but arter a while de 'spiracy got deeper, and
mas'r tole me dat Gin'ral Washington wanted ter see if he
couldn't tuck de fort some dark night. So I put on a long
face de nex' time I went, and said,

"'Can't git here no mo' in daylight. Hoein' corn time's
come; mas'r can't spare me;' and dey said, 'Mus' hab
our berries. You come ebenin's, and we'll let you in and
out; for you'se an innercent darkey, and wouldn't do no
more harm dan a mule.' I said, 'Yes, mas'rs, I'se jes' as
innercent as a mule.' An' I tole de truf; for you know,
Mas'r Brown, you neber can tell when a mule is a-gwine to
kick up.

"Well, I tuck de berries in at night, an' all went smooth
as ile a few days, an' de countysign let me in an' out in de
dark jes' as well as in de light. On de fourteenth ob de
month my mas'r said, 'Pompey, you'se got a long head.
We don't want a dorg nowhar near Stony P'int, kase dey
might bark de wrong time, you know. Can you fix 'em so
dey won't bark to-morrow night?' an' den he wink one eye
jes' dis way.

"Den I knew de 'spiracy was a-gittin' deeper yit, an'
takin' in de dorgs. Wheneber dey wanted some strogedy
dey allers come to me, an' dey knowed dat de only way dey
could eber git aroun' dem ar dorgs was by strogedy. I tink
po'ful strong a few minutes, an' den I said, 'Mas'r Lamb,
jes' leave dem dorgs to me. If any ob 'em barks to-morrow
night, den dorgs hab ghosts jes' as much as oder folks.'
Dat night I tuck down de berries in one basket an' sumfin'
for de dorgs in anoder. Whar I knowed people lived dat

thought 'mo' ob dare dorgs dan ob de country I jes' drapped a chunk ob seasoned meat, an' watched till I seed it tucked away whar it would be werry quietin'. To de trueblue Whigs I says, ' Gin'ral Washington doesn't want no dorgs barkin' ter-morrow night.' Den I winked jes' as mas'r did an' dat was enuff.

" I'se been 'tickler in 'latin' dese parts, kase here's whar de strogedy comes in, an' it all 'pended on strogedy. Anybody kin fight an' git knocked on de head, but in dis case eberybody, even Gin'ral Washington, had to wait till I'd done up de strogedy.

" Well, de fifteenth come, an' it was a big day an' a bigger night. You heerd de guns, but dare had ter be a po'ful lot ob strogedy afore dey was fired, an' all de great gin'rals an' kunnels an' captings foun' dat dey couldn't git on widout Pompey. Gin'ral Wayne, de one dey call ' Mad Anterny,' was at de head ob it all, an' he 'rived sumfin' less dan two mile below de P'int arter dark, an' he had quite a lot ob Continentals wid him, not so wery many, dough, for he was 'pendin' on my strogedy more'n hard fightin'.

" Gin'ral Wayne stopped his men out ob sight, an' was jes' a-startin' wid a lot ob his big ossifers to take a squint at de Britishers an' de kaseway leadin' to de fort, when we heerd a hos comin' as if de debbil was arter him, an' some 'un dashed up like mad. ' Why, Saville,' said Gin'ral Wayne, ' how in de name ob wonder did you git here?' ' I jes' heerd what was on foot, an' I stole away to jine de 'spedition as a wolunteer.' ' Kunnel De Fleury says you're mo' reckless dan I is,' ~nid de gin'ral, ' an' it won't do ter hab too many hot heads in dis ticklish bizness ; so I'll put you in charge ob de kunnel, and you must keep back and 'bey orders.' ' I promise, gin'ral, to keep back,' said de one dey call Saville, 'till you say de fust man dat gits to de center ob de fort is de best man,' an' den dey let him go."

Vera had been listening with a half smile upon her face, for she could not help being amused by the negro's droll manner and boundless egotism ; but, at the mention of Saville's name, she became deathly pale and very faint ; by great effort, however, she controlled herself sufficiently not to interrupt the narrative.

" Now, you mus' know, Mas'r Brown, dat de Britishers was a little careless, kase dey said de 'sition ob de fort was so po'ful strong dat de rebs couldn't tuck it ; an' no mo' dey couldn't, widout strogedy, an' dat was de reason dey wanted me all de time. De fort is on a great, high, rocky hill, an' de water ob de ribber comes all aroun' in front ob it, an' to'rd de land dere's wide, nasty mash, whar de mud is deeper nor de water, an' you'd go down inter it kerchunk ! right ober yer head. Stony P'int is a kind ob island, an' de only way to git dare is by a long, narrow kaseway, whar my ole missus, wid a broomstick, could keep back a reg'-ment. We could only git across dat ar place by strogedy, an' so dey all was a 'pendin' on me.

" Well, Gin'ral Wayne an' Kunnel De Fleury, an' him dey call Capting Saville, look all aroun' as near as dey an' could not be seen, an' all was still. De dorgs was wery quiet, an' dey seed dat I had fixed eberyting jes' right.

" About de middle ob de night all de sogers started, an' I goes on ahead wid de gin'ral an' all de big men, kase I had de countysign, an' was to keep on doin' de 'portant part of the strogedy. I had to lab de help now ob two oder 'spirators ; so dey had two big men fixed up like ole farmers, an' dey was to go along wid me. When de sogers got near de fort, de gin'ral stopped dem agin, an' he sent me an' de ole farmers on ahead, while he an' some ossifers follered slow like. Capting Saville wanted to go wid me, but de gin'ral called him back.

"Well, I had my basket ob berries jes' de same as eber —Tascar here pick 'em fer me—an' de ole farmers was each a-carryin' a sheep; an' so we trudged along up to de fust sentinel, as innercent as mules, sure 'nuff. De man knowed me, an' had let me by often afore. So I steps up to him to guv de countysign, which was ' De fort is our own,' an' de' ole farmers follered close on my heels. While I was a-whisperin' de countysign an' a-talkin', dey was to carry out de rest ob de strogedy.

"' De fort's our own,' says I to de Britisher. 'Correct, hand hit'll stay hour hown,' says de Red-coat. 'You doesn't tink I'm a-gwine to take it away in my basket, ternight, does yer?' 'What hab you hin de basket?' says he. 'Help yerself,' says I, an' while he was a-fumblin' about de basket, de two old farmers jump on him an' tuck away his muskit an' stopped his mouf so tight he couldn't git no berries in nor no sound out. Down by de kaseway dere was anoder sent'nel, but we come de strogedy on him, de same way.

"But de tide was so high dat even de kaseway was kivered wid water, an' strogedy couldn't help dat, an' so dey all had ter wait till de tide lowered. But Capting Saville wouldn't wait, and was a-gwine to feel his way ober through de water when de gin'ral call him back agin. Po'ful brave man, dat Capting Saville, but no good at strogedy.

"At last we all got ober, sabe a big lot ob men dat was to stay on dis side for a resarve, dey said. De gin'ral tole me dat I needn't go no furder; but I telled him dat I'd done my part, an 'bout de same as guv him de fort, and now I'se was a-gwine along wid him and see how he did his part. He larfed and says, 'Pompey, p'raps you is de biggest gen'ral ob de two.'

"Well, he d'wides de sogers into two big parties, and he tucks one and Kunnel De Fleury de oder, and he sent ahead ob each party an ossifer wid twenty men, who was to cut away what dey call de 'batis, or a strong, scragly fence ob tree-tops, all sharpened and stuck in front ob de fort. Dare was two thick rows ob dese, an' I pitied dem po' fellers who had ter go ter wood-choppin', while de Red-coats was a-cut-tin' dem up. Dey called dese twenty men ahead ob each party de ' 'lorn hope.' Who should jine one ob dese 'lorn hopes but Capting Saville. ' Come back,' says Kunnel De Fleury ; ' Come back,' says Gin'ral Wayne ; ' you'se no bizness dar.' ' I'll 'bey de lieutenant in command, and will disconsort no un,' says Saville, an' away he goes up de steep hill wid de 'lorn hope.

" I wanted ter see it out ; but I wasn't 'sessed, like Cap-ting Saville, ter get knocked on de head ; so I crep around one side, away from bof de parties, kase I knowed de Red-coats wouldn't fire whar no one in 'tickler was comin' agin' 'em, an' I could see by de flashes how tings was goin'. Gittin' 'round in a safe place, while oders was bein' cracked on de head, was de difference between havin' strogedy an' not havin' strogedy."

" But Captain Saville," cried Vera, seizing his arm ; " what became of him ?"

The sharp interruption, and Vera's bloodless, agonized face, checked Pompey's historic flow of thought, and sug-gested a new and quite distinct idea to him.

" Law sakes, missy," he began, " I didn't know you cared in 'tickler 'bout him. Tascar, you orter—"

" Speak, man !" she said, with an importunity that was almost fierce. " Was Captain Saville wounded ? was he— O God ! I cannot utter that word !"

" Missy Vera, Capting Saville's safe at West Point. I seed him yesterday. He wasn't hurt, dough it 'pears like as if he tried to be," said Tascar hastily.

" Ah ! thank God ! another awful danger is past. Please

hasten your story, for I cannot bear to hear of these awful scenes.''

"I'se near through, missy, for what happened arter whar I lef' off all seemed to be in a minute. Our folks went up de hill as still like as if dey was ghosts. On a sudden dey come on de Red coats, an' dey fired on our men, but no flashes came from our side. I was tole dat dare wasn't a loaded musket 'mong de 'Mericans, an' I tinks it was so ; for dey jes' put dere bay'nets in front an' run for'ud like mad. In a minute de 'lorn hope nex' me was cuttin' away de 'batis, or big, ugly fence. De place dat was so still as if dey was all sleepin' became full of drefful sounds. De drums beat de long roll, de ossifers was a shoutin' ' To arms ! to arms !' de cannons began to beller, and dev filled dem wid grape-shot, an' all de Britishers was a-firin' dare muskets fas' as dey could load. It 'peared to me dat ebery un ob our folks would be killed twice ober. A minute later I seed Capting Saville, by de light ob a big flash, jump on an' ober de 'batis, a-cuttin' an' a-slashin' wid his sword. Away went a crowd ob our sogers arter him. In less time dan I kin tell you our two parties come togedder, kerslap, right in de middle ob de fort. Dey hauled down de flag ; dey stuck ebery 'un dat was oncivil— Well, Mas'r Brown, ter make a long story short, dey jes' picked up, on de p'ints ob dare bay'nets, de fort dat I had already got for 'em by my strogedy. But, Missy Vera, if Capting Saville is a friend ob your'n, you orter look arter him, kase he can't do what he did dat ar night twice, strogedy or no strogedy.''

Vera fled to her room.

Her father looked after her with an expression of deep commiseration, and having dismissed Pompey with a few words of thanks, turned on his heel, and strode away into the forest, muttering,

"The curse resting on me will crush her also, and seems

to be falling on Saville. His pride will not permit him to marry the daughter of such a wretch as I am, and yet his thwarted love makes life a burden that he would gladly be rid of. Oh! the malign power of one evil deed! Who can tell when and where its deadly influence will cease? I have destroyed myself ; I am destroying Vera and Saville ; my crime dug poor Esther's early grave. How many others shall I blight before the curse dies out? Would to God I had never been born!''

NOTE.—A shrewd negro slave, by the name of Pompey, obtained the countersign, and guided the American forces to the causeway leading to Stony Point, in the manner described in the foregoing chapter. He belonged to Captain Lamb, a staunch Whig who resided in the neighborhood.

CHAPTER XXXVII.

SEEKING LIFE.

ON reaching the seclusion of her own little closet, Vera did not give way to helpless grief. She recognized the necessity of prompt action. Saville must again feel her strong yet gentle grasp, or he might be lost to her and to himself. Another battle would soon occur, and another opportunity for the carrying out of his dreadful purpose. He must be shown at once that such reckless exposure was a virtual violation of his promise of which her mother's ring was the token. She resolved to write to him and appeal to all the noble, generous traits which she knew he possessed, and to chide him for the unmanly weakness which he was now displaying. She even determined to risk the loss of her dearest treasure, Washington's Bible, in the hope that he would read it, and be led by its teachings to doubt the skepticism which had so little power to sustain and comfort. Thus, she was a sleepless watcher through the night, often writing earnestly and rapidly, and again thinking long and deeply between the sentences of the following letter :

" Theron, my more than brother, have I lost my influence over you ? The fear that I have adds greatly to a burden that is already too heavy. Your influence over me loses none of its power. It would be hard for me to say when the thought of you is absent from my mind. The greatest sacrifice you could ask would be a joy did not conscience forbid. Theron, I am trying very hard to do right. There are many days in which I can only cling desperately to God's hand ; but He has sustained me in a manner so wonderful that my confidence in Him, not myself, is continually increasing. He is very gentle and patient with me also, for He knows I am a ' bruised reed.'

" But, Theron, you are making my burden heavier than I can bear, even with God's compassionate help. You know well that in my shadowed life I have become acquainted with suffering, and yet never before have I endured such agony as pierced my heart to-day. You are the cause. Theron, in every unordered, uncalled-for, reckless step you took, in the attack on Stony Point, you trod upon my heart. When you are called upon to face danger by just authority, do your duty, and your whole duty, as I am asking God to help me do mine, in the face of a temptation that assails me relentlessly and almost continuously. I say this much, though well aware that if you receive wounds, I shall be more sorely wounded, and that if you are killed, it will be worse than death to me. But, did duty compel you to take part in that desperate midnight assault ? Was it love of country that thrust you forward beyond the bravest who were acting under orders ? When I pained and disappointed you, I did so under a compulsion the strongest and most sacred that the human soul can recognize. Was your motive in seeking death, that awful night, noble and sacred ? Theron, it was the first cowardly act I ever knew you to commit, and it was an act so cruel as to be utterly unlike you. It was an unmanly effort to escape from a burden which I, in case you had accomplished your purpose, would have had to bear alone, and which was made infinitely greater by your act. Granting that your belief is true, and that death is dreamless sleep, can you long for a rest which means unspeakable agony for me? I do not say it boastingly, but from the depths of my heart, I could welcome pain, loss, disaster, anything save sin, which would bring you rest. You should be stronger and braver than I. Why are you not? Theron, there must be something wrong in your philosophy when a man naturally as noble and good as you are sinks, fails, and is overborne; and if your philosophy cannot sustain one peculiarly strong and favored like yourself, of what use would it be to average humanity? How utterly it would fail the weak and tempted! But my faith in God sustains even me in as sore a stress, I think, as ever a woman was called to endure. It sustained my dear mother, and you know how sad her lot was in so many respects. If your creed cannot make a strong, noble man like yourself brave and patient, it is so poor that I am sure it is unfounded.

"Theron, I know you honestly think you are right, but are you sure you have full reason to think so. Pardon me if I, in love and sympathy, touch for a moment on your past experience. You once believed that the woman who is your wife was worthy of your affection. You assumed that she was, and acted honestly and naturally in view of your belief. If you had studied her character carefully and patiently you would have found that you were mistaken. Forgive me for saying it, Theron; but I cannot help thinking that any view, creed, or philosophy which can permit you to make a cowardly flight from life's burden, from the duties you owe to your mother and country, is equally unworthy of respect. We are now, as it were, meeting the same cruel misfortune side by side. Will you run away and leave me to suffer it all alone?

"I have a favor to ask. Your response will show whether I have still any influence over you, and whether you will do a comparatively little thing for one who will do for you everything in her power save that which is wrong. I listened patiently to all your arguments, and I tried very hard to believe them. Oh ! how I wished that I could think as you did ; but I had known and seen the power of God's living truth, and it was impossible. Will you in fairness honestly consider the grounds of my faith ? As a proof of my all-absorbing interest in you, I send the dearest thing I have, Washington's Bible, with the one request that you read it through, patiently and thoughtfully, and that you dwell especially on the New Testament. I suppose that there are wise men who could argue with you and tell you something about the Bible, how it was written, and why people think it is God's Word ; but I do not ask you to seek them. I only ask that you sit down by yourself, and, putting aside all prejudice, that you read this Bible with the candor and sincerity which have always been among your noblest traits. I feel sure the book will make its own impression, and contain all the arguments that are needed. I leave the issue with God, to whom I pray in your behalf more often than in my own. I hope my pencilings here and there will not mar the pages for you.

" Theron, is my mother's ring still on your finger ? It means now all that it did when I placed it there. But you made a promise then as truly as I did. Do not keep its letter but break its spirit. Farewell.

" VERA."

Early the next morning she summoned Tascar, and giving him the letter and package containing the book, said, with a decision which he could not fail to understand,

" Find Mr. Saville, and give him these as soon as possible. Mark my words, Tascar, *find him*. Go to him wherever he is, and give this letter and book into his own hands ;

remember, his *own* hands.   There is money.   If need be, travel days and weeks till you find him.   I must take no risks in this matter.   Wait for his answer.''

Having done her part, Vera was able, more calmly and trustingly, to leave the result in God's hands.

Tascar reached West Point at about noon, and found Saville in his quarters.   His gloomy face lighted up as he saw the boy.

'' Missy Vera tole me to give you dese, an' wait for an answer.''

Saville eagerly took the missive and package, and shutting himself up in a small room back of the main one, opened the letter with a hand that now trembled as it never had in the shock of battle.   He soon reappeared with a note in his hand, and said to Tascar, wno had zealously complied with the request that he should eat the untasted dinner on the table,

'' Take this to your mistress, and come to me again in a week, for I shall have something to send to her.''

'' Did you find him ?'' asked Vera, surprised at his speedy return.

'' Yes, Missy Vera, an' here is what he guv me.''

Vera hastened to her room, tore open the note, and, with tears of joy, read as follows :

'' My loyal Vera, I have read your letter, and am overwhelmed with shame and self-contempt.   How strong you are !   How weak I have been !   If I am not a *man* after this, let even my memory perish.   I now promise you to keep the spirit of my pledge.   If anything happens to me, it will be in the performance of what you even would esteem—duty.   And, Vera, I will even read the book which has broken my heart and blighted my life, in separating you from me.   I cannot now trust myself to say anything more. You are as much above and beyond me as your fancied heaven is above the earth.

" Yours, to command henceforth,

" SAVILLE."

The long, dark night was passing, and Vera saw in these few words the faint dawning of hope.   •

Did her pencilings mar the pages of the little Bible ?   Saville, on his return to his quarters that evening, turned at first only to such pages, and to the words indicated, which were thus made to seem as if spoken directly to him by the maiden.

One text struck him with peculiar force, in the circumstances.   It was heavily marked, and Vera had written under it, " May not this be true ?"   It was, " There is a way which seemeth right unto a man, but the end thereof are the ways of death."

" Is it possible that I am mistaken ?" he asked himself for the first time.   " At any rate, I shall be more bigoted than the bigots themselves if I do not accede to Vera's request, and give her side a careful, unprejudiced hearing."

Saville was too honest a man to bestow on Washington's Bible a careless, hasty perusal ; and he was too large-natured and fair to read it with his mind steeled against its truth by dislike, contempt, or the pride of preconceived opinion.   It was his sincere intention to be receptive, judicial, and let the book speak for itself, according to its capability.

Some things in Vera's letter strongly tended to promote a condition of mind favorable to the reception of the truth. Her reference to the blindness which he had shown, at first, to the character of his wife, made him wince, but the effect was wholesome.   He certainly had been mistaken then in a matter of vital importance, and how disastrous had been the consequences !

"If Vera is right, and this book is true ; if I am mistaken again," he thought, "the evil will be without remedy.   If death is not a dreamless sleep, but rather an eternal, waking consciousness of all that one has lost ; if there is the faintest possibility of this, I had better consider it at once."

He moreover felt that he had justified Vera's contempt for his philosophy.   What had it done for him, save to prompt to unmanly, cowardly action ?   Her faith, in contrast, had sustained her in patient, heroic endurance.   He was humbled, and truth is ever ready to be the guest of humility.

It does not come within the scope of this story to follow closely his mental changes during the days and weeks that followed.   It is sufficient to say that the grasp of the Divine mind upon his grew continually more masterful and firm. The Bible, as Vera said, did prove itself, as it ever does to the candid reader ; as it ever does to those who are not absorbed in their own little 'isms, or befogged by their own pet theories, or intrenched in opinions already formed.   Few of the Bible's opponents have ever followed the example of Saville, for he permitted the book to do all it could with him.

"My reason," he often resolved, "shall be like a judge upon the bench, and neither pride, prejudice, my wishes, nor an unfair hearing, shall bribe or dispose it to a false decision."

As he read and carefully re-read the book, and at last was able to grasp, to some extent, its scope and meaning ; as he discovered its wonderful unity in the seeming diversity ; as he saw that the verbal husk in the early parts of the Old Testament had a kernel of rich, spiritual meaning, and that the New Testament clearly taught a philosophy too lofty for a merely human origin, he gradually became convinced that there was a God, and that the Bible was His guiding word to His earthly children. The " Man of Sorrows'' fascinated him with irresistible power, and he followed Him in all His patient journeying through Palestine, wondering, fearing, hoping, but unhealed.

With the conviction of the Bible's truth, a distress of mind, such as he had never known before, began to develop itself. How must the all-powerful and holy God regard him, who had so arrogantly, and with so little proof and reason, assumed that His Word was a myth, and Himself a fiction of the superstitious ? And when he thought how he had tempted Vera, and caused her to waver in her faith, he was ready to despair.

" What have I learned from the Bible ?'' he exclaimed one day, in agony, " save that I am justly and irretrievably lost. I now know what poor, tempted Vera meant when she trembled at the words, ' A certain fearful looking for of judgment.' '' .

As early as possible, after receiving the Bible Vera had sent him, Saville had procured another, which he sent out to her by Tascar, as he had promised. While Vera welcomed this gift as a proof that he was relenting in his bitter hostility to' the book, she was left in ignorance of the radical changes taking place in his mind. Saville did not wish to commit himself until fully convinced. But when, after intellectual conviction, he commenced drawing practical inferences from its truth, and saw the fate which threatened him ; when his awakened and instructed conscience revealed to him that the penalty of sin is not arbitrary and externally imposed, but inevitable and natural, in the one sinning, from the very law and principle of creation ; the man was overwhelmed with rational fear. The dark question, which all the penances of the Romish Church, and the cruelties of superstition, have vainly tried to answer, rose for his personal solution, How shall I be rid of my sin ?

Only the flippant and shallow-minded make light of this question, and they but for a brief time.   The student of history and humanity knows that it has been the burden of the heart among all races and in every age ; and that to-day men are inflicting upon themselves inconceivable suffering in the vain hope of answering it.

Saville had learned from the Bible only part of the truth. He saw what evil was and what it involved ; but he had not yet discovered the remedy, which is usually overlooked at first from its very simplicity.

His despairing self-condemnation became so great that he determined to write to Vera, and see if she could not give him some clue of hope.   So, one day several weeks after the time he had commenced reading the Bible, at her request, he wrote the following brief letter, knowing that he would soon have an opportunity of sending it out to the cabin by Tascar, who was often down to the garrison.

" My faithful Vera, I fear the gift of the Bible, which cost you so much to send, but which I tried to make good by sending another, has been but of little service to me.   Will you be full of joy when I tell you that I believe it to be the true Word of the all-powerful God ?   Can you be, when you remember the doom which this Bible pronounces on me who so long scoffed at it, and (what is far worse to me) who tempted you ?   I am no longer in the darkness of unbelief, but stand in the searching, consuming light of God's truth, trembling at the thought that I have lost myself—that I have lost you—forever.   Is there no remedy ?   In my despair I turn to you, the one I have wronged most.

                              " SAVILLE."

" Mas'r Saville looked sick," said Tascar, as he gave the letter to Vera, one evening.

In a few moments Vera came to the cabin door again and summoned Tascar. The boy thought the expression of her face indicated that something unusual would be required, and he was prepared for the request.

" Tascar, will you go to West Point for me again to-night ?"

" Yes, Missy Vera, if it's anyting 'tickler."

" Give that letter to Mr. Saville, and you won't be sorry for the trouble it costs you. I will reward you."

Late in the evening, Saville received a missive which contained only these words :

" Theron, I wish to see you. Come to the place where we parted on the hill-side, the first evening your duties will permit.   VERA."

He briefly wrote in reply, " I will come to-morrow evening. How faithful you are !"

He put a broad piece of gold in the wearied messenger's hand, and said,

" Keep that yourself, Tascar."

It was with feelings difficult to be described that Saville looked down into the wild, secluded glen once more. Over a year had passed since he had seen it, or its inmates. The mellow autumn sunlight shimmered through the trees and upon the rocks, softening the rugged wildness of the scene. But in its dreariest wintry garb it would be the one attractive spot of earth to him.

" Will Vera be much changed ?" he had asked himself again and again. Ages seemed to have passed since he had seen her.

He could not surprise her now. She was waiting for him.

with her hand upon her side, as was her custom when deep feeling caused her heart to flutter too strongly. To one watching them from a little distance their meeting would have appeared very quiet and undemonstrative ; but to each other, trembling hands and moistened eyes revealed the depths of feeling in reserve.

" You are pale and thin, Theron," said Vera, her tears gathering visibly.

" These are the least of my troubles," he replied, half smiling. " I dreaded lest you had become shadowy and spirit-like under the discipline of sorrow. Since I have come to believe there is a heaven, I have been constantly wondering why you are not taken there at once. But I am inclined to think that you have become womanly during this long year, rather than angelic."

" I am glad to hear you say so," she answered, trying to smile also ; " for the reason that I am a woman, if for no other. I have no desire to be anything else at present."

" Vera," he could not forbear saying, " I did not know that faith and sorrow could make a human face so beautiful."

She could not have been a woman did not a smile of pleasure illumine her face now. Almost instantly it was followed by an expression of deep pain, and she turned away for a moment.

He understood her ; she could not drink at the ever-full fountain of his love and admiration, though the waters were so sweet.

But when she turned to him again, there was no prudish restraint in her manner. She took his hand as a sister might do, and said,

" Theron, I want to help you. You as yet only believe the poorest and most meagre part of God's truth."

He looked at her with some surprise, and said,

" Why, Vera, I now believe the Bible as it reads substan-tially. I admit that there is much that I do not understand, and cannot reconcile. It grows clearer, however, as I study it. The difficulty in understanding it all is an argument in its favor. It's a revelation of an infinite mind ; mine is finite. If I could grasp the whole book, I should say at once, ' It is the work of human intellects like my own.' "

" The simple parts are those which you do not believe. You do not understand the parts. that mother taught me when I was a little child."

" Then teach me as if I were a child."

" How strange that you should say that ! It's a good omen. Read those words." And she pointed out the fol-lowing text in the Bible he had given her :

" Verily I say unto you, whosoever shall not receive the Kingdom of God as a little child shall in no wise enter therein."

" We must come to the point, Theron, of believing what our Heavenly Father says, with the trust of a little child."

" But what does the Bible say of those who offend, or cause one of God's little ones to offend ? How sorely I tempted you, Vera," and he covered his face with his hands.

" But you have no wish to make me offend now ?"

" No. Whatever becomes of me, I shall thank God that He preserved you."

" Can you not see what a difference this fact makes ? Besides, you did not deliberately and consciously tempt me to evil."

" But that made the temptation tenfold harder for you to resist."

" You were not to blame for that. But why dwell on the unhappy past ? I said truly that you, as yet, believe and understand but the poorest part of the Bible. If the Bible is true, is not God true ?"

" Certainly."

" Must He not keep His word ?"

" Yes."

" Then listen : ' Let the wicked forsake his way and the untighteous man his thoughts, and let him return unto the Lord, and He will have mercy upon him ; and to our God, for He will abundantly pardon.'   You are willing to forsake your unbelief, and all the evil that grew naturally out of it."

" How sweetly those words sound as you read them," said Saville musingly ; " but can God, consistently with justice and His threatenings against evil, forgive my years of blasphemy, and my———"

" O Theron ! surely He will and can.   Did He not teach His disciples to forgive each other seventy times seven ? Will He do less ?"

He looked at her very earnestly, and she saw from the expression of his face that the light was coming.

" Vera, my good angel, lead me on a little further," he said.   " Even if I were forgiven, it seems to me the memory of what I have been and what I have done will oppress me with gloom forever."

" Read those words, Theron."

He took her Bible and read, " The next day John seeth Jesus coming unto him and saith, Behold the Lamb of God which taketh away the sin of the world."

" The Bible also says," she added, " ' The blood of Jesus Christ cleanseth us from all sin.' "

" Where is that ?"

She showed him.

" Theron," she said tearfully, " can you remember the scenes of Calvary and doubt God's love ?   That is the part of the Bible you don't understand and believe.   You never can understand God, or this, His book, until you make these words the key to all, ' God is love.'   I shall test you now whether you believe the Bible or not," and she repeated earnestly these words :

" If we confess our sins, He is faithful and just to forgive us our sins, and to cleanse us from all unrighteousness."

" There is no escape here, Theron. It's either God is true, or He is not true, and will not keep His word. You have acknowledged your sin with grief and sorrow, and you have no wish to continue in it. With this clear promise before you, what must be your inevitable conclusion ? Ah, Theron ! I read your answer in your face. You take God at His word. You believe. Can any happiness of heaven surpass this moment ?"

" O God !" he said, in a low, deep tone, " I thank Thee for mercy which is as boundless as Thyself !"

" Did I not tell you once, Theron, that Shakspeare echoed the Bible ? He writes thus of mercy, you remember :

> 'It is twice bless'd ;
> It blesseth him that gives and him that takes :
> 'Tis mightiest in the mightiest.'

" I believe that God finds more joy in showing you mercy, than you in receiving it."

" I can almost believe it." he said ; " for the Being I dreaded inexpressibly an hour ago now seems the source and fountain of tenderness. O Vera !" he added, with an expression which warmed her heart, and cheered her through the long, lonely years that followed, " I am glad to owe heaven to you. This is better than saving me from death in Fort Clinton. I can wait patiently now."

An hour flew by and another like brief moments. The full moon filled the wild gorge with beautiful lights and shadows ; but they were too deeply absorbed to heed the witchery of nature.

At last Saville reluctantly rose to go. " No ; I will not

go to the cabin," he said. "After these words to you I wish to speak to no other human being to-day."

He then commenced looking for something on the ground, and said,

"Where was it that I, in my wicked passion, trod that ring into the earth?"

"Here, Theron," said Vera promptly. "I have watched the place ever since as if it were a little grave."

He soon recovered it, and taking her hand, said hesitatingly,

"Vera, can you not wear this ring as a token of my boundless gratitude to you?"

"Yes, Theron."

"It is tarnished and warped like myself."

"But it's made of gold, Theron, gold that has been tried in the fire."

"This is a very different parting from our last," he said, after a moment; "and we now have the earnest in our hearts that the time will come when these sad farewells shall cease. Good-by. Good-by once more, my true, loyal Vera. I will watch till I see you enter the cabin door."

"Theron, you never made me so happy before. Good-by."

He watched her as she passed through the alternate light and shadow that fell upon the path. He saw the flutter of her handkerchief as she waved him a farewell at the cabin door, but still he did not go. The dawn was tinging the sky before he could bring himself to leave the place where heaven had opened to him in the stony desert of his despair.

.

CHAPTER XXXVIII.

A MYSTERY SOLVED—GREAT CHANGES.

ON the day following his visit to the mountain valley, Saville received orders which occasioned one of those suoden changes that are characteristic of military life ; for he was directed to report as soon as possible at Charleston, South Carolina. He wrote quite a long letter to Vera, in which he recognized the kind Providence which had brought about his new and happy belief and feelings before this wide separation took place.

" I must go this very day," he wrote, " for my orders are urgent. Your promptness gave me our interview last evening, and the peace, hope, and faith which grew out of it. I now feel that my feet are on the rock, Vera, and no distance, time, or disaster can finally separate me from you. How much I owe to you !"

The winter of 1779–80 was one of unprecedented severity. Even the great bay of New York was frozen over, and the British ships were ice-bound at their anchorage. If Washington's army had been strong and thoroughly equipped, he could have attacked the men-of war as if they were inland fortresses. New York city was no longer on an island, and the heaviest artillery could approach it on every side. General Knyphausen, in command, was greatly alarmed, apprehending that Washington would attempt a *coup de main*, and he made extraordinary efforts to secure himself against a sudden attack from the Continentals. But Washington's troops were half naked, shivering, and starving among the snow-clad hills of Morristown. For weeks at a time the whole army was on half allowance, and this at a period when the intense cold made generous diet most necessary.

"For a fortnight past," Washington wrote on the 8th of January, "the troops, both officers and men, have been almost perishing with want. Yet," adds he, feelingly, "they have borne their sufferings with a patience that merits the approbation, and ought to excite the sympathies, of their countrymen."

In addition to all other horrors, the loathsome disease of small pox became epidemic, and often there was not even a blanket with which to cover a sick and dying man. Thus the Continental army could scarcely keep soul and body together, much less strike vigorous blows at their ice-bound enemies, who were at least comfortably housed and well fed.

In this dark hour Washington entreated Heaven continually in behalf of his country.* He was often seen bowing in prayer in some retired place of the forest, and it is rational to believe that we witness the answer to his petitions in his sublime and more than human fortitude.

Had such a winter occurred at the time when Vera was chiefly dependent upon her own exertions, it might have been fatal to her and all the inmates of the cabin. It certainly would have been so, in the condition in which Saville found them in the autumn following the burning of their first home. But his forethought and liberality, and the labors of Tascar, had provided against such an emergency, and though she and her father suffered somewhat from the

---

* A soldier in the regiment of which the writer was chaplain during the late war, stated that his grandfather had seen Washington at prayer, in the woods near his quarters at Morristown, more than once.

cold during this interminable winter, they had food in abundance.

It passed away at last, and spring brought another long campaign, during which she heard from Saville but very seldom.

Another winter and summer passed, and there were long, anxious intervals, with no tidings from the South. Letters were rare and uncertain luxuries in those days.

At last the thrill of joy which went through the land at the surrender of Lord Cornwallis at Yorktown was felt, even in the secluded mountain cabin. Tascar, half wild with excitement, brought the news from West Point. Vera was profoundly thankful, as the event promised to hasten the day of peace ; while her father was more elated than he had ever been before with the hope that he would soon be, without doubt, beyond British law. As the war continued, and the colonies had maintained the struggle from year to year, his hope had gradually strengthened, that even the enormous power of England might at last be wearied into yielding the liberty which her colonies claimed. Under the influence of this hope he grew somewhat less moody and depressed, and at times he even tried, in a grim, poor way, to be more companionable to Vera, whom he pitied profoundly in her loneliness.

In the winter of 1781–2 a letter, that had been long on the way, came from Saville, stating that he had been wounded in the siege of Yorktown, but that he was now out of danger and recovering. It breathed the same quiet, hopeful spirit which had pervaded all his letters during this long absence. His faith was strengthening with time and trial.

Vera immediately wrote fully and feelingly in reply, and Surgeon Jasper, who was still at West Point, and a friend that could be depended upon, promised to make great efforts to secure her letter a safe transit. Its receipt did much to hasten Saville's recovery ; but such was the feeble and exhausted condition of his system, that his surgeon insisted upon his remaining in the South during the winter.

The spring of the auspicious year of 1782 again clothed the Highlands with beauty, and rumors of peace were gladdening the hearts of the people.

One day Tascar came up from West Point in an unusual state of excitement.

" I'se a-tinkin', Missy Vera," he said, " dat peace mus' hab come ober de water, for dey's gitting ready for wonderful doin's at de P'int. Nebber see de like afore. Dey's buildin' a kind ob arbor wid trunks ob trees, and de branches all twisted togedder, and it's as big—why de hull army could git under it. An' dey tells me dat dere's a-gwine to be *a big dinner, an' a dance, an' a ' few de joyful,'* an' no end to wonderful tings. I seed Capting Molly, too, an' she said we mus' all come down an' see, kase eberybody would be dar. Gin'ral Washington and big ladies and eberybody else."

Vera saw that her father was as greatly interested as herself.

" Do you think that it does mean peace, Vera?" he asked.

" We will go and see."

" Oh, no ; I cannot——"

" Father, I am going, and you would not let me go alone."

So, on the morning of the 31st of May, the strange little group, consisting of the tall and grizzled exile, carrying his long rifle ; his beautiful daughter, with her golden hair falling in wavy fullness far over her shoulders, and the delighted Tascar, who capered along the path like a frolicsome spaniel, often exposing their basket of lunch to imminent danger from his odd freaks, started for the plain of West Point, where the celebration was to be held.

They reached the vicinity of their old cabin during the forenoon, and Vera said,

" Father, we will rest and eat our lunch by the spring near mother's grave."

" Oh, no, Vera, not there," he answered, with a remorseful face.

" Yes, father, there. Mother is not lost to us. She is only absent now ; but I am sure she would like us to remember her, and to be near her resting-place."

He yielded. He was forming the habit of yielding to her more and more, for, since her will had governed, he recognized the fact that he had enjoyed both security and the comforts of life.

Vera left her lunch untasted for some time, as she gazed wistfully around the familiar place, now so changed in consequence of the fort having been built. With a deep sense of gratitude she saw that the grave had not been molested or trampled.

" I would rather spend the day here, recalling the past," she said, as they were preparing to leave, " than in witnessing the grand festival. But come, the longer I remain, the harder it will be to go."

" O Esther, my wife I would to God you had seen these better days," sighed her father. " Would to God you had seen the time when we could begin to feel safe."

" She does see it, father. I feel sure she is rejoicing in everything that brings us hope and joy."

He shook his head, but followed silently.

Vera was young, and still had the keen interest of youth in all that was new, strange, and beautiful ; and her eyes kindled and her face flushed with delight as the wide plain of West Point, lined with barracks, tents, and officers' quarters, all decorated with flags and gay streamers, opened before her. Across this plain, groups of people, and battalions of soldiers with their weapons glittering in the bright, early summer sunlight, were moving in what seemed from her distant place of observation to be bewildering confusion.

The magnificent colonnade, or arbor, which was built on a slight rise of ground in the rear of Fort Clinton, seemed to her a structure more wonderful and beautiful than even the imagination could create.

It was indeed one of the most remarkable edifices of the kind ever erected, and had required the supervising skill of an eminent French engineer by the name of Major Ville-franche, and the labors of a thousand men for over ten days. It was two hundred and twenty feet long and eighty feet wide, and was composed of the simple materials which the trees in the vicinity afforded. A grand colonnade of one hundred and eighteen pillars, which were simply the trunks of tall, stately trees, ran down the center, and supported the lofty roof, that was formed by curiously interwoven boughs and leafy branches ; the fragrant evergreens, in which the region abounds, being the chief components. Rafters sloped beneath this leafy canopy from the ridge to two lighter rows of supporting pillars on either side, and from these were suspended wreaths of evergreens and flowers. The ends and sides, up to a lofty height, were left open, so that the guests could pass in and out unimpeded, and also from every part command a view of the plain and surrounding scenery. This openness of formation also caused the immense structure to give the impression of light, airy grace.

As Vera approached, and saw that groups of people were passing unhindered under and through the beautiful bower, she induced her father to go thither also. He seemingly had come to the conclusion that he would humor Vera to her heart's content on this occasion, though it cost him a greater effort than even she realized to face the curious stare he saw on every side. At first she was so absorbed and delighted with the new and wonderful scenes, that she did not notice how many eyes were following her. Wherever they went,. faces were turned toward them, on which were the blended. expressions of surprise, admiration, and curiosity. But Vera was so utterly free from vanity and self-consciousness that she did not notice this till the fact was forced upon her. With her lovely features aglow with pleasure and intelligent interest, she strolled through the arbor at the side of her father, calling his attention to the festoons of flowers, the garlands encircling the rustic pillars, the emblematical devices, fleurs-de-lis, and other decorations significant of the American alliance with France.

As she was examining the fanciful manner in which the central pillars were surrounded by muskets and bayonets bound together by the intermingled colors of each nationality, she suddenly became conscious of a dark, bloated face directly before her, and the rude, leering stare of two evil eyes. She sprang back as if she had seen a viper coiled among the devices about the pillar, for she recognized in the stranger the tipsy officer who had insulted her by trying to snatch a kiss at the time she went to Constitution Island in search of tidings from Saville.

'' Ha ! my pretty one, I see you remember me,'' he said brassily. '' I hope you are now prepared to make amends for your coyness then. If so, I will forego the grudge I might naturally hold against you.''

Vera gave him no other answer than a look of aversion and contempt, which her expressive features made very un· mistakable, and hastening to her father, she induced him to follow the people who were streaming across the plain to the northern side, as if something of interest were taking place there.

They had not gone very far before the fellow, captivated by Vera's beauty, determined to make another attempt to break down her reserve. She started violently as she found him walking coolly at her side.

"Upon a gala occasion like this," he said, "a fair lady needs a gallant. I am an officer and a gentleman, and I can make the day pass more pleasantly."

"You are not a gentleman, sir, or you would not thrust yourself upon those to whom your society is evidently unwelcome."

"Nay, my lovely charmer; your frowns and coyness only stimulate my desire to win your favor."

Almost before the words were spoken a blow laid him prostrate on the plain, and the enraged father stood over him and said, with significant emphasis,

"As you value your life, do not approach my daughter again to-day."

The scene was drawing a curious crowd, and Vera, taking her father's arm, hastened to escape, leaving her insulter to explain his plight as he pleased. The scene explained itself, however, and the prostrate officer picked himself up and skulked off amid jeers and shouts of laughter.

But among those who had witnessed the incident was no other than the redoubtable Captain Molly herself, who, with quite a following of "swatehearts," was about as jolly a widow as one could imagine. She hastened after Vera, and soon overtook her, crying volubly,

"The top o' the mornin' to ye, Misthress Vera, and the same to yerself, sur. It did me heart good, sur, to see how ye gave that capting a lesson in manners. That clip at the side o' his head is the fust wound he's got in the war, for they say he's moighty discrate wid men, though bould as a lion or some wusser baste wid women. Faix, and I'm honest glad to see ye agin, an' a-lookin' as petty as a wild rose, too. I don't wonder the fellers is all a-starin' at ye."

Vera's greeting was cordial though quiet. For some reason she felt safer since Molly was within call ; but she shrank sensitively from the attention she drew, for the " captain," in her blue petticoat, cocked hat, and the scarlet coat of an artilleryman, was the cynosure of all eyes, being followed by a crowd of gaping country people wherever she went.

" This festival is not in honor of peace after all," said Vera.

" Did ye think that it was ? Well, yez live so far behoind the mountings that ye're a little behoind the times. Pace is comin' soon, but they call this a fate, and it's to the honor of the Dolphin of France. "

" The Dolphin of France ?" said Vera, turning to her father with a look of inquiry.

" Yis, it's in honor of the birth of the Dolphin of France. That's what ivery one's a-sayin'. It's not meself that knows what kind of a craythur it is that's been bourn, but I'm a-hopin' its mother'll have a lot more, if we are to have as big a day as this ivery toime ǃ"

" She means that the *fête* is in honor of the birth of the Dauphin of France, the child who is heir to the French throne," said Vera's father, his grim face re axing at Molly's words and manner.

" Now ye've got it straight, Misther Brown. It's nothin' but a baby we're makin' sich a fuss about. But niver ye moind, since we're goin' to have the fuss and frolic. An' now I must go back to me swatehearts. But belave me, Misthress Vera, none on 'em comes up to the fust 'un. I've thried many a one since poor Larry got his head shot off, but I shall niver git his loikes agin," and with that she scampered off, to Vera's great relief. And yet the maiden had cause to bless the meeting ever afterward.

Escaping from the staring, laughing crowd which Molly's appearance and words drew around them, they soon reached the northern edge of the plain facing the river, from which

point they witnessed a beautiful spectacle. Approaching
the shore were parallel lines of barges decorated with flags
and streamers, and the water around them was flashing and
sparkling under the strokes of multitudinous oars. These
boats contained General and Lady Washington and his suite,
Governor Clinton and his wife, eminent generals with their
staffs, and a large number of prominent citizens and ladies
of rank and fashion. A band of music led the way, and accompanied the distinguished guests up the hill to Major-
General McDougall's quarters, while the artillery thundered
out its salvo of welcome.

Vera watched everything with the wonder and delight of a
child, and it was a relief to her, and especially to her father,
that the pageant absorbed all attention, and that they, for a
time, were utterly unnoticed. It gave them a chance to recover from the nervousness and disquietude which their encounter with the rude officer and the irrepressible Molly had
occasioned. As Washington approached, Vera recognized
him with a strong thrill of pride and gratitude.

" He has the same quiet, noble face," she thought ; " he
is too great to be elated by all this pomp and show."

After his Excellency, his wife, and suite had disappeared,
Vera was annoyed at finding so many glances turning toward
her again. Unlike, perhaps, the majority of her fair sisters
who have since visited West Point she did not realize that
her own lovely face was the chief cause. In fact, both father
and daughter appeared as if they might have stepped out of
some old story for book of fairy tales ; and Tascar, as he
followed them, would have answered very well as a hobgob-
lin page. Many young officers lingered near, and cast wistful
glances at the maiden, but their manner was respectful and
unobtrusive.

Vera now suggested that they should find some quiet nook
near to the great colonnade, whence they could see all with-

out attracting notice themselves ; and her father was only too glad to accede, for this exposure was taxing his resolution to give Vera a day of pleasure, at every cost to himself, almost beyond his power of endurance.

Soon after their arrival, Vera had directed Tascar to find Surgeon Jasper ; but he returned, saying that the doctor had been summoned home, on important matters, a few days previous ; so they had no other resource than to do the best they could themselves.

They at last found a spot a little off at one side, from which, under a clump of trees, they had a good view of the plain, the colonnade or arbor, and surrounding heights. Plain country people and utter strangers, who, like themselves, were bent on seeing the pageant, and had no other thought, sat down around them, hiding them, in part, from view, and shutting away the curious and obtrusive. It was not long before they felt a sense of security and retirement in this sheltered place, which was decidedly reassuring, and even the poor exile became interested in the brave scenes before him, especially as they gave evidence that the Americans were gaining rather than losing the power to cope with their most formidable enemy.

At two o'clock in the afternoon, it seemed to them that an innumerable host appeared. The hills on the eastern side of the river were covered with troops, while from every side of the plain, and on the circling heights around, bayonets began to gleam, led forward by that music which chiefly has the power to set the nerves tingling with excitement. The earth beneath them trembled under the heavy, rumbling wheels of the artillery. Within an hour the plain and hills adjacent, on both sides of the river, were covered with serried ranks of men, their burnished weapons lighting up the scene with flashing brilliancy, by their vivid reflection of the genial sunlight.

About the middle of the afternoon, three cannons were fired as a signal. All the troops around the immense circle advanced simultaneously in grand and glittering array ; and, after a brief display, in full view of the arbor, the men were permitted to stack their arms, and throw themselves upon the ground, or stroll about near the line of their position.

All the officers, except one field officer to each brigade, and one battalion officer to each regiment, repaired to the colonnade, where, they had been informed, " General Washington expected the pleasure of their company at dinner." From every part of the plain, and in barges on the river, the gallant veterans of seven years of war were gathering to the banquet—a most unwonted experience to them.

But, while Vera was enjoying every moment beneath the shelter of her tree, and in the shadow of the honest, home-spun people, who were wondering, with breathless interest, at the rapidly shifting scenes, she was the object of plots and counter-plots. The officer whose insolence had been punished, in part, went away with oaths of vengeance. As far as he could learn, Vera was friendless, and her father under a cloud of some kind, so that there would be no one to resent any indignity he might offer them. He knew well where to find men of the basest sort like himself, and, as liquor flowed like water that day, the evil-disposed were ready for any reckless deed. He resolved that if Vera stayed until the dusk of the evening, he would carry her off to his quarters up the river. He laid his plans cunningly, rapidly, and secretly, taking into his plot only a sufficient number to carry it out. It was briefly this : After night obscured everything, he and his party would suddenly crowd up and around his victim, separate her from her father, tie a handkerchief over her mouth, so that she could make no outcry, and spirit her off to the shore, where a boat would be in waiting. But it so happened that a bad fellow of this officer's company was one of Captain Molly's satellites ; for she still was not over choice in her company. She saw this man summoned away for a few moments by his captain, and the whispered conference that followed ; and the quick witted camp follower surmised that a plot against Vera was on foot.

" What did that spalpeen say to ye ?'' she asked the man on his return to her side.

" He was a-tellin' me what a handsome woman ye is.''

" If ye don't tell me what he said, ye may take yerself off.''

" Now, Molly, me darlint, why should ye care what he said ?''

" I don't care ; I've only took a notion to see how good a friend ye're to me.''

" Well, ye won't tell, thin, nor do anythin' to sthop the fun that's up ?''

" Of course not.''

" Well, the capting, who is moighty swate on the women, is a-gwine to carry off a perty little gall to-night, and I'm to help him,'' he whispered in her ear.

" Is that all ?'' she said carelessly.

" I tould ye it was somethin' ye wouldn't care nothin' about.''

Molly made no further reference to the subject, but not long after she casually, and with no apparent motive, took a position where she could keep Vera and her father constantly under her eye, and she continued to maintain such a position.

As the sun declined toward the western highlands, General and Lady Washington, his suite, and the most distinguished guests moved from General McDougall's quarters, through lines of saluting soldiers, to the arbor, where was spread as elegant a dinner as the times and circumstances permitted. Five hundred guests, ladies and gentlemen, sat

down to the dinner, and the thousands who looked on, kept
by the guards at a respectful distance, regarded these favored ones as among the immortals. Vera saw Washington
at the head of the table, and she wondered how one so exalted in station could have been so simple and kind in his
manner toward her. She found herself watching him, and
thinking about his interview with her, during the time he
was presiding over the banquet.

But there was another, seated toward the further end of
the table, who would have absorbed her thoughts completely
had she known of his presence. Pale, thin from much suffering, and with the sleeve of his left arm hanging empty at his
side, Saville sat quietly among the guests, equally in ignorance that the one never far from his thoughts was but a few
rods away. He had heard of the proposed *fête* in honor of
the Dauphin, had hastened his journey, and arrived just in
time to sit down with his brother officers beneath the rustic
arbor. The insignia upon his uniform showed that he had
been promoted to the rank of colonel ; but the expression
of his face revealed that he had achieved a character which
is above all earthly rank and distinction.

He had not written to Vera of the serious nature of his
wound, and of the irreparable loss it had occasioned, knowing that it would pain her to no purpose. She would grieve
over it continually ; but, when she came to see him, he
could, in a measure, make light of it.

Saville found himself seated next to an officer possessing
the same rank as himself, and of a very noble mien, and distinguished bearing. There was a peculiar gravity in his
manner and expression, and he seemed to have no disposition to become convivial, as was the case with the majority.
This made him all the more a congenial companion to Saville, and they both speedily became interested in each other.
Saville thought he had never met a man of more wide and

varied information, or one bettei 'ble to express himself with elegance and force. He also no. .1 that he was treated with deference by those who knew him. The stranger soon introduced himself as Colonel Wellingly, adding, with fine courtesy, "I have long known you, Colonel Saville, by reputation as an accomplished engineer officer, and I have heard of your gallantry at Yorktown."

"I feel highly honored," Saville replied, "that my name has ever had favorable mention to you ; but I confess that I am thoroughly tired of war, and would be glad to devote what there is left of me to the arts of peace."

"Well," said Colonel Wellingly musingly, "I suppose the war is practically over, and I am glad, on account of the evils and suffering it ever occasions. But I am at a loss to know to what I shall devote myself, unless it be to the erection of a hunting-lodge among these magnificent mountains. I have never seen a better place in which to while away the useless remnant of a life."

From the first Saville had detected a low undertone of sorrow and disappointment in the man's words and accent. Colonel Wellingly evidently knew that he had suffered deeply in the past, for he said, as the cloth was being removed, preparatory to the drinking of toasts,

"We have both seen trouble in our day, Colonel Saville ; but I envy you the hopeful spirit you possess, and the purpose still to accomplish something in life. I am growing listless and tired."

Thirteen toasts, appropriate to the occasion, were announced successively, and each one was followed by the discharge of artillery and joyous music, and, by not a few, with long, deep potations, which made their march to their quarters anything but steady.

After the thirteenth toast was drank, the guests rose from the tables, which were rapidly cleared away in preparation for the dancing of the evening, and the regimental officers joined their respective commands.

As the twilight deepened, the *feu-de-joie* which had been ordered commenced with the thunder of thirteen cannon, followed by volleys of musketry along the whole line of the army on the surrounding hills. Three times the circling lines of fire flashed out, and the hills and mountains were kept resounding with the mighty echoes, until they gave way to another and more awe-inspiring sound—the thrice-repeated shout of acclamation and benediction for the Dauphin, by the united voices of the entire army, on every side. The poor boy was destined to soon hear, and from his own people, volleyed curses, instead of benedictions, and a pitiless cry for his blood, instead of loyal acclamations.

As the last vehement shout died away, the night was illuminated by a brilliant display of fireworks from Fort Webb. The discharge of three cannon concluded the ceremonies of the day, and was the signal for the troops to march to their cantonments.

In the mean time the arbor or colonnade had been brilliantly lighted up, and the dancing was about to commence. Vera had been almost overwhelmed with awe at the deep reverberations of the artillery and the impressive closing scenes. She now persuaded her father to let her see Washington open the ball, and then she would return home fully content. And when his Excellency, with dignity and grace, having Mrs. General Knox for partner, carried down a dance of twenty couples in the stately minuet, she felt as if the grandest visions which her old friend Will Shakspeare had ever raised in her mind, had been more than fulfilled.

But all was growing confused and somewhat disorderly where they stood, and her father had said more than once,

"Come, Vera, it is getting late, and we have far to go."

Vera turned away with a deep sigh; she had ever felt a

longing for social pleasures and the companionship of people of culture. The beautiful and brilliant scene before her showed how attractive such occasions were in reality, and she had looked on with the natural desires of a young and healthful mind. She had once hoped to participate in such social reunions at the side of Saville, and even the thought had been ecstasy. But now she felt that the deep shade, which fell so early across their humble mountain cabin, was the type of the somber shadow that would ever rest upon her life.

"Come, Vera," said her father still more urgently to the girl, who was lingering, for she saw in the gay throng beneath the arbor a face that reminded her of Saville.

They found their steps impeded ; the confusion around them increased ; suddenly her father was struck down by a blow from some one behind him, and before Vera could cry out, a handkerchief was passed around her mouth, two men seized her hands on either side and thrust them within their arms, and she was being forced away in the darkness, she knew not whither ; but she could not help associating the dark, bloated-faced officer who had twice before insulted her, with the outrage.

The assault had been cunningly conceived and skillfully carried out, for the villainous accomplices were making loud demonstrations around the prostrate father, thus drawing the attention and the crowd thither, while the daughter was being hurried off unperceived.

Never, perhaps, had Vera been in greater peril before. She was so overcome by terror and a sense of suffocation that she was almost fainting, when the handkerchief was snatched from her mouth, and she wrenched violently from the grasp of her captors.

"Ye spalpeens !" cried Captain Molly, with a wild Irish howl, and she drew her nails across the eyes of one of the men. No wildcat of the neighboring mountains could have given a deeper or more vindictive scratch, and he was glad to stumble off in the darkness away from the crowd which Molly's shrill voice was rapidly gathering.

But it was toward the principal villain that the redoubtable "captain" directed her chief attention, and she laid upon him a clutch from which he vainly sought to escape.

"I'll tache ye a lesson," she yelled. "Ye shall have some wounds afore the war is over, I warrant ye, an' they won't be in yer back 'nuther, but on yer big bloated face, where yer grandchildren kin see the scars;" and she clawed him like a tigress, and until his cries made a duet with her own shrill voice.

On being released, Vera had looked around a moment in hesitating terror. She could not see her father, and she knew not where he was. All around were dark, strange faces, and hurrying forms of men and women, and the air was filled with confused cries, above which arose Molly's loud vituperation, for with every blow and scratch she fired a volley of epithets. But a few rods away, the bewildered girl saw the lighted arbor, with Washington full in view. If she could reach him she knew that she would be safe. She darted through the intervening throng, past the startled and astonished guests, and knelt at his feet.

"Officer of the guard," cried Washington sternly, "what means such ruffianly disorder without that women must fly to us for protection? Arrest all concerned in it. What do you wish, madam? Do not be afraid," he said to Vera.

"Your Excellency," cried Saville, stepping eagerly forward, "I will answer for that maiden with my life."

At the sound of his voice Vera sprang to his side and clung, panting, to his arm.

"Indeed, Mr. Saville, I think that she is capable of answering for herself. If I mistake not, I have met this young girl before.''

'' Yes, your Excellency,'' faltered Vera, with her hand upon her side ; ''and you were kind to me and therefore I fled to you for protection now.''

' And you shall have full protection, my child ; so, calm your fears. Indeed, Mr. Saville looks as if he might defend you against the world.''

By this time the attention of all was directed to Colonel Wellingly. With a face as pallid as that of Vera's, he came forward and asked, in a husky voice,

'' Will you please tell me your name ?''

'' Vera—Vera Brown.''

'' Is that your only name ?''

'' Yes.''

The colonel looked at her a moment, shook his head despondently, and muttered, as he stepped back,

'' It's very, very strange. I never saw such a resemblance ; and the same old habit, too, of putting her hand to her side.''

'' O Theron ! you have lost an arm. You did not tell me.'' said Vera, bursting into tears.

'' That is a small loss compared with all I have gained. I did not wish to pain——''

'' My daughter, where is my daughter ?'' cried a loud, agonized voice from without, and wrenching himself away from the guards who had arrested him as one of the disturbers of the peace, the exile rushed into the lighted arbor. All fell back before his tall form, and wild, threatening aspect, for the expression of his face was a terrible blending of anguish and rage.

'' She is here, Mr. Brown,'' said Saville promptly. '' You are both among friends ;'' and he led Vera to him and placed her hand in his ——

"Come," said her father eagerly; "let us go. Let us escape while we can."

Again Colonel Wellingly stepped forward and confronted the exile.

"Who are you?" he asked excitedly.

The moment Mr. Brown's eyes fell on the questioner, he staggered back as if he had received a heavy blow.

"Are you Arthur Wellingly?" he asked, in a strange, hoarse whisper.

"I am," was the agitated answer.

"You did not die, then?"

"No, Guy; and I have been searching for you all these years. O my brother!" and he clasped the trembling exile to his heart.

"O Esther, Esther! my poor, dead wife! why could you not have seen this day?" Guy Wellingly groaned, with remorseful memories.

"She is dead, then?" his brother said, in a low, shuddering tone.

"Yes, dead."

At this moment, Vera, to whom the strange scene began to grow intelligible, stepped forward and said earnestly,

"No, father—no, uncle—not dead, but in heaven."

"This is a remarkable scene," said Washington, with moistened eyes. "Colonel Wellingly, I congratulate you on the success of your long search, of which I have often heard with sympathy. I already esteem myself as among the friends of your niece, and think you will have just cause to be proud of her; and I shall hope to make the acquaintance of your brother. I now suggest that you take your relatives to your quarters, for you must have much to speak of in which strangers have no part."

"I thank your Excellency," was the grateful reply. "I

have been so overwhelmed by this unexpected meeting that I am not myself."

" Your emotions are most natural, sir, and are to your credit."

" Vera," said Saville, coming to her side and taking her hand, " I am overjoyed at your good fortune. I thank God from the depths of my heart. My little wild flower has become a great lady."

He felt her fingers seeking her mother's ring, and she answered in a low tone, " No outward changes can change that of which this ring is the token. You shall ever be first. Good night."

But before they could move away, a shrill voice just without the arbor cried,

" Ye didn't arrist him at all ; I arristed him meself, and I'm a goin' to take him afore his Ixcellency. Git out o' the way, ye spalpeens, or I'll tear yer eyes out ;" and she broke from the guards, dragging her bleeding. half-murdered captive with her, and did not stop till she stood before Washington.

" This is the spalpeen, your Ixcellency, as was carryin' of the perty Misthress Vera. I heerd the hull plot, and I cotched him in the very dade."

" What does all this mean ?" demanded Washington sternly, and yet with difficulty maintaining his gravity, for the wretched officer looked like a torn quarry in the claws of some strange bird of prey.

" Indeed, sir, all we can tell your Excellency is that we found him on the ground, and this woman on top of him pounding him within an inch of his life."

At this there was a general and irrepressible burst of laughter, in which even Washington joined for a moment. But, instantly recovering his gravity, he asked,

" Miss Wellingly, does this woman state the truth about this man ?"

"She does, your Excellency ; but I think that he has been sufficiently punished and humiliated already."

"I cannot agree with you upon this occasion," said Washington, his face becoming almost terrible in his indignation. Then addressing Captain Molly, he asked,

"You are the woman who took her husband's place at his gun in the battle of Monmouth ?"

"I be, your Ixcellency ; an' it was moighty swate in ye to give me the pay and rank of sergeant."

Washington's face twitched a moment, but he managed to say, with his former sternness,

"You are a far better soldier than the craven whom I am glad to see in your clutches. Will you oblige me by taking from his uniform all insignia of rank ?"

"Faix, yer Ixcellency, I will. Barrin' the presence of the foine leddies, I'd take ivery stetch off him as I'd skin an eel."

A roar of laughter followed this speech, and her miserable victim looked as if he would indeed be glad to have the mountains fall and cover him from the universal scorn.

"Now," continued Washington to an officer, ' take him to the guard house, and to-morrow I wish him drummed out of camp with the Rogue's March ;" and the culprit was led away.

"Come, my dear niece, my heart is too full to endure this publicity any longer," said Colonel Wellingly.

"In one moment," Vera replied ; and crossing to Captain Molly, she took her hand in both of hers, saying,

"I thank you from the depths of my heart. If you ever need a friend, come to me."

"Have ye become a great leddy ?"

"I should not be a lady at all did I fail to remember, with grateful affection, all who were kind to me in my need. Good-by for the present, my brave, true friend. I owe you more than words can express."

" An' ye pay me in the coin I loikes best. Faix, ther's nothin' that goes furder wid man nor baste than a koind word. Though I'm a bit rough and reckless loike, I'd ruther have ye spake to me as ye does than a hatful of crowns. "

" The money shall not be lacking either," said Colonel Wellingly, offering her his purse.

" Not a penny will I iver take for anythin' I've done for Misthress Vera," and she darted away.

With a low courtesy to General and Lady Washington, and a swift glance to Saville, Vera permitted herself to be led away with her father ; and the wondering guests were boundless in their admiration, and almost equally so in queries that could not as yet be answered.

Tascar, who had been watching all in a state of excitement that made him almost as explosive as one of the cartridges of the *feu de-joie*, was sent to inform old Gula that her master and mistress would not return that night ; and the tale he told his mother, and acted out in pantomime that night, was more marvelous than any of her weird imaginings.

A few hours later the beautiful colonnade or arbor was darkened, and echoed only to a lonely sentinel's tread.

CHAPTER XXXIX.

EXPLANATIONS.

EVEN the rude temporary quarters which Colonel Wellingly occupied, at West Point, gave evidence that he was a man of wealth and culture ; for, as far as possible, he had surrounded himself with objects that ministered to refined and luxurious tastes. He had been the more inclined to carry out his bent, from the fact that his duties would, in all probability, keep him at his present location for a long time.

In the fullness of his heart it seemed as if he could not do enough for his brother and niece ; and, for one naturally stately and reserved, his manner was affectionate in the extreme. He embraced Vera again and again, and his eyes rested on her with an expression of wistful tenderness, which proved that she was the embodiment of a very dear memory.

When he heard that they had not partaken of any refreshment since their frugal lunch early in the day, he brought out a bottle of rich old madeira, and ordered his servant to prepare as sumptuous a supper as could be provided promptly.

" I cannot realize it all," said Vera again and again ; and her father ejaculated, more than once,

" Thank God ! your blood, Arthur, is not on my soul. It is now possible that I may again become a man." After a few moments he asked hesitatingly,

" Shall we tell Vera ? She does not know."

" Yes, Guy ; it's right she should know. I will tell her, for I feel that I am as much, if not more, to blame than you.''

" No, Arthur ; no. There is no excuse for the murderous blow I struck you, and the remorse and fear, that have followed me through all these years, have nearly destroyed my reason. I sank lower than the beasts ; for they, at least, provide for their own. I wonder that you can forgive me. I can never forgive myself.''

" I do forgive, and in the same breath ask forgiveness. Henceforth we must be to each other all that she who is dead would have wished. I shall seek to make reparation to you and Vera to the extent of my ability, and you shall share in all I possess. It is best that Vera should know everything, for with those who are as closely united as we shall be, there should be no mysteries. Vera, the highest praise I can give you is, that you closely resemble your mother when she was of your age. Never did a maiden live who had greater power to win and keep affection than Esther Ainsley. She was of humble station, being the daughter of a curate, who had a small charge near to our estate ; but she was dowered with a beauty of person and character which I have never seen equalled. Our mother died when Guy and myself were children, and our father died before I was through with my studies, so that I as eldest son, became heir to a large property, at a time when I needed restraint, guidance, and counsel, more than wealth and independence. The lessons of self-control and patience, which should have been taught us in childhood and youth, were left to the schooling of bitter experience ; and bitter, in truth, it has been to us both. I valued my untrammeled position chiefly because there was no one to prevent me from marrying the daughter of this obscure and penniless curate. Only her own will, which was as strong as she was gentle, did prevent the marriage, for I sought in every possible way to shake her resolution. There was not a trace of gratified vanity in her refusal, but only the keenest distress. At last she told me that she loved some one else, and I think she was about to inform me who it was, but my darkly vindictive face prevented her. Egotistic and passionate fool that I was, I felt that no one had a right to thwart me, and I determined to discover the one, whom I at once regarded as a personal enemy. To be brief, I was not long in learning that it was Guy, my younger and only brother ; but, in the infatuation of my passion, this fact made no difference, and, as the eldest, I would brook no rivalry. I confronted him one evening, as he was returning from a tryst with Esther, and arrogantly informed him that he could not cross my path in this matter. I first made him a large offer, if he would quit the country and leave the field clear for me. But he said, and with good reason, that he would not relinquish Esther Ainsley for the wealth of England, much less for the pitiful sum I offered. One word led to another. We both became enraged, and at last I sprang toward him in a transport of passion, and he, equally unmanned, struck me on the head with a heavy cane that he carried and for weeks thereafter I was unconscious.''

Guy Wellingly, who was sitting with his face buried in his hands, groaned deeply.

"You see, Vera,'' continued her uncle, "I was even more to blame than he. I had it in my heart to strike just as heavy a blow. Indeed, we were both beside ourselves at the time, and scarcely responsible. The trouble was that neither of us had ever learned the first lesson of self-restraint.''

"O Arthur ! I was sure I had killed you. I brought water from the brook, but I could not revive you, and then came the one desperate, all-absorbing desire to fly and hide, which has been my curse ever since. I felt that I had upon me the mark of Cain.''

'' We have both paid dearly for that rash quarrel, in which I insist that I was to blame more truly than yourself. I had a narrow escape from death. My body servant found me late at night, and I revived only to pass into a brain fever, and then after I regained consciousness came the dreary weeks of slow convalescence, in which recovery was retarded by my restlessness and self-reproach. For a time I tried to forget my sorrow and disappointment in dissipation, but I soon turned from sensual excess with loathing. In every sane moment I saw Esther's pure, reproachful face. I do not think that a man, who has been absorbed by a love for a pure, good woman, can ever make a beast of himself, unless there is something essentially gross in his nature.

'' As soon as I was able, I traced you and Esther to Liverpool, and all I could learn was that you had been married and had sailed for America. Her father and mother were quite broken hearted at the loss of their child. The only alleviation of their sorrow that I could give was to secure to them a competence for life. As time passed on, and I brooded over the past, quiet life in England became hateful to me. I resolved that I would come to this country and try to find you. As the years passed, this search. became a passion with me, and the increasing difficulty and doubt only stimulated my purpose. It was a good thing for me, for it absorbed my sad thoughts, and kept my mind from preying on itself. I would often follow a supposed clue for months, only to be disappointed. I have often passed up and down this river, little dreaming that the objects of my search were but a few hundred rods away. Oh ! that I had found you in time to have seen Esther, and asked her forgiveness.

" But a few words more will explain how I happen to be in the Continental service. In my wandering over this country, I became greatly enamored with its beauty and magnificence, while the wildness of many of its vast solitudes accorded with my moods and tastes. I am very fond of hunting, and I could gratify that bent here to my heart's desire. I have no special ties in England, so I returned thither, sold my estate to advantage, and, to insure myself, invested large sums in France and Holland, as well as England, in addition to that which I brought with me to this country. When the American struggle for independence commenced, my heart took sides with this people. They had been so kind and sympathetic in every case, as they learned that I was trying to find relatives who had migrated hither, that I identified myself with their cause from the first. Besides, my long residence here convinced me of its justness. On seeing that the struggle was inevitable, I instructed my English agent to transfer my funds to Holland, and from thence I have drawn them largely hither, and the American Government is, to some extent, in my debt. During the war, I sought the duty of a staff officer, as it brought me in contact with many troops from all parts of the country, and enabled me to continue my inquiries concerning any one answering to your name and description. But you escaped me utterly, until our most unexpected meeting to-night. I was getting weary and discouraged in my search. I was becoming oppressed with my loneliness, and life began to drag heavily ; but now that I have found you, Guy, and have this dear girl, who is the image of her mother, to provide for, I shall find abundant zest in living."

As he finished his narration, Vera put her arms around his neck, and said,

" I am equal to mother in only one thing. I can love very deeply, and you have won my heart already. I won't let you regret having found me, uncle." Then going to her father's side, she added, with reassuring caresses,

"After this night, do not again doubt that God is good, father. Though I never before knew what the deed was that led to your flight from England, I have been sure that Mr. Saville's words were true, and that your 'remorse was greater than your crime.'"

"No, Vera," replied her father, in strong emotion. "If I had in fact slain this generous and forgiving brother, I should never have known peace in this or any other world. As it is, Arthur, I am but a miserable wreck of a man, warped, by base fear and years of brooding remorse, from all good and noble uses. There is nothing that makes such awful havoc in the soul as a constant sense of guilt. The knowledge that you are living has brought me inexpressible relief, and I ask nothing more, and nothing better than this fact. But Vera still has life before her. I have at times meditated self destruction, in the hope that she might thus escape the curse which I felt resting on me ; but something held me back."

"Thank God !" murmured Vera shuddering.

"Now she can be very happy," continued her father. "Since I am not the foul criminal that, in justice to Mr. Saville, I told him that I was, his pride will no longer be an obstacle in the way of their marriage."

"Vera marry Colonel Saville !" exclaimed her uncle. "He is married already."

"Saville married !" ejaculated her father, in unbounded surprise and rising anger. "Then I have an account to settle with him ;" and his tall form towered up instinct with passion.

At the mention of Saville's name Vera's face became scarlet ; then, at her father's words, her pallor was equally marked.

"Vera," said her uncle, in a tone of deep distress, "what trouble have we here?"

But the maiden, strong in her conscious rectitude, rallied promptly, and, in a firm, quiet tone, said,

"We have no trouble whatever, except we make it. Uncle, Mr. Saville is a true, honorable man, and he has never asked me to do a thing that *he* thought wrong. Both father and myself would have been dead years ago were it not for his unspeakable kindness. Father, be calm. You cannot strike Theron Saville without striking me. He is my brother, my more than brother, and I love him better than life."

"But, Vera," remonstrated her uncle, with a gravity almost approaching to sternness; "in your secluded life you have not learned how rigid the proprieties of life are in these matters. You bear the proud name of Wellingly, and——"

"Uncle," interrupted Vera, with a dignity and firmness of which her gentle mother had never been capable, "I bear a prouder name than that of Wellingly. I am a Christian, and, in the light of God's truth, and not the fashion of this world, I have thought this matter out to its right issue, and I shall stand by my decision. Rather than permit any one to come between me and Mr. Saville, I will go back to the poverty and obscurity of our mountain cabin for the rest of life. I do not speak these words as a willful, ignorant child, but as a woman who has been matured and sobered by years of bitter sorrow. Mr. Saville is my dearest friend—nothing more; and he never can be anything more. I have known for years that he is married. He told me himself, and he never cherished one dishonorable thought toward me. I declare to you both that there is nothing in our relationship to which my sainted mother would object. But I would rather perish by slow torture than stand aloof from him or treat him coldly."

" This is very extraordinary," said her uncle.

" I cannot reconcile his conduct with your words," added her father, in deep agitation.

The strain of the eventful day had at last become too great for Vera. and she felt herself growing faint.

" Be patient," she said wearily ; " you shall know all. As uncle said, we shall have no mysteries. But I can say no more to-night. In pity, uncle, remember what I have passed through to-day."

" Forgive me, my child," he said remorsefully, and bringing her a glass of wine. " I will trust you, Vera," he added ; " for your words and manner are those of truth and purity. My only fear is lest you should be misled through your innocence and ignorance of the world."

She looked him steadily in the face a moment as only the innocent could do, and then replied,

" Uncle, my honor and good name are as safe in Mr. Saville's hands as in yours or father's. He is a Christian gentleman, in the truest and strongest sense of the word."

" There, my dear, I am satisfied, and your father must be, too, until he can have fuller explanation. Calm yourself now, and let me show you to the best resting-place which a soldier can provide for a guest who is as loved and welcome as she was unexpected ;" and, without listening to her remonstrances, he gave her his own room, and kissed her tenderly as he said good-night.

Vera was too exhausted to think ; but she was dimly conscious that, after all, it would be difficult to make her father and uncle understand the honest skepticism from which Saville's course was the natural outgrowth. What was so clear to her mind might seem dubious, or worse, to theirs. She was not so weary, however, but that she thanked God, with a boundless gratitude, that He had led her safely through that season of doubt and strong temptation. If she had yielded, she saw plainly that her proud and stately uncle would have cast her away in bitter contempt ; or, what was far worse, her father might have killed her lover.

Early the next morning Saville sought an interview with Colonel Wellingly, and, to secure privacy, took him to Jasper's quarters, which he was occupying, in the surgeon's absence.

Vera's words and manner had convinced her uncle that she had not consciously erred from the path of rectitude, but he was not so sure of Saville ; and it must be confessed that he was not a little anxious, for he saw that Vera was a girl of unusual force and decision, and he feared that if Saville chose to take advantage of the strong hold he had upon her affections, he could make them trouble indeed. Although he had been very favorably impressed with Saville, his knowledge of the world made him slow and cautious in trusting men who are under strong temptation. And yet he was pleased with the fact that the young man had come to him so promptly, feeling that it might give him a chance to prevent difficulties.

"Colonel Wellingly," said Saville, after they were alone, "I have sought the first opportunity possible that I might make explanations which are your due, and which it might cause your niece pain and embarrassment to give. I have no fears that my good name would suffer through any words of hers ; on the contrary, she would excuse conduct for which I have only bitter condemnation. I owe to her my life, and much more than life, and it is a privilege to save her from the least pain and annoyance. Are you willing to listen to an honest statement of all that has occurred between us ?"

"Colonel Saville," was the reply, "I am gratified that you have thus early sought this interview, for it tends to assure me that my niece's confidence in you as a Christian gentleman is not misplaced. I admit that, from her father's words and manner, last evening, after he learned that you were a married man, I feared that I might have a quarrel with you. The Wellingly blood has ever been over hot upon certain kinds of provocation, and on no point more sensitive than that of our women's honor.''

"You may still think that you have cause to quarrel with me ; but, be that as it may, I shall not gloss the truth. You cannot condemn me more bitterly than I do myself Nor shall I shrink from any punishment or course which you may impose.'' And he gave a faithful history of his acquaintance with Vera from the first. While, in justice to himself, he showed how his wrong conduct was the natural fruit of his erratic views, he did not in the least extenuate it ; but, on the contrary, spoke of it with a censure so strong as to be almost fierce. It was evidently the one thing for which he could never forgive himself. Indeed, in his boundless admiration for Vera, he forgot himself, and became her advocate rather than his own. He argued that she had been tempted as no woman ever was before—tempted by one to whom she was profoundly grateful, not only for much kindness, but for the fact that he had stood by her after her father's statement that he was a criminal. She had been tempted by one upon whom she was almost utterly dependent for existence and the necessities of life. And, what made resistance tenfold more difficult, he had not sought to beguile her as a villain might have done, but he had been open and honest in his error, full of plausible arguments ; and he had, for long months, and with all the skill he possessed, sought to undermine what he regarded as her baseless faith.

"Moreover,'' Saville concluded, "there was much in my own unhappy relations and in the conduct of my wife which excited her womanly sympathies in my behalf ; but, in the face of all, she was loyal to truth and duty. I have now

been through a long war ; but I have seen no heroism, no
fidelity, and all-enduring fortitude equal to that which she
has displayed through long, weary years, and I love and
honor her next to God in whom she led me to trust.   I am
through, sir, and I have told you the truth.''

As Saville had warmed with his narrative, and spoke with
graphic earnestness and power, Colonel Wellingly walked
the floor in deep excitement, with strong and varying emotions contending on his face.   When Saville concluded, he
said,

"This is a most extraordinary statement, and yet I cannot doubt its truth.   I have been inclined by turns to embrace you in the profoundest gratitude, and to shoot you on
the spot.   Poor child, poor child !   What a strange, sad lot
she and her mother have had !   Heaven grant that I may
shield Vera from any more of such dark and terrible experiences.''

"I shall ever echo that prayer, sir,'' Saville added earnestly.

"Colonel Saville,'' continued Colonel Wellingly, after a
few moments of deep thought, "I cannot doubt, after hearing all that you have said, that Vera is correct in believing
you are *now* a Christian gentleman ; but you were once a
very dangerous man, sincere as you evidently were in your
errors.   As a matter of curiosity, I have read some of the
writings of your old masters, and, though very friendly to
the French people, I predict for them terrible evils, as the
result of this destructive and disorganizing philosophy.''

"I can believe you, sir.   Were it not for a firm, gentle
hand, that stayed and rescued me, it would have brought
evils into two lives that would have been irreparable.''

"Your own strong self-condemnation,'' said Colonel
Wellingly, "has disarmed me of censure.   Your feelings
and motives are now evidently honorable, and it would be

wretched folly to drag forward the evils of the past to mar the present. But, Colonel Saville, you know the way of the world, and how ready it is to suspect of evil. Even now I fear that rumor may couple your name with that of my niece in a sense that neither of us can wish.''

'' I recognize and respect your wish. I will not even see Miss Wellingly again, if you think such a course wise.''

'' No,'' Colonel Wellingly replied, after a little thought. '' I do not think such a course would be wise,'' for he remembered Vera's decisive words. '' I think it would be better for you to see her occasionally. But a gentleman of your tact could easily give the impression that your rela-tion to my niece was only that of frank, cordial friendship. At the same time, it might be well to apply for duty else-where.''

'' I look upon you,'' Saville answered, '' as Miss Wel-lingly's guardian, and shall be guided strictly by your judg-ment. Believe me, sir, I should regard it as the greatest mis-fortune that I could suffer, if any act of mine should cast a shadow on her fair name. You are at liberty to state to her father all that I have told you ; and I sincerely hope that his mind will now rapidly recover a serene and healthful tone.''

'' I will satisfy him,'' was the reply, '' as you have satis-fied me. Please do us the favor of dining with us at six this evening.''

When Vera awoke, late in the day, her thoughts again reverted to the explanation which she supposed she must make, and she dreaded the ordeal unspeakably. But when she emerged from her room, her uncle took her in his arms, and said,

'' Vera, Mr. Saville has told me all, and I am proud of you, as the best and noblest little girl that ever breathed.''

'' That's like Mr. Saville,'' said Vera, coloring deeply.

" He has been making me out an angel, and himself almost
a villain."

" Well," said Colonel Wellingly, laughing, " the more
he called himself a villain, the more sure I became that he
was an honorable man.   At any rate, I have invited the villain to dine with us this evening."

She rewarded him so promptly and heartily that the wary
colonel was filled with alarm.

" She is too demonstrative," he thought, "and will show
all the world that Saville has her heart ;" so he began, very
gravely, " Vera, my dear, when in Mr. Saville's presence, I
hope you will——"

She put her hand over his lips, and said smilingly,
" Don't fear, uncle ; a sensitive woman's nature is a better
guide in these matters than the soundest advice."

During the hour of dinner Colonel Wellingly was abundantly satisfied that he had nothing to fear, for the most evil-
disposed of gossips would not have seen anything in Saville's
or Vera's manner toward each other to which exception
could have been taken.   But, as he gave her his hand, in
taking leave, she touched her mother's ring upon his finger
so significantly that he went away with his heart warmed and
comforted by the thought, " She will be unchangeable amid
all changes."

Immediately after Captain Molly left the arbor, the
evening before, Saville joined her, and said, in a low
tone,

" Molly, my brave girl, will you do for me one more good
deed to night ?"

" Faix, an' I will ; a dozen on 'em, if I've toime."

" Promise me, by all that took place in Fort Clinton, that
you will never mention my acquaintance with Miss Vera to
any one.   It's not the world's business, and the world sus-
pects evil where there is no evil."

"Misther Saville," was her reply, "may that big Hessian that ye killed cotch me agin if I iver say a word."

Tascar had often been warned, but the boy was perfectly safe, for he had a habit of dense ignorance on any subject concerning which he did not choose to speak.

Only enough of Vera's romantic story got abroad to lend an increased charm and interest to her beautiful person. If at first there had been some disposition to ask what had been her relations with Saville, their frank, unaffected manners in society banished the thought of evil from all save those who, being wholly bad themselves, have no faith in anything good.

In spite of herself, Vera speedily became a belle, and, instead of being a hunted, frightened animal of the mountains, as she once described herself to Saville, she was now established in the highest social position, and soon became a special favorite with General and Lady Washington. In addition to her beauty, she possessed unusual solid attractions, as heiress of her uncle's large wealth, and suitors began to gather from far and near, as, in her favorite comedy, they had beset the door of Portia, in Belmont ; and, like Portia, she often sighed, "By my troth, Nerissa, my little body is a-weary of this great world." But the casket which contained Vera's image was Saville's heart, and that was closed to all the world. She instructed her father and uncle to give a courteous but firm refusal to all who asked of them permission to pay their addresses, and those who sought to lay siege without such formality were speedily taught that any attentions that were not merely friendly were most unwelcome.

Colonel Wellingly had been much pleased with the situation of the mountain cabin, and at once commenced enlarging it as a hunting-lodge. He saw that his brother, from long habit, would be much happier there than anywhere else, and it was a place in which he felt that he could while away many months of the year when his duties would permit. The incubus, in a very great measure, lifted from Guy Wellingly's mind, and he was no longer subject to his old fits of gloom, which bordered on horror and despair ; but it was evident that he would always be a grave, silent man, finding the shadows of the forest more congenial than the haunts of men.

CHAPTER XL.

HUSBAND AND WIFE.

SAVILLE, at Colonel Wellingly's request, did not apply to be sent from West Point ; but, before many weeks elapsed, he was summoned away for the most unexpected and painful reasons. Papers came through the lines, from New York, containing the following statement :

" A DOUBLE CRIME IN HIGH LIFE. —Mrs. Julia Saville, the wife of Colonel Saville, of the American Army, has eloped with Captain Vennam, the officer whom she married with such indecent haste, on receiving from him the report of her husband's death. Captain Vennam had obtained leave of absence, on the pretext of visiting some friends in Nova Scotia, whither the guilty pair have sailed. This was bad enough. But, on the night before their departure, an event occurred which seems to give proof of a malice and vindictive hate, of which it is difficult to believe a woman capable, save on the theory that when she does fall, she surpasses man in wickedness. In the middle of the night, flames broke out in Colonel Saville's mansion, which has been occupied by his mother during the war. Mrs. Saville barely escaped with her life, and found refuge in a small cottage on the estate, and she is now quite ill from fright and exposure. But the worst part of the story is, that a short time before the fire manifested itself, she was sure that she heard the voice of her son's recreant wife beneath her windows, and also the unrecognized voice of some man. She also asserts that the house did not take fire from within, but from the front piazza, and that it swept up the main stairway. She and the servants escaped by a rear staircase and entrance. The night was dark and windy, and favorable for the fiendish deed. Everything was lost. The authorities should thoroughly investigate," etc.

Colonel Wellingly, as he read it, unconsciously exclaimed, " Shameful !   Poor Saville !''

In a moment Vera was at his side, and, before he could prevent it, also read the paragraph.

" Uncle, I wish to see Mr. Saville."

" But, Vera, my dear, it may not be prudent to——''

" O uncle ! if Mr. Saville has friends, should they not show themselves such now ?''

" I will go to him with all my heart.   There are many things which a man can do which are not proper for a young lady.   The very thought of that vile creature, his wife, is soiling to you."

" I do not think of her, but of him in his cruel chains,'' she replied, weeping bitterly.   " Never was there a more hideous bondage than his.''

But her uncle was relieved of all perplexity, for his servant brought him a note from Saville to Vera, containing a copy of the paper, but in his care.

" I am so overwhelmed with shame and sorrow," Saville had written, " that I cannot trust myself to see you.   Were it not for the faith which you taught me, I could not have survived this last blow and disgrace.   By the time this reaches you, I shall be on my way to New York, and shall make every effort to induce the British authorities to permit me to visit my mother, and provide for her comfort.   I have not seen her now for years, and, if necessary, I will throw up my commission and become a citizen in order to reach her side at once.''

The English commander, after a little delay for explanations, courteously acceded to Saville's request, on condition that he would not do anything during his residence prejudicial to his majesty's service. Peace was now almost assured, and there was a disposition to relax the rigid military rule of the city.

The son found that he had not reached his mother a day too soon, for she was sinking under the effects of her fright, loss, and loneliness. His presence revived her, however; but she rallied slowly, and was a feeble invalid for the remainder of the summer and autumn. He hoped to move her to West Point; but she was not equal to the journey, and most reluctant to leave the spot where she had spent so many years. He made the gardener's cottage, which she occupied, as comfortable as he could with his limited means; for his property, lying chiefly in the city, had melted away during the war, and the money he had deposited in Paris was now inaccessible. He denied himself everything that he might make his mother comfortable, and devoted himself to her, trying to make amends for his long absence, and she slowly regained health and strength under his care.

And yet those long months of watching and poverty taxed Saville's faith and fortitude to the utmost. The open shame of his wife did not make her less his wife in the legal sense. Her offense gave no cause for divorce before the laws as then existing. In his intense desire to escape his chains, he had the legal archives searched for some precedent; but found that for over a hundred years no divorce had been granted, in the province of New York, on the ground of his wife's crime.

The future grew darker and more uncertain than ever.

His wife had disappeared utterly from his knowledge. There was a rumor that Captain Vennam had gone to England. But Saville knew that it was ever the custom of satiated lust to cast away its victims, and Vennam, of all men, was the one to coolly abandon a woman of whom he had wearied. Therefore Saville's wife would probably become a wanderer on the face of the earth, and might perish in some miserable place and way, and still he remain in ignorance of the event. If she filled a nameless grave in a foreign land, so long as the fact could not be proved, Saville would still remain bound, and the chances were now that he would wear out his life in this slow torture of uncertainty. He could never approach the proud Colonel Wellingly and ask for his niece while such a doubt hung over him, even if his own jealous regard for Vera's honor would permit.

As the dreary winds of November began to blow, he became deeply depressed. Captain Vennam's regiment had been ordered to England, and there was not the slightest chance for his return. Saville did not know to what part of Nova Scotia he had taken his wife. He had lost all clues. In frequent and painful reveries he saw himself growing old in doubt and uncertainty, ever chained to a possible, supposititious woman, who might be living a vile life of crime in some of earth's slums. He saw Vera's bright youth and beauty fading into dim and premature age under the blight of hope deferred. Then, after life had nearly passed, and the chance for happiness was gone, he pictured to himself the return of his wife as a hideous, shrunken hag, as loathsome in appearance as in character. And he shuddered at the thought that he could neither refute nor escape her claim —" *My* husband !"

A letter from Surgeon Jasper, that came in with a flag of truce, greatly increased his despondency, for it contained the incidental statement that " the young officers were half wild over Miss Wellingly, and that she might take her pick from the army."

One dreary day, when even the wild storm without was a cheerful contrast to his thoughts and feelings, he came to the deliberate conclusion that Vera's future should not be destroyed with his own, and, knowing that a flag of truce would go out the following morning, he sat down and wrote, telling her just how he was situated.

He told her that he was a cripple, that the war had consumed his property, and that the sum deposited in Paris, even if he should be able to get it, would not be more than sufficient to support his mother. These facts in themselves formed a good reason why she should be released from the promise of which her mother's ring was the token. He then stated plainly the uncertainty he would always probably be under in regard to the fate of his wife, and he earnestly urged Vera not to lose her chance of happiness. "I will wear you. mother's ring henceforth as your friend and brother, hoping and asking for nothing more."

He inclosed this letter to the care of her uncle, and intimated that she had better show him the contents.

He went out in the storm, and made it certain that the letter would go the next morning, and then returned to his humble home, chilled, cold, and wet. But he had achieved a great self-sacrifice, and he felt better. He now believed that Vera would form new ties and interests, and eventually become happy in them. For himself he must look beyond the shadows of time.

He did his best to make his mother pass a cheerful evening, and succeeded. She did not dream that he had given up the dearest hope of his life, and that his genial manner was like sunlight playing upon a grave. She had been ill and weak, and he had not burdened her with his sorrow.

They were just about retiring, when a light, uncertain step

was heard upon the little porch. There was a low, hollow cough, and then came a hesitating knock.

Saville took a candle and went to the door, and the form of a woman stood in the driving sleet. The candle flared in the wind, and nearly went out.

" Who are you, madam, and what do you wish ?" he asked.

" I am your wife," said the woman, in a low, desperate tone.

He knew from her voice that she was ; but, in his surprise and strong feeling, he could not immediately speak, and she continued,

" I suppose you will thrust me out to die also, as I have been turned from the door of my own home, and by my own father, this bitter night. I deserve nothing better at *your* hands. I said I would never cross your threshold again, but I must or perish, and I dare not die. If you will only give me shelter in some out———," but here a paroxysm of coughing interrupted her.

" I cannot turn you away in such a night," said Saville, in an agitated tone. " Indeed, I pity you from the depths of my heart. I will give you food and shelter here for tonight, and in the morning will try to find a refuge for you."

" No, Theron," said his mother, who had drawn near to the door and overheard all ; " if that woman comes in, I will go out."

" O mother ! you women have no mercy on each other."

" I will not pass the night under the same roof with that creature," said his mother sternly.

" As I am a Christian man, she shall have shelter somewhere," he said ; and throwing a large cloak over her shoulders, he took her to the cottage of a poor man living near, who was under great obligations to Saville, and, with much difficulty, secured a room for her there. He then took her food and wine with his own hands.

"Why do you do this?" she asked.

"Julia," he said kindly, "if I had been a Christian instead of an unbeliever when we were married, you might never have come to this wretched state."

"Will you forgive the past, and take me back as your wife again?" she asked, her old trait of self-seeking promptly showing itself.

"I will and do forgive you," he said gravely, "and I will do all for your comfort that I can in my poverty; but you can never be my wife again save only in name."

"Well," she muttered, "that's more than I could expect; and it's a great deal better than dying in the street like a dog."

The next day she was very ill and feverish, and Saville summoned a physician. After a brief examination, he told Saville that she could live but a short time under any circumstances, since she was in the last stages of hasty consumption.

Her wretched history after leaving New York was soon told. Vennam left her penniless in a northern city, and, after a brief life of crime, she became ill from exposure in the rigorous climate. A British officer who had known her in New York secured her a steerage passage thither. She arrived in the storm, but did not dare to go to her father's house till after dark. He had sent her from his door with curses, and then she came to the one whom she had wronged most.

She was in great terror when the physician told her that she could not live, and the scenes at her bedside were harrowing in the extreme. Saville patiently and gently tried to lead her to the Merciful One who received and forgave outcasts like herself; but her mind was too clouded by terror and too enfeebled by disease to understand anything clearly save the one dreadful truth that she must die. Her delirious words were even worse than her partially sane cries and moans ; but Saville, with patient endurance, remained at her bedside almost continually, and ministered to her with his own hand to the last. All that medical skill and faithful care could accomplish was done to alleviate her suffering and add to the number of her days. With earnest words and prayer he sought to instill into her guilty and despairing heart something like faith. But that had happened to her which may happen to any who persist in the ways of evil : she had passed so far down into the dark shadow of moral and physical death that no light could reach her. Her end was so inexpressibly sad, that, although by it Saville was relieved from his cruel bondage, he yet sat down by her lifeless body and wept as only a strong man can weep.

CHAPTER XLI.

WEDDED WITH HER MOTHER'S RING.

VERA was alone with her uncle when she received Saville's letter. She read it with a blending of smiles and tears, and then passed it to Colonel Wellingly, saying,

" Mr. Saville wished you to see this, and I am very glad to have you do so, for it will satisfy you more fully than ever what kind of a man he is."

Her uncle read the contents with great interest, and then said, " This letter does Mr. Saville much credit, and, I must say, I think he takes a correct and sensible view of things. Your promise was a rash one, at best, and it was extorted from you in a moment of dire emergency. Moreover, what he says is true, and it is probable he will never hear a word from his wife again. And yet Vera Wellingly cannot marry a man whose wife *may* appear any day."

" I do not expect to marry him, uncle."

" Now that is sensible, too. You must be quite well convinced by this time that you can take your pick, and make a very brilliant match."

" Where is your wife, uncle ?" said Vera, with tears in her eyes. " You are the kind of man who can always take his pick."

He was silent, for she had touched a very tender chord in him, as he had in her heart.

" It may be that some can manage these things in a sensible, thrifty way," she continued ; " but it does not seem to run in our blood to do so. Forgive me, uncle, for touching a sensitive chord : but I wish you to learn to interpret my heart by your own ; then this question will be finally settled, and you can shield me from many unwelcome attentions."

" Well," said her uncle, trying to give a lighter turn to the conversation, " somebody's loss is mine and your father's great gain."

" Yes," said Vera ; " I intend to make myself so necessary to you both, that you will be like two dragons toward every one with suspicious designs. I am satisfied that it is money that most of them are seeking, at best ; and Theron loved me and was kind when I was hungry and in rags. Foolish fellow ! I suppose he was in a state of high tragedy when he wrote this letter, and thought that I would take him at his word. He will never make such a blunder again after receiving my answer."

But one day, before she found a chance of sending her reply to New York, her uncle entered his quarters in a state of great excitement, and said, producing a city paper,

" Vera, it is due to you that you should see this at once." And he pointed out the following paragraph :

RARE MAGNANIMITY.—The Saville tragedy has at length ended, and ended strangely. As might have been expected, Captain Vennam soon abandoned the wretched woman who eloped with him, and she returned to this city in a sick and dying condition. In the pitiless storm of the night of the 25th ult., she was repulsed from her parents' door and, in her despair, sought help from her most deeply wronged husband. Strange to say, he has treated her with wonderful kindness. He could not give her a refuge under the same roof with his mother ; but he procured for her a comfortable room, and was untiring in his attentions, doing everything in his power to alleviate her sufferings during the few days she survived.

We have these facts from the citizen at whose house she died, and can vouch for their correctness."

Vera dropped the paper and fled to her room, and several hours elapsed before she reappeared. When she did, her eyes gave evidence that many tears had mingled with her joy. In curious and feminine contradiction to her plainly expressed purpose, she did not write to Saville by the next flag of truce. " He is now at liberty to write to me another and a very different letter," she said to herself ; " and I shall wait till he does."

But when Saville's letter came, as it did in time, it breathed only a quiet and friendly spirit, such as he would naturally write on the supposition that she had accepted his last letter as the basis of their future relations. It was not in Vera's nature to write and inform him that he was all at fault, and that she was like a rose waiting to be plucked. " He will have to find out all for himself," she thought ; " but I fear he will be ridiculously blind, and continue his high tragedy until some unforeseen circumstance opens his eyes."

Early in the spring Mrs. Saville so far regained her health that her son was able to return to the army, a step rendered specially necessary by his pecuniary circumstances. He called promptly on Vera after his return to West Point ; but it so happened that there were several strangers calling at her uncle's quarters at the time, and his manner was somewhat formal and distant. She was provoked at herself that she permitted her bearing to be tinged by his.

After the guests were all gone, her uncle found her in tears, and said,

" Foolish child ! as if you had cause to worry. You are both like gunpowder, and only need a spark to set you off."

" You are very much mistaken, uncle. Theron is worse than a spiked cannon."

The next evening, she and her father were taking a walk by the river, near the extreme point of land where Saville had first discovered her nearly eight years before, on the June afternoon, now memorable to both.   Footsteps caused her to glance up the bank, and then she pulled her father into the concealment afforded by a clump of cedars.   In a few moments, Saville came out on the point and threw himself down upon the grassy plot where he had seen Vera reclining before he caused her hasty flight.   She put her finger to her lips, and made a sign to her father not to move, and then she stole up toward him as he had before approached her, and reached the same low cedar over which he had peered wonderingly and admiringly at her childish face and form.

"O stupid Theron ! can't you feel that I am here ?" she thought.   " I felt your presence even then before I saw you. I am so near that I can almost touch you, and yet there you lie at lazy length."

He commenced singing, in a low tone,

"I know a bank whereon the wild thyme blows."

She waited no longer, but, in her sweet voice, repeated the old refrain, which had been the signal for so many of their trysts.   He sprang up, and catching a glimpse of her laughing and blushing face back of the cedar, came instantly to her side.

" See what a whirligig time is," she said.   " I surprised you on this occasion."

" But I shall not run away as you did, Vera."

" Indeed !   Now it is my turn to be surprised again.   I had fears lest, in your desire to escape, you might plunge into the water."

He looked at her very earnestly, and her eyes drooped under his gaze, as they had, years before, in the early dawn, after she had rescued him from Fort Clinton.

" Vera," he said hesitatingly, " I am very poor."

" What has that to do with the subject ?" she asked, with a sudden mirthfulness in her eyes.

" I am but a cripple," he continued. sadly, " and there is a dark stain upon my name."

Her laughing eyes became full of tears.

" Circumstances have greatly changed. You are now Vera Wellingly, and the heiress of large wealth."

" I would rather be the ragged, friendless Vera Brown you found at my mother's grave, than have you talk in this way, Theron."

" Would to heaven you were !" he said with passionate earnestness ; " for then I would kneel at your feet and beg you to be my wife."

She dashed her tears right and left, and taking his hand, asked,

" Theron, what right have you to this ring ? You have become a skeptic again, and I shall have to teach you a new and stronger faith."

" And may I give this old, bent ring which you are wearing its first meaning ?" he said eagerly.

" It never had any other meaning to me," she said, with a low laugh, and then she added, with an exquisite touch of pathos, " We could not help loving each other, Theron, after all that had happened ; we could only help doing wrong. Do not grieve that you have lost an arm, for you shall have both of mine in its place. That which you call a stain upon your name has come to be, in my eyes, the most flashing jewel in the crown of your manhood. When that poor creature fled to your door from her father's scorn and curses, you, who had been most wronged, acted as the Divine Man would have done. If you could be so kind to her, how sure I am of patient tenderness ! I will conclude my long homily with this plain exhortation : Never forget that Vera Wellingly and Vera Brown are one and the same person. It will save you a world of trouble.''

Then she called her father, but he had stolen away and left the lovers to themselves.

The long and terrible war was over. The last British soldier had embarked from the city of New York, and Washington, who had become the foremost general of the age, was about to repair to the seat of government, that he might resign his commission and become a simple American citizen. But, before doing so, he attended a wedding in a beautiful uptown villa which had been hastily prepared for the occasion.

It was a magnificent affair for those primitive and war-depleted times. Sam Fraunces and his buxom daughter Phœbe presided over the *cuisine* and entertainment, and the best military band of the army discoursed gay music. Many of the leading men of the country, State, and city, were present, and among them, it might almost be said, was Captain Molly, for she persisted in wearing her cocked hat and artilleryman's coat. Surgeon Jasper found himself an honorable master of ceremonies, and Tascar was charged with so many important duties that he at last was satisfied that he utterly eclipsed his old friend, Pompey. His mother, old Gula, in her lofty red turban, looked as if she might have been in very truth an African dowager queen.

Mrs. Saville was so happy that she quite renewed her youth, and would have been perfectly ready to admit that heaven had made a better match than she had thriftily compassed, as she had once supposed. Vera's gentle and affectionate manner had won her heart at once, while she, at the same time, complacently remembered the ducats of the bride.

The tall, bent form of the father was conspicuous, even though, in accordance with his old shrinking habit, he ever sought the background in the brilliant scene. Peace sat serenely on his brow, where gloom had lowered for so many years. He believed that the curse had passed away from him and his, and he was daily becoming more grateful for recognized blessings.

But Colonel Wellingly was the genius of the occasion, and, with a genial, high-bred courtesy, he moved among the guests, bestowing words of welcome and graceful attentions, with the tact of one whose thorough knowledge of men enabled him to make every utterance and act timely and appropriate. To each one he gave the sense of being recognized and cared for ; and his fine breeding made him at ease in addressing Governor Clinton, or the Commander-in-chief, and no less so in speaking to some subaltern, or Captain Molly herself.

Soon a breezy and expectant rustle and hum of voices announced that the bride and groom were descending the grand stairway.

As Vera entered, leaning upon the arm of her father, there was a deep murmur of admiration.

Her heart was filled with unspeakable gratitude, for God's minister was before her, and in his hand God's Holy Word. And when Saville spoke the words, '' With this ring I thee wed,'' and put upon her finger the plain gold band with which her father had espoused her mother, she thought she felt that mother's hands resting upon her head in blessing. Even in that supreme moment, her mind flashed back to the hour of her strong temptation, when her mother's charge that she should be wedded with this ring came to her help like an angel's hand. While the clergyman was offering the concluding prayer, her mind wandered a little, and harbored the thought,

'' If on earth God can thus richly reward patient obedience, what will heaven be ?

As Washington was about to take his leave, with strong expressions of his regard and kindly interest, Saville asked him if he would grant them a brief private interview.

With some surprise he consented, and was conducted into a beautiful little room, to which no guests had been admitted. On a stand of inlaid wood of rare value, and resting on some exquisitely embroidered velvet, lay a little book.

"Does your Excellency recognize this?" asked Vera, pointing to it.

As Washington took it up, a quick ray of intelligence lighted up his face, and he said,

"It is my old Bible, which I have carried through many a battle."

"God bless your Excellency!" said Vera, taking his hand in strong emotion. "This book, which is your gift, carried me through the one sore battle of my life."

"And this happy wedding to-night," added Saville, in a tone of deep feeling, "at which I feel the Son of God is present, as truly as He was at Cana, is due to your gift of this Bible, and the Christian counsel which accompanied it. I was then an unbeliever, and was tempting this dear wife to a union in which she must have thrown away her mother's wedding-ring. But this Bible saved us both, and we bless you for it with a gratitude that shall never cease."

Tears gathered quickly in Washington's eyes, and taking Vera in his arms, he kissed her tenderly, saying,

"The words which you and your husband have spoken form one of those memories which grow dearer to the last hour of life."

One quiet summer evening, Arthur and Guy Wellingly issued from the door of the rustic hunting-lodge into which the mountain cabin had been developed, and, following a path, they came to a lovely and secluded spot, embowered in the primeval trees of the forest. From a pedestal arose a light shaft of white marble, around which was entwined the clinging ivy. It bore no name. That was engraved on the hearts of the brothers.

Was she a weak woman who had thus enchained two such men ? Is not that faith rational which affirms that love so faithful must have a spiritual and eternal fruition ?

THE END.